British Social Attitudes

The 24th
REPORT

The **National Centre for Social Research** (NatCen) is an independent, non-profit social research organisation. It has a large professional staff together with its own interviewing and coding resources. Some of NatCen's work – such as the survey reported in this book – is initiated by NatCen itself and grant-funded by research councils or charitable foundations. Other work is initiated by government departments or quasi-government organisations to provide information on aspects of social or economic policy. NatCen also works frequently with other institutes and academics. Founded in 1969 and now Britain's largest social research organisation, NatCen has a high reputation for the standard of its work in both qualitative and quantitative research.

The contributors

Jillian Anable
Research Fellow at The Centre for Transport Policy, The Robert Gordon University

Tracy Anderson
Research Director at NatCen

Anne Barlow
Professor of Family Law and Policy in the School of Psychology at the University of Exeter

Frank Bechhofer
Emeritus Professor of Social Research at the University of Edinburgh

Carole Burgoyne
Senior Lecturer in the School of Psychology at the University of Exeter

Elizabeth Clery
Senior Researcher at NatCen and Co-Director of the *British Social Attitudes* survey series

Chris Creegan
Research Director at NatCen

Rosemary Crompton
Professor of Sociology at City University

Alexandra Cronberg
Researcher at NatCen

John Curtice
Research Consultant at the *Scottish Centre for Social Research* and Professor of Politics at Strathclyde University

Simon Duncan
Professor of Social Policy at the University of Bradford

Peter John
Hallsworth Chair of Governance at the University of Manchester

Robert Johns
Lecturer in Politics at Strathclyde University

Mark Johnson
Senior Researcher at NatCen and Co-Director of the *British Social Attitudes* survey series

Clare Lyonette
Research Officer at City University

Ann Mair
Computing Officer in the Social Statistics Laboratory at Strathclyde University

Rose Martin
Research Associate in the School of Social Policy, Sociology and Social Research at the University of Kent

David McCrone
Professor of Sociology at the University of Edinburgh

Stephen Padgett
Professor of Politics at Strathclyde University

Alison Park
Research Director at NatCen and Co-Director of the *British Social Attitudes* survey series

Miranda Phillips
Research Director at NatCen and Co-Director of the *British Social Attitudes* survey series

Chloe Robinson
Senior Researcher at NatCen

Janet Smithson
Research Fellow in the Schools of Law and Psychology at the University of Exeter

Stephen Stradling
Professor of Transport Psychology at Napier University

Peter Taylor-Gooby
Professor of Social Policy in the School of Social Policy, Sociology and Social Research at the University of Kent

Katarina Thomson
Research Director at NatCen and Co-Director of the *British Social Attitudes* survey series

Paul F Whiteley
Professor of Government at the University of Essex and Co-Director of the British Election Study

British Social Attitudes

Attitudes

The 24th
REPORT

EDITORS
Alison Park
John Curtice
Katarina Thomson
Miranda Phillips
Mark Johnson
Elizabeth Clery

SAGE Publications
Los Angeles · London · New Delhi · Singapore

NatCen
National Centre *for* Social Research

First published 2008

Apart from any fair dealing for the purposes of research or private study, or criticism or review, as permitted under the Copyright, Designs and Patents Act, 1988, this publication may be reproduced, stored or transmitted in any form, or by any means, only with the prior permission in writing of the publishers, or in the case of reprographic reproduction, in accordance with the terms of licences issued by the Copyright Licensing Agency. Enquiries concerning reproduction outside those terms should be sent to the publishers.

 SAGE Publications Ltd
1 Oliver's Yard
55 City Road
London EC1Y 1SP

SAGE Publications Inc.
2455 Teller Road
Thousand Oaks, California 91320

SAGE Publications India Pvt Ltd
B 1/I 1 Mohan Cooperative Industrial Area
Mathura Road
New Delhi 110 044

SAGE Publications Asia-Pacific Pte Ltd
33 Pekin Street #02-01
Far East Square
Singapore 048763

Library of Congress Control Number: 2007931629

British Library Cataloguing in Publication data

A catalogue record for this book is available from the British Library

ISBN 978-1-4129-4774-9

Printed in Great Britain by The Cromwell Press Ltd, Trowbridge, Wiltshire
Printed on paper from sustainable resources

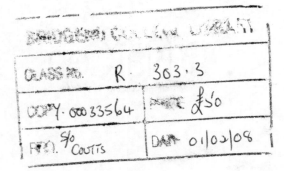

Contents

6   Prejudice and the workplace

Chris Creegan and Chloe Robinson   **127**

7   Car use and climate change: do we practise what we preach?

Stephen Stradling, Jillian Anable, Tracy Anderson and Alexandra Cronberg   **139**

List of tables and figures

Chapter 4

Chapter 5

Chapter 9

Chapter 10

Chapter 11

Appendix I

Introduction

The *British Social Attitudes* survey series began nearly 25 years ago, in 1983. In this *Report*, we focus on the results of the 2006 survey, and assess what this can tell us about the attitudes and behaviour of the British public, and how they have changed over time.

Our first three chapters focus upon the family and relationships within it. In Chapter 1, we examine the extent to which views about the 'traditional' family are changing and whether alternative family forms are increasingly seen as valid. Chapter 2 assesses whether an increasingly common form of relationship, cohabitation, is seen as distinct from marriage. It also explores the extent to which people understand the different legal rights enjoyed by married and cohabiting couples and what they think these should be. Meanwhile, Chapter 3 assesses whether the division of labour between men and women at home is changing, and examines the extent to which people's attitudes are reflected in their actual behaviour.

Chapters 5 and 6 shift our focus from the home to the workplace. In Chapter 5, we examine whether there is a distinct public service ethos among those who work in the public sector, and ask if this has changed in the light of new forms of public sector management. Chapter 6 focuses upon prejudice in the work place, a particularly timely topic given the new and emerging legislative and policy framework in this area.

Chapter 7 concerns transport and the choices people make as to how they travel between the different elements of their lives. In particular, it examines how far we practise what we preach when it comes to car use and concern about climate change.

Two chapters assess national differences in opinion. In Chapter 4 we examine whether devolution within the UK has had any impact upon how people in England and Scotland describe their national identities. Chapter 9 broadens its scope by assessing attitudes to citizenship in 37 countries, using data collected as part of the *International Social Survey Programme* (ISSP).

Chapter 10 also uses data collected as part of the ISSP but confines its attentions to Britain alone. Its focus is upon whether changing attitudes about the role of government and the welfare state reflect more deep-seated changes in

British 'core' values. Views about welfare are also explored in Chapter 11, which considers how attitudes to poverty and inequality have changed over the last two decades and what views people now have as to how government should address these issues.

In Chapter 8 we chart the extent to which newspaper readership has declined over the last 20 years and assess whether this can be seen as good or bad for Britain's democracy.

Most of the tables in the *Report* are based on *British Social Attitudes* data from 2006 and earlier years. Conventions for reading the tables are set out in Appendix II of this *Report*.

Our thanks

British Social Attitudes could not take place without its many generous funders. The Gatsby Charitable Foundation (one of the Sainsbury Family Charitable Trusts) has provided core funding on a continuous basis since the survey's inception, and in so doing has ensured the survey's security and independence. A number of government departments have regularly funded modules of interest to them, while respecting the independence of the study. In 2006 we gratefully acknowledge the support of the Departments for Health, Transport, and Work and Pensions. We also thank the Department of Education and Skills (now split into the Department for Children, Schools and Families and the Department for Innovation, Universities and Skills) and the Department of Trade and Industry (now part of the Department for Business, Enterprise and Regulatory Reform). Our thanks are also due to the Hera Trust.

The Economic and Social Research Council (ESRC), the body primarily responsible for funding academic social science research in Britain, has regularly provided the funds needed to field modules on the survey. In 2006 it continued to support the participation of Britain in the *International Social Survey Programme* (ISSP), a collaboration whereby surveys in over 40 countries field an identical module of questions in order to facilitate comparative research. Further details about ISSP can be found on its website (www.issp.org). The ESRC also funded questions in 2006 about gender roles (designed as part of the Gender Equality Network, or GeNet, part of the ESRC's Priority Network Programme), as well as a module of questions about the 'new family'.

Thanks are also due to The Nuffield Foundation and The Leverhulme Trust, both of whom have provided invaluable support to the series. In 2006 the former funded a module on attitudes towards cohabitation, which forms the basis of Chapter 2. Meanwhile, the latter supported a module of questions about national identity on both the *British Social Attitudes* survey and its sister survey, *Scottish Social Attitudes*. These questions provide much of the evidence reported in Chapter 4. Further information about the *Scottish Social Attitudes* survey itself can be found in Cleghorn *et al.* (2007).

We would also like to thank Professor Richard Topf of London Metropolitan University for all his work in creating and maintaining access to an easy to use website that provides a fully searchable database of all the questions that have ever been carried on a *British Social Attitudes* survey, together with details of the pattern of responses to every question. This site provides an invaluable resource for those who want to know more than can be found in this report. It is located at www.britsocat.com.

The *British Social Attitudes* survey is a team effort. The research group that designs, directs and reports on the study is supported by complementary teams who implement the survey's sampling strategy and carry out data processing. This year, the team bid farewell to Mark Johnson, who has left NatCen and will be much missed. The researchers in turn depend on fieldwork controllers, area managers and field interviewers who are responsible for all the interviewing, and without whose efforts the survey would not happen at all. The survey is heavily dependent too on staff who organise and monitor fieldwork and compile and distribute the survey's extensive documentation, for which we would pay particular thanks to Neil Barton and his colleagues in NatCen's administrative office in Brentwood. We are also grateful to Sandra Beeson in our computing department who expertly translates our questions into a computer assisted questionnaire, and to Roger Stafford who has the unenviable task of editing, checking and documenting the data. Meanwhile the raw data have to be transformed into a workable SPSS system file – a task that has for many years been performed with great care and efficiency by Ann Mair at the Social Statistics Laboratory at the University of Strathclyde. Many thanks are also due to David Mainwaring and Kate Wood at our publishers, Sage.

Finally, we must praise the people who anonymously gave up their time to take part in our 2006 survey. They are the cornerstone of this enterprise. We hope that some of them might come across this volume and read about themselves and the story they tell of modern Britain with interest.

The Editors

References

Cleghorn, N., Ormston, R. and Sharp, C. (2007), *Scottish Social Attitudes survey 2006: Core module technical report*, Scottish Executive Social Research (online publication)

1 New families? Tradition and change in modern relationships

Simon Duncan and Miranda Phillips[*]

Family life is traditionally seen as central to the well-being of both individuals and society in general. As Gordon Brown put it, in announcing the creation of a new 'super-ministry' for Children, Schools and Families in June 2007, "children and families are the bedrock of our society".[1] In setting up this new ministry Brown was securing New Labour's continuing interest in families, formally expressed as early as 1998 in the Green Paper *Supporting Families*: "Family life is the foundation on which our communities, our society and our country are built" (Home Office, 1998: 2). At around the same time, the Conservatives restated their concerns about 'family breakdown' (Social Justice Policy Group, 2007).

This current political interest reflects the fact that contemporary understandings of family revolve around the themes of dramatic social change and flux. The bedrock of family, it is assumed, is rapidly shifting, perhaps even collapsing, and is being replaced by looser, and more individualised, arrangements for loving and caring. There are two contrasting poles in this debate: while some commentators describe a 'breakdown of the family' resulting in social and moral dislocation, others describe its resilience, albeit in different forms to before, and see its new forms as offering increasing opportunity for choice, tolerance and family democracy. Certainly there is a broad context of public disquiet, with close attention to family affairs, their rights and wrongs, and about how to 'do' family and relationships. This is supported by what MacLeod (2004) calls a 'burgeoning family industry' of family services, counselling, self-help and therapy, campaigning groups, policy and research.

At the heart of this debate are what social theorists like Beck (1992) and Giddens (1992) have called 'individualisation'; the notion that traditional social structures of class, gender, religion and family are withering away, so people no longer have pre-given life-worlds and life trajectories.[2] Instead, individuals are

[*] Simon Duncan is Professor of Social Policy at the University of Bradford. Miranda Phillips is a Research Director at the *National Centre for Social Research* and is Co-Director of the *British Social Attitudes* survey series.

'condemned to choose' their own biographies. Meanwhile, the 'project of self', with an emphasis on individual self-fulfilment and personal development, comes to replace collective, social aims. This has a profound impact upon the family, with modern society being seen as having dissolved "the social foundations of the nuclear family" (Beck, 1992: 153). We no longer need, or expect, to get engaged and marry as young adults, to acquire a given set of relatives, to have children and live together till death do us part. Of course, we still search for love and intimacy, and still need to give and receive care, but now this search is seen to lead to 'families of choice'. Caring and loving relationships are consciously developed and built up on the basis of what they do, rather than depending on a pre-given biological or kinship status. Gender is important here; according to individualisation theory it is women who often lead change, as they break away from traditional and 'undemocratic' relationships and seek fairer and more equal ones. At the same time, the significance of romantic coupling is lessened and friendships become more important. These developments contribute towards the 'decentring' of the married, co-resident, heterosexual couple. It no longer occupies the centre-ground statistically, normatively, or as a way of life (Beck-Gernsheim, 2002; Roseneil and Budgeon, 2004). Rather, other ways of living – living alone, lone parenting, same-sex partnerships, or 'living apart together' – which in earlier periods were both relatively infrequent and seen as abnormal, become more common and are both experienced and perceived as equally valid. In summary, family life is no longer equated with the married couple.

There is a glaring problem with this vision of how family life is developing: how far it exists in reality is largely uncertain (Jamieson, 1998). The individualisation theorists themselves are notorious for asserting their almost millenarian scenarios on the basis of sketchy evidence. Subsequent research in Britain has shown that other family forms can provide everyday alternatives to the married couple (see Williams, 2004). While these studies point to many of the issues covered in this survey, they largely rest on the evidence of small samples of particular social groups in particular places. We still need to assess how far this 'new family' extends throughout the population, and how far it is accepted as a 'normal' and valid way of partnering and parenting.

True, we know a lot about statistical changes. For example, heterosexual married or cohabiting couples accounted for 57 per cent of British households in 2006, a decrease of 13 percentage points since 1971. Conversely, one person households increased by 10 points from 18 per cent in 1971 to 28 per cent in 2006 (Office for National Statistics, 2007). More and more couples cohabit outside marriage (accounting for 25 per cent of adults under 60 by 2005 – double the 1986 rate), divorce is at record levels, and by 2007 the number of marriages have declined to the lowest figures since 1896 – although weddings have become all the more fashionable, ornate and expensive. Over four in ten (43 per cent) births in 2005 were outside marriage, compared to just 12 per cent in 1980, most of which were to cohabiting couples (*ibid.*). But what do trends like these actually mean for the nature of family life? Are they evidence that it is breaking down into individualised 'projects'? Or do they suggest a continuing commitment to family life, if often expressed in different, and perhaps more democratic, forms than before?

In this chapter we will tackle this question by assessing whether, and how far, the public's views of family, partnering, parenting and friendships show that the 'traditional' centre of 'the family' – the married, co-resident, heterosexual couple – is no longer central, and how far alternative family models are seen as equally valid. Put simply: is marriage seen as the best form of relationship for partnering and parenting, or are other family forms seen as being equivalent? To assess this, we focus on public attitudes towards four key areas: heterosexual partnering; divorce and separation; non-conventional partnering and solo living; and friendship. This allows us to address a range of issues. What, for instance, does marriage mean to people, and is it much different to living together unmarried? Does marital breakdown mean tragedy, or can it be seen as a positive step forward? Are non-conventional forms of relationship seen as being just as good as heterosexual, co-residential partnerships when it comes to commitment and parenting? And are chosen friends seen as a replacement for given family?

Where relevant, we examine the extent to which views vary between different social groups. A number of characteristics are of interest here. Age is likely to be important, as we are assessing a social issue that has changed notably in recent decades, and therefore we might expect to find that older people are more traditional in their views. Gender also matters, as individualisation theory stresses the role that women can have in leading change as they break away from traditional homemaker roles through careers and divorce. In contrast, individualisation theory sees religion as prescribing a traditionally determined and 'externally imposed' moral code for social behaviour, particularly in relation to sexual relations, marriage and parenting. Social class may also be of interest, for while professional groups can be liberal on some social issues (and individualisation theorists often imply they form a vanguard for change), they can display more traditional behaviour when it comes to family practices (Duncan and Smith, 2006). Because some of these characteristics are themselves interrelated (for example, older people are more likely than younger ones to be religious), we also report where necessary on multivariate analysis that allows us to assess the importance of each of the characteristics while taking others into account.

Marriage and cohabitation

Marriage has traditionally been the socially accepted, legally sanctioned and religiously sanctified means of having sex, at least since the triumph of 'Victorian values' in the mid-nineteenth century. In contrast, sex outside marriage has normatively been perceived as both risky and deviant, however common it might have been in practice.

The *British Social Attitudes* survey has asked about this over a number of years:

> *Now I would like to ask you some questions about sexual relationships. If a man and woman have sexual relations before marriage, what would your general opinion be?*

> *What about a **married person** having sexual relations with someone other than his or her partner?*

> *[Always/Mostly/Sometimes/Rarely wrong/Not wrong at all]*

Table 1.1 shows how this 'traditional' view is both changing and stable. On the one hand, there is a developing consensus that marriage is not a prerequisite for legitimate sex. The proportion who think that pre-marital sex is "rarely wrong" or "not wrong at all" increased from 48 per cent in 1984 to 70 per cent by 2006 (and the proportion thinking it was "always wrong" shrank from 15 per cent to just six per cent). But on the other hand, opinion about extra-marital sex has barely changed over the last two decades, with around 85 per cent thinking this "mostly" or "always wrong" (and around 55 per cent going so far as to judge this "always wrong").

Table 1.1 Views on sex and marriage, 1984–2006

% who think that ...	1984	1989	2000	2006
Pre-marital sex is rarely or not wrong at all	48	55	71	70
Extra-marital sex is mostly or always wrong	85	84	85	84
Base	*1675*	*1513*	*3426*	*1093*

These figures immediately indicate what will become a theme throughout this chapter. In some respects there is no longer much commitment to the 'traditional' view (in this case, people are no longer expected to get married in order to have sex), but in other respects 'traditional' views are maintained (overwhelmingly, sexual faithfulness continues to be valued as a key part of commitment within marriage).

A similar story of change and stability is shown in relation to attitudes about cohabitation outside marriage. Barlow *et al.* in *The 18th Report* (2001) demonstrated that there was widespread acceptance of unmarried cohabitation; indeed, over half the adult population thought this was a 'good idea' before marriage. Almost half thought that there was no need to get married in order to have children; cohabitation was good enough. And even those who were less accepting (such as the elderly and the more religious) were becoming more so over time. In the 2006 survey we went on to examine how far unmarried cohabitation was perceived as an equivalent of marriage. Table 1.2 presents data for four questions on this subject:

These days, there is little difference socially between being married and living together as a couple

These days, a wedding is more about a celebration than life long commitment

Living with a partner shows just as much commitment as getting married to them

Married couples make better parents than unmarried ones

There is a consensus that marriage and unmarried cohabitation are *socially* similar (two-thirds agree), and there is considerable scepticism about weddings as a symbol of lifelong commitment – only 28 per cent think that they are, whereas a majority see them more as a celebration. Around half agree that unmarried cohabitation shows just as much commitment as marriage. While a sizeable minority (around a third) retain a more traditional view, disagreeing with the view that those who live together are just as committed to one another as those who get married, this 'traditional' stance is outweighed by the less traditional position on all of these questions.

Table 1.2 The equivalence of unmarried cohabitation and marriage

		Agree	**Neither**	**Disagree**
There is little difference socially between being married and living together	%	66	12	**19**
A wedding is more about a celebration than life long commitment	%	53	16	**28**
Living with a partner shows just as much commitment as getting married	%	48	13	**35**
Married couples make better parents than unmarried ones	%	**28**	28	40

Base: 2775

Most traditional view emboldened

These results tally with earlier quantitative and qualitative research (Barlow *et al.* 2001, 2005; Lewis 2001) which suggests that it is personally expressed commitment that is seen as significant by most people, not the public display of commitment as expressed in a marriage and a wedding. This overall consensus on the social and personal equivalence of unmarried cohabitation and marriage presumably helps account for the continuing (and incorrect) majority view that cohabiting couples have legal rights afforded by their 'common law marriage'. It also lends support to current attempts to reform the law to give unmarried cohabitants a greater measure of legal rights in the event of separation or death (as discussed in more detail in Chapter 2).

However, public opinion is more ambivalent about the importance of marriage when it comes to parenting. While only 28 per cent agree that married couples make better parents, just 40 per cent disagree – figures virtually unchanged since 2000.

What is the social distribution of these 'traditional' and 'non-traditional' attitudes on marriage? To help summarise views about marriage, we constructed a scale of traditional views,[3] using responses to the four questions presented above. Each respondent scored between 1 (most traditional views) and 5 (least traditional) and then the scores on the scale were grouped into three bands.

Table 1.3 shows the results broken down by related social characteristics.[4] Our expectations about relationships between social groups and views about marriage generally hold true. Those most likely to hold traditional views include religious respondents (20 per cent of those belonging to a religion and attending services compared to six per cent of those with no religion) and those who are married (15 per cent compared to two per cent of cohabitants). By way of example, 48 per cent of those belonging to a religion and attending services *disagree* that cohabitation shows as much commitment as marriage, compared to 28 per cent of those with no religion. And 43 per cent of married respondents disagree, compared to just 15 per cent of cohabitants. Age is significant in its own right, with older groups most likely to be traditional in their views. This applies even if we take into account other related characteristics such as religion and marital status.

Men are more likely to take the more traditional position on marriage than women, with, for example, 34 per cent of men agreeing that married couples make better parents than unmarried ones, while just 23 per cent of women take this view (perhaps reflecting the distribution of 'hands-on' experience). This tallies with the claim of individualisation theory that it is women who often lead change, as they break away from their traditional role as homemaker. Interestingly, both on the summary variable, and on our specific question on parenting, those at the 'coal face' – parents with dependent children – are notably *less* traditional than non-parents; just 17 per cent of parents agree that married couples make better parents than unmarried ones, compared to 32 per cent of non-parents. This is likely to be a function of age, religiosity and marital status, as the relationship between parenthood and attitudes to marriage is no longer significant once these factors are controlled for. Finally, social class is a factor, with professionals being more likely to take the traditional view than those in lower supervisory and technical occupations, or in semi-routine or routine jobs. This confirms other research which has shown that this group can show more traditional behaviour in their family practices than might be assumed from their somewhat more liberal social attitudes (Duncan and Smith, 2006).

Table 1.3 Traditional views on marriage, by socio-demographic groups

	% most traditional	Base
All	11	2775
Religion		
Belongs to religion, attends services	20	884
Belongs to religion, doesn't attend	9	610
No religion	6	1281
Marital status		
Married	15	1343
Widowed	13	269
Cohabitants	2	271
Separated/divorced	4	338
Single, never married	9	553
Age		
18–24	9	223
25–34	12	443
35–44	8	555
45–54	10	446
55–59	8	261
60–64	13	220
65+	17	623
Sex		
Male	13	1220
Female	10	1555
Parent status		
Parent of dependent child in household	9	725
Not parent	12	2049
Social class		
Managerial & professional	14	1032
Intermediate	12	349
Employers in small org	11	218
Lower supervisory & technical	7	335
Semi-routine & routine	9	760

So far we have seen that, for many, marriage does *not* have normative centrality, and unmarried cohabitation is seen as its equivalent. However, the way in which people think about cohabiting couples suggests that many traditional norms about relationships still hold true. Indeed, qualitative research shows that, for many cohabitants, living together is seen as a form of marriage rather than an alternative (Barlow *et al.*, 2005). Moreover, just as the majority think that sex outside marriage is wrong, the same applies to sex outside cohabitation: the large majority of cohabitants, over 80 per cent, think that sex outside a cohabiting relationship is wrong, according to the 2000 *National*

Survey of Sexual Attitudes and Lifestyles (Erens *et al.*, 2003). These findings give little support to the notion that many people cohabit outside marriage because cohabitation is more congruent with a project of the self, as individualisation theory would have it (Hall, 1996).

The importance of tradition, alongside change, is also suggested by responses to a set of questions on marriage as an ideal (see Table 2.2 in Chapter 2 for results of the first three):

> *There is no point in getting married – it's only a piece of paper*

> *Even though it might not work out for some people, marriage is still the best kind of relationship*

> *Marriage gives couples more financial security than living together*

> *With so many marriages ending in divorce these days, couples who get married take a big risk*

Here (in contrast to our first four statements), the traditional view is the consensus on all but the last of these questions, suggesting that marriage is widely perceived as an ideal. Overwhelmingly, the idea that marriage is just a piece of paper is dismissed: just one in ten (nine per cent) agree with this proposition, figures hardly changed since 2000. Meanwhile, just over half (54 per cent) see marriage as the best form of relationship, although a sizeable minority disagree or choose the 'neither' option. Furthermore, six in ten (61 per cent) think that marriage is more financially secure than living together – something which fits uneasily with the assumed social and emotional equivalence displayed in Table 1.2. This financial non-equivalence, in contrast to the consensus that cohabitation and marriage are socially equivalent, presumably helps fuel public support for legal change. It is also something of a change since 2000, perhaps reflecting the recent profile of high income divorce cases, or possibly increasing awareness of the common law marriage 'myth' (see Chapter 2). In contrast to the consensus in responses to the first three questions, our fourth splits opinion. A third (34 per cent) see marriage as risky because of the high likelihood of divorce (especially those who are themselves separated or divorced, 47 per cent of whom agree), and this is matched by a similar proportion who disagree (36 per cent).

While marriage is held up as an ideal by many, we should remember the blurred lines seen earlier between marriage and cohabitation in everyday life, if not in law. Unmarried cohabitation may be included as part of this 'married' ideal by some; cohabitants may be re-creating a form of marriage, albeit informally.

Partnering and commitment

We have seen that in terms of everyday life and commitment, many people see cohabitation and marriage as more or less equivalent, rather than alternatives.

What then is the nature of this commitment? This question lies at the heart of the individualisation debate, where theorists claim that people can no longer rely on partners and relatives (Bauman, 2003 is perhaps an extreme example).

Qualitative studies report that by the 1960s the couple (which was assumed to mean marriage) had moved to the centre of many people's social and emotional lives – at least normatively (Lewis, 2001). However, in 2006 most respondents think that relationships are much stronger if both partners have independence. We asked respondents to choose between these two options:

> *Relationships are much stronger when both partners have the independence to follow their own careers and friendships*
> *OR*
> *Partners who have too much independence from each other put their relationship at risk*

As many as 62 per cent choose the first option, with just 28 per cent thinking that social independence for partners poses a risk. So, yet again, we see a departure from the 1960s' normative model – the majority think partners can and indeed should be socially independent. Even a majority (54 per cent) of those with the most 'traditional' views on marriage take this view. Note, however, that this does not necessarily mean the decentring of conjugal partnership itself, as the questions asked presume that partnership remains in the middle of an individual's emotional life; indeed, the 'decentred' option in this question was framed in terms of independence *strengthening* partnership.

To try and further understand the strength and nature of this 'emotional centre' we asked respondents how much they agreed or disagreed with two questions about the importance of partners relative to support from relatives and love for, and from, children:

> *Relatives are always there for you in a way that partners may not be*

> *The relationship between a parent and their child is stronger than the relationship between any couple*

Only small minorities *disagree* with these statements (31 and 20 per cent respectively), thereby seeing relationships with partners as more dependable than those with relatives or stronger than those with children. In both cases, the most popular response, given by around four in ten is "agree" or "strongly agree" (41 and 42 per cent). Perhaps, surprisingly, parents with dependent children are little more likely than non-parents to see the relationship with a child as stronger. These responses both confirm and contradict individualisation theory. On the one hand, its theorists claim that children become the last source of unconditional love in an uncertain world of risky commitment. On the other hand, they would hardly see the 'given families' of relatives as providing an alternative (e.g. Giddens, 1992, Weeks *et al.*, 2001). It may also be the case that people have always seen relatives and children as more reliable than partners;

on this point, our survey – like individualisation theory – is limited by a lack of historical perspective. But we can say that, in 2006, we find elements of both continuity and change when it comes to 'traditional' notions of the relationship between couples.

The couple relationship, then, is not seen by most as necessarily the most durable source of support, nor the strongest bond. Perhaps reflecting this, there is an overwhelming consensus (75 per cent) that "many couples stay in unhappy relationships because of money or children". Even a majority of those most committed to marriage more generally (the religious, those who have separated/divorced and those with more traditional views) agree, although they are less likely to do so than their less traditional counterparts. Clearly, then, most people see the world of families and relationships as potentially involving severe structural constraints to personal choice. This is hardly a case of 'choosing one's own biography', as individualisation theory would have it.

Divorce and separation

To those taking a 'traditional' view, one that stresses the centrality of the married and co-residential couple, divorce and separation are clearly a family tragedy. Both significantly undermine the traditional model of marriage which has lifelong commitment at its centre; indeed, those taking the pessimistic position cite divorce and separation rates as evidence of family breakdown (for example, Social Policy Justice Board, 2007). Alternatively, a 'decentred' view would see divorce and separation as a normal, perhaps even beneficial, part of the life-course (Smart, 2004). Meanwhile, when divorce does occur, individualisation theory sees a developing ideal where both father and mother become equally active and lifelong parents, with traditional assumptions about roles and rights questioned (Giddens, 1992). We turn now to see how far the views of the general public support or refute these claims.

The majority of respondents, as Table 1.4 shows, take the 'decentred' view. We might expect widespread agreement with the proposition that divorce is the only response to violence – only 14 per cent disagree – but even fewer disagree with the idea that divorce can be a positive step towards a new life (just seven per cent). Nearly two-thirds agree with this statement. This suggests that, for most, lifelong commitment through marriage is not seen as a necessary part of a successful life, a result that undermines the traditional view of marriage. Overwhelmingly, 78 per cent agree with the view that it is not divorce in itself that harms children, but parental conflict. This supports other research in this field (Smart, 2003). In this respect, our respondents are confronting some recent media comment and political shibboleths about the harm caused by divorce *in itself*. Rather, they appear to see children's welfare as being most affected by the process of 'doing' family (that is, what actually happens in parenting). Dysfunctional families are seen as the problem, not the actual separation.

Table 1.4 The normality of divorce

		Agree	Neither agree nor disagree	Disagree
If either partner is at all violent then divorce is the only option	%	64	18	14
Divorce can be a positive first step towards a new life	%	63	26	7
It is not divorce that harms children, but conflict between their parents	%	78	12	7

Base: 2775

Despite these findings, people are more likely to question the 'normality' of divorce when children are brought to the foreground. Table 1.5 shows responses to a question which asked respondents whether they agreed or disagreed that:

It should be harder than it is now for couples with children under 16 to get divorced

As many as 30 per cent agree (the more traditional view) and a quarter remain undecided. As the table also shows, unsurprisingly, those with traditional views about marriage in general are more likely to support making divorce harder for parents. Once again, those who might actually face this scenario – parents themselves – are actually *less* likely than non-parents to take the 'make divorce harder' position (although this relationship appears largely to reflect the marital status and age profile of parents).

Table 1.5 Divorce should be harder if children are under 16, by views on marriage and parental status

		Agree	Neither agree nor disagree	Disagree	Base
All	%	30	26	38	2775
Views on marriage					
Most traditional	%	48	25	24	289
Least traditional	%	24	26	47	1302
Parental status					
Parents	%	26	26	43	725
Non-parents	%	32	26	37	2049

As we will see later in the chapter, children seem to hold a particular, 'morally absolute' position in people's attitudes to family. While less fixed and less definite family arrangements may find widespread acceptance when it comes to adults, this is less likely to be the case when children are involved.

Just as the married couple with children used to be normatively central, so too was the assumed position of the mother if divorce did take place. Children, it was assumed, should and would live with the mother and both normal practice and court decisions reflected this norm. We do not have time-series data to see how views have changed over time on this, but it is notable that in 2006 under a quarter (23 per cent) of respondents opt for "the mother" (and a mere 0.2 per cent opt for the "the father") when asked:

> *If a couple with children divorce, who do you think the children should normally live with for most of the time?*
>
> *[Spend equal time with both parents/Live with the parent who is best able to look after them/the father/the mother]*

For some leading individualisation theorists, the ideal is lifelong parenting by both father and mother, where children live with both the separated parents equally. At the same time, family law has been moving towards this 'norm'. However, just 18 per cent of respondents choose this more rigidly 'democratic' option of "equal time with both". Rather, the majority, 57 per cent, opt for the more open and contextual option "with the parent who is best able to look after them". Both age and social class are significant here. Those most likely to take this pragmatic view of parental rights and children's welfare are those aged 25–64 (the age groups most likely to have dependent children), and professionals. This pragmatism also questions current trends in family law towards joint residence after divorce.

Individualisation theory sees families as becoming steadily more democratic, with children also having their say in important family decisions. This should clearly apply to where they should live post-divorce, and indeed family courts are increasingly taking children's views into account when reaching decisions like this. But what do the public think – we asked the following question to assess this:

> *... imagine a 9 year old child whose parents are divorcing. How much say should a child of this age have over who they will live with after the divorce?*
>
> *[A great deal/Quite a lot/Some/Not much/None at all]*

An overwhelming majority – 84 per cent of respondents – think that the child should have at least some involvement in choosing whom they would live with after the divorce. But this idea of family democracy is not unequivocally accepted, for only 44 per cent opt for much influence ("a great deal" and "quite a lot"). In this case at least, family democracy is seen as more 'consultative'.

If divorce is largely normalised, then so too should be 'reconstituted' families after divorce with step-parents and stepchildren. After all, step-families accounted for 10 per cent of families with dependent children in 2005, according to Social Trends (Office for National Statistics, 2007). This normalisation did seem to be the case, at least for the usual pattern of a stepfather and biological mother (86 per cent of all step-families in 2005 – *ibid.*). We described this as follows:

> *I would like you to think about a family where the parents separated some time ago. The children are all under 12 years old and now live with their mother and her new partner. Do you think that these children could be brought up just as well by their mother and her partner as they could be by their mother and father?*

Fully 78 per cent agree that this sort of family 'definitely' or 'probably' could bring up children just as well as two biological parents. Perhaps, surprisingly, being a parent or a step-parent did not particularly relate to views on this topic (81 per cent of both groups take this view).

This acceptance of stepfathering then begs the question of the balance of rights and responsibilities between the 'household' stepfather and the 'absent' biological father. Individualisation theory expects that 'lifelong parenting' by separated biological fathers is one part of the development of democratic families, although qualitative research suggests that some stepfathers rather see stepchildren as 'their children', hence excluding the biological father from this role (Ribbens-McCarthy *et al.*, 2003). We gave respondents a scenario to assess their views. Following the question about step-parenting, we asked:

> *Still thinking about the same family, where the parents separated some time ago and the children now live with their mother and her partner. The children's mother and her partner don't have very much money and are worried that the children are being spoilt by their father because he regularly buys them expensive gifts and pays for outings that the children's mother and her partner cannot afford Which of these statements comes closest to your view about this situation ...*

> *... the father should be allowed to spend what he likes on his children,*
>
> *OR*
>
> *the children's mother and her partner should have the right to insist that the children's father spends money on things the children need, rather than expensive gifts?*

Most respondents – 63 per cent – give the household stepfather and the child's residential mother primacy in this situation (which, after all, portrays them as more in touch with children's needs), with only half as many – 30 per cent –

supporting the primacy of the biological father. Those most likely to support the biological father include men, younger respondents, cohabiting and single respondents and those with the most traditional views on marriage. That more traditional groups (men and those with traditional views on marriage) are more likely to support the biological father is unsurprising. The more surprising support by some in less traditional groups (younger and cohabiting/single people) suggests the question taps into a different dimension than the marriage questions considered earlier – perhaps an idea of equity in terms of the rights of the absent father – as well as their likely inexperience in the actual practice of bringing up children.

So far we have found that the centrality of the married couple has diminished; marriage is no longer seen as necessary for legitimate sex, unmarried cohabitation is seen as more or less equal to marriage – in everyday life, if not in law – partners should have social independence, divorce is usually seen as a normal, even beneficial, part of the life-course, and step-parenting is acceptable. Earlier norms about marriage as a lifelong commitment have been undermined and replaced by a preference for serial monogamy. However, throughout we often find caveats and doubts where children are concerned. In a sense what appears to have happened is that the social rules surrounding marriage have relaxed – 'marriage' may not be expressed formally through legal and public ceremony, and it can be interrupted through divorce and separation – but it continues informally in cohabitation and is rebuilt in reconstituted 'second' families. Extra-marital sex, and sex outside a cohabiting relationship, remain widely condemned. The emotional centre continues to be the residential couple, even if children and relatives are seen as more dependable over the long term. The question therefore remains of how far the 'married' couple in this wider sense – in other words the co-residential heterosexual partnership – is also 'decentred' in contemporary Britain. This is the subject of the next section.

Beyond the family

In previous sections we showed how the centrality of marriage itself has diminished in contemporary Britain, but that nevertheless the co-residential partnership (whether married, cohabiting or reconstituted) remains an emotional centre for many. Marriage, as a social institution, may have simply been reformed, widened and 'modernised' rather than being 'decentred'. The question remains, therefore, of how far co-resident heterosexuality remains at the normative centre of family life. If this family form were indeed 'decentred', we would expect to find that those who live apart from their partners, solo living and same-sex partnerships are seen as equivalent, rather than inferior family forms. Indeed, individualisation theory sees living 'beyond the family' in these ways as the vanguard of change (Roseneil and Budgeon, 2004). In this section we will examine how far these family forms are seen as adequate, or indeed equivalent, to the co-residential partnership.

Living apart together (LAT)

'Not living with a partner' does not necessarily mean not *having* a partner – they might simply live elsewhere. However, a traditional view which places co-residential partnership at the centre of a relationship can hardly recognise this logic, and would see living apart from one's partner as both abnormal and, if it happened at all, a temporary phenomenon forced by external causes, such as one partner obtaining a job a long distance away. This is perhaps why the idea of people *choosing* to 'live apart together' (LAT) has only recently been recognised (Roseneil, 2006). In fact, living apart from your partner is not that uncommon. Previous studies estimate that around a third of adults in Britain between 16 and 59, who were neither married or cohabiting, were living away from their partners (Haskey, 2005). Our latest survey (which includes people aged 18 or over only) is in rough agreement with these overall figures, and nine per cent of respondents (n = 320)[5] report that they are in a relationship but not living with their partner, compared to 65 per cent who are married or cohabiting and 26 per cent who do not have a current partner, either in the household or outside it. This equates to 25 per cent of those outside a co-residential (married or cohabiting) partnership.

Like previous surveys, we find that living apart from one's partner is more common among younger respondents. As many as four in ten respondents aged between 18 and 34 and outside a co-residential partnership have a partner who lives elsewhere (38 per cent of 18–24 year olds; 37 per cent of 25–34 year olds). However, this situation is to be found across all ages; for example, 13 per cent of respondents aged 55–64, and outside a co-residential partnership, report a partner living elsewhere. Non-parents (those without dependent children) are significantly more likely than parents to live apart from their partner. We cannot tell from our data whether the higher likelihood of living apart among younger groups is a cohort, period or generational effect, but taken together with the evidence on parents and non-parents, these findings suggest that for many living apart coincides with a particular life-stage or set of circumstances.

The majority of respondents with a partner living elsewhere (seven per cent of the full sample) had been in the relationship for six months or more, so if we use time as a measure of relationship status then these appear to be relatively established 'living apart together', or LAT, relationships. However, we were able to conduct a more incisive assessment of the status of living apart relationships by asking questions about *why* people were in this position, and about what partners living apart do together socially.

By far the main single reason for living apart, given by four in ten of those respondents with a partner living elsewhere, is that they are not ready to live together, or that it is too early in their relationship. This is not because these respondents are waiting to get married – a mere five per cent cite this as a reason for living apart (also underlining the normalcy of unmarried cohabitation discussed earlier). This gives a different impression of the status of these relationships than our more simplistic measure of length – we can perhaps see these as akin to the old-fashioned notion of 'going steady' boyfriend/girlfriend relationships, rather than full-blown partnerships. Half indicate clear external constraints on living together: this includes a quarter who cannot afford to do so and a fifth whose partners are working or studying elsewhere. Only around a third cite 'choice'-type reasons for living apart, including not wanting to live together, and wanting to keep their own home (both 14 per cent). In terms of activities, just over a half act as long-term partners in a social sense, for example, in terms of seeing relatives together (53 per cent), or going on holiday together (55 per cent). Putting all this together suggests that only a minority of respondents who live apart from a partner are LATs in the sense of both being in a significant relationship and *choosing* to live apart. While we do not have time-series data to assess whether more people choose to live apart now than in recent decades, the relative paucity of such relationships does not easily support the impression given in some of the individualisation literature of a developing rejection of conjugal relationships.

Statistically, then, couples who live apart are not as uncommon as some might expect, although this often seems to reflect constraint rather than a preference for living apart. But how are these non-residential relationships regarded in a normative sense? A majority (54 per cent) agree that "*a couple do not need to live together to have a strong relationship*", with only 25 per cent disagreeing. Not surprisingly, those with traditional views on marriage are twice as likely to disagree (48 per cent); conversely only 15 per cent of the youngest 18–24 age group do so. While choosing to live apart seems quite rare, many more people find themselves living apart from a mixture of circumstances, and this is generally seen as good enough for partnering. Indeed, other research has found that a significant minority of people describe 'living together apart' as their 'ideal relationship', compared to over 40 per cent for exclusive marriage and just under 20 per cent for unmarried cohabitation (Erens *et al.*, 2003).

Solo living

There has been a substantial rise in the number of people living alone in Britain over recent decades; by 2005, 17 per cent of adults aged over 16 were in one-person households, compared to just eight per cent in 1971 (*General Household Survey*, 2005). Although many elderly people are forced to live on their own because of the death or infirmity of a partner, this recent increase is almost entirely accounted for by a rise in solo living among younger age groups. Indeed the proportionate increase has been greatest among those in the 25–44 age group, rising from just two per cent in 1971 to 12 per cent in 2005 (*ibid.*). As Roseneil (2006) points out, it is precisely this age group which traditionally would be most expected to be married and having children. By 2005, over a quarter of adults over 30 had lived alone at some stage in their lives (Wasoff *et al.*, 2005).

As we have seen, some of these people classified as 'living alone', particularly in younger age groups, will in fact be in 'living apart together' relationships with partners living elsewhere. In these cases it is still the intimate *couple* which forms a central part of life. What, then, of those who live alone, without a partner living elsewhere? When the centrality of married couples was taken for granted, such people often attracted 'spinster' and 'confirmed bachelor' stereotypes – people who in some way had failed at normal life, and were inadequate at making relationships (although this had different connotations for men and women). These particularly negative stereotypes have now been replaced in common parlance, and in official documents like marriage and birth registers, by the less pejorative appellation 'single'. Going even further, individualisation theory sees single women as in the vanguard for change in personal relationships – they are voting with their feet in rejecting the traditional, undemocratic, heterosexual couple and choosing to build 'families of choice' outside it. Nonetheless, qualitative research shows that this 'choice' is often difficult to sustain (Reynolds *et al.*, 2007). The question remains of whether solo living is still seen as a 'deficit identity', defined negatively by *lack* of a partner and 'normal' family life, or whether it is seen as a viable way of living where those who live alone are as socially accomplished as those who live as a couple. To assess this, we asked respondents how far they agreed or disagreed with the following statements. The first two relate to normality of single living, the second two address the issue of solo parenting:

You do not need a partner to be happy and fulfilled in life

People who choose to live alone just aren't good at relationships with others

There is nothing wrong with a single woman who lives alone having a child if she wants one

One parent can bring up a child as well as two parents together

As shown in the first two rows of Table 1.6, there is little support for the 'deficit identity' image of solo living; 69 per cent agree that it is not necessary to have a partner to live a happy and fulfilled life. Similarly, six in ten reject the idea that people who choose to live alone are not good at relationships (and only one in ten agree). But when we turn to parenting, this picture changes, as the next two rows in Table 1.6 show. Less than half are supportive of solo parenting: only 44 per cent think that there is nothing wrong with a single women who lives alone having a child if she wants one, and just 42 per cent think that single parents are as good as two parents at bringing up children. (Although this does show some change since 1994, when only 35 per cent agreed that single parents could be as good). The notion of solo living as 'deficit' returns for many when it comes to parenting.

Table 1.6 The normality of living alone and solo parenting

		Base
Living alone		
% agree do not need a partner to be happy and fulfilled in life	69	2775
% disagree people who live alone aren't good at relationships	60	2775
Solo parenting		
% agree nothing wrong with a single woman who lives alone having a child	44	2775
% agree one parent can bring up a child as well as two	42	2775
Donor sperm		
% think donor insemination should be allowed …		
… for single woman	61	3197
… for co-residential heterosexual couple	90	3197

We forced the issue of solo parenting by asking respondents for their views about donor insemination for a single woman (implying that she had made an overt choice to be a single parent), and in comparison, for a heterosexual couple. The scenarios were described as follows, and the results are shown in the last rows of Table 1.6:

> *These days it's possible for women to get pregnant by paying a clinic and using sperm from a donor. I'm going to read out two scenarios about different people. For each, assume that they can afford to pay for the treatment and bring up the child without relying on benefits.*

> *First, do you think that a single woman who lives alone, who wants to have a child, should be allowed to have this treatment?*

> *And what about a man and woman who live together as a couple, and who want to have a child, but the man can't have children. Should the woman be allowed to have this treatment?*

> *(IF NECESSARY REPEAT: Assume they can afford to pay for the treatment and bring up the child without relying on benefits)*

As many as 61 per cent think that single women "definitely" or "probably" should be allowed to use donor sperm in order to become pregnant – at least if she is financially self-supported. This somewhat contradicts our earlier finding that just 42 per cent think that single parenting is as good as two parents together. Perhaps the question appeals to feelings about the importance of private choice and freedom for individual adults, which are less influential when faced with perceived moral absolutes of actual parenting, not to mention some media stereotyping of single parents. Nevertheless, this majority approval is significantly below the overwhelming consensus, at 90 per cent, that heterosexual couples should be allowed such treatment. Overall, then, we have found considerable support for the idea that solo living is not seen as deficient, though the issue of solo parenting is far more likely to divide public opinion.

Same-sex partnerships

According to the 2001 census, only 0.3 per cent of co-residential couples in Britain defined themselves as same-sex partners (Duncan and Smith, 2006). This is likely to be a significant underestimate of the actual number of same-sex partnerships, for many will be in 'living apart together' relationships. In addition, there was probably a high degree of under-reporting in the census, especially as it relied on self-definition (although this reluctance in itself might indicate some fear of intolerance). Nonetheless, individualisation theorists have seen gay men and lesbians in general, and same-sex partnerships in particular, as pioneers for individualisation. This is because they already lie outside traditional family life and so have been almost forced to create alternative 'families of choice' (Weeks *et al.*, 1999). Not only this, but theorists claim that gay men and lesbians have become a role model for heterosexuals in changing family life more generally (Roseneil and Budgeon, 2004). Symptomatically, these claims beg the question of how widespread this pioneering and proselytising role actually is (Duncan and Smith, 2006).

For a number of years *British Social Attitudes* has asked questions about the rightness and wrongness of homosexuality, and these provide some initial answers. The following questions were asked in separate places in the questionnaire:

> *Homosexual relations are always wrong*
> *[Agree strongly – Disagree strongly]*
>
> *... what about sexual relations between two adults of the same sex?*
> *[Always/Mostly/Sometimes/Rarely wrong/Not wrong at all]*

The initial impression is of widespread tolerance. By 2006, only 18 per cent agree with the first question, taking the view that homosexual relationships are always wrong. On this measure, attitudes have become more liberal since 1996 (when 24 per cent agreed). Those who remain disapproving in 2006 are most likely to be older men, those in lower supervisory and technical occupations or in semi-routine or routine jobs, people with traditional views about marriage and the religious (defined as those belonging to a religion and attending services). Young women, and those in professional jobs, were most liberal.

Tolerance declines, however, when we ask our second question, which focuses on actual sexual relations, rather than relationships in general terms. The results are shown in Figure 1.1. Now a third (32 per cent) of respondents see sex between adults of the same sex as always or mostly wrong – which must leave some respondents in a 'Church of England' position, where homosexuality is all right as long as sex is not involved. This inconsistency suggests a difference between tolerance – something not approved of can be tolerated – and acceptance – where there is no disapproval. However, the largest proportion (49 per cent) still think sex between same-sex adults is rarely or never wrong. Furthermore, the figure shows substantial liberalisation over the last 15 years; before that, around two-thirds or more thought that homosexual sex was wrong.

Figure 1.1 Views on sex between same-sex adults, 1983–2006

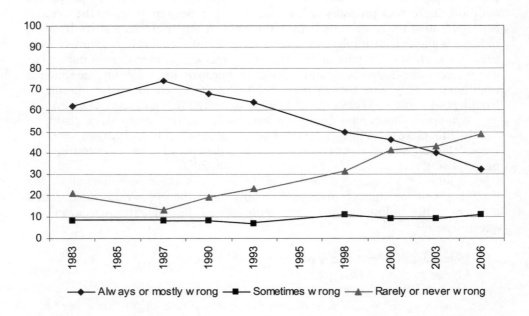

The fact that a significant minority do not accept same-sex relationships is clear when we examine responses to the statement "civil partners should have the same rights as married couples". Over a quarter (27 per cent) disagree with this view, though the majority, 58 per cent, agree. So even when the issue is about rights rather than sexual activity, the acceptability of same-sex relationships is still rejected by a substantial minority.

To what extent are same-sex partnerships seen as adequate for partnering and parenting? Table 1.7 echoes the patterns found earlier for solo living. There is strong consensus for the 'private' matter that same-sex couples can be as committed as heterosexual couples (63 per cent), with few disagreeing (12 per cent). But there is no consensus for the more 'public' issue of parenting – an issue where it seems 'non-individualist' moral absolutes or imperatives are still pervasive (Ribbens-McCarthy *et al.*, 2003). Indeed the larger proportions, around two in five, see same-sex couples as less adequate parents than heterosexual couples. Disapproval is little more for gay men than for lesbians, indicating that it is sexuality, not gender, that is largely at issue.

Table 1.7 The capability of gay men and lesbians as partners and parents

		Agree	Neither agree nor disagree	Disagree
A same sex couple can be just as committed to each other as a man and a woman	%	63	19	12
A lesbian couple are just as capable of being good parents as a man and a woman	%	36	21	38
A gay male couple are just as capable of being good parents as a man and a woman	%	31	20	42

Base: 2775

Intolerance and disapproval of any particular social group is often linked to its stereotyping as an abstract and unknown (and hence threatening) 'other'. Significant contact with 'real' people from that group allows more inclusive and less stereotypical judgement. We can examine this to some extent through a question which asked whether respondents knew someone who was gay or lesbian and, if so, what the status of this relationship was (respondents could choose more than one answer):

> *Do you personally know anyone who is gay or lesbian?*
> *[No, I don't know anyone who is gay or lesbian/Yes – a member of my family/Yes – a friend I know fairly well/Yes – someone I do not know very well/Yes – someone at my work/Yes – someone else/Not sure]*

While over two-thirds of respondents (69 per cent) say they know at least one gay man or lesbian, far fewer can claim what might be *significant* relationships – only nine per cent refer to a family member who is a gay man or lesbian, and 29 per cent to a friend they know 'fairly well'. In total, only 35 per cent of respondents have experience of these possibly closer relationships (some of course are overlapping). Another third (36 per cent) refer only to a more 'distant' acquaintance (to someone they do not know very well, someone at work, or some other person). This leaves a final third (30 per cent) who do not know any gay men or lesbians at all (or are unsure). Older groups (especially aged 65 or more), married respondents, and those in lower supervisory and technical occupations or in semi-routine or routine jobs are the least likely to have significant personal contact through relatives or closer friends This relative lack of significant personal contact, in contrast to more widespread acquaintance, seems to link to the 'tolerance–acceptance' dichotomy noticed above. Certainly the degree and nature of personal contact is strongly associated with rates of acceptance. As Table 1.8 shows, those with 'close' personal contact are substantially more likely to take the accepting or tolerant view than those without any contact.

Table 1.8 Personal contact and accepting gay men and lesbians

	Personal knowledge of gay man or lesbian		
	Close (friend/relative)	Not close, but a more distant acquaintance	None
% disagree homosexual relations always wrong	73	52	30
Base	632	603	447
% agree gay male couple are just as capable of being good parents as a man and a woman	47	28	19
Base	957	931	657

Earlier we outlined the way in which individualisation theorists can see gay men and lesbians as role models for more widespread change (e.g. Roseneil and Budgeon, 2006). While this may be the case, it does seem that this effect may be limited by the relative paucity of significant personal contact between many straight people and gay men and lesbians. Moreover, while there has been a substantial liberalisation of attitudes towards homosexuality, this may reflect public tolerance rather than active approval and personal acceptance.

  In this section we have seen that different forms of 'non-conventional' relationships, whether 'living together apart', same-sex, or solo living seem fine for consenting adults. In this sense, the heterosexual, co-residential couple is no longer particularly central as a social norm. However, when it comes to the more public, and morally absolute, issue of children and parenting the picture remains fairly traditional.

Friends and families of choice

Friendship is an important social relationship that has been neglected by research and policy alike, partly because of the normative centrality of the heterosexual couple. In contrast, individualisation theorists place some considerable emphasis on friends, for, of course, friends are 'chosen' to a much greater degree than 'family'. It is not, according to this view, just the heterosexual couple that has become decentred, but also its surrounding family. Given 'families of fate' – the whole panoply of parents, siblings, in-laws, uncles, nieces, great aunts, and so on – will be increasingly replaced by more freely chosen 'families' of friends (Weeks *et al.*, 2001).

The simple polarities set up by this view have been questioned in empirical research. *The 19th Report*, for instance, found that family ties are 'seemingly in robust good health' (Park and Roberts, 2002). The majority of people were in close contact with immediate family members, and family members were a very important source of help to whom most would turn first. Friends, while also important in most people's lives, were far less likely to be a first port of call, even for the young and single. Moreover, those who had most family contact also had more friends. This picture fits in well with other research which suggests that it is not a case of 'family' simply being replaced by 'friends'. Rather there is a 'suffusion' of the two (Pahl and Spencer, 2004). People do indeed tend to choose members of their personal communities – those that are important to them for love, care, support and friendship – but these are as likely to include kin as much as non-kin.

We found some support for the idea that friends can act like family. Three-quarters of respondents claim to have at least one "particularly close friend you can share your private feelings and concerns with" (leaving aside partners or anyone in their family). As many as 41 per cent have more than one such close friend, while a quarter of respondents have no particular close friend at all, as defined here. While those who are married are more likely to lack a close friend (31 per cent), this is no doubt largely a matter of age rather than partnership status, as cohabitants (who, on average, are younger) are far less likely to be in this position (just 17 per cent). Men are less likely than average to have a close friend (33 per cent lack one), as are those aged 65 or above (40 per cent do not have one), and those in lower supervisory and technical occupations or in semi-routine or routine jobs (around 30 per cent do not have a close friend).

Of those with close friends, 84 per cent had received help or support from them when "facing a difficult problem in your life". Not surprisingly, then, as Table 1.9 shows, most people reject the notion that:

Friends are for fun, not for discussing personal problems with

Friendship is seen by most as an important part of their social support, not something peripheral in their lives. But when it comes to weighing up friends *versus* family, only a minority of three in ten see friends as more dependable than family in times of crisis, although only four in ten see family as more dependable than friends.

This belief in the relative dependability of family probably relates to the persistence of norms about family obligations, as the last two rows in Table 1.9 suggest. The majority think that people should make time for relatives, even if they have nothing in common with them. Even when it comes to more distant relatives, as many as 55 per cent of respondents subscribe to this view, and seven in ten agree in the case of close relatives.

Table 1.9 Family and friends

		Agree	Neither agree nor disagree	Disagree
Friends are for fun, not for discussing personal problems with	%	12	14	71
When things go wrong in your life, family is more likely to be there for you than friends	%	42	26	29
People should make time for relatives like aunts, uncles and cousins, even if they don't have anything in common	%	55	26	15
People should make time for close family members, even if they don't have anything in common	%	68	20	9

Base: 2775

To explore the relative importance of friends and family further, we attempted to force respondents into a somewhat artificial choice between family and friends:

> *Some people feel that having close friends is more important than having close ties with their family. Others disagree. Where would you put yourself on this scale between these two positions?*
> *[5-point scale, from 1 'Friends most important' to 5 'Family most important']*

Given the persistence of norms about given obligations to family, it is perhaps not surprising that around half (48 per cent) feel that maintaining close ties with family is more important than having close friends (choosing 4 or 5 on the scale), with just 13 per cent choosing close friends (choosing 1 or 2). However, the fact that a large minority (39 per cent) choose the mid-point between the two positions supports the 'suffusion' idea that friends are becoming more like family and *vice versa*. Gender and whether or not a person themselves has a close friend – but not age nor marital status – are related to this view: women are more likely than men to choose the mid-point (41 per cent compared to 36 per cent), while those with more than one close friend are 15 percentage points more likely to choose this 'neutral' position than those with no close friend (45 per cent *versus* 30 per cent).

Overall, friends are important to most people for support and closeness as well as for fun, and in this way friends can take on 'family' functions. At the same time, many people retain a sense of obligation to family and, reciprocally, see family members as more dependable in the long run. If 'families of choice' are replacing 'families of fate', then these chosen families are likely to have partners and kin at the centre.

Conclusions

We started this chapter by asking how far the 'traditional' core of 'the family' – the married, co-resident, heterosexual couple – was no longer central, and how far alternative family models are seen as equally valid. Is marriage still seen as the best form of relationship for partnering and parenting, does marital breakdown still mean tragedy, are other forms of relationship just as good, and can friends replace family?

Certainly the centrality of the formally married couple has diminished. While marriage is held up as an ideal by most, it is no longer seen as necessary for legitimate sex, and a majority see unmarried cohabitation as more or less equal to marriage in everyday life. Most think partners should have social independence, divorce is usually seen as a normal part of the life-course – even beneficial in some instances, and step-parenting is viewed as a good enough alternative to a child being brought up by both his or her biological parents. We have found, therefore, that on all of these issues public attitudes do not conform to normative expectations of the 'traditional' family model of the mid-20th century – although we also find caveats and doubts where children are concerned.

But in many ways this is a case of *'plus ça change, c'est la même chose'*. For in a sense what has happened is that the social rules surrounding marriage have relaxed rather than vanished entirely. 'Marriage' may not be expressed formally through legal and public ceremony, and it can be interrupted through divorce and separation, but it continues informally in cohabitation and is rebuilt in reconstituted 'second' families. Sex outside cohabiting and living apart relationships are as widely condemned as extra-marital sex. Marriage, as a social institution, may have simply been widened more than 'decentred'.

The same theme of decentring within continuity is repeated when it comes to alternative forms of relationship. Living apart together, living alone without a partner, and same-sex couples are not seen by most as inadequate or deficit family forms. In this way the heterosexual, co-residential couple is no longer that central as a social norm. But the picture becomes more traditional when it comes to the more public issue of children and parenting. Children seem to hold a particular, 'morally absolute' position in people's attitudes to family. While less fixed and definite family arrangements may find widespread acceptance when it comes to adults, this is less likely to be the case when children are involved. Similarly, friends can take on 'family' functions, but at the same time many people retain a sense of obligation to family and, reciprocally, see family members as more dependable in the long run.

If 'families of choice' are replacing 'families of fate', then most of these chosen families are likely to have partners and kin at the centre. Theories of individualisation and their negative reflection through ideas of 'breakdown of the family' both rely on assumptions of dramatic and universal social change. While we have been hampered in that we must rely for the most part on cross-sectional data for 2006, our evidence suggests a more mixed picture. Certainly there is evidence of change and evolution – one example where we do have longer time-series data is the widespread tolerance, if not always acceptance, of same-sex relationships developing since the 1980s. Attitudes and practices also vary between different social groups and, we might add, vary in different places (Duncan and Smith, 2006). And yet while theories of individualisation may have heuristic value, they seem partial and exaggerated as a description of norms and attitudes about family life in contemporary Britain. Rather, if we take a broader view, norms about the content and nature of family life seem quite durable. People ascribe centrality to maintaining good relationships and functional family lives, not to their own self-projects in isolation. This also means that most people seem to place the emphasis on successfully 'doing' family in practice, whatever situation people find themselves in, rather than on the supposed functionality of different family forms. In this way there seems to be as much 'recentring' as 'decentring'.

Notes

1. In "Balls takes charge of new ministry for children", *The Guardian*, 29th June 2007.
2. For an examination of this claim in relation to social class, political and religious identity, we refer readers to Heath *et al.*, (2007).
3. Scores were created by reversing the numerical values for the first three statements, so that the most traditional view was changed from 5 to 1 and so on; the values for the four statements were summed, divided by four, and rounded. The 1 to 5 scale was then recoded into most traditional views (1 and 2), middle (3) and least traditional (4 and 5). Not answered or "don't know" at any of the four questions was excluded. We repeated this analysis with a larger number of statements included in the scale (the additional statements were the final three statements listed on page 8. However, the 'most traditional' group using this increased scale was larger and more diverse, and therefore less useful in identifying our most traditional respondents. It did, however, produce similar results in terms of identifying broad social patterning of views about marriage. Indeed, the only social group which was not related to the second scale, but was to the first, was parent status.

4. All of the characteristics shown in Table 1.3 are significantly related to views on marriage, even after controlling for the effect of the other factors through regression analysis. The results of the regression are available from the authors on request.
5. In addition, nine did not answer definitively (DK/RF); these are included in the base for the follow-up questions, meaning the unweighted base for those is 329.

References

Barlow, A., Duncan, S., James, G. and Park, A. (2001), 'Just a piece of paper? Marriage and cohabitation in Britain', in Park, A., Curtice, J., Thomson, K., Jarvis, L. and Bromley, C. (eds.), *British Social Attitudes: the 18th Report*, London: Sage

Barlow, A., Duncan, S. Grace, J. and Park, A. (2005), *Cohabitation, Marriage and the Law: Social Change and Legal Reform in the 21st Century*, Oxford: Hart

Bauman, K. (2003), *Liquid Love: on the Frailty of Human Bonds*, Cambridge: Polity

Beck, U. (1992), *Risk Society: Towards a New Modernity,* London: Sage

Beck-Gernsheim, E. (2002), *Reinventing the Family: in Search of New Lifestyles*, Cambridge: Polity

Duncan, S. and Smith, D. (2006), 'Individualisation *versus* the geography of new families', *21st Century Society: the Academy of Social Sciences Journal*, (**1/2**): 167–189

Erens, B., McManus, S., Prescott, A., Field, J. with Johnson, A.M., Wellings, K., Fenton, K.A., Mercer, C., Macdowall W., Copas, A.J. and Nanchahal, K. (2003), *National Survey of Sexual Attitudes and Lifestyles II: Reference tables and summary report*, London: NatCen/UCL/LSHTM

Giddens, A. (1992), *The Transformation of Intimacy: Sexuality, Love and Eroticism in Modern Societies*, Cambridge: Polity Press

Hall, D. (1996), 'Marriage as a pure relationship: exploring the link between premarital cohabitation and divorce in Canada', *Journal of Comparative Family Studies*, (**27/1**): 1–12

Haskey J. (2005), 'Living arrangements in contemporary Britain: having a partner who lives elsewhere and living apart together (LAT)', *Population Trends*, **122**: 35–45

Heath, A., Martin, J. and Elgenius, G. (2007), 'Who do we think we are? The decline of traditional social identities', in Park, A., Curtice, J., Thomson, K., Phillips, M. and Johnson, M. (eds.), *British Social Attitudes: the 24th Report – Perspectives on a changing society*, London: Sage

Home Office (1998), *Supporting Families: a Consultation Document*, London: Stationery Office

Jamieson, L. (1998), *Intimacy: Personal Relationships in Modern Societies*, Cambridge: Polity Press

Lewis, J. (2001), *The End of Marriage? Individualism and Intimate Relationships*, Cheltenham: Edward Elgar

Macleod, M. (2004), 'The state and the family: can the government get it right'. Paper presented at the CAVA conference 'Rethinking care relations: Family lives and Policies', Leeds, December

Office for National Statistics (2007), *Social Trends 37*, Basingstoke: Palgrave Macmillan

Pahl R. and Spencer, L. (2004), 'Personal communities: not simply families of 'fate' or 'choice', *Current Sociology*, **(52/2)**:199–221

Park, A. and Roberts, C. (2002), 'The ties that bind', in Park, A., Curtice, J., Thomson, K., Jarvis, L., and Bromley, C., (eds.), *British Social Attitudes: the 19th Report*, London: Sage

Reynolds, J., Wetherell, M. and Taylor, S. (2007), 'Choice and chance: negotiating agency in narratives of singleness', *Sociological Review*, **(55/2)**: 311–330

Ribbens-McCarthy, J., Edwards, R. and Gillies, V. (2003), *Making Families: Moral Tales of Parenting and Step-Parenting*, Durham: sociologypress

Roseneil, S. and Budgeon, S. (2004), 'Beyond the Conventional Family: Intimacy, Care and Community in the 21st Century', *Current Sociology*, **(52/2)**: 135–159

Roseneil, S. (2006), 'On not living with a partner: unpicking coupledom and cohabitation', *Sociological Research Online*, **(11/3)**

Smart, C. (2003), 'New perspectives on childhood and divorce: introduction to special issue', *Childhood*, **(10/2)**: 123–9

Smart, C. (2004), Changing landscapes of family life: rethinking divorce', *Social Policy and Society*, **(3/4)**: 401–8

Social Justice Policy Group, Chair: Callan, S. (2007), *Breakthrough Britain: Ending the costs of social breakdown, Volume 1: Family Breakdown – Policy Recommendations to the Conservative Party*, available at
  http://standupspeakup.conservatives.com/Reports/BreakthroughBritain.pdf

Wasoff, F. and Jamieson, L. with Smith, A. (2005), 'Solo living, individual and family boundaries: findings from secondary analysis', in McKie, L. and Cunningham-Burley, S., *Families in Society: Boundaries and Relationships*, Bristol: Policy Press

Weeks, J., Donovan, C and Heaphy, B (1999), 'Everyday Experiments: Narratives of Non-Heterosexual Relationships', in Silva, E.B. and Smart, C. (eds.), *The New Family?* London: Sage

Weeks, J., Donovan, C. and Heaphy, B. (2001), *Same Sex Intimacies: Families of Choice and Other Life Experiments*, London: Routledge

Williams, F. (2004), *Rethinking Families*, London: Calouste Gulbenkian Foundation

Acknowledgements

The authors would like to thank Anne Barlow, Rosalind Edwards, Ray Pahl, Sasha Roseneil, Carol Smart and Fiona Williams for help and advice. Thanks also to the Economic and Social Research Council (ESRC) for providing funding that allowed us to include questions on the 'New Family' in the 2006 *British Social Attitudes* survey, grant number RES-000-23-1329.

2 Cohabitation and the law: myths, money and the media

Anne Barlow, Carole Burgoyne, Elizabeth Clery and Janet Smithson[*]

The 2000 *British Social Attitudes* survey confirmed a growing social acceptance of heterosexual cohabitation as a partnering and parenting choice and identified strong public support for reform of cohabitation law (Barlow *et al.*, 2001). It also established the existence of a 'common law marriage' myth whereby the majority of the public, and cohabitants in particular, falsely believe that cohabiting couples who have lived together for some time have the same legal rights as married couples (Barlow *et al.*, 2001). Even among those cohabitants who were aware of their vulnerable legal position, it was found that very few had taken appropriate steps to gain or provide legal protection despite, as we found in subsequent research, often having good intentions to do so (Barlow *et al.*, 2005).

These findings prompted widespread media interest and government concern. This led the Department for Constitutional Affairs (now the Ministry of Justice) to fund their 2004 Living Together Campaign, aimed at advising cohabitants about their legal rights and indicating practical steps they could take to gain marriage-like protection where possible.[1] Subsequently, in 2005, with Scotland having already decided to reform the law relating to cohabiting couples (see Family Law (Scotland) Act 2006), the government decided to refer the issue of whether cohabitation law should be reformed to the Law Commission for England and Wales, a decision which sparked further media interest.

The attention paid to cohabitation over the last few years makes it worth revisiting the subject, to see whether, and how, behaviour and attitudes are changing.[2] So our first aim in this chapter is to examine the evolving prevalence and role of cohabitation as a relationship form in British society. Our second aim is to establish whether attitudes to cohabitation have changed, and whether legal knowledge and actions have increased following a period of sustained

[*] Anne Barlow is Professor of Family Law and Policy, Carole Burgoyne is a Senior Lecturer in the School of Psychology, both at the University of Exeter. Elizabeth Clery is a Senior Researcher at the *National Centre for Social Research* and is Co-Director of the *British Social Attitudes* survey series. Janet Smithson is a Research Fellow in the Schools of Law and Psychology at the University of Exeter.

government and media focus. Finally, we consider public beliefs about cohabitants' legal rights and financial practices. This latter issue is vital, as the courts may now take into account how cohabiting couples manage their money in deciding appropriate legal remedies on separation. Some of our key findings have already informed the deliberations of the Law Commission, due to report to Parliament in 2007, but this is the first full account of our research.[3]

Who cohabits, and for how long?

Certainly, we have not detected any decline in the popularity of cohabitation as a partnering choice. On the contrary, more than one third (36 per cent) of the public have been in a cohabiting relationship at some point, with more than a tenth (11 per cent) currently cohabiting. This represents a slight but statistically significant increase in experience of this form of relationship since 2000, when 33 per cent had cohabited (and nine per cent were currently doing so). It also reflects the gradual long-term increase in the proportion of the public currently cohabiting, identified through analysis of demographic data (Haskey, 2001).

There are a number of possible explanations as to why cohabiting is gradually increasing. These are not mutually exclusive. Attitudes to relationships may be shifting in favour of cohabitation, making this a viable option for sections of the population who would not previously have considered it. Some groups who would previously have got married may now therefore decide to cohabit instead, at least in the short term. Indeed, the cost of a 'proper wedding' has been found in recent research to be a common reason for delaying marriage and engaging in short-term cohabitation (Barlow *et al.*, 2005). Alternatively, or additionally, we may be seeing a generational effect, with cohabiting becoming more common as younger generations, who are known to be more likely to cohabit, gradually replace older ones. Or it may be that the intended purposes of cohabiting relationships are changing, resulting in them being engaged in more widely and over longer periods.

Our evidence does indeed suggest that cohabitation has increased slightly in popularity as a relationship form, and that this increase has taken place at the expense of marriage. Firstly, there is no evidence that people are becoming less keen on relationship forms that involve living with a partner (whether in the form of marriage or cohabitation). Overall, two-thirds of our respondents (65 per cent) fell into this category in 2006, the same proportion as we found in 2000. Secondly, there has been a small but significant decline in the proportion of married people over the same period, from 56 per cent to 54 per cent, and an increase in the proportion who cohabit from nine per cent to 11 per cent.

We turn now to examine the characteristics of those who cohabit and those who marry. Clearly, these groups are not mutually exclusive. Cohabitation and marriage may be engaged in by the same individuals at different life-stages, on more than one occasion and in different sequences. For instance, 31 per cent of cohabitants in 2006 had been married previously and 27 per cent of those who are married had previously cohabited. It is notable that trends in the movement between cohabitation and marriage reflect the gradual rise in the former and decline in the latter relationship form. Thus, the proportion of cohabitants who have previously been married has declined by five percentage points since 2000 (from 36 per cent) and the proportion of the married who have previously cohabited has risen by three percentage points (from 24 per cent in 2000).

Despite the overlaps between those who cohabit and those who marry, in 2000 we found considerable variations in the proportions of particular social groups in these relationship forms. In particular, cohabitants were much more likely to be young, to have no religious faith and to have earnings as their main source of income (as opposed to benefits or a pension). As shown in the next table, these trends persist. Now, more than a quarter aged between 25 and 34 cohabit, compared to a tenth aged between 45 and 54 and just one in twenty-five aged between 55 and 64. Almost a fifth of those with no religion are currently cohabiting, compared to less than one per cent of those who belong to a non-Christian religion. And the link between main source of income and relationship form also remains – with those whose main income source is earnings or benefits being more than 10 times as likely as those who rely on pensions or another source of income to be cohabiting.

Clearly, the latter difference will to some extent result from the fact that an individual's main source of income is strongly linked to their age, with younger respondents (who are much more likely to cohabit) being more likely to rely on earnings or benefits. As there is no obvious theoretical reason for these differences, it may be that the main source of income is acting as a proxy for another factor which links to levels of engagement in different relationship forms.

As those in older age groups are much more likely to belong to a religion, it may be that only one factor out of age and religion independently predicts rates of cohabitation and marriage. However, multivariate analysis (presented in Table A.1 in the chapter appendix) indicates that, even when the interaction between age and religion is controlled for, both independently predict whether an individual is currently cohabiting.

As Table 2.1 shows, not all groups are increasing their levels of cohabitation and decreasing their levels of marriage at the same pace. Cohabiting is increasing at a similar rate in all except the very oldest and youngest age groups. This suggests that the gradual increase in cohabiting can be explained by a 'period' effect (where behaviour changes across all age groups at the one time) rather than a 'generational' effect (where cohabiting increases as younger generations, who are more likely to cohabit, gradually replace older ones).

However, with the exception of those defined by age, the social groups amongst whom cohabiting was most prevalent in 2000 have, by 2006, increased their cohabitation rates the most. The cohabitation rates of those belonging to no religion, Catholics and other Christians, which were the highest in 2000, have all increased by three percentage points; conversely, levels of cohabitation among Anglicans and non-Christians, which were the lowest in 2000, have each declined by one percentage point. The same observation applies to different income groups. We found that cohabitation was most common in 2000 among those whose main source of income was earnings or benefits; by 2006, cohabitation rates for these two groups had risen by two and four percentage points respectively (while, for those relying on pensions or another main source of income, cohabitation rates have remained constant).

Table 2.1 Changes in levels of cohabiting and marriage, by age, religion and main source of income

% cohabiting and married in 2006	Cohabiting	Change since 2000	Married	Change since 2000	Base
All	11	+2	54	-2	4290
Age					
18–24	11	0	5	+1	344
25–34	26	+4	42	-2	682
35–44	16	+4	61	-3	850
45–54	10	+3	69	-1	693
55–64	4	+2	73	-5	727
65+	1	0	60	+5	989
Religion					
Church of England	6	-1	64	+1	1038
Catholic	11	+3	54	-1	391
Other Christian	8	+3	58	-1	676
Non-Christian	<1	-1	64	+8	222
No religion	17	+3	47	-1	1937
Income source					
Earnings	15	+2	59	-2	2556
Pension	1	0	65	+5	1096
Benefits	11	+4	28	-2	433
Other	1	0	18	-8	164

Our findings for marriage follow a similar pattern to those observed for cohabitation; that is, an increase in this form of relationship between 2000 and 2006 in those groups among whom marriage is most prevalent (for instance, the older, those with a non-Christian religion and those living on pensions). In most other groups, the proportion that are married has fallen very slightly between 2000 and 2006 or stayed the same.

These findings suggest that, while those who cohabit and those who marry are not two mutually exclusive groups, if these trends continue cohabitants and the married may become increasingly distinct from one another.

We turn now to consider whether the reasons why people cohabit might be changing. We know that the average age for marriage has been increasing year on year, with the average age at marriage for men being 36 and 33 for women in 2004 as compared with 27 and 25 in 1990.[4] But are cohabiting relationships being formed less often as a prelude to, and more frequently as a long-term alternative to, conventional marriage? Such a trend, as well as resulting in a reduction in the proportion of the public that are married, would lead to cohabitations lasting longer, meaning a higher proportion of the public would be cohabiting at any one particular time.

Cohabiting relationships are certainly now lasting longer. For current cohabitants, the mean average length of relationship in 2006 is 6.9 years, compared to 6.5 years in 2000.[5] For cohabitants with children, the mean increases to 8.5 years (with a median of 7 years), which indicates that such relationships cannot merely be dismissed as fleeting and insignificant when compared to marriage. This is particularly important as cohabitants with children are the group where the primary carer potentially stands to lose most legally from not marrying. And, although there has been a small decrease in the proportion of cohabitants who have a child with their partner (from 42 per cent in 2000 to 39 per cent in 2006), more than a quarter of children are now born to cohabiting couples.[6]

We also find evidence of longer relationship duration among former cohabitants – in 2000, previous cohabitations had lasted an average of 4.3 years whereas in 2006 they have lasted an average of 4.6 years. So one explanation for the increased number of cohabiting relationships we found in 2006 is simply that the same numbers of people are involved in cohabiting as before – they are just doing so for longer, meaning that at any single point in time a greater proportion of the public are cohabiting. And the fact that cohabiting relationships are becoming longer may mean that, for a greater proportion, they are being established as a long-term alternative to or, at the very least, an increasingly long prelude to marriage.

Further weight is added to this conclusion by the fact that slightly fewer cohabitants now go on to marry their partners. In 2000, 59 per cent of previous cohabiting relationships ended in marriage; by 2006 this proportion has declined to 56 per cent. So, for an increasing number, cohabitation may be an end in itself – an alternative to marriage. In 2000, we observed that, in some instances, cohabitation might be a refuge for those disillusioned by previous experiences of marriage. Certainly, the tendency for cohabitants to be more likely to have been married previously persists; 31 per cent of current cohabitants have been married before compared to 17 per cent of those who are currently married. Moreover, cohabitants who have been married before tend to have been cohabiting for longer (an average of 8.3 years, compared to 5.9 years for those who have not), giving further support to the conclusion that, for this group at least, cohabitation is indeed a long-term alternative to marriage.

The fact that cohabiting is becoming more common, particularly in distinct social and religious groupings, may additionally be the result of changes in attitudes towards cohabitation and its main alternative – marriage. It certainly appears that cohabitation is increasingly considered to be a valid partnering life-style choice, one which has taken on many of the functions of marriage, including parenting. So we next turn to examine if and how attitudes towards cohabitation and marriage have changed in recent years, and how these attitudes relate to take-up of these forms of relationship.

Attitudes to marriage and cohabitation

In order to assess attitudes towards marriage and cohabitation, we asked respondents how far they agreed or disagreed with four different statements about marriage, each focusing on a positive or negative element of this relationship form, as compared (either implicitly or explicitly) with living together. We had asked the same questions in 2000 and, by comparing responses, we can ascertain whether an increase in cohabiting and decline in marriage has been accompanied (and perhaps prompted) by the development of more positive attitudes towards cohabitation and less positive ones towards marriage. The responses obtained in 2000 and 2006 are presented in the next table.

On two measures, there has been little change since 2000. Less than one tenth in both years agreed that "there's no point getting married – it's only a piece of paper", indicating a continued and widespread belief in the functional importance of marriage. Slightly more than one quarter thought that married people made better parents, a similar proportion as in 2000, leaving almost three-quarters rejecting the view that married parenting is necessarily the best.

While significant changes have taken place on the other two measures, these do not both point in the same direction. The proportion who think that marriage is still "the best kind of relationship", while still a majority, has declined slightly from 59 per cent to 54 per cent. But far more dramatically, and moving in the opposite direction, more than two-fifths now agree that "marriage gives couples more financial security than living together", whereas slightly less than half thought this was the case in 2000. It is likely that the widespread publicity in the intervening period regarding the different legal positions of married and cohabiting couples has played a key role in this change. The government-sponsored Living Together Campaign has since summer 2004 targeted information at the mass media in order to raise public awareness and try and 'debunk' the 'common law marriage' myth.[7] Other organisations providing advice to families (for example, One plus One and the National Family and Parenting Institute) also drew attention to the legal position of cohabitants on their websites. Moreover, great media interest was generated by the Law Commission's proposals to reform cohabitation law as set out in their consultation paper in May 2006, just before the start of the survey (Law Commission, 2006). Lastly, there has been considerable publicity surrounding the increased level of financial awards made to wives on divorce. As we will see, this has had the effect of *widening* the gulf between the financial positions of married and unmarried couples on relationship breakdown, as the law currently takes quite different approaches to functionally similar couples.

In summary, therefore, heightened government and media focus on the fact that marriage gives couples greater financial security than cohabiting has probably contributed to increased public recognition of this fact, although it should not be forgotten that a sizeable minority are still seemingly unaware of this.

Table 2.2 Attitudes to marriage and cohabitation, 2000 and 2006

% agree	2000	2006
Married couples make better parents than unmarried ones	27	28
Even though it might not work out for some people, marriage is still the best kind of relationship	59	54
Marriage gives couples more financial security than living together	48	61
There is no point getting married – it's only a piece of paper	9	9
Base	2980	2775

How do different groups of people respond to the attitude statements posed? We might expect cohabitants to respond differently to those who are married as both groups have effectively selected one relationship form as their preferred type, at least for the time being. The next table compares the responses of those currently cohabiting and those who are married to the four statements.

In each case, cohabitants and the married have very different attitudes towards the advantages and disadvantages of marriage, as compared to cohabitation. These differences are in the direction we would expect – that is, those who cohabit are less likely than those who are married to have a positive view of marriage, while for those who are married the reverse is true. For instance, two-thirds of those who are married agree marriage is the best kind of relationship, compared to just one quarter of cohabitants. And, while only minorities of any group think marriage is "only a piece of paper", cohabitants are almost five times more likely to do so than those who are married. Those who are married are also substantially more aware of the fact that marriage gives couples more financial security than living together – almost two-thirds agree this is the case, compared to slightly less than half of cohabitants. Of course, awareness of the lack of financial security associated with cohabiting may be one of the factors that prompts people to get married. What is perhaps more surprising is the fact that more than two-fifths of cohabitants are aware that marriage gives couples more financial security, yet have still apparently chosen to cohabit. Of course, it may be that they have taken steps to address this situation within their cohabiting relationships, a possibility that the next section explores in detail.

Table 2.3 Attitudes to marriage and cohabitation, by marital status

% agree	All	Cohabitants	Married
Married couples make better parents than unmarried ones	28	7	32
Even though it might not work out for some people, marriage is still the best kind of relationship	54	24	66
Marriage gives couples more financial security than living together	61	45	65
There is no point getting married – it's only a piece of paper	9	19	4
Base	2775	269	1343

We know from qualitative studies that many couples see cohabitation as a step towards marriage whilst a minority view is that cohabitation is a preferable alternative for ideological or practical reasons (Barlow *et al.*, 2005, 2007). Some cohabitants might recognise the benefits of marriage and treat short-term cohabitation as a form of 'engagement', with marriage being their ultimate goal, whilst others have actively rejected marriage. This might go some way towards explaining why those with particularly negative attitudes towards marriage tend to have cohabited for longer. Just seven per cent of those who have cohabited for less than three years think marriage is "only a piece of paper", compared to 15 per cent of those who have cohabited for between three and six years and 21 per cent of those who have cohabited for more than seven years. This pattern is replicated across cohabitants' responses to all four statements. Perhaps long-term cohabitants are more likely to have rejected marriage altogether or over time have formed the view that marriage differs little from long-term cohabitation in what it offers.

To what extent are attitudes linked to behaviour? To examine this, we repeated the multivariate analysis described earlier, adding in responses to the four marriage statements shown in Table 2.2. This allows us to assess whether these attitudes independently predict whether an individual is currently cohabiting, once we take account of age and religion. The results of this analysis are presented in the chapter appendix. While age and religion continue to independently predict whether an individual is cohabiting, attitudes also appear to make a difference (although we must remember, of course, that people's attitudes are sometimes a consequence of their choices, rather than a cause). In our model, the belief that married couples make better parents than unmarried ones and the view that marriage is "only a piece of paper" were both significant predictors of whether or not a person currently cohabits.[8]

So far, then, we have seen that cohabitation remains an important and increasingly popular family form, although marriage continues to be more prevalent. More couples are cohabiting and these relationships (particularly those of cohabiting parents) are lasting longer. Attitudes to marriage as compared with cohabitation remain broadly similar, although there does seem to be a growing awareness of the fact that marriage provides greater financial security.

Beliefs about cohabitation and money management

The style of money management adopted by cohabiting couples has recently gained significance in the context of legal reform, both as a possible indicator of commitment within a relationship, and as being relevant to the appropriate legal remedies that should apply on relationship breakdown or death of a partner. Thus, a recent House of Lords decision used the fact that the couple had *not* merged their finances as evidence that the couple were not operating as a single financial entity.[9] This was contrasted with the pattern of management more typical of married couples, where the most common form of money management is the joint pool (Pahl, 1995).

So we turn now to consider how the *public* think cohabiting couples with children should behave financially during their relationship, and how views about this compare with those held about married couples. Do, for instance, people believe that a cohabiting couple with children should treat their finances as if they were two separate individuals, or in the more collective manner associated with marriage? We focus on this in the expectation that our findings will provide important insights into the extent to which marriage and cohabiting are seen as functionally equivalent relationships.

To address these issues, we presented respondents with the following scenario:

> *Imagine an unmarried couple living together with young children. Both the man and woman work part-time, but he earns more. They share the childcare between them. Which of the options… do you think is the best way for them to organise their money as a couple?*

We asked respondents to choose from a number of different options. These included approaches which involve pooling all income together, found previously to be the most common financial practice among married couples (Pahl, 1995). More recently we have witnessed an increase in the use of partial pooling and independent management of finances, especially amongst younger married and unmarried couples (Burgoyne *et al.*, 2006, 2007; Ashby and Burgoyne, 2007). So we also included options that allowed people to express a preference for these approaches instead. We also allowed respondents to indicate whether contributions to the household finances should be equal or unequal, depending on income, as these more nuanced aspects of money management have been found to be important in recent research (Ashby and Burgoyne, 2007). The full range of options offered to respondents is shown below, with our shorthand label for each option shown in brackets:

They pool some of their income, with each giving the same amount, and keep the rest of their income separate (partial pooling – equal contributions)

They pool some of their income, with the man giving more, and keep the rest of their income separate (partial pooling – higher earner more)

They keep their incomes separate and deal with bills when they come in, with each paying the same amount (independent management – equal contribution)

They keep their incomes separate and deal with bills when they come in, with the man paying more (independent management – higher earner more)

They pool all their income together (pooling)

Some other arrangement

Of the six options, just over half (53 per cent) think the couple should pool all of their income (Table 2.4). The second most popular option, favoured by 17 per cent, is partial pooling, with the man contributing more. Since the man in this scenario is depicted as the higher earner, this arrangement helps to offset the disparity in partners' earnings, though, of course, it leaves the precise degree of adjustment unspecified. Partial pooling with equal contributions is slightly less popular and was chosen by 14 per cent of respondents. There is far less support for either form of independent management. These findings serve to underline the strength of the norm of sharing in families, especially when there are dependent children (Sonnenberg *et al.*, 2005). It seems that even when a couple are not married, the idealized view is that money should be pooled to a greater or lesser degree and used as a joint resource, regardless of financial contribution.

There are some differences of opinion between different social groups (though notably men and women do not have different views on this matter). There is less support for pooling all income among the young (particularly those aged 18 to 24). Total pooling of income is favoured by a third (34 per cent) of 18 to 24 year olds and 45 per cent of 25 to 34 year olds. Support for pooling increases for each older age group, with the exception of the over 65s where it declines slightly to 55 per cent. These patterns reflect the recent trend towards greater separation in finances amongst younger couples, many of whom will have two independent incomes and, certainly among the 18 to 24 year olds, will be less likely to have dependent children.

As Table 2.4 shows, cohabitants are less inclined than the general public to endorse the pooling of all household income, with 48 per cent favouring this compared to 53 per cent of the public as a whole. There may be two possible explanations for this. Firstly, the average age of cohabitants is lower than that for the sample as a whole, and total pooling is less popular in the under 35s. Secondly, cohabitants who are conscious that they have different rights to married couples, and who have chosen cohabitation deliberately, may be less willing to endorse pooling in the absence of additional safeguards.

Table 2.4 Attitudes to money management for a cohabiting couple with children, by cohabitation status

	All	Cohabitants
	%	%
Pooling	53	48
Partial pooling – higher earner more	17	19
Partial pooling – equal contributions	14	13
Independent management – equal contribution	7	9
Independent management – higher earner more	6	8
Some other arrangement	1	1
Don't know	2	1
Base	*2909*	*267*

How do these findings compare with what cohabitants actually do in practice? Previous research (Vogler *et al.*, 2007) shows that childless cohabitants are more likely than married couples to use one of the more independent systems such as partial pooling or independent management, though these authors also found that 40 per cent of the childless cohabitants in their sample were using the 'joint pool'. However, cohabiting parents were much more similar to married parents, with 52 per cent and 59 per cent respectively using a joint pool approach.

Our findings suggest that a majority of people believe that pooling income (whether fully or partially) is the most appropriate financial arrangement for cohabiting couples with children. This mirrors behaviour among both cohabiting and married parents, and lends support to the view that the public view these two forms of relationship as functionally very similar to one another. We next turn to consider how these two forms of relationships are treated by the law and how the public believe they are treated.

Cohabitants and the law

We begin by considering the current legal status of cohabitants in England and Wales, and examine the prevalence of the 'common law marriage' myth. We then examine the legal actions taken by those who are currently cohabiting.

In Scotland, the recent Family Law (Scotland) Act 2006 has given cohabitants cohesive marriage-like remedies on relationship breakdown, and has provided new remedies on death of a cohabitant partner. In England and Wales, the law has developed *ad hoc* and is yet to adopt a consistent approach to the treatment of cohabiting couples (see Barlow and James, 2004).[10] At present, cohabitants in England and Wales are treated as if they were married in some situations. Examples of this would include the claiming of means-tested benefits or tax credits, and the transferring of, or succeeding to, the rented tenancy of the family home on relationship breakdown or death. In other situations, the law gives cohabitants rights that are similar to those that apply to people who are married but are usually less generous from the perspective of the financially weaker partner. Examples here would include claiming an inheritance from a partner's estate where that partner has died without making a will under the Inheritance (Provision for Families and Dependants) Act 1975. In yet other situations cohabitants are treated as quite separate and unconnected individuals. Examples would include inheritance tax from which property transfers between spouses are exempt, or claiming a state retirement or widowed person's pension on their partner's national insurance contributions. Perhaps the starkest difference between married and cohabiting couples, however, is on relationship breakdown. Rented tenancies of the family home aside, there is no divorce equivalent for cohabitants, who are dependent on strict and complex property law rather than family law based on principles of 'fairness' to resolve their disputes concerning the owner-occupied family home or other property. As previously observed, this situation has become more anomalous due to the more generous financial provision available to the weaker financial spouse on divorce. Indeed, the gulf between the legal treatment of these two functionally equivalent family forms is one that has widened considerably even since the 2000 *British Social Attitudes* survey and has received a good deal of media coverage.[11]

The 'common law marriage' myth

Data from the 2000 *British Social Attitudes* survey highlighted the fact that, in the broadest terms, the legal position of cohabitants outlined above is not widely understood. Over half, 56 per cent, of the public thought there was such a thing as common law marriage, whereby unmarried couples who have lived together for some time have the same legal rights as married couples. Moreover, this figure could not simply be explained by the fact only a minority of the public were cohabiting; almost six in ten (59 per cent) of those cohabiting in 2000 believed in common law marriage.

As we have noted, there has been a concerted effort by government, accompanied by intense media coverage, to publicise the disparity in the legal rights and treatment of cohabitants as compared with married couples. Given these activities, we asked respondents to the 2006 survey the same question about common law marriage to see if and to what extent public understanding of the legal position of cohabitants has improved. Specifically, we asked respondents:

As far as you know do unmarried couples who live together for some time have a 'common law marriage' which gives them the same legal rights as married couples?

The responses obtained are presented in the next table. They suggest that only a limited inroad has been made into the myth. True, there has been a slight though significant decline of five percentage points in the proportion who believe that common law marriage "definitely" or "probably" exists; around half now believe this is the case. However, this decline cannot be explained by a rise in the public's knowledge of the legal position of cohabitants. Rather, as often happens when an issue has received extensive publicity, there has been an increase in public uncertainty, with the proportion who could not choose an answer rising from six per cent to 10 per cent. As a result, the proportion who (correctly) answered that common law marriage does not exist has remained almost identical between 2000 and 2006 (at 37 per cent and 38 per cent respectively).

Table 2.5 Belief in existence of common law marriage, 2000 and 2006

	2000	2006
Belief in existence of common law marriage	%	%
Definitely do	17	14
Probably do	39	37
Probably do not	23	23
Definitely do not	14	15
Can't choose	6	10
Base	*2669*	*2775*

Base: England and Wales only

As much of the publicity around cohabitants' rights has been aimed at cohabitants themselves, it may be that an increase in knowledge has been confined to this group. This is partially true; the proportion of cohabitants who correctly believe that there is no such thing as common law marriage went up from 35 per cent to 39 per cent between 2000 and 2006. While this increase is comparatively small and not statistically significant it may indicate that the publicity geared towards cohabitants has, as intended, impacted particularly on the knowledge of this group. However, it is important to note that the same proportion of cohabitants as married people still falsely believe that common law marriage exists (53 per cent in both cases).

Belief in the existence of common law marriage is not equally pervasive across all sections of society. Age is significantly linked, with those in the youngest age group being *less* likely to believe in its existence, the opposite of what we found in 2000. Forty-four per cent of those aged between 18 and 24 believe common law marriage exists; this lower level of belief can be explained by the fact that almost one fifth (18 per cent) in this group could not choose an answer to the question. It is also notable that belief in common law marriage declines as the level of educational qualifications increases; 39 per cent of graduates believe cohabiting and married couples have the same legal rights, compared to 56 per cent of those with no qualifications. This might reflect a tendency for graduates to be more adept at interpreting the legal position of cohabitants from the range of information available. In contrast to 2000, when men were more likely than women to believe in the existence of common law marriage, we found no difference by gender.

While there has not been a marked increase in public understanding of the legal position of cohabitants, we found earlier that there *has* been a substantial rise in the proportion of the public who recognise that marriage gives couples more financial security than living together. This security is, of course, itself a consequence of the legal rights associated with the two statuses. So, whilst we cannot conclude that the public has a better understanding of the legal rights of cohabitants than six years ago, there is some evidence that understanding of the impact of these differential rights may have increased.

Taking legal action

Given that the legal position of cohabitants continues to be poorly understood, we might expect few legal steps to have been taken by cohabitants to address their vulnerable position. Indeed, more than half appear to believe they have the same legal rights as they would have if they were married. What is more, even among those who are aware that legal steps are needed, the assumption that legal knowledge leads to appropriate legal action may not necessarily be correct. The 2000 *British Social Attitudes* survey and follow-up study identified only a small increase in legal action by cohabitants who were aware of the need for it, with legal costs and an optimism bias (as a consequence of which they believed they were unlikely to split up or die prematurely) being cited as key reasons for inaction (Barlow *et al.*, 2001, 2005). Since 2000, it may be that the increased availability of online legal advice and appropriate legal forms from organisations such as the Living Together Campaign,[12] as well as publicity about cases where inaction proved ill-advised, has prompted a greater proportion of legally aware cohabitants to take appropriate legal steps. So we asked current and previous cohabitants a number of questions about any legal steps which they or their partner had taken with regard to their relationships: whether those who own their accommodation have a written agreement with their partner about their share in the ownership; whether either partner has ever made or changed a will because they were living together or has sought advice about their legal position as a cohabiting couple.

Only a minority of current or previous cohabitants or their partners in 2006 had taken any of these steps. One ninth (11 per cent) of those who own their accommodation had a written agreement about their share in the ownership, a similar proportion (12 per cent) had changed a will as a result of their cohabiting relationship and one fifth (19 per cent) had sought advice about their legal position as a cohabiting couple.

We found no strong evidence that legal actions by cohabitants are increasing, which raises the issue of whether the law's expectation of people taking the 'legally rational' steps available is itself over-optimistic and unlikely to be realised (Barlow and Duncan, 2000; Duncan *et al.*, 2005). For instance, the proportions of previous and current cohabitants who have changed a will as a result of their cohabitation remained almost identical between 2000 and 2006, although this action is slightly (but not significantly) more common among current than among past cohabitants, suggesting that it might be becoming more common over time. We also asked for the first time in 2006 whether cohabitants had sought legal advice about their relationship; however, the proportions of current and previous cohabitants who had done so are identical, suggesting little change over time.

One action has increased in prevalence; that of having a written agreement about each person's share in the ownership of the home. Among current cohabitants where one or both partners own their home, 15 per cent now have such an agreement, up from eight per cent in 2000. This increase is almost certainly due in part to the requirement that declarations of shares in jointly owned property should now be made before a purchase of a home can be registered at the Land Registry.[13] However, there is no such requirement if just one partner owns the home; any decision to share ownership in these cases would have to be initiated and negotiated between the cohabitants themselves without any prompting, leaving the non-owner legally vulnerable.

Each of the three legal actions we examined are more likely to have been taken by cohabitants in longer relationships. Thus, six per cent of those who have cohabited for less than three years have changed a will as a result of their relationship, compared to 11 per cent and 25 per cent of those who have cohabited for between three and six years and more than seven years respectively.

Are legal actions more likely to be taken by the legally aware minority of cohabitants? While the small size of our samples of cohabitants greatly limits the identification of significant differences, there is certainly some evidence of a link between legal knowledge and legal actions. For instance, of those cohabitants who own their homes, 42 per cent of those with an agreement about their share in the ownership believe the 'common law marriage' myth, compared to 51 per cent of those with no agreement. Similarly, those who have sought legal advice about their cohabiting relationships are significantly less likely to believe in common law marriage; this was the case for 43 per cent, compared to 55 per cent of those who had not sought advice. The knowledge that common law marriage does not exist could, of course, have prompted some cohabitants to investigate their legal position, or could have been the consequence of this investigation. It is notable, however, that the levels of knowledge about the legal position of cohabitants are very similar among those who have and have not changed a will as a result of their cohabiting relationship.

Clearly, then, the majority of the public currently believe cohabitants have a far more extensive set of rights than they actually do. This may be because, in the absence of knowledge of the actual legal position, they assume this is what the situation logically should be, given the social acceptance of cohabitation. In addition, the legal steps needed to gain marriage-like protection between cohabitants are not always straightforward, although efforts have been made through government funding and media exposure to make advice and appropriate action more available than was the case previously. Certainly we have found little evidence to suggest that any more than a minority of cohabiting couples have made legal arrangements to protect themselves in the light of relationship breakdown or the death of one partner.

Perceptions of what cohabitants' legal rights should be

We turn now to examine public views about how the law *should* treat cohabitants in a variety of situations, irrespective of how it currently operates. Our aim is to examine attitudes to the current law in situations where it treats functionally similar married and cohabiting couples differently and to ascertain what might be publicly acceptable in terms of reform in these areas.

To achieve this, respondents were presented with a number of scenarios describing a range of relationships. For instance, one scenario asked respondents to:

> *Imagine an unmarried couple who have lived together for 20 years and have three children. The woman had reduced her working to part-time when the first child was born but gave up work entirely after the second child was born in order to care for the family and home. The man has supported the family financially throughout and also owns the family home. The youngest child recently left home and the couple's relationship has now broken down. The woman has no income and poor job prospects.*

The scenarios differed in certain key aspects: duration; the presence or absence of children; and the level and types of investment which the two partners had made in the relationship. We asked respondents whether the less well off partner in each scenario should have a right to "financial provision" from the better off partner on separation, firstly in situations where the couple had been married and secondly when they had been cohabiting. Currently, in each situation described in the scenarios, the law provides a remedy only for the married. However, the Law Commission is considering what remedies, if any, might be appropriate in cohabiting relationships which are functionally similar to married ones, particularly where one partner suffers financial disadvantage as a result of the relationship.

The responses are presented in Table 2.6. Focusing firstly on those situations involving an unmarried couple, we can see major differences in the proportions of people who think that the less well off partner should be entitled to financial provision. These differences appear to relate to the length of the relationship and how much the less well off partner has invested in it. Thus, when the couple have lived together for 20 years, have three children and the woman gave up work completely to look after the family and home, almost nine-tenths agree she should be entitled to financial provision on separation. However, when the couple have lived together for just two years with one partner having a much higher income and owning the family home (and when no clear investment in the relationship by the less well off partner is indicated), less than four-tenths agree that the less well off partner should have a right to financial provision.

Table 2.6 Attitudes regarding rights to financial provision on separation for married and unmarried couples

% agree partner should have right to financial provision on separation if ...	If couple not married	If couple married
... couple living together for 20 years, three children, woman reduced work to part-time and then gave up work to look after family and home, man supported family financially and owns home, woman has no income and poor job prospects	89	n/a
... couple living together for 10 years, no children, one partner worked unpaid to build up other partner's business, partner who runs business also owns family home, other partner has no property or income of own	87	93
... couple living together for 10 years, one partner has well-paid job requiring frequent moves, other partner has worked where possible but has not had a settled career	69	81
... couple living together for two years, one has a much higher income than the other and owns the family home	38	62
Base	*3197*	*3197*

n/a = not asked

We can see a similar level of differentiation when the couple in question are married. While a higher proportion in each scenario think the married partner should have a right to financial provision on separation, as compared to the cohabiting partner, differentiation between the two types of relationship is most marked when its duration and the partners' investments in it are at their lowest. So, for the couple who have lived together for 10 years with one partner working unpaid to build up the other's business, there is a difference of just six percentage points between the proportions who think that the less well off partner should be entitled to financial provision, if married as compared to cohabiting. However, for the couple who have been together two years where one has a much higher income than the other and owns the family home, there is a difference of 34 percentage points, with almost twice as many respondents agreeing the partner should be entitled to financial provision if he or she is married than if he or she is not. Clearly, then, the public's perception of what separating partners should be entitled to is not simply informed by the status of their relationship but relates strongly to its length, as well as the nature and level of the investment in it made by the less well off partner. It could be concluded that when cohabitations become more 'marriage-like', with partners living together for a long time, having children and sharing earning and caring responsibilities between them or prioritising one partner's career, the public are much more likely to feel they should receive the same level of treatment as that given to partners separating from marriage.

The previous questions focused upon financial provision after separation. Of course, some relationships will end because of the death of one of the partners, rather than separation. As we outlined earlier, unless specific measures have been taken, this can leave cohabiting partners vulnerable. To assess what people think should happen in this sort of situation, we asked:

> *Imagine an unmarried couple without children who have been living together for two years in a house bought in the man's name three years ago, before their relationship began. Say the man died without making a will. Do you think the woman **should** or **should not** have the same financial rights regarding his property as she would if she had been married to the man?*

In this instance, two-thirds (66 per cent) of people think that the woman in the scenario should have the same financial rights she would have done were they married, even though the relationship was short and she has not suffered any apparent financial disadvantage.

These findings show that a majority of the public think that cohabitants should have a far more extensive set of legal rights than they currently do. However, they do not necessarily think cohabitants should have the *same* rights on separation as married couples – instead they differentiate substantially on the basis of individual circumstances, with the presence or absence of children, 'investment' in the relationship and duration all proving important factors. Clearly, then, it is not just the public understanding of the legal position of cohabitants which is at odds with current legislation; so too are public beliefs about what cohabitants' legal position should be.

Conclusions

What light do our findings shed on the way forward for reform of cohabitation law? Both the strong continued existence of the 'common law marriage' myth and our findings as to what the public think cohabitants' rights should be, lend very strong support for reform of cohabitation law and this has been recognized by the Law Commission (Law Commission, 2007). People are very confused by the disjuncture between the social acceptance of marriage-like cohabitation and its often unmarriage-like legal consequences. Where legal advantage or disadvantage has been gained or suffered by a partner at the expense of another because of their cohabiting relationship, there is strong public support for a legal remedy, with support depending on factors such as the length of the relationship, the presence of children, and the nature of a person's 'investment' in the relationship. The Law Commission's approach to relationship breakdown has public endorsement. The data also reveal a clear case for differentiating between short childless marriages and short childless cohabitations of two years, although it is worthy of note that the case for a claim to financial support after such a marriage has far less endorsement than claims for financial support after longer relationships where economic advantage or disadvantage is demonstrated (as shown in Table 2.6). In the public's mind, the case for a distinction between cohabitation and marriage appears to decrease as the relationships in question lengthen, but a minimum qualification period for such rights of between two and five years as suggested by the Law Commission would seem appropriate. Conversely on death, the data reveal support for a greater generosity than exists currently towards a childless cohabitant of two years standing. Here a majority of two-thirds favour such a cohabitant having the same claim to a deceased partner's property as she would have had if she had been married. Taken with findings from the 2000 *British Social Attitudes* survey which showed near unanimous support for equal treatment between a childless cohabitant of 10 years standing and a married counterpart, there does seem to be public support for a marriage-equivalent approach consequent upon the cohabitation relationship, rather than one based on proof of economic advantage and disadvantage on death of a cohabitant partner as recommended by the Law Commission (Law Commission, 2007).

Our findings as regards money management issues are also important. Our data show pooling is seen as the ideal when a couple have a child, irrespective of whether a couple are married or cohabiting. This lends some support to the view that the public see these forms of relationship as functionally very similar. However, we would urge caution in placing too much emphasis on this when deciding legal outcomes. Despite the House of Lords decision, some research suggests that financial arrangements cannot and should not always be relied on as a transparent indicator of the nature of an intimate relationship nor of the intentions of the two partners (Ashby and Burgoyne, 2007, Douglas *et al.*, 2007). There may be a host of pragmatic reasons for keeping finances separate, such as the need to clear individual debts incurred before the start of the relationship, avoiding the involvement of a current partner in an assessment for maintenance or child support for a previous relationship, or simply inertia and a delay in changing the existing bank accounts. Ashby and Burgoyne found that some couples who appeared to have entirely separate accounts, in practice treated all their money as a collectively owned resource in the same way as is the common practice in marriage.

Overall, our findings confirm that cohabitation is very much here to stay, both as a partnering and a parenting form. However, as the increased duration of cohabiting partnerships makes clear, it is no longer appropriate to regard it is a relatively brief and transitory arrangement (Ermisch and Francesconi, 1999). Cohabitation continues to take on many of the functions of marriage and is seen as a valid lifestyle choice which is socially accepted in virtually all sections of society. Whilst making legal information available to cohabitants is important, there are many people it has not reached. The 'common law marriage' myth lives on, despite the wealth of media exposure the issues have enjoyed in recent years. Perhaps this is because there is no great distinction made by the majority of the public between what the legal remedies available to cohabitants should be as compared to married couples on death or even, in most situations, on relationship breakdown. Where there has been a long-term cohabiting relationship functionally equivalent to marriage, or where there has been a joint enterprise relationship where one partner suffers disadvantage or gains advantage as a consequence of the relationship, there is strong support for legal remedies to be made available. How marriage-like these should be, is at the end of the day, a policy decision for government, but there seems to be little public appetite for the continuation of the deep legal divisions drawn between married and unmarried cohabiting families.

Notes

1. See http://www.advicenow.org.uk/livingtogether run by the Advicenow organisation and funded by the Department of Constitutional Affairs (now the Ministry of Justice).
2. The *British Social Attitudes* survey questions on cohabitation reported here are the first phase of a project, funded by the Nuffield Foundation, which goes on in its second phase to further explore issues raised by means of in-depth qualitative research interviews with a purposive sample.
3. The Law Commission's report to Parliament (Law Com. No. 307), which drew upon *British Social Attitudes* survey data, was published on 31st July 2007.
4. ONS Marriage, Divorce and Adoption Statistics 2004 (Series FM2 No. 32)
5. The median is five years for 2006 and four years for 2000.

6.   ONS, Birth Statistics Series FM1 No. 33 (2005) Table 3.10 shows that 42 per cent of all live births were to unmarried parents in 2004, with 76.4 per cent of these registrations by couples living at the same address and presumed to be cohabiting.

7.   The most intense media publicity took place in May and early June 2006 just before the survey went into the field. The Living Together Campaign featured on BBC Breakfast television, Channel 4 lunchtime news, Radio 5 Live breakfast programme, 33 local radio stations and 5 national newspapers. Following the publication of the Law Commission's consultation paper (Law Commission, 2006) on 31st May 2006, the Living Together Campaign's website was visited 50,000 times over a four day period.

8.   As those with a pro-marriage attitude on any particular statement are more likely also to register pro-marriage views on the other three measures, we should exercise caution in concluding that these two specific measures influence individuals' decisions to cohabit.

9.   In *Stack v. Dowden* [2007] UKHL 17 the (unmarried) couple's treatment of money and other assets *was* taken into account as an indicator of their (non)intention to operate as a single financial entity.

10. Consequently, our subsequent analysis excludes responses from Scotland as the legal position of cohabitants there is quite different from that in England and Wales.

11. For in a recent case, the House of Lords has confirmed that where there are surplus assets, dependent spouses' claims are no longer limited to their reasonable needs even following a short marriage. Rather, all other things being equal, matrimonial asset division is guided by the overarching principle of fairness which is achieved by addressing the parties' needs, compensation for disadvantage caused to one party by the relationship and sharing. It should reflect the fact that marriage is a partnership of equals regardless of who was the breadwinner and who was the homemaker and primary carer of the children (see *Miller v. Miller; McFarlane v. McFarlane* [2006] UKHL 24).

12. See www.advicenow.org/livingtogether. By the end of May 2006, just less than two years from when the Living Together Campaign was launched, one million Living Together Guides providing free and accessible legal information to cohabitants had been downloaded from their site.

13. See Land Registry documents TR1 and FR1. This was introduced by changes to the Land Registration Rules in 1977 (see SI 1997/3037 rules 19 and 98) and so more cohabitants purchasing a property jointly would have had their attention drawn to this by 2006 than was the case in 2000.

References

Ashby, K. and Burgoyne, C. (2007, forthcoming), 'Separate financial entities? Beyond categories of money management', *Journal of Socio-Economics*

Barlow, A., Burgoyne, C., and Smithson, J. (2007), *The Living Together Campaign –
An investigation of its impact on legally aware cohabitants,* London: Ministry of
Justice, available at www.justice.gov.uk/publications/research250707.htm

Barlow, A. and Duncan, S. (2000), 'Family law, moral rationalities and New Labour's
communitarianism: Part II', *Journal of Social Welfare and Family Law,* **22(2)**: 129–43

Barlow, A., Duncan, S., James, G. and Park, A. (2001) 'Just a piece of paper? Marriage
and cohabitation in Britain', in Park, A., Curtice, J., Thomson, K., Jarvis, L. and
Bromley, C. (eds.), *British Social Attitudes: The 18th Report – Public policy, social
ties,* London: Sage

Barlow, A., Duncan, S., James, G. and Park, A. (2005), *Cohabitation, marriage and the
law. Social change and legal reform in 21st Century Britain,* Oxford: Hart Publishing

Barlow, A. and James, G. (2004), 'Regulating Marriage and Cohabitation in 21st
Century Britain', *Modern Law Review,* **67(2)**: 143–176

Burgoyne, C., Clarke, V., Edmunds, A. and Reibstein, J (2006), '"All my worldly goods
I share with you?" Managing money at the transition to heterosexual marriage', *The
Sociological Review,* **54**: 619–637

Burgoyne, C., Dolman, V., Edmunds, A. and Reibstein, J. (2007), 'Money management
systems in early marriage: factors influencing change and stability', *Journal of
Economic Psychology,* **28**: 214–228

Douglas, G., Pearce, J., Woodward, H. (2007), *A Failure of Trust: Resolving Property
Disputes on Cohabitation Breakdown,* available at
www.law.cf.ac.uk/researchpapers/papers/1.pdf

Duncan, S., Barlow, A. and James, G. (2005), 'Why don't they marry? Cohabitation,
commitment and DIY marriage', *Child and Family Law Quarterly,* **17(3)**: 383–398

Ermisch J. and Francesconi, M., (1999) 'Cohabitation in Great Britain: Not for long but
here to stay', *Working Paper of the Institute for Social and Economic Research,*
Colchester: University of Essex

Haskey, J. (2001) 'Cohabitation in Great Britain: Past, present and future trends – and
attitudes', *Population Trends* **103**, available at
www.statistics.gov.uk/CCI/article.asp?ID=547&Pos=7&ColRank=2&Rank=144

Law Commission for England and Wales (2006), *Cohabitation: The Financial
Consequences of Relationship Breakdown (consultation paper 173),* London: The
Stationery Office

Law Commission for England and Wales (2007), *Cohabitation: The Financial
Consequences of Relationship Breakdown (Law Commission No. 307),* London: The
Stationery Office

Pahl, J. (1995), 'His money, her money: Recent research on financial organisation in
marriage', *Journal of Economic Psychology,* **16**: 361–376

Sonnenberg, S., Burgoyne, C. and Routh, D. (2005), 'Income disparity and choice of
financial organisation in the household', Proceedings, 30th Annual Congress of
IAREP, International Association for Research in Economic Psychology: Czech
Republic

Vogler, C., Brockmann, M. and Wiggins, R. (2007, forthcoming), 'Managing money in
new heterosexual forms of intimate relationships', *Journal of Socio-Economics*

Acknowledgements

The *National Centre for Social Research* is grateful to the Nuffield Foundation for their financial support which enabled us to ask the questions reported in this chapter from 2006, although the views expressed are those of the authors alone.

Appendix

Table A.1 Logistic regression (dependent variable whether respondent currently cohabits) – socio-demographic and attitudinal characteristics

Predictor variables	Model A	Model B
	Socio-demographic characteristics	Socio-demographic characteristics and attitudinal characteristics
Nagelkerke R²	0.158	0.212
Age (increase by one year)	-.053**	-.044**
Religion (no religion)		
Church of England	-.488	-.148
Catholic	-.271	-.131
Other Christian	-.595**	-.105
Non-Christian	-2.667**	-1.671*
Married couples make better parents than unmarried ones		.496**
Decrease in agreement by one unit (agree strongly, agree, neither agree nor disagree, disagree, disagree strongly)		
Even though it might not work out for some people, marriage is still the best kind of relationship		.145
Decrease in agreement by one unit (agree strongly, agree, neither agree nor disagree, disagree, disagree strongly)		
Marriage gives couples more financial security than living together		.028
Decrease in agreement by one unit (agree strongly, agree, neither agree nor disagree, disagree, disagree strongly)		
There is no point getting married – it's only a piece of paper		-.292**
Decrease in agreement by one unit (agree strongly, agree, neither agree nor disagree, disagree, disagree strongly)		
Base	*4260*	*2585*

* = significant at 5% level
** = significant at 1% level

3 Who does the housework? The division of labour within the home

Rosemary Crompton and Clare Lyonette[*]

Although it might appear to be an uncontentious term, the idea of 'work' has long been debated. Should 'work' primarily be thought of as something done for pay, hence separate and distinct from other aspects of life? That view has been strongly contested by feminists, who have argued that unpaid domestic work and caring are necessary to human reproduction and should also be treated as 'work' (Glucksmann, 1995; Sevenhuijsen, 2002). More generally, others have argued that contemporary transformations in the world of paid employment are increasingly blurring the boundaries between work and non-work. Consumerism and the growth of services mean that an increasing proportion of the population is engaged in flexible working and have non-standard work hours. The emergence of the global corporation, and associated technological developments such as electronic communications, can mean that colleagues are located in different time zones, and the worker is expected to be available at all times. Meanwhile, increased competitiveness and target setting, together with the development of high-commitment management techniques, have led to pressures on employees to maintain a focus on their work even outside paid working hours (Burchell *et al.*, 2002).

Increasingly, more women are in employment: today the proportion of dual-earner households in Britain far exceeds old-style male-breadwinner households. Yet gender differences in the home persist. Two different sets of theories have been developed to explain the nature of, and trends in, the division of domestic labour between men and women (Bianchi *et al.*, 2000; Coltrane, 2000; Baxter *et al.*, 2004). The first set, which we refer to as economistic or material theories, stress the significance of both time availability and relative resources within the household. Time availability models suggest that those household members spending most time in market work (usually men) will have the least time available for household work. Those spending most time in market work will also bring the most resources into the household, and as a

[*] Rosemary Crompton is Professor of Sociology, Clare Lyonette is a Research Officer, both at City University.

consequence, their superior relative material power will also result in their spending less time on housework – the relative resource hypothesis (Blood and Wolfe, 1960). Furthermore, neoclassical economists (Mincer and Polachek, 1974; Becker, 1991) have argued that the household as a unit will operate to its best advantage if men specialise in market work and women specialise in caring and domestic work. According to these kinds of theories, therefore, women's increased involvement with market work (which will both reduce the time they have available and increase the resources they bring into the household) should result in men's increased involvement in domestic work.

These kinds of rational economic accounts of the division of domestic and market labour have been challenged by normative or gender construction theories. Feminists have argued that the allocation of the primary responsibility for housework to women is the key to the reproduction of gendered traditionalism, as the roles of wife and mother are intimately tied to expectations for doing housework (West and Zimmerman, 1987). Thus order and cleanliness within the home are reflections on women's competence as a "wife and mother" – but not on men's competence as a "husband and father" (Bianchi *et al.*, 2000: 195). According to these arguments, given that the construction and reconstruction of gendered identities is the major factor in the determination of who does domestic work, its allocation is not necessarily rational and women will almost invariably do more of it, even when in full-time employment. It should be noted, however, that normative theories are not necessarily feminist in their inspiration. Theories may be informed by conventional ideas regarding sex roles, including morality theories that argue that women, because of their essential nature, are uniquely well qualified to perform these tasks (Coltrane, 2000; Crompton and Lyonette, 2005).

In this chapter, we shall examine the gendered division of labour in the home in the light of these theories, using data from the *British Social Attitudes* survey series. We shall also examine the related topic of the association between women's reported happiness and the domestic division of labour. Empirical research has suggested that women are happier if there is less domestic traditionalism in the home, but morality theories would suggest, on the contrary, that women are happier when they accept their traditional domestic roles.

The questions we look at were asked in identical format in the 2002 and 2006 surveys. In order to have a sufficient sample size for our analyses, we have combined the two datasets. This is, of course, only possible because the changes in attitudes and behaviour over this period have been relatively small. Where this is not the case, we make mention of this. Some of the questions were also asked on the *International Social Survey Programme* modules on *Family and Gender* in 1989 and 1994. We use these to look at longer-term trends.

Changes over time

Attitudes to gender roles, central to which are ideas about the proper kinds of work for men and women, are moving in a more gender liberal direction amongst all social groupings. As shown in the next table, the proportion of men who say that "a man's job is to earn money; a woman's job is to look after the home and family" fell from around a third in 1989 to one sixth in 2006.

In particular, women's employment, even amongst mothers of young children, is now widely accepted in Britain. In 1989, over half of men still thought that "a pre-school child is likely to suffer if his or her mother works", but this has fallen to two-fifths. Indeed, changes in attitudes to women's employment have followed closely on actual increases in women's (and mothers') paid work. In Britain, women's employment rates increased rapidly during the 1980s. Although still on an upward trend, the rate slowed somewhat during the 1990s, a decade in which "increasing female participation in the labour market was entirely concentrated among women with children" (Dench *et al.*, 2002: 31).

Table 3.1 Attitudes to women's employment, by sex, 1989–2006

	1989		1994		2002		2006	
% agree	Men	Women	Men	Women	Men	Women	Men	Women
A man's job is to earn money; a woman's job is to look after the home and family	32	26	26	21	20	15	17	15
A pre-school child is likely to suffer if his or her mother works	53	42	42	34	42	31	41	29
Base	*587*	*720*	*448*	*536*	*852*	*1108*	*834*	*1011*

However, as has been widely observed, men's involvement in household work has not increased to the same extent as women's involvement in paid employment. Men's share of domestic work rose from the 1960s onwards, but this increase appeared to reach a plateau in the 1990s (Bianchi *et al.*, 2000; Coltrane, 2000; Gershuny *et al.*, 2005). This pattern is found across a wide range of countries (Blossfeld and Drobnic, 2001). Indeed, previous research has shown that the major reason for the closing of the gendered "domestic labour gap" between the 1960s and the 1980s was because women substantially reduced their hours of domestic work, rather than that men increased theirs (Coltrane, 2000:1211). The *British Social Attitudes* survey has only asked a limited number of questions on this topic that have been asked in identical format over the years, but where data are available they paint a similar picture. As seen in the next table, the proportion of respondents with partners who reported that the woman usually or always does the laundry fell from just over four-fifths to just over three-quarters over the period 1994 to 2006 – hardly a major social shift – while the proportion who reported that the woman usually or always shops for groceries was unchanged at just under half. Most of the rest of the respondents say that the chores are shared equally, leaving only a small minority reporting the man as doing the brunt of the housework.

Table 3.2 Gendered allocation of household tasks, 1994, 2002 and 2006

% "always"/ "usually" done by woman	1994			2002			2006		
	Men	Women	All	Men	Women	All	Men	Women	All
Laundry	77	84	81	78	82	81	71	80	77
Shopping for groceries	39	45	42	43	49	46	38	45	42
Base	*448*	*536*	*984*	*491*	*578*	*1069*	*524*	*549*	*1073*

Base: partnered respondents only

The previous table also illustrates another pattern commonly found in research on the division of domestic labour: men tend to report that they spend more time on domestic work than women report that men do. For example, in the combined data from 2002 and 2006, we find that 25 per cent of partnered men report that they carry out between six and ten hours of domestic work a week, while only 18 per cent of partnered women reported that their men do so. (Although the men and women in the *British Social Attitudes* survey do not come from the same couples, we should expect the average reports across the sample to tally if everyone is doing their reporting in the same way.) It has been suggested that "men may inflate their estimates more than women because of cognitive biases relating to salience effects and ego-enhancement" (Coltrane, 2000: 1217). These systematic differences between men and women in the reporting of the gendered division of routine household work present us with a problem. Is it that men are over-reporting their domestic work, or are women under-reporting the household work done by their men? As the *British Social Attitudes* survey is an individual level survey, which relies on the respondent's reports of their partner's contribution, we have no way of checking the reports given by couples living in the same household against each other. Given that the reporting differences between men and women are so large (and as we shall see, they are particularly large in the case of some sub-groups in our analysis), we decided that the only sensible option was to carry out separate analyses for men and women.

In summary so far, the *British Social Attitudes* survey data thus suggest a general stability in the gendered division of household labour since the middle of the 1990s – and it should be remembered that women's employment, particularly that of mothers, was still increasing during this period. Although, as highlighted in Table 3.1, attitudes to gender roles have changed markedly since 1989, men's participation in household tasks has not changed very much. Overwhelmingly, women still do the washing and ironing. Although food shopping is more likely to be shared, women still do more of it. Women may have gained formal equality with men in respect of employment, but they nevertheless remain normatively assigned to the responsibility for domestic work and caring. These responsibilities mean that, in practice, many women do not compete on equal terms with men in the labour market. As Coltrane (2000:1209) has summarised:

> In general, women have felt obligated to perform housework, and men have assumed that domestic work is primarily the responsibility of mothers, wives, daughters and low-paid female housekeepers. In contrast, men's participation in housework has appeared optional, with most couples … characterising men's contributions as 'helping' their wives or partners.

Others, however, have argued that many (if not most) women choose to retain the major responsibility for domesticity and are in fact happier when they do so (see discussion in Crompton and Lyonette, 2005).

Measuring domestic work

Several measures of domestic work are available on the 2002 and 2006 *British Social Attitudes* surveys.[1] In this chapter we concentrate on a set of questions which asked the respondent to report who usually caries out various household chores:

> *In your household, who usually does:*
> *The laundry*
> *Cares for sick family members*
> *Shops for groceries*
> *Household cleaning*
> *Prepares the meals*
>
> *(always me, usually me, about equal, usually spouse/partner, always spouse/partner)*

We base our analysis only on those respondents who are married or living as married, and we also include only those respondents who are not retired, as our interest is in the combined effects of paid and unpaid work.

Note that the list includes four items (cooking, cleaning, shopping and laundry) that have been identified as the most time-consuming household tasks and, it has been argued, are "less optional and less able to be postponed than other household tasks such as gardening and household repairs" (Coltrane,

2000:1210). Described as "mundane", "repetitive", "onerous" and "boring", Coltrane has labelled them as "routine housework".

The next table shows that the majority of respondents say that within their household the woman "always" or "usually" does the laundry, cleaning and cooking. However, it is also clear that certain items are less feminised than others: for example, grocery shopping and caring for sick family members both have lower proportions of respondents saying that the woman is "always" or "usually" responsible. However, the proportion of men "always" or "usually" carrying out each task was relatively low, so most of the remaining respondents report that the task was shared equally.

As in Table 3.2, we can also see gender differences in reporting: in all cases, women are more likely than men to report that women do the bulk of the work.

Table 3.3 Domestic division of labour items and mean index scores, by sex

% say task "always" or "usually" done by the woman	Men	Women
Laundry	72	80
Care for sick family members	39	54
Grocery shopping	42	49
Cleaning	54	68
Prepare the meals	55	61
Mean index score for all items	18.1	19.4
Base	768	908

Base: not retired, partnered only, 2002 and 2006

We used the five questions to compute a division of domestic labour (DDL) index. On each question, responses were scored as follows: always the woman = 5, usually the woman = 4, about equal = 3, usually the man = 2, always the man = 1. The scores were summed across the five questions. Hence a high score of 25 indicates that all five tasks are always carried out by the woman, while a low score of 5 implies that all tasks are always done by the man. Working on the conventional assumption that these can be considered 'women's tasks', we label those with high scores as most traditional and those with low scores as most liberal.[2] The mean scores for men and women respondents are shown in the final line of Table 3.3.

What factors shape the gendered division of domestic labour?

Previous empirical research has demonstrated that the extent to which caring and domestic work is shared by men and women within the household is dependent on a number of inter-related factors (Bianchi *et al.*, 2000; Coltrane, 2000). Many studies are concerned with institutional influences – different national policies in respect of labour markets, welfare states and mothers' employment are all associated with systematic differences in the domestic division of labour (Crompton and Lyonette, 2005; Geist, 2005). These do not concern us here, however, as we are focusing only on Britain. Another important factor is age and the life-course. Many studies indicate that the "transition to parenthood is associated with movement toward less sharing of family work between men and women" (Coltrane, 2000: 1222), and older women also do less housework than younger women.

As economistic/material theories would predict, other studies have consistently found that the most important factor affecting the gendered division of household work is whether or not the woman is in employment, and whether she works full-time. Women who work full-time do less routine domestic work, and their partners do more. As women earn more, there is an increase in domestic sharing between partners, and "In general, wives who make more money enjoy more equal divisions of labour" (Coltrane, 2000: 1220). However, it has been demonstrated (for the US and Australia) that when women provide more income than their husbands, then 'gender trumps money' (Brines, 1994; Bittman *et al.*, 2003) and women do more housework, or men's housework hours go down. That is, "where men are not enacting masculinity through providing money, women pick up more of the housework" (Bittman *et al.*, 2003: 203).

Marriage (as opposed to cohabitation) has also been found to make a difference (married women do more housework than cohabiting women and married men do less than cohabiting men). Women with more education do less housework, and better-educated men do more, and social class (which is closely associated with educational level) also has an impact. Finally, "women's egalitarian gender ideology is a consistent predictor of household labour sharing" (Coltrane, 2000: 1221). Some studies show that gender egalitarian men also do more housework, although as previously indicated in Table 3.1, women have – at least in the past – tended to be less likely than men to think that women should have primary responsibility for domestic work.

With few exceptions, these factors affecting the domestic division of labour are also found to be significant in the *British Social Attitudes* surveys and we look now in detail at these findings.

Employment status

As shown in the next table for both male and female respondents, whether or not the woman works full-time has a significant impact on the division of domestic labour: men whose partners work full-time have an average index score of 17.2 – significantly lower (i.e. less traditional) than the figure of 18.7 for those whose partners do not work. The equivalent figures for female respondents are 18.3 and 20.3. However, women's part-time work seems to have little impact and the index scores are indistinguishable from those who do not work at all.

Table 3.4 Division of domestic labour index, by woman's work status

		Mean DDL score	Base
Men	**Partner's work status**		
	Full-time work	17.2	297
	Part-time work	18.8	222
	Not in work	18.7	239
	All	18.1	758
Women	**Own work status**		
	Full-time work	18.3	356
	Part-time work	20.0	290
	Not in work	20.3	203
	All	19.4	849

Base: not retired, partnered only, 2002 and 2006

Hours of paid work (for both men and women) are also significantly associated with the division of domestic labour index. Men work an average of 46 hours per week, and longer hours of work are related to a more traditional index score. For women, the average number of paid work hours is much lower at 33 (this figure includes all full-time and part-time women), and greater hours are related to lower (less traditional) index scores. In other words, the longer the hours worked by a man, the more traditional the division of domestic labour in his home, but the longer the hours worked by the woman, the less traditional the division of domestic labour in her home.

Education and class

Better-educated women report a less traditional division of domestic labour in their homes than those with lower levels of education, although there are no significant differences between men with different levels of education. Occupational class, however, has a significant effect on the division of domestic labour for both men and women. Moreover, this is one area where there appears to have been some change between 2002 and 2006. As seen in the next table, for men, there was very little difference between the social classes in 2002. However, by 2006, men from both the professional/managerial and the manual class had moved in a more liberal direction, leaving men in the intermediate class to stand out as being the most traditional.

The story is different for women: here there is little change between 2002 and 2006, but women from the professional/managerial class are less traditional on both occasions. The discrepancy in men's and women's reports is greatest between routine and manual men and women, particularly in 2006.[3] It should be noted, however, that male and female respondents from the same class may not be directly comparable because men tend to 'marry equal' or 'marry down' while women tend to 'marry equal or 'marry up'. Moreover, social class may be related to various other factors that affect the division of domestic labour, so we should perhaps not put too much store by this weak and somewhat inconsistent relationship with class. We shall return to this point shortly in an analysis combining a number of these factors.

Table 3.5 Division of domestic labour, by class, sex and year

	Class	2002 mean DDL score	Base	2006 mean DDL score	Base	2002/2006 combined mean DDL	Base
Men	Professional/ managerial	18.5	164	17.7	181	18.1	345
	Intermediate	18.6	76	18.9	72	18.8	148
	Routine/ manual	18.4	124	17.4	146	17.9	270
	All	18.5	364	17.8	399	18.1	763
Women	Professional/ managerial	19.0	184	18.8	167	18.9	351
	Intermediate	19.7	115	19.8	101	19.8	216
	Routine/ manual	19.7	166	19.9	151	19.8	317
	All	19.4	465	19.4	419	19.4	884

Base: not retired, partnered only

Marital status

At first sight, the *British Social Attitudes* data appear to confirm that marriage is a significant factor as far as domestic traditionalism is concerned. Respondents who are cohabiting – men and women – report a significantly less traditional division of domestic labour than those who are married. For married men the mean index score is 18.3, compared with 17.4 for cohabiting men; for married women the mean index score is 19.6, compared with 18.5 for cohabiting women. However, it should be borne in mind that marital status may be related to other factors like age and a combined analysis is needed to disentangle this.

Age and parental responsibilities

Rather surprisingly, having a child under 11 in the household is not associated with variations in domestic traditionalism for either men or women. As shown in the next table, age did have an effect, however, with older respondents reporting a more traditional division of domestic labour than younger respondents.

Table 3.6 Division of domestic labour, by age and sex

	Age	Mean DDL score	Base
Men	18–34	17.4	161
	35–54	18.2	431
	55 and over	18.6	176
	All	18.1	768
Women	18–34	18.6	247
	35–54	19.6	498
	55 and over	19.9	162
	All	19.4	907

Base: not retired, partnered only, 2002 and 2006

We should note that the men included in this analysis are older on average than women overall. That men should be older than women, and that more women report non-earning partners in our sub-sample, is not surprising. Although the *British Social Attitudes* survey sample as a whole is designed to be representative of the British population, this is not necessarily true for the sub-sample used in this analysis. Here we focus on respondents in partnerships only. As women tend to marry, or enter into partnerships with, men who are older than themselves, we would expect the average age of the men to be greater than that of the women. Women's partners are also more likely to have retired than men's partners, and therefore not be reported as 'earning'.

Gender role attitudes

Finally, for both men and women, expressing less traditional gender role attitudes is significantly associated with a less traditional division of domestic labour in their own home (especially for men). Men with liberal gender role attitudes report an average division of domestic labour index score of 17.7, compared with traditional men who score 18.9. Women with liberal attitudes report an average index score of 19.2, compared with more traditional women who score 19.8.

Multivariate analysis

As noted at several points, the various factors associated with the division of domestic labour are not unrelated to each other. In order to establish which are the key ones, we need to perform multivariate analysis, which establishes the influence of each of these factors when the others are taken into account. Separate linear regressions were performed for men and women, using those variables shown to be significantly associated with the division of domestic labour index in earlier analyses. Full details of the results are given in the appendix to this chapter.

For men, having a full-time working spouse is the most significant predictor of the index score, followed by the woman earning more and the male respondent not working himself. These are all predictive of a more liberal domestic division of labour within the household. On the other hand, having more traditional gender role attitudes, answering in 2002 (as opposed to 2006) and being older are all predictive of a more traditional domestic division of labour. As suspected in the earlier discussion, marital status and class proved not to be significant predictors of the index score once the other factors were taken into account.

For women, working full-time and earning more than her partner are significant predictors of a more liberal domestic division of labour. Being older and having a full-time working spouse, however, are significantly predictive of a more traditional situation. Class, gender role attitudes and marital status were found not to be predictive once the other factors were taken into account.

These findings lend support both to the economistic and to the normative theories outlined earlier. Men do increase their housework inputs when women are in full-time employment, as economistic theories would predict, but nevertheless, women still retain the major responsibility for routine domestic chores, even when in full-time work – and, as we have seen, part-time work for women makes hardly any difference to the domestic division of labour. This continuing gender imbalance in the domestic division of labour would be predicted by normative theories.

Reported happiness and the domestic division of labour

Previous research has shown that in general, the sharing of domestic work is associated with greater happiness for women, although not for men. When women are responsible for the major share of the housework:

> their perceptions of fairness and marital satisfaction decline, and depending on gender ideology and other mediating factors, marital conflict and women's depression increase. For men, in contrast, divisions of household labour and perceptions of fairness are typically unrelated to personal well-being or marital satisfaction. (Coltrane, 2000: 1209)

However, populist gender conservatives have argued that women are actually happier if they assume traditional gender roles within the home (Doyle, 2001). Our data tend to support the former argument – that is, that women are happier when domestic burdens are shared. A question asking respondents how often they disagree about housework shows no association between disagreement and domestic traditionalism for men. However, the 63 women who report that they disagree about housework several times a week report a more traditional division of labour score (20.2) than average (19.2).

In a similar vein, although only 32 women report that they are actually unhappy, these women also report a more traditional division of labour score (20.3) than average (19.4). The 31 women who say they are dissatisfied with their family lives also have an average index score of well over 20, in contrast with those women who are satisfied. Finally, although there is no association between reported levels of stress at home and index scores for men, the 68 women who strongly disagree that "life at home is rarely stressful" have index scores of 20.6, as against an average of 19.4.

As the above summary of results indicates, only a small minority of people report that they are actually unhappy or dissatisfied, but for women, unhappiness, dissatisfaction and stress are associated with a more traditional division of domestic labour in their home. Nevertheless, another possible explanation might be that a contradiction between attitudes and practice in relation to domestic work is in itself a source of dissatisfaction. For example, an individual might have liberal or non-traditional gender role attitudes, but be involved in a rather traditional domestic division of labour, which may be a source of resentment. We explore this possibility by developing a combined measure of gender role attitudes and the division of domestic labour. Responses relating to gender role attitudes (using the single question: "A man's job is to earn money; a woman's job is to look after the home and family") were dichotomised and cross-tabulated with a dichotomised version of the division of domestic labour index.[4] This generated four categories:

- 'congruent traditionals', those respondents with less liberal gender role attitudes and a more traditional division of domestic labour in their home;
- 'incongruent traditionals', those with traditional gender role attitudes but a less traditional division of domestic labour in their home;
- 'incongruent liberals', those with less traditional gender role attitudes but a more traditional division of domestic labour in their home; and
- 'congruent liberals', those respondents with liberal gender role attitudes and a less traditional division of domestic labour in their home.

As would have been anticipated, the distribution of congruence categories, presented in the next table, varies by both sex and class.

Table 3.7 Congruence, by class and sex

| | | Social class | | | |
		Professional/ managerial	Intermediate	Routine/ manual	All
	Congruence category	%	%	%	%
Men	Congruent traditional	16	25	25	21
	Incongruent traditional	15	17	18	16
	Incongruent liberal	24	24	17	21
	Congruent liberal	45	34	41	42
	Base	*341*	*145*	*261*	*747*
		%	%	%	%
Women	Congruent traditional	11	20	24	18
	Incongruent traditional	9	8	12	10
	Incongruent liberal	40	44	41	41
	Congruent liberal	41	28	24	32
	Base	*346*	*212*	*306*	*864*

Base: not retired, partnered only, 2002 and 2006

As shown previously, men are rather more traditional in their gender role attitudes than women and the men in our sub-sample are rather older. There are, indeed, rather more congruent traditionals amongst the men than among the women. However, the most frequently occurring category for men (42 per cent) is congruent liberal – liberal gender role attitudes combined with a less traditional division of domestic labour in their own home. For women, the most common situation is incongruent liberal (41 per cent) – liberal gender role attitudes, but combined with a more traditional division of domestic labour in their own home. In respect of this category, there is a difference of 20 percentage points between men's and women's reports, with only 21 per cent of men falling into the 'incongruent liberal' category. (This finding would tend to lend support to the suggestion that men are over-reporting their domestic involvement.)

As far as the females are concerned, class differences in congruence categories are patterned in a manner that might have been anticipated – significantly fewer professional and managerial women are congruent traditionals while a much higher proportion are congruent liberals. There are also significant class differences in the discrepancy between men's and women's reporting of congruent liberalism. For the professional/managerial and intermediate groupings, there is a difference of about five percentage points between men's and women's reporting, but for routine and manual respondents, the gender discrepancy in reporting is 17 percentage points.

As shown in the next table, couples' work status also has a significant impact as far as the distribution of congruence categories are concerned, although gender differences in reporting are still very apparent.

Table 3.8 Congruence, by couples' work status and sex

		Couples' work status			
		Both full-time	Man full-time, woman part-time	Man full-time, woman not working	All
	Congruence category	%	%	%	%
Men	Congruent traditional	12	22	32	21
	Incongruent traditional	13	13	19	15
	Incongruent liberal	18	32	24	24
	Congruent liberal	57	33	25	41
	Base	*260*	*190*	*168*	*618*
		%	%	%	%
Women	Congruent traditional	6	20	36	17
	Incongruent traditional	8	6	11	8
	Incongruent liberal	38	49	42	43
	Congruent liberal	47	25	11	33
	Base	*298*	*236*	*120*	*654*

Base: not retired, partnered only, 2002 and 2006

For both men and women, women's full-time employment is most strongly associated with congruent liberalism – liberal gender role attitudes and a less traditional division of domestic labour in their own home. Almost half of women who are working full-time are in the congruent liberal category, compared with only a tenth of those who are not working. However, it is of particular interest that women who work part-time are the most likely to be in the incongruent liberal category – that is, liberal gender role attitudes, but a more traditional division of domestic labour at home.

One of our objectives in developing this congruence analysis was to establish whether a lack of fit between attitudes and behaviour is associated with lower levels of satisfaction and marital agreement. As can be seen from the next table, incongruent liberal women, that is, those with liberal gender role attitudes but a more traditional division of domestic labour in their home, do report more disagreement over household work, suggesting some conflict between gender role aspirations and actual behaviour as far as women are concerned (this association just failed to reach statistical significance, however). For men, there is no association between congruence and disagreement over household work.

Table 3.9 Congruence, by disagreement over household work and sex

% who disagree over housework "several times a month" or more	Men	Base	Women	Base
Congruent traditional	14	155	14	156
Incongruent traditional	15	123	16	90
Incongruent liberal	11	162	21	358
Congruent liberal	17	312	15	283
All	14	752	17	887

Base: not retired, partnered only, 2002 and 2006

The patterns in the previous table may be less than startling, but there *is* an interesting association for women between congruent liberalism and stress at home, as shown in the next table. In general, men are more likely to report their home life as lacking in stress than women. However, congruent liberal women are significantly more likely to report a lack of stress at home than other women. This suggests not only that a fit between attitudes and behaviour is associated with less stress for women, but also that the sharing of domestic work is beneficial as far as women are concerned – congruent traditional women report similar levels of home stress to women in the incongruent categories.

Table 3.10 Congruence, by reported stress at home and sex

% who agree "My life at home is rarely stressful"	Men	Base	Women	Base
Congruent traditional	44	155	37	156
Incongruent traditional	43	123	37	90
Incongruent liberal	53	162	35	358
Congruent liberal	47	312	48	283
All	47	752	40	887

Base: not retired, partnered, 2002 and 2006

It would seem, therefore, that women who hold liberal gender role attitudes and experience a less traditional division of domestic labour in their home, are less stressed at home than other women. These women are also more likely to be in full-time employment. Holding liberal gender views but having a more traditional division of domestic labour leads to more disagreement about household work for women – these women are more likely to be in part-time employment. Together with the evidence of higher levels of domestic traditionalism amongst the (admittedly small) number of women who reported they were actually unhappy, these findings suggest that an increased sharing of domestic work is, indeed, better for women.

Women who earn more than men

Although women still do more domestic work than men, even when they are in full-time employment, the situation is changing, albeit at a rather slow pace. It has been argued that a process of 'lagged adaptation' is occurring (Gershuny *et al.*, 1994). That is, men's participation in household work is responding to the changes in women's employment status (although not to the same extent as women's), and

> we may expect, in future, greater convergence in men's and women's
> daily hours of domestic work, around lower weekly hours of domestic
> work. (Gershuny *et al.*, 2005: 664)

However, what about the relatively unusual situation where the woman earns more money than the man? Exchange bargaining models suggest that the spouse who brings more resources to the partnership will have the power to get the other spouse to do more housework, as the partner with lower resources will have more to lose if the partnership ends through separation or divorce (Brines, 1994; Bittman *et al.*, 2003). However, as noted earlier, previous research from Australia and the US suggests that the exchange bargaining model works up to the point of about equal earnings, with men progressively doing more housework. But as women earn even more this association breaks down, and as men become economically dependent, they actually carry out *less* housework. Specifically, Bittman *et al.* found that in Australia, men's hours of unpaid work were virtually unaffected by relative contributions to household income. For women, as their relative contribution to household income increased, so their hours of household work went down. However, as Australian women's contribution to the household income rose beyond the point of equal shares, their hours of household work went up – that is, the relationship between women's income contribution and their unpaid work hours was curvilinear.[5] They explain this result as being part of an effort to neutralise gender deviance for male (non)-providers:

> when men are earning substantially less than their wives, this violates gender norms and leads either the wife or the husband (or both) to move to more traditional behaviour in the realm of housework in order to neutralise the deviance. (Bittman *et al.*, 2003: 192)

Previous investigations of this topic have drawn upon time diary data including many thousands of respondents. Our data are less extensive and less detailed than this. However, previous research relied on information that was gathered some time ago (e.g. Bittman *et al.* use 1992 Australian data). We feel justified, therefore, in making a contribution to this debate, although we are aware that our evidence cannot be conclusive.[6] Moreover, this is a topic of increasing contemporary relevance. As women's educational and economic activity levels continue to rise relative to men's (Crompton and Lyonette, 2007), we may anticipate that in the future, in an increasing minority of households, the woman will earn more than the man.[7]

We do not have information on partners' income (although we do have information on household income). However, we do have access to a question which asked: "Considering all sources of income, between you and your partner, who has the higher income?" The next table summarises the division of domestic labour index scores depending on the answers to this question.

Although our data are substantially less robust than that available to Bittman *et al.*, the table tells a rather different story to theirs. In the first place, the contribution of the female partner to household income has an impact on reported division of domestic labour for both women *and* men. Indeed, for men, there is a linear relationship between the woman's contribution and the division of domestic labour – the more money the woman contributes, the less traditional the domestic roles reported by male respondents. For women respondents, too, domestic traditionalism declines the more she contributes – and this decline continues when a higher income is reported. Admittedly, the level of domestic traditionalism appears to increase somewhat when women report much higher incomes, or when the man has no income (based on a very small number of respondents), but it still does not reach that of same-income respondents and is considerably lower than that of women with no income/man much higher income.

Table 3.11 Division of domestic labour index, by who earns more and sex

	Who earns more in household	Mean DDL score	Base
Men	Man no income, woman much higher income	15.2	21
	Woman higher income	16.7	63
	Both same income	17.2	63
	Man higher income	18.4	186
	Man much higher income, Woman no income	19.0	296
	All	18.3	629
Women	Man no income, woman much higher income	18.6	47
	Woman higher income	17.4	57
	Both same income	19.2	73
	Man higher income	19.5	300
	Man much higher income, Woman no income	20.2	217
	All	19.4	694

Base: paid work or looking after the home (respondent and spouse), 2002 and 2006

Higher-earning women, therefore, report a less traditional division of domestic labour – and men whose partners earn more than they do report near gender equality as far as domestic work is concerned (15 being the mid-point of the division of domestic labour index). These results would lend general support to exchange-bargaining models of domestic work, although in aggregate, even women making the major economic contribution to the household still do more housework than men. Given that our numbers are so small, we can only speculate as to why our findings should be different from those of previous research in this area. However, on the assumption that our findings are valid, the most likely explanation is the passage of time: gender role attitudes are changing, more women are earning higher salaries, and it has been suggested that there is a slow convergence in the contribution of men and women to domestic work (Gershuny *et al.*, 2005).

Nevertheless, although there are grounds for some optimism, it must be emphasised that households where the woman earns more than the man remain a very small minority. Of those who are in paid work or looking after the home, 10 per cent report that their partners earn the same income, and 12 per cent that the woman earns more or much more. In contrast, 69 per cent of respondents are in households where the man earns more, and of these, 32 per cent are in households where the man earns much more than the woman. In total, therefore, we have only just under two hundred cases (193) where it can be firmly established that the woman is earning more than the man., Nevertheless, it seems worthwhile to examine in more depth the characteristics of this small – but likely to be expanding – grouping.

In the first place, and as might be expected, females in households where the woman is earning more than the man are overwhelmingly (78 per cent) in the managerial and professional category, as compared with 43 per cent of employed women in the sub-sample as a whole. A similar pattern is found amongst men with higher earning partners. We only have details of partners' occupation for the 2006 sample, but over 69 per cent of men who report that their partners earn more than they do have managerial/professional partners. (On the other hand, 43 per cent of male respondents in 'woman earns more' households were in the professional/managerial category, a proportion fairly similar to the sub-sample average of 49 per cent.)

Gender-related attitudes, household stress and satisfaction with family life

We have already established that the division of domestic labour in households where the woman earns more is significantly less traditional than in higher male-earner households. However, in what other respects do they differ from more conventional (in earnings terms) households? Although numbers are small, we can see from the next table that the presence of a higher-earning woman really does make a difference.

First, women who earn more than their partners are much less likely to think that a man's job is to earn money, or that family life suffers if a woman works, than women in more conventional households. A similar pattern is found amongst men with higher-earning partners, although, as is usual in these matters, men are slightly more traditional than women. In these households, both women and men are more likely to think that women should work full-time when there is a child under school age. Women in households where men earn more are rather more likely to be stressed at home than women who earn more, although their satisfaction with family life is greater. Interestingly, however, women in households reporting that they earn more than their partners disagree more often over housework, suggesting that they are, indeed, more likely to be using their greater bargaining power to increase the domestic contribution of their partner.

Women earning more than their partners may be considered to be pioneers in relation to gender relations in the home, and although our numbers are very small, our results do suggest that these 'gender pioneers' have markedly less traditional attitudes and behaviour than women in more conventional earning partnerships. To a lesser extent, a similar case might also be argued in relation to men with higher earning partners.

Table 3.12 Attitudes to work and family, by relative earnings of man and woman within the household

	Men	Women	All
% disagree man's job to earn money; woman's to look after home/family			
Woman earns more	73	90	82
Same income	61	74	67
Man earns more	66	75	71
% disagree family life suffers if woman works			
Woman earns more	56	70	62
Same income	38	56	48
Man earns more	45	43	44
% agree women should "work full-time" when child under school age			
Woman earns more	11	15	14
Same income	3	2	3
Man earns more	3	4	3
% disagree life at home rarely stressful			
Woman earns more	25	36	31
Same income	24	38	32
Man earns more	32	45	39
% "very" or "completely satisfied" with family life			
Woman earns more	75	64	70
Same income	70	76	74
Man earns more	71	71	71
% disagree over housework "several times a week" or more			
Woman earns more	16	29	23
Same income	27	15	20
Man earns more	14	17	16
Bases			
Woman earns more	*81*	*82*	*163*
Same income	*63*	*73*	*136*
Man earns more	*429*	*476*	*905*

Base: respondents with a partner where both partners are working

We also examined the influence of women earning more on each of the separate items making up the division of domestic labour measure. Although male respondents again significantly over-report their own contribution (in comparison with women's estimates of their male partners' contributions), in each case, women are less likely to do the majority of tasks than other women (either earning the same amount as their partners or less). In some cases, such as laundry and cleaning, this difference between women was of more than 15 percentage points (see the chapter appendix for further details).

Outsourcing domestic work

One possibility we considered was that in households with women earning more, paid domestic help, that is, the outsourcing of particular tasks – such as laundry and cleaning – would be more frequent. Reliable data on this topic are notoriously problematic to obtain, as much of this employment is informal, cash in hand, and not registered for social insurance purposes. Nevertheless, we have some information available on this topic, as, for each of the domestic tasks included in our measure, a further option was available: "is done by a third person". No details were available on the identity of the other person. Most likely, this other person represents paid domestic help, but it could also be another family member, or an unpaid friend or volunteer. However, none of the men in households where the woman earns more report outsourcing of laundry and only three report that the cleaning was done by a third person. For women earning more, only two report outsourcing of laundry and six said that the cleaning was done by a third person. From this limited evidence, therefore, it appears that although there are increased pressures to get domestic work done, given the increase in women's employment, this is rarely being taken up by paid domestic help to any great extent.

Table 3.13 Outsourcing of cleaning, by class and sex

	% say cleaning done by another person	
Social class	**Men**	**Women**
Professional	7	7
Base	*345*	*352*
Intermediate	2	4
Base	*148*	*216*
Manual	1	1
Base	*270*	*317*
All	4	4
Base	*763*	*885*

Base: partnered only, not retired, 2002 and 2006

In fact, the data reveals a very low level of outsourcing of domestic chores –
although it is possible that there is substantial under-reporting on this topic.
Only household cleaning is reported as "is done by a third person" for more
than one per cent of respondents, and as the previous table demonstrates, this is
concentrated amongst managerial and professional respondents.

Conclusions

In general, data from the 2002 and 2006 *British Social Attitudes* surveys tends
to confirm what has been established in other quantitative studies that have
investigated the division of domestic work between men and women. This is
that, although women have substantially increased their participation in paid
employment, men's participation in domestic work has yet to catch up.
Nevertheless, there are also clear signs of change.

One major problem we face in this analysis is that as compared with women's
reports of their partners, men appear to be substantially over-reporting their
share of domestic work. Whereas 'congruent liberalism', that is, liberal attitudes
and a relatively non-traditional division of domestic labour, is the most frequent
combination amongst male respondents, 'incongruent liberalism' is most
frequent amongst women. This entails liberal attitudes but a traditional division
of domestic labour in practice in their home. It would seem that attitudes to
gender roles have changed to a greater extent than behaviour in respect of
domestic work – it is possible that men who profess gender liberalism might
feel constrained to report behaviour in line with these attitudes. This gendered
difference in the reporting of domestic work is particularly marked in the
'routine and manual' social class. We can only speculate as to the origins of
these differences. It is possible that domestic responsibilities are more important
as a source of gender identity amongst routine and manual women, who might
as a consequence over-report their domestic responsibilities – but we have no
way of actually demonstrating this.

In line with previous research, we find that age, class, level of education,
marital status, and gender role attitudes may all play some part in levels of
traditionalism in the domestic division of labour. But by far the most significant
factor, swamping the others in a combined analysis, is whether or not the
woman is employed, especially whether she works full-time, and the extent of
her earnings. Part-time work for women would seem to perpetuate a 'modified
male-breadwinner' model, and the division of domestic labour reported by
respondents in these households is very similar to that of male-breadwinner
households. British women, it should be remembered, have the second highest
level of part-time working in Europe.

Full-time working amongst women makes a significant difference as far as
gender traditionalism in the home is concerned. However, although the numbers
are rather small, our data suggest that the extent of the woman's earnings is also
crucial for gender equality. In households where women earn more than men
(and particularly according to the men's reports), men do more housework.

These households are more gender liberal, and higher-earning women argue more about housework. In short, 'money talks', and rather than compensating for 'gender deviance' by reverting to a more traditional division of domestic work (as previous studies have argued), women who earn more than men have a less traditional division of labour in the home.

Nevertheless, in aggregate, women remain normatively associated with domestic work and caring and, as has been argued elsewhere, this fact will restrict their 'agency freedom' as far as their employment choices are concerned (Lewis and Giullari, 2005). Thus it is unlikely that more than a minority of women will earn more than their male partners for as long as this normative association persists. However, it is not simply a matter of changing norms, but also behaviour, in both the home *and* in the workplace. British men work amongst the longest hours in Europe, and long working hours make it very difficult for men to do more in the home (Crompton and Lyonette, 2006). Gender equality is unlikely to be achieved unless domestic sharing between men and women becomes more generalised, but domestic sharing is problematic as long as men work longer hours than women. The answer would seem to be shorter hours for both.

Notes

1. An alternative series of questions provide an estimate of domestic work hours (excluding childcare) done by the respondent and by their partner. However, survey estimates of hours spent in domestic work are known to be less reliable than time diary data, especially for men. In a recent paper that compared stylised (questionnaire-based) estimates and diary-based estimates of housework time collected from the same respondents, Kan shows that the gap between the two types of estimate tend to be smaller for women (Kan, 2006). As survey estimates of domestic work hours are relatively unreliable for both men and women (Coltrane, 2000; Bittman *et al.*, 2003; Gershuny *et al.*, 2005), we have chosen to use the task-based measures in this chapter.
2. Respondents who had answered less than three questions (including "can't choose") were excluded (n = 23). The remaining cases where "can't choose" was selected or the question was not answered were then allocated an imputed score (listwise): DDL1 = 3.16; DDL3 = 3.66; DDL4 = 3.50; DDL5 = 3.80; DDL6 = 3.70. A further option "is done by a third person" was included in the questionnaire. Previous research (Geist, 2005) has coded this response as 'shared'. However, we have argued that this allocation is misleading (Crompton and Lyonette, 2007). We therefore allocated an average score for all respondents in cases of the "done by another person" response. All five items load on to one factor, explaining about 55 per cent of the variance. All five items contribute to the DDL scale (all above +0.6 using Principal Components Analysis). Reliability analysis showed that all items contributed to the reliability of the scale (Cronbach's Alpha = 0.79).
3. A closer analysis of the change in the pattern of men's reporting revealed that between 2002 and 2006, two groups of men were more likely to report less

traditional DDL in 2006. These were men with liberal gender role attitudes whose partners were in full-time work, and men with traditional gender role attitudes whose partners were either part-time or not employed. In the case of the first category identified, routine and manual men were over-represented, whereas in the case of the second category, it was professional and managerial men.

4. Congruence based on DDL scale with missing coded 1 (liberal DDL) = 1–18.95 (50%); 2 (traditional DDL) = 19–25 (50%); gender role based on 2-category recoding of "A man's job is to earn money; a woman's job is to look after the home and family".

5. Using American data gathered in 1985, Brines (1994) also found a similar curvilinear relationship for men – that is, beyond equal earnings, men whose partners earn more than they do reduce their hours of unpaid work.

6. Although our numbers are small, and a replication of the Bittman *et al.* (and similar) analyses is impossible, we have introduced similar controls on our data. Thus we have included only respondents whose partners are below retirement age (as women tend to enter into partnerships with older men, it would not be unusual for her to continue in employment after he had retired). For both men and women, we have excluded those who are long-term sick or disabled, and those reporting long-term sick and disabled partners, as this may well affect one's ability to perform housework. We have also excluded the unemployed, and those reporting unemployed partners. Our sub-sample, therefore, includes only those in paid work or looking after the home, and similar restrictions apply to their partners.

7. In fact, there had been an increase in 'woman earns more' households in the *British Social Attitudes* data between 2002 and 2006, although it was not statistically significant.

References

Baxter, J., Hewitt, B. and Western, M. (2004), *Post-familial families and the domestic division of labour*, Queensland: University of Queensland, School of Social Science

Becker, G. (1991), *A Treatise on the Family*, Massachusetts: Harvard University Press

Bianchi, S., Milkie, M., Sayer, L. and Robinson, J. (2000), 'Is Anyone Doing the Housework? Trends in the Gender Division of Household Labor', *Social Forces*, **79(1)**: 191–228

Bittman, M., England, P., Folbre, N., Sayer, L. and Matheson, G. (2003), 'When does Gender Trump Money? Bargaining and Time in Household Work', *American Journal of Sociology*, **109(1)**: 186–214

Blood, R. and Wolfe, D. (1960), *Husbands and Wives: the Dynamics of Married Living*, Illinois: Free Press

Blossfeld, H. and Drobnic, S. (eds.) (2001), *Careers of Couples in Contemporary Societies*, Oxford: Oxford University Press

Brines, J. (1994), 'Economic Dependency, Gender and the Division of Labor at Home', *American Journal of Sociology*, **100(3)**: 652–688. Burchell, B., Ladipo, D. and Wilkinson, F. (eds) (2002), *Job insecurity and work intensification*, London: Routledge

Coltrane, S. (2000), 'Research on Household Labor: Modeling and Measuring the Social Embeddedness of Routine Family Work', *Journal of Marriage and Family*, **62**: 1208–1233

Crompton, R. and Lyonette, C. (2005), 'The new gender essentialism – domestic and family "choices" and their relation to attitudes', *British Journal of Sociology*, **56(4)**: 601–624

Crompton, R. and Lyonette, C. (2006), 'Work–life balance in Europe', *Acta Sociologica*, **49(4)**: 379–393

Crompton, R. and Lyonette, C. (2007). 'Are we all working too hard? Women, men, and changing attitudes to employment', in Park, A., Curtice, J., Thomson, K., Phillips, M. and Johnson, M. (eds.), *British Social Attitudes: the 23rd Report*, London: Sage

Dench, S., Aston, J., Evans, C., Meager, N., Williams, M. and Willison, R. (2002), *Key indicators of women's position in Britain*, London: Department of Trade and Industry

Doyle, L. (2001), *The Surrendered Wife: a Practical Guide For Finding Intimacy, Passion and Peace With a Man*, Australia: Simon and Schuster

Geist, C. (2005), 'The welfare state and the home: regime differences in the domestic division of labour', *European Sociological Review*, **21**: 23–41

Gershuny, J., Bittman, M. and Brice, J. (2005), 'Exit, Voice and Suffering: Do Couples adapt to Changing Employment Patterns?', *Journal of Marriage and Family*, **67**: 656–665

Gershuny, J., Godwin, M. and Jones, S. (1994), 'The Domestic Labour Revolution: a Process of Lagged Adaptation', in Anderson, M., Bechhofer, F. and Gershuny, J. (eds.), *The Social and Political Economy of the Household*, Oxford: Oxford University Press

Glucksmann, M. (1995), 'Why "work"? Gender and the "Total Social Organisation of Labour"', *Gender, Work and Organisation*, **2(2)**: 63–75

Kan, Man Yee (2006), 'Measuring Housework Participation: The Gap between "Stylised" Questionnaire Estimates and Diary-based Estimates', Institute for Social and Economic Research Working Paper 2006–11, Colchester: University of Essex

Lewis, J. and Giullari, S. (2005), 'The adult worker model family, gender equality and care: the search for new policy principles and the possibilities and problems of a capabilities approach', *Economy and Society*, **34(1)**: 76–104

Mincer, J. and Polachek, S. (1974), 'Family investments in human capital: earnings of women', *Journal of Political Economy*, **82**: 76–108

Sevenhuijsen, S. (2002), 'A third way? Moralities, ethics and families: an approach through the ethic of care', in Carling, A., Duncan, S. and Edwards, R. (eds.), *Analysing Families*, London: Routledge

West, C. and Zimmerman, D. (1987), 'Doing Gender', *Gender and Society*, **1**: 125–151

Acknowledgements

The *National Centre for Social Research* and the authors are grateful to the Economic and Social Research Council (grant number R000239727 and Genet Research Network) for their financial support which enabled us to ask the questions reported in this chapter.

Appendix

We ran separate linear regressions for men and women, the results of which are given in the tables below. The dependent variable was the domestic division of labour (DDL) index score.

Table A.1 Regression on DDL index score (men, not retired, 2002 and 2006)

Predictor variables	Beta (standardised)
Intercept	
Woman earns more	-0.133***
Woman does not earn more	-
Traditional gender role attitudes (agree that "A man's job is to earn money; a woman's job is to look after the home and family")	0.147***
Non-traditional gender role attitudes	-
2002	0.083*
2006	-
Married	0.010
Cohabiting	-
Age	0.079*
Spouse works full-time	-0.196***
Spouse does not work full-time	-
Respondent not working	-0.113***
Respondent working	-
Intermediate class	0.050
Not intermediate class	-
Base	*679*

* = significant at 5% level
** = significant at 1% level
*** = significant at 0.1% level

Table A.2 Regression on DDL index score (women, not retired, 2002 and 2006)

Predictor variables	Beta (standardised)
Intercept	
Woman earns more	-0.115***
Woman does not earn more	-
Traditional gender role attitudes (agree that "A man's job is to earn money; a woman's job is to look after the home and family")	0.047
Non-traditional gender role attitudes	-
Married	0.056
Cohabiting	-
Age	0.176***
Spouse works full-time	0.169***
Spouse does not work full-time	-
Professional/managerial class	-0.059
Not professional/managerial class	-
Respondent not working	0.233***
Respondent working	-
Base	*778*

* = significant at 5% level
** = significant at 1% level
*** = significant at 0.1% level

Table A.3 DDL items by who earns more and sex

% say "always" or "usually" done by the woman		**Men**	*Base*	**Women**	*Base*
Laundry	Woman higher income	51	*77*	64	*76*
	Same income	57	*59*	75	*72*
	Man higher income	77	*346*	81	*403*
Cares for sick family members	Woman higher income	28	*77*	35	*76*
	Same income	32	*59*	48	*72*
	Man higher income	41	*346*	56	*403*
Grocery shopping	Woman higher income	35	*77*	43	*76*
	Same income	33	*59*	49	*72*
	Man higher income	45	*346*	52	*403*
Cleaning	Woman higher income	32	*77*	52	*76*
	Same income	42	*59*	60	*72*
	Man higher income	60	*346*	70	*403*
Prepares the meals	Woman higher income	40	*77*	51	*76*
	Same income	57	*59*	61	*72*
	Man higher income	55	*346*	61	*403*

Base: those in paid work, married and with a spouse also in paid work, 2002 and 2006

4 Talking the talk: national identity in England and Scotland

*Frank Bechhofer and David McCrone**

The death of 'Britishness' has become the hot topic of everyday commentary in British politics and the media. Whereas once the focus tended to be on the constitutional *Break-up of Britain* (the title of Tom Nairn's iconic book published in 1977), in recent years these dramatic predictions of change have receded somewhat. True, the constitutional relationships that govern the United Kingdom have undeniably changed, and English regional government may once more be on the agenda. However, although nationalists now have varying but considerable degrees of power and influence in Scotland, Wales and Northern Ireland, concern about the imminent disintegration of the United Kingdom has largely evaporated to be replaced by a more subtle debate about whether people in Britain no longer 'feel' British and, instead, prefer to describe themselves using 'national' epithets, such as Scottish and English. *British Social Attitudes* surveys have helped to chart this change (see, for example, Curtice and Heath, 2000; Heath *et al.*, 2007).

Why might there have been changes in the balance between national identities?[1] Popular commentary attributes this to a number of causes, including the impact of devolution. The argument is that the Scottish Parliament, arguably expected to head off independence (and espoused by some for this reason), has actually stoked demand for it. The election of an SNP government, albeit a minority one, at Holyrood is seen as further evidence for this view. A second supposed cause is the anticipated succession, now a reality, of Gordon Brown, a Scottish MP, as leader of the Labour Party and hence Prime Minister. The legitimacy of a Scottish MP becoming Prime Minister is especially challenged by the so-called West Lothian Question, a paradox which is seen to affect all MPs sitting for Scottish seats since devolution. Gordon Brown, sitting at Westminster for a Scottish seat, can vote to determine all legislation in England, but English MPs cannot vote on a whole range of legislation which is devolved to the Scottish Parliament. Indeed, it is notable that Brown organised his campaign to be Prime Minister under the rubric of 'Brown for Britain'. The

---

* Frank Bechhofer is Emeritus Professor of Social Research, David McCrone is Professor of Sociology, both at the University of Edinburgh.

tercentenary of the Union between Scotland and England adds a further context, heightening the debates about who, these days, feels British and why.

All things considered, then, this is a good moment to survey in some detail attitudes to national identity. Our focus here is on Scotland and England, whose partnership in 1707 founded the British state.[2] In this chapter, we address four key questions. First, whether national identity, being either British or English or Scottish, actually matters to people in the context of other social identities they have. Second, to *whom* national identity matters, and whether the English and the Scots differ in their perception and use of national identity. Third, what evidence there is that national identities are changing over the longer term. Are the English and the Scots becoming less British, for example, an issue of seeming importance to the long-term future of the United Kingdom? Finally, we ask how much association, if any, there is between people's national identity and their party political and constitutional preferences. These are questions not simply of academic interest but central to the cohesiveness of the British state, particularly at a time when politicians and commentators are addressing the idea of Britishness, how British the citizens of the United Kingdom feel, whether a sense of being British should be encouraged, and if so, how this might best be done. The nature of Britishness is generally treated uncritically as self-evident and undisputed. If this is not so, the implications are considerable.

Unlike other studies, in which people living in Scotland have usually been compared straightforwardly with people living in England, we are able to identify residents who were *born* in England and Scotland, and those residents who were not. The latter groups (13 per cent in both countries according to 2001 census data) are important; it is possible, for instance, that an apparent shift away from 'being British' simply reflects the fact that the proportion of non-British-born people has grown. Further, we know from census data that there are substantial numbers of people born in Scotland living in England (around 800,000) as well as people born in England living in Scotland (around 400,000). Thus, in order to focus our study more sharply and provide a more rigorous comparison of national identity in the two countries, the questions on national identity in the 2006 surveys, both British and Scottish, departed from previous ones by focusing on birthplace rather than residence. In this way we can confine our main analysis to 'natives', that is, people who were born and who currently reside in each country. This makes our comparisons between Scotland and England sharper and, over time, if there is a shift among 'natives' in terms of how they talk about their identities, we can be more sure that this is a significant trend rather than simply an artefactual one resulting from greater geographical mobility.

Our previous research has shown clearly that place of birth is an important marker of national identity, determining both whether people claim a particular national identity, and whether others accept their claims (see, for instance, Kiely *et al.*, 2005a). This qualitative research showed that for people born and living in Scotland, being Scottish was a pragmatic matter of birthplace and that most English migrants to Scotland adopted an unproblematic view of their own national identity based, in a matter of fact way, on where they were born. We also know that the Scots in England and the English in Scotland, especially the latter, differ somewhat in their views on national identity from the Scots in Scotland and the English in England.

Does national identity matter?

And so to our first question: does national identity actually matter to people? Or are discussions about national identity the preserve of politicians and the chattering classes, something confined to parliament and newspapers, and the media generally, but of little concern to ordinary people in England and Scotland as they go about their daily business? Our interest here is in the priority that people give to being Scottish, English or British in relation to other social identities – being a parent, being a partner, their gender, their social class, and so on. Respondents were first asked to choose from a list of identities other than national ones, and only thereafter asked whether they would describe themselves as English, Scottish, British, and so on in place of identities already chosen. This second question then focuses the respondent's attention sharply on and forces them to think about national identity.[3]

We began by asking:

> *People differ in how they think of or describe themselves. If you had to pick just one thing from this list to describe yourself – something that is important to you when you think of yourself – what would it be?*

Respondents were asked to choose the first, second and third most important identity from the following list.

Working class	*Middle class*
Elderly	*Black*
A woman/A man	*Retired*
Not religious	*Religious*
A wife/A husband/A partner	*A working person*
A Catholic	*Young*
A country person	*White*
A city person	*Asian*
A Protestant	*Unemployed*
A mother/A father	*Other*

The choices for respondents *born and living in* England and Scotland (who we refer to throughout this chapter as English and Scots) are shown in Table 4.1. For each group we show the proportion that choose a particular identity as their most important identity, and then the proportion that choose that identity as one of their top three identities overall. So, for example, 22 per cent of the English and 26 per cent of the Scots saw being a parent as their most important identity, while 49 per cent and 55 per cent respectively choose parenthood as one of their top three.

The table shows that what one might call family-related identities, being a parent (chosen by around half the sample) or a partner (chosen by two out of five) are the most popular. Gender-, class- or employment-related responses are chosen by around a third of respondents. There are some small differences between our English and Scottish respondents but, on the whole, the broad similarities between the English and Scots are more striking than any differences. When comparing the combined responses the largest difference between the two groups is found for mother/father and working class; on both measures the results for the Scots are six percentage points higher than for their English counterparts, whereas Scots are less likely to mention gender (five percentage points lower).

Table 4.1 Identity choices of the English and Scots (five most frequently chosen categories)

% choosing identity	English 1st choice	English all choices combined	Scottish 1st choice[+]	Scottish all choices combined[+]
A mother/father	22	49	26	55
A wife/husband/partner	8	41	8	43
A woman/man	16	37	11	32
A working person	11	34	12	37
Working class	13	27	19	33
Base:	*2366*	*2366*	*1286*	*1286*

Base: respondents born and resident in England/Scotland
[+]Source: *Scottish Social Attitudes*
Options shown in order of popularity (for second column), not questionnaire order

Next we presented respondents with a list of *national* identities and asked:

> *If the list had also included the things on this card would you have chosen one or more of these **instead of** the ones you did choose?*
> *[British/English/European/Irish/Northern Irish/Scottish/Ulster/Welsh]*

As Table 4.2 shows, national identity is clearly an identity of some importance. Overall, a third of English respondents would choose a national identity instead of one of the other social identities listed on the previous page, making it less salient than family-related identities and gender, what one might perhaps think of as the most everyday identities, but comparable with the other most frequently chosen identities. Among the Scots, national identity is of higher salience still, with nearly a half choosing it as one of their identities (making it the second most important identity, after parenthood).

Among the English who *would* choose a national identity, nearly six in ten say they would choose "English" and around half would choose "British". In both cases, around half say this is their most important identity. The balance is very different among their Scottish equivalents; only one in ten of whom mentions "British" whereas nine in ten choose "Scottish" (with around half of those choosing "Scottish" describing this as their most important identity).

Table 4.2 National identity choices of English and Scots

	English	Scots[+]
% choosing national identity instead of $1^{st}/2^{nd}/3^{rd}$ choice identity	33	46
Base	*2366*	*1286*
Of which …		
… % choosing "English"/"Scottish"	57	92
… % choosing "British"	49	10
Base	*759*	*594*

Base: respondents born and resident in England/Scotland
[+]Source: *Scottish Social Attitudes*

Three key conclusions emerge from this discussion. Firstly, national identity does matter to people in both England and Scotland but is a more important identity in Scotland. Secondly, when people do choose to emphasise their national identity, the Scots are much more likely than the English to choose the 'national' (Scottish or English) and are much less likely to choose the 'state' identity (British). And, thirdly, in all other respects, people in Scotland and England are very similar in their choice of identities.

Migrants and natives

What of Scots-born people living in England, and English-born people living in Scotland? Does the context in which they now find themselves affect their sense of identity and, if so, how? Do migrants resemble more the society they have left behind or the one to which they have migrated? Do Scottish and English migrants respond differently to the society in which they find themselves?

As far as Scots and English migrants are concerned, the proportions choosing the various social identities are very similar. When it comes to their choices as regards national identity, however, there are striking differences. Some of these mirror the differences we have already seen among 'native residents'. Thus, 53 per cent of Scots living in England would describe their national identity as an important aspect of who they are, compared with 33 per cent of English-born people in Scotland. This is roughly the same proportion as we found earlier among comparable 'natives' (46 per cent and 33 per cent). Perhaps unsurprisingly, of those who choose a national identity to describe themselves, most Scots living in England opt for "Scottish", a minority say "British", and none describe themselves as "English". On the other hand, among English-born people living in Scotland who see their national identity as important, there is a fairly even split between those who describe themselves as "British" or "Scottish", far higher than the proportion who feel they are "English".[4]

This suggests that English-born migrants to Scotland and Scots-born migrants to England may adopt different identity strategies.[5] Most striking is that one third of English migrants in Scotland would have chosen the 'national' identity of their hosts (Scottish); no Scots-born migrant would have chosen "English". This tendency for English-born migrants to Scotland to make claims to be Scottish is also evident from qualitative research (Kiely et al., 2005a: 160–166). While most Scots migrants to England continue to say they are Scottish, many come to acknowledge that they are also British, possibly as a way of fitting in to the new territorial context. It seems that the context in which those born in Scotland or England find themselves does affect their choice of national identity but while the shift among the Scots is modest, that among the English is considerable.

We turn now to look at the characteristics of those native-born people – those respondents *born and living in* England or Scotland – who choose national identity as an important way of describing themselves (Table 4.3). Firstly, we find a clear gradient from young to old in both countries, while at each age level men are more likely than women to choose a national identity, though small bases mean these results need to be treated with caution. Thus, while 48 per cent of English men aged 18–24 would choose their national identity as an important way of describing themselves, the same is true of only 28 per cent of English men over the age of 65. The comparable figures for English women are 44 per cent and 27 per cent respectively. For Scots, the figures are 68 per cent for young men and 40 per cent for older men, and for women, 58 per cent and 30 per cent.

We can only speculate as to the reasons for this age gradient, assuming, at least plausibly, that it is a genuine cohort effect and not an age effect. It is certainly the case that, as we have already pointed out, national identities, English, Scottish and British, are more discussed in the public arena partly as a result of constitutional change and partly as a tool of political mobilisation. It may be that younger persons, especially younger men, who are more likely to favour their 'national' identity than their 'state' identity are more enthused about this and thus more inclined to wish to include national identity along with their other identities. People may also realise that constitutional change is a long-term process and the older generation may then feel that any resulting changes will come too late to be of any great importance to them in their lifetimes.

Table 4.3 National identity choices of different social groups, English and Scots

	% choosing national identity instead of 1st/2nd/3rd identity	Base	Of which …		Base
			… % choosing "English"/ "Scottish"	… % choosing "British"	
English					
Age & sex					
18–24 Men	48	143	65	57	69
18–24 Women	44	132	57	55	58
65+ Men	28	205	58	42	57
65+ Women	27	273	60	40	75
Education					
Degree level	40	372	44	57	148
No qualifications	26	537	69	41	142
Scots[+]					
Age & sex					
18–24 Men	68	72	96	2	49
18–24 Women	58	71	86	29	42
65+ Men	40	112	71	22	45
65+ Women	29	166	94	10	48
Education					
Degree level	54	198	93	9	107
No qualifications	41	314	87	10	130

Base: respondents born and resident in England/Scotland
[+]Source: *Scottish Social Attitudes*

Educational background also appears to make a difference, with 40 per cent of English graduates opting for a national identity, compared with 26 per cent among those with no educational qualifications. Among Scots, the figures are 51 per cent and 41 per cent respectively. Social class, on the other hand, is not linked to people's propensity to see their national identity as important.

We will return later to the relationship between national identity and party identification, but suffice it to say at this point that, contrary to what one might expect, those who would include 'national identity' in their list of identities are not especially marked out in their support for a political party.

Importance of place

We have shown that 'national identity', taken to mean territorial identity at the level of the nation (England or Scotland) or the state (Britain) matters to people, certainly in relation to other social identities they may have such as social class, gender, parenthood, and so on. We are not saying, of course, that national identity is at the forefront of people's minds and is a salient consideration all the time as they go about their everyday lives.[6] Rather, we know from previous qualitative research that national identity comes into play in certain contexts and in interaction with others under various circumstances. In everyday life, for most people, the local and regional levels may generally matter more than the national. 'I'm not English, I'm from Yorkshire' may be somewhat apocryphal, but it makes the point. In order to get a grip on this issue, we evoked a childhood game (at least for the authors of this chapter) and we asked people in both countries:

> *Sometimes for their amusement, children give their address as Home Street, My area, This town, Localshire, My country, Britain, United Kingdom, Europe, The World. Thinking about where you live now, which* **one** *do you feel is most important to you generally* **in your everyday life?**
>
> *[The street in which you live/The local area or district/The city or town in which you live/The county or region, for instance, Yorkshire, Lothian or Glamorgan/The country in which you live, for instance, England, Northern Ireland, Scotland, Wales/Britain/The United Kingdom/Europe]*

Responses are given in Table 4.4.

Table 4.4 Importance of place in everyday life to English and Scots

Most important place in everyday life	English	Scots[+]
	%	%
Street	10	10
Local area/district	34	29
City/town	27	31
County/region	10	6
Country (e.g. England/Scotland)	7	17
Britain	4	1
UK	5	2
Europe	1	1
Base	*2366*	*1286*

Base: respondents born and resident in England/Scotland
[+]Source: *Scottish Social Attitudes*

What is striking is, as suggested earlier, how much locality matters to both Scots and English. The same proportion of both groups (around 70 per cent) say their street, local area or district, or town/city is most important to them. In other words, it is the sub-national level which matters most to people whether they are Scots or English. That said, as one might expect from the previous discussion, two and a half times more Scots than English rate the national level as important. Similarly, when it comes to the state level, English people are three times as likely as Scots to say "British" or "UK" (nine per cent to three per cent), but that is still less than one in ten.

Nevertheless, we must stress that context is crucial. Our previous work has led us to think that one situation in which national identity certainly comes to the fore is when people go abroad. To test this we asked respondents which option they would choose (using the same categories as shown in Table 4.4) if they were in the following situation:

> *If you were abroad and someone who knew this country asked you 'where do you come from?'*

For Scots and English alike, the national and state levels become far more important than before (see Table 4.5). However, major differences between the two groups also emerge. Almost three times as many Scots say "Scotland" as English people say "England", and more than three times as many English as Scots say "Britain/UK"; as many English give this latter response as say "England". Once again, 'national' identity is far more salient for Scots; 'state' identity for the English.

Table 4.5 Importance of place when abroad to English and Scots

"Where do you come from?"	English	Scots[+]
	%	%
Street/local area/district	8	6
City/town	33	28
County/region	21	8
Country (e.g. England/Scotland)	18	52
Britain/UK	18	5
Base	*2366*	*1286*

Base: respondents born and resident in England/Scotland
[+]Source: *Scottish Social Attitudes*

So far we have seen that national identity does matter to people in relation to their other social identities, and that this is so both in England and in Scotland. We have also found that certain groups, particularly the young, are more likely to see their national identity as important. National differences are also important, with Scots being much more likely to choose a 'national' (that is, Scottish) identity than they are to choose a 'state' identity (British). Finally, within people's everyday lives, the locality in which they live is more salient than their national identity, but context is important. In particular, when people go abroad, country of origin becomes important, as opposed to a more local identity. This is especially true for the Scots.

Choosing national identity

National identity clearly matters to people, especially in Scotland but also in England. It is not an imagined construct dreamed up by those in the media or indeed academics. These data confirm our findings from a great deal of qualitative research carried out over the last decade (see, for instance, Kiely *et al.*, 2005a, 2005b). So we turn now to our next question: how the English and Scots vary in their choices when it comes to national identity.

In this section we will consider *three* different approaches to asking people about their national identity. The first presents people with a list of alternative national identities and asks them to choose as many as they wish. We will refer to this as the 'multiple choice' question:

> *Please say which, if any, of the words on this card describes the way* **you** *think of* **yourself**. *Please choose as many or as few as apply.*

> *[British, English, European, Irish, Northern Irish, Scottish, Ulster, Welsh, other answer]*

The second approach involves asking a 'forced choice' question of anyone who chooses more than one national identity (for example, a person who chooses both "British" and "English" at the previous question):

> *And if you had to choose, which one* **best** *describes the way you think of yourself?*

Of course, our multiple choice question gives us no sense of the relative balance between different national identities, in cases where a person picks more than one. And, while our forced choice question achieves this, forcing people to choose just one national identity can be seen as a somewhat blunt instrument with which to measure something as complex as national identity. We address this difficulty by asking respondents a more subtle third question, one which allows them to weigh 'national' and 'state' identities equally or give priority to one over the other (the so-called 'Moreno' question):

Which, if any, of the following best describes how you see yourself?
[English/Scottish] not British
More [English/Scottish] than British
Equally [English/Scottish] and British
More British than [English/Scottish]
British not [English/Scottish]
Other description

At our multiple choice question, nearly all (95 per cent) of the Scots choose the national identity "Scottish" while rather fewer but still the great majority (80 per cent) of the English sample choose "English". When we turn to the choice of "British" the differential is far greater; seven out of ten (71 per cent) of the English choose this identity, compared with only four in ten of the Scots. When forced to choose just *one* of these identities, the difference becomes even sharper. Among the Scottish sample, nine out of ten choose "Scottish" as their sole identity whereas fewer than six out of ten of the English sample choose "English" (57 per cent). On the other hand, 'state' identity, "British", is chosen by only eight per cent of the Scots compared with 36 per cent of the English.

Finally, when we look at responses to the more subtle Moreno question (Table 4.6), differences between the English and the Scottish groups are immediately apparent. The response in Scotland is more skewed: a mere three per cent choose to prioritise their British 'state' identity whereas four times as many do so in England, while three-quarters choose to prioritise their 'national' identity of "Scottish", nearly twice as many as in England.[7]

Table 4.6 'National' and 'state' identities (Moreno measure) for English and Scots (summary)

	English		Scots[+]
	%		%
Only/mainly English	37	Only/mainly Scottish	73
Equally English & British	46	Equally Scottish & British	21
Only/mainly British	13	Only/mainly British	3
Base	*2366*		*1286*

Base: respondents born and resident in England/Scotland
[+]Source: *Scottish Social Attitudes*

If we compare responses to the Moreno question with those given to the multiple choice list of national identities, we find some striking anomalies. For example, 39 per cent of those English people who say they feel "English, *not* British" nonetheless choose "British" as one of their identities at the multiple choice question. Only 16 per cent of Scots give the analogous contradictory response. There are even greater contradictions among those responding to the Moreno question by saying they feel "British *not* English", 50 per cent of whom choose "English" at the multiple choice question.

These contradictions between responses to the Moreno question and the multiple choice question have been observed before.[8] We have no simple explanation for this, and indeed surveys are not as effective as qualitative research in illuminating the reasons behind responses albeit we have made a first attempt at collecting such data in the 2006 surveys.[9] However, a range of possible explanations exist: that the multiple choice national identity question encourages people to include rather than exclude responses; that the terms 'English' and 'British' are not distinguished in a hard and fast manner in public (and private) discourse south of the border;[10] and, lastly, that saying you are 'British' may simply be recognition of a constitutional fact of life (like having a passport) rather than something to which you feel emotionally attached.

In summary, this section has shown that, whichever measure of national identity we use, Scots are more likely than the English to describe themselves in 'national' terms, and are far less likely to describe themselves as being "British". We have also found that, when people are forced to choose a national identity, the difference between Scotland and England becomes even more pronounced. The Moreno measure, which is more subtle because it permits people to weigh 'national' and 'state' identities, reinforces these points about Scottish–English differences.

Are national identities changing?

We turn now to examine whether, and how, national identities are changing over time. What can we say about changes over time? Our main focus in this chapter is on 'natives' – people born and currently living in a country – because if there are significant shifts over time in the choice of national identities this focus minimizes the effect of migration. We start with multiple choice responses because they do not presume that people have only one national identity. We have data on place of birth at four time points in the new millennium: 2000, 2003, 2005[11] and 2006, and hence can see whether 'natives' are changing identities or not. For comparison, the percentages for everyone resident in England and Scotland are given in brackets (Table 4.7).

Two key points emerge. First, whereas English natives describe themselves as "British" in more or less equal numbers at the four time points, there was a major increase in those describing themselves as "English" between 2005 and 2006, a greater increase than found among those resident in England over the period. Second, almost everyone born and living in Scotland describes themselves in 'national', that is, Scottish, terms, but those describing themselves as "British" decrease between 2005 and 2006. This shift away from state identity is mirrored among Scottish residents more generally rather than simply being true of natives, possibly suggesting that the general climate of political and constitutional change in the last few years is having an effect on people living in Scotland rather than simply on those born there. This is in line with the tendency, on which we have already commented, of English people in Scotland to adapt their identity claims to those of the host country.

Table 4.7 National identity (multiple choice) for English and Scots natives (data for residents of England and Scotland in brackets), 2000–2006

Identity choice	2000		2003		2005		2006	
	English	Scots[+]	English	Scots[+]	English	Scots[+]	English	Scots[+]
% choosing "British"	69 (67)	51 (52)	72 (70)	56 (58)	73 (70)	50 (52)	71 (68)	40 (43)
% choosing "English"/ "Scottish"	69 (59)	95 (87)	68 (59)	94 (84)	67 (59)	96 (85)	80 (67)	94 (84)
Base	1660	1439	1584	1231	1538	1263	2366	1286
(Base)	(2887)	(1663)	(3709)	(1508)	(3643)	(1549)	(3666)	(1594)

Base: respondents born and resident in England/Scotland
(Base): respondents resident in England/Scotland
[+]Source: *Scottish Social Attitudes*

Over the same time points, a similar picture of strengthening 'national' identity and weakening 'state' identity in both countries can be seen from data on forced choice national identity (Table 4.8), a cruder measure, but one which underlines the shift.

Table 4.8 Forced choice national identity for English and Scots natives (data for residents of England and Scotland in brackets), 2000–2006

	2000		2003		2005		2006	
	English	Scots[+]	English	Scots[+]	English	Scots[+]	English	Scots[+]
% choosing "British"	47 (47)	9 (13)	49 (48)	15 (20)	51 (48)	10 (14)	36 (39)	8 (14)
% choosing "English"/ "Scottish"	49 (41)	89 (80)	45 (38)	83 (72)	44 (40)	88 (77)	57 (47)	90 (78)
Base	1660	1439	1584	1231	1538	1263	2366	1286
(Base)	(2887)	(1663)	(3709)	(1508)	(3643)	(1549)	(3666)	(1594)

Base: respondents born and resident in England/Scotland
(Base): respondents resident in England/Scotland
[+]Source: *Scottish Social Attitudes*

Between 2000 and 2006, considering Tables 4.7 and 4.8 together, among English natives, both the measures, multiple choice (+11 per cent) and forced choice (+8 per cent) show a trend towards being "English". However, while the forced choice measure shows a decline in being "British", the multiple choice question on the other hand shows a small increase (two per cent). Among Scots natives, on the other hand, the multiple choice measure shows a decline in being "British" (11 per cent) but the forced choice question shows little change. This suggests that when forced to choose, Scots since 2000 form two polarised groups, the one unlikely to go significantly above its present level of 90 per cent and the other unlikely to fall below 10 per cent.

If we focus on all residents in each country, rather than upon the views of those who were born there, the forced choice question, crude though it is, is the longest running measure in *British Social Attitudes* surveys. The results are shown in Table 4.9. This shows that people living in England have become less "British" since the early 1990s. In 1992, nearly two-thirds chose this description of their national identity, now only 39 per cent do so. There has been a corresponding rise in the proportion of people who describe themselves as "English"; the main shift appeared to take place between 1997 and 1999, when the proportions opting for this national identity increased from 34 to 44 per cent. There followed a period of relative stability, but between 2005 and 2006 there was another rise in the proportion of people saying they were "English", to 47 per cent. Year on year changes of this sort, of course, may simply reflect the importance of contextual effects such as cultural or sporting events (England's participation in the 2006 World Cup, for example, which took place during the fieldwork for that year's survey).

Table 4.9 National identity (forced choice), England and Scotland (residents), 1974–2006

	1974	1979	1992	1997	1999	2001	2003	2005	2006
England	%	%	%	%	%	%	%	%	%
"English"	n/a	n/a	31	34	44	43	38	40	47
"British"	n/a	n/a	63	59	44	44	48	48	39
Other/none	n/a	n/a	6	7	12	13	14	12	14
Base			*2442*	*3150*	*2718*	*2761*	*3709*	*3643*	*3666*
Scotland[+]	%	%	%	%	%	%	%	%	%
"Scottish"	65	56	72	72	77	77	72	77	78
"British"	31	38	25	20	17	16	20	14	14
Other/none	4	6	3	8	6	7	8	9	8
Base	*588*	*658*	*957*	*882*	*1482*	*1605*	*1508*	*1549*	*1594*

Base: respondents resident in England/Scotland
[+]Source: 1974–1997 Scottish Elections Surveys; 1999–2006 *Scottish Social Attitudes*
n/a = not asked

The picture in Scotland is similar, but starker. Comparable data go back further, to 1974, and show that the proportion of people living in Scotland and describing themselves as "British" has halved over 20 years, from 31 per cent in 1974 to 14 per cent in 2006. It seems safe to conclude that people in Scotland are less likely to call themselves "British" than ever before, or at least since surveys began 30 years ago.

Trend data for the Moreno question confirms the pattern in England of a gradual decline in 'Britishness' and an increase in the proportion opting for an identity that gives greater weight to being "English" (Table 4.10). The trend we observed earlier towards a rise in 'Englishness' between 1997 and 1999 is evident here, followed by a slower and more modest rise between 1999 and 2006. However, the proportion choosing the 'only/mainly British' option (that is, who say they are "British more than English" or "British not English") is stable until 2003, after which the data suggest a move away from this choice to the mid-point of the scale.

Table 4.10 National identities (Moreno measure) in England (residents), 1997–2006

	1997	1999	2003	2006
	%	%	%	%
Only/mainly English	24	32	36	37
Equally English & British	45	37	31	45
Only/mainly British	23	25	24	14
Base	*3150*	*2718*	*1929*	*2432*[++]

Base: respondents resident in England

++2006 base: respondents born and resident in England[12]

In Scotland (Table 4.11), the results of the Moreno question differ sharply from those shown in Table 4.10 and broadly show stability. In particular, the proportion of people describing themselves as 'only/mainly British' varies only slightly over time and indeed rises slightly over the entire period. We take the view that the Moreno question, because it enables respondents to strike a balance if they so wish, between their 'national' identity (English or Scottish) and 'state' identity (British), is a better guide to what is going on than forced choice.

Table 4.11 National identities (Moreno measure) in Scotland (residents), 1992–2006

	1992	1997	1999	2000	2001	2003	2005	2006
	%	%	%	%	%	%	%	%
Only/mainly Scottish	59	61	67	68	66	65	64	64
Equally Scottish & British	33	27	22	21	24	22	22	21
Only/mainly British	6	8	7	7	6	8	9	9
Base	957	882	1482	1663	1605	1508	1549	1594

Base: respondents resident in Scotland
Source: 1992 & 1997 Scottish Election surveys; 1999–2006 *Scottish Social Attitudes*

In summary, there has been a slow but significant shift in England towards people describing themselves in 'national' terms, with evidence of a sharp jump between 2005 and 2006. Meanwhile, those in Scotland continue to emphasise strongly their Scottishness. In addition, over the last few years there has been a decline in the proportion of people in both England and Scotland who opt for a "British" national identity, although when English 'natives' respond to the multiple choice question, the proportion saying they are British has not declined since the turn of the century. None of these changes can be accounted for by changing patterns of immigration, as they remain even when we focus only upon those who are native born and bred.

Does politics matter?

To what extent is national identity affected by political change? The last 10 to 15 years should offer us an ideal opportunity to explore this issue as they represent a period of unprecedented constitutional change, culminating in the setting up of the Scottish Parliament (and the National Assembly for Wales) in 1999. In short, how 'political' is national identity? Is it a driver of constitutional change, an outcome or, indeed, neither?

The first thing to note is that respondents who would include a 'national identity' in their list of identities are not especially distinctive in their support for particular political parties. Thus, in England, 37 per cent of Conservatives would have included national identity in their list of important identities, compared with 31 per cent of Labour supporters, and 36 per cent of Liberal Democrats. In Scotland, even among SNP identifiers, only 56 per cent would have included national identity, compared with 45 per cent of Labour supporters, 44 per cent of Conservatives and 42 per cent of Liberal Democrats. It is interesting that only just over half of Scottish Nationalists would have done so, suggesting that the relationship between national identity and people's party political views is by no means straightforward.

Our prime focus in this section will be on Scotland where there has been the greatest constitutional change, but where the data for England allow, we shall make appropriate comparisons. By and large, we have assumed that the direction of causality leads from national identity to, for example, party identification and constitutional preference, on the grounds that how people think about their own identity will have been formed by many factors over a long period of socialisation and is more likely to drive their politics and constitutional views than *vice versa*. For example, it might be argued that if you define yourself as Scottish – and not British – this will lead you towards being more likely to vote SNP and to favour independence. Conversely, if you see yourself as British, you are more likely to vote for one of the 'Unionist' parties. In fact, though there is some association between national identity and a person's party political choices, there is less than one might expect. As far as being "British" is concerned, Liberal Democrats and Conservatives are somewhat more inclined to describe themselves in this way (56 per cent doing so in both cases) than are Labour supporters (42 per cent) or Nationalists (30 per cent). It is somewhat surprising that nearly a third of SNP identifiers think of themselves as British, possibly reflecting constitutional realities and the possession of a British passport (Kiely *et al.*, 2005b: 74–75). On the other hand, supporters of all parties, including Conservatives, are overwhelmingly likely to call themselves Scottish.

What of the more subtle Moreno measure, given that most Scots opt for a combined national and state identity? The first column in Table 4.12 shows that, among those who describe themselves either as "Scottish not British" or as being "Scottish more than British", just over a third (36 per cent) are Labour party identifiers, while 23 per cent identify with the SNP. By comparison, among those who see themselves as "equally Scottish and British" the only significant shift is that they are less likely to favour the SNP. The 'only/mainly British' group is numerically small, and all that can be said is that the differences are again in the expected direction.

Table 4.12 Party identification by national identity (Moreno measure) among Scots

	Only/mainly Scottish	Equally Scottish & British	Only/mainly British
	%	%	%
Conservative	8	14	36
Labour	36	38	18
Liberal Democrat	7	7	13
SNP	23	9	13
None	13	17	7
Others	12	15	13
Base	*941*	*273*	*47*

Base: respondents born and resident in Scotland
Source: *Scottish Social Attitudes*

Is England different when it comes to the relationship between national identity and party identification? If anything, national identity is an even weaker predictor of party identification than in Scotland. Thus, in terms of responses to our multiple choice national identity question, the gradient runs from 69 per cent of Conservatives describing themselves as British, to 75 per cent of Liberal Democrats, with Labour at 74 per cent. Similarly, supporters of <u>all</u> parties also describe themselves as "English", from 75 per cent of Liberal Democrats, 82 per cent of Labour and 83 per cent of Conservatives. As far as the Moreno measure is concerned, while people who think of themselves as 'only/mainly English' are more likely to be Conservatives than Labour identifiers (35 and 28 per cent respectively), positions are somewhat reversed for the 'only/mainly British' group, among whom 33 per cent support Labour and 25 per cent the Conservatives.

All in all, one finds only weak associations between national identity and party political support, in both Scotland and England. In Scotland, only 27 per cent of those who describe themselves as "Scottish, not British" are supporters of the SNP, while 34 per cent support Labour, a useful indicator of the weak association between party support and national identity.

Considering oneself a supporter (or not) of a political party, however, might be seen as only one part of the story. What of the relationship between national identity and constitutional change? Surely, in Scotland at least, one might safely predict that supporting devolution or independence is linked to national identity, and that the more Scottish a person feels, the more likely he or she is to support self-government? To assess this we asked the following question:

> *Which of these statements comes closest to your view?*
>
> *Scotland should become independent, separate from the UK and the European Union*
>
> *Scotland should become independent, separate from the UK but part of the European Union*
>
> *Scotland should remain part of the UK, with its own elected parliament which has **some** taxation powers*
>
> *Scotland should remain part of the UK, with its own elected parliament which has **no** taxation powers*
>
> *Scotland should remain part of the UK **without** an elected parliament*

We can use people's responses to place them in one of three broad categories. The first comprises those who would prefer independence (and includes the first two of the answer options shown above); the second comprises those who would rather see some form of devolution (the third and fourth categories above); the third those who would rather devolution did not exist (the fifth category).

Among those who describe themselves as "Scottish, not British", half (49 per cent) opt for independence, a similar proportion to those preferring devolution (47 per cent). Virtually the same proportion (46 per cent) of those describing themselves as "equally Scottish and British" prefer devolution, one in three no parliament and one in five independence. Even among the very small minority who are in the 'only/mainly British' group, the most popular option is devolution (50 per cent), with only a third opting for no parliament at all (33 per cent). This shows nicely the lack of relationship between national identity and constitutional preference.

We also asked those born and living in England a rather different but analogous question, which asked people to choose between continuing with a UK Parliament, having regional assemblies or having an English Parliament.[13] Overall, 22 per cent think an English Parliament would be the best way to govern England, a figure which only rises to 28 per cent among those who define themselves as "English not British".

In short, while there is some weak association between national identity and political and constitutional attitudes, it is clear that national identity, however measured, is neither a strong predictor of views on constitutional questions nor on party identification. Put even more starkly, if we focus on those defining themselves as "Scottish, not British", we find that only one in five both supports the SNP <u>and</u> favours independence. If we adopt a more generous measure of national identity, namely, those who choose "Scottish" on the multiple identity measure, the ratio falls to almost one in eight. In other words, it is the *lack* of association between national identity and political–constitutional attitudes which is striking.

We can gauge the absence of association more directly from the responses to questions asked of people in England and in Scotland who said that they were "only" or "mainly" English or Scottish.[14] We asked them to respond to the following statement.

> *I feel more English now that Scotland has its own Parliament and Wales its National Assembly*

A third (34 per cent) of the English respondents agree, 35 per cent are neutral, and 29 per cent disagree. If anything, the replies from the Scots to their comparable question[15] were even less 'political': 29 per cent agree, 30 per cent are neutral and 40 per cent disagree. In other words, it seems that devolution in and of itself has not made the English feel more English nor, indeed, the Scots more Scottish. We might construe that as indicating that national identity is perhaps more 'cultural' than 'political', at least at the time of writing. There is always the possibility that circumstances may arise whereby matters of national identity become more politically charged, offering political entrepreneurs the opportunity to mobilise and manipulate such issues, but that does not seem to be the present situation in Scottish – and British – politics.

Conclusions

We began this chapter by pointing out that, as the 'break-up' of Britain has stubbornly failed to materialise, the discussion of constitutional politics in these islands has come to be founded on a belief that people are no longer as 'British' as they once were. Much of the current interest in national identity appears politically driven, especially by a fear among the chattering classes, notably politicians, that people living in the UK no longer feel 'British', or not sufficiently so for their purposes.

Politicians of a Unionist slant have reacted to this belief in 'the decline of Britishness' by suggesting a 'British Day', classes in Britishness, and so on. While much of this debate is angled at non-white people and economic migrants – the so-called 'multicultural' question – it also has a strong territorial focus, what we might call the 'national' question. Given that Britain was forged 300 years ago by the Treaty of Union between England and Scotland, it is appropriate to ask whether these two 'core peoples', the English and the Scots, still feel British, and if so, to what degree. It is especially appropriate because fears about what the posited decline in Britishness may lead to have doubtless been intensified by the recent elections in Scotland resulting in an SNP minority administration.

If, of course, ordinary people do not care about what we have called as shorthand their 'national' or 'state' identity, whatever they may believe it to be, these alarms would be pointless. However, we have seen that this is not the case; in both England and Scotland, people rank national identity just below everyday identities such as family and gender, and on a par with class and employment status.

We have found that considerable numbers of English and Scots do indeed still feel British: on multiple choice, as many as 71 per cent of the former and 40 per cent of the latter. What we have seen is a steady long-term shift away from being British towards being English and being Scottish, though for most people it is still a question of being both English (or Scottish) and British, rather than either/or. Nevertheless, over the long duration – 30 years – there has been a perceptible shift towards 'national' rather than 'state' identity. Does this mean that the assertion of national identity vis-à-vis state identity will lead to the demise of the UK in a constitutional sense? We have seen that for those of a Unionist disposition these changes are to be feared. The reverse of this coin is that for Nationalists they may be seen as encouraging, and even the cause of their recent successes.

Whatever has happened or may happen in the realm of party politics, our data suggest that people themselves do not connect their politics, be they the party they identify with or the way in which they would like their country to be governed, to their national identities. It is pretty clear to us that the person in the street does not make these sorts of connections, at least in the way that politicians might think, and fear or rejoice in. In short, it seems that people have a more 'cultural' as opposed to 'political' understanding of their national identities, whatever they think the future of the UK as a constitutional unit should be.

Has devolution, notably the creation of a Scottish Parliament, had much impact on how people describe their national identities? The picture that emerges in England and Scotland is complex. If anything, Scotland has shown less change in the period 1999 to 2006 than England. However national identity is measured, by Moreno, multiple choice or fixed choice questions, the advent of devolution has not led to a large increase in the numbers saying they are Scottish, if only because substantial proportions did so to start with. In England, on the other hand, there has been a general strengthening of Englishness and a decline in being British, although when English 'natives' respond to the multiple choice question, the proportion saying they are British has not declined since the turn of the century.

Will these trends continue? Time, as always, will tell. We cannot know how political entrepreneurs will try to manipulate and shape people's sense of national identity, and whether or not they will be successful. And it is not simply the 'national' level which matters. The data show unequivocally that most people, in Scotland as well as England, relate most to the local level, their street, district, town or city, and only thereafter to their nation. To be sure, it's not a matter of either/or, for people have a sophisticated and nuanced awareness of the different levels in which they lead their lives, and the more local these happen to be, the more meaningful they are.

Nevertheless, there have been slow but considerable changes in people's sense of national identity over the last 30 years. In that respect, and possibly in that respect only, politicians who talk identity talk are correct to do so, but possibly not for the reasons they choose.

Notes

1. In this chapter, we will use the term 'national identity' to refer to territorial or 'state' identity such as British as well as Scottish and English.
2. Our focus in this paper is on Scotland and England, whose partnership in 1707 founded the British state. Whether the Welsh are more likely to describe themselves as Welsh rather than British requires specifically Welsh data and is therefore beyond the scope of this paper. We draw readers' attention to *The 23rd Report* which presented data on national identity for Wales (alongside England and Scotland) (Heath *et al.*, 2007).
3. In 2003, the question was asked with national identities included in the list from the outset. We made this change to provide a more direct test of the importance people attach to national identity.
4. These results need to be treated with caution because of the sizes of the bases involved. In total, 153 English people living in Scotland and 74 Scots living in England were interviewed. Overall, 70 per cent of Scots in England who say their national identity is important to them opt for a "Scottish" identity, while 37 per cent opt for "British". Among the English living in Scotland who say their national

identity is important, 18 per cent describe themselves as "English", 40 per cent as "British" and 34 per cent as "Scottish".

5. The greater willingness of Scottish migrants, when compared with Scots in Scotland, to say they are British may reflect a wish to express common identity with the host country, and the modest decline in choosing British identity among English migrants a sensitivity to what they perceive, probably wrongly, as Scottish ambivalence about this choice. In a recent paper (2007) based on *Scottish Social Attitudes* 2005 data ('Being British: a crisis of identity?' Political Quarterly, **78(2)**: 251–260), we argued that Scots, even those who did not see themselves as British, were not particularly hostile to British cultural and political symbols.

6. The Scottish novelist, Willie McIlvanney, expressed this well: "Having a national identity is a bit like having an old insurance policy. You know you've got one somewhere but often you're not entirely sure where it is. And if you're honest, you would have to admit you're pretty vague about what the small print means." (*The Herald*, 6th March 1999)

7. In Table 4.6 the data are shown with the two extreme categories on either side of the mid-point merged, and the analysis restricted to those making a choice of one of the five categories. The full results for the Moreno question can be found in the appendix to this chapter (Table A.1).

8. In their article in *The 17th Report*, Curtice and Heath (2000: 155–174), used the difference between Moreno and multiple choice responses to differentiate between 'unambiguously English' and 'ambiguously English' (and correspondingly extending the 'British' end of the scale), thereby producing a seven- rather than a five- point scale. We have not followed this procedure, because we think that in sociological terms it conflates the results from two different stimuli and as we suggest in the text it is possible to offer explanations for the contradictions which throw doubt on the procedure.

9. In a future paper based on these surveys we will explore in detail some of the reasons behind people's Moreno choices.

10. By way of illustration, *The Guardian* (7th June 2007) carried a headline: "Britain faces 20-year house boom that will split nation, says report". The report was about England only.

11. The 2005 *British Social Attitudes* survey asked respondents where their parents were living when they were born rather than directly about their own place of birth. We can treat the data as a rough proxy, nevertheless.

12. In the 2006 *British* and *Scottish Social Attitudes* surveys, questions on identity were generally asked of those born in England, Scotland or Wales rather than those resident in these countries. In the Scottish survey, the Moreno question was asked on both bases and we compared the results. The figures do not differ greatly, giving us some confidence that the 2006 data for England in Table 4.10 are not wide of the mark.

13. *With all the changes going on in the way the different parts of Great Britain are run, which of the following do you think would be best for England ... for England to be governed as it is now, with laws made by the UK Parliament, for each region of England to have its own elected assembly that makes decisions about the region's*

economy, planning and housing, or, for England as a whole to have its own new Parliament with law-making powers?

14. That is, who said they were either "English, not British" or "more English than British" on the Moreno question; and the parallel questions in the Scottish survey.

15. *I feel more Scottish now that Scotland has its own Parliament*

References

Curtice, J. and Heath, A. (2000), 'Is the English lion about to roar? National identity after devolution', in Jowell, R., Curtice, J., Park, A., Thomson, K., Jarvis, L., Bromley, C. and Stratford, N. (eds.), *British Social Attitudes: the 17th Report*, London: Sage

Heath, A., Martin, J. and Elgenius, G. (2007), 'Who do we think we are? The decline of traditional social identities', in Park, A., Curtice, J., Thomson, K., Phillips, M. and Johnson, M. (eds.), *British Social Attitudes: the 23rd Report – Perspectives on a changing society*, London: Sage

Kiely, R., Bechhofer, F. and McCrone, D. (2005a), 'Birth, blood and belonging: identity claims in post-devolution Scotland', *Sociological Review*, **53**: 150–171

Kiely, R., Bechhofer, F. and McCrone, D. (2005b), 'Whither Britishness? English and Scottish people in Scotland', *Nations and Nationalism*, **11**: 65–82

Nairn, T. (1977) *The Break-up of Britain*, London: New Left Books

Acknowledgements

The authors are grateful to The Leverhulme Trust which has supported their research into national identity since 1999 and in particular for their most recent grant (F/00/158/AY) which has enabled them to commission *The National* and *The Scottish Centre for Social Research* to ask the questions from 2006 reported in this chapter. Frank Bechhofer produced the first draft of this paper, but it is the product of a collegiate form of working in which the data, the analysis and the drafts have been discussed by both authors throughout, and they are equally responsible for it.

Appendix

Table A.1 National identities (Moreno measure) for English and Scots, 2003 and 2006

English	2003 %	2006 %	Scots[+]	2003 %	2006 %
English not British	19	21	Scottish not British	35	38
English more than British	22	16	Scottish more than British	38	35
Equally English & British	34	46	Equally Scottish & British	22	21
British more than English	14	7	British more than Scottish	2	2
British not English	8	6	British not Scottish	1	1
Base	*1584*	*2366*		*1231*	*1286*

Base: respondents born and resident in England/Scotland
[+]Source: *Scottish Social Attitudes*

5 Is there still a public service ethos?

Peter John and Mark Johnson[*]

For many people, the choice between working in the public and private sector is a fundamental one. On the downside, public sector pay is on average lower for equivalent jobs than in the private sector, and public sector employees may feel constrained by a larger number of rules and regulations (Boyne, 2002; Allington and Morgan, 2003). But on the upside, the public sector may have one unique advantage to offer: the chance to do a socially useful job. Public sector bodies are supposed to advance outcomes that societies care about. Such beliefs and values are often thought to be shared by those who work there – in contrast with the supposedly more selfish outlooks of those who are employed in the private sector whose individual rewards tend to be tied to profits and sales. If so, this publicly orientated set of values may help compensate for lower levels of remuneration and generally worse working conditions in the public sector.

This so-called 'public service ethos' is valued by policymakers. The cynical commentator may say that it can help keep wages down. But even those who do not take that position would tend to agree that a motivated staff, who are keen to do their most for the public realm, can help to ensure that the large spending increases of recent years translate into improved public policy outcomes. Workers in the public sector face considerable challenges, whether it is teaching children in an urban school or nursing walk-in cases at an NHS Accident and Emergency clinic. These are the kinds of jobs that cannot be done by people who are just there for the extrinsic benefits and financial rewards. They need a public service ethos for employees to engage with this demanding but intrinsically rewarding work.

Talking about the public service ethos is also a way of recognising the wider contribution these workers make to society in the number of unpaid hours and extra effort they put in beyond what is laid down in their contracts. It provides an answer to the populist and right-wing critique of the public sector as being less efficient because there is no profit motive driving productivity. Another

[*] Peter John is the Hallsworth Chair of Governance at the University of Manchester. Mark Johnson was formerly a Senior Researcher at the *National Centre for Social Research* and Co-Director of the *British Social Attitudes* survey series.

benefit is supposed to be the ability of the civil service to attract some of the brightest graduates away from more lucrative city careers to take up careers in the civil service. So it is no surprise that decision makers and opinion leaders think the public service ethos should be cultivated for the benefit of society as a whole (see Public Administration Committee, 2002).

There has been a lot of academic attention paid to the public service ethos in recent years. Survey and case study evidence suggests that those working in the public sector have a more altruistic motivation than those in the private sector (Crewson, 1995; Pratchett and Wingfield, 1996; Steele, 1999; Houston, 2000; Public Services Productivity Panel, 2002; Norris, 2003; Buelens and Broeck, 2007). Many researchers regard the public service ethos as an attachment to the intrinsic elements of a job, which includes feelings of accomplishment and self-worth. But here we offer a simpler definition of wanting to work for the public interest, which is similar to the approach of Rainey and Wittmer (Rainey, 1982; Wittmer; 1991). The advantage of this definition is that it focuses on the key purpose of the public sector and how its mission can become part of workers' own views and motivations.

One important issue addressed by previous research is whether the public service ethos is a result of self-selection (possibly as a result of certain educational pathways) or post-entry socialisation. While neither approach necessarily undermines the altruistic nature of the values, the latter seems to be more about how organisational power shapes values, particularly if these are needed for career advancement. Linked to this is the importance of hierarchy. Do those in managerial grades have more public service ethos than others? If you are at the bottom of the pile, like a manual worker in the National Health Service, are you more interested in pay and conditions than in doing public good? But, it seems this is not the case: many studies show similarity between the public and private sectors among those at managerial grades (Rainey and Bozeman, 2000; Buelens and Broeck, 2007).

Another unresolved question is whether it is working in the public sector *per se* or the kind of job that is important. This is particularly hard to investigate because some jobs exist only in the public sector (e.g. social work, university teaching) or are mainly in it (e.g. doctors and nurses). Too few studies compare the same kind of employees in both sectors, but Buelens and Broeck conclude that it is job content rather than working in the public sector itself that counts, which suggests that public sector ownership is not a necessary condition for a public service ethos (Buelens and Broeck, 2007).

The academic literature also focuses on the different bases of the public service ethos. Gender is a particularly interesting example because of the large number of women employed in the public sector (DeHart-Davis *et al.*, 2006). Less discussed are age or cohort effects but these can be very influential if a particular age group has a different vision for society than the rest (Jurkiewicz and Brown, 1998). This chapter is particularly interested in this dimension to the ethos as it may be a component of how it changes over time.

Many policymakers and commentators think that the public service ethos has declined. Perhaps the public service ethos was a feature of a more collectivist or traditional society, reflecting the values of the post-1945 welfare state reforms and their Webbian antecedents. The idea is that the state – and by implication its employees – could be harnessed for public purposes (Plant, 2003). An extreme example of this view was the idea that the coal miners would increase productivity when the mines were transferred from the private to the public sector. Another common argument is that as the institutions of the state are reformed by privatisation, new public management, quasi-markets, contracting out and private finance projects, the public service ethos would weaken, because traditional bureaucracy is no longer the central means of state intervention. It is argued that the public service ethos is in danger of being replaced by self-interested behaviour driven by performance-related pay and sanctions of performance measurement (Public Administration Committee, 2002). The more public sector workers are treated like self-interested actors working for their short-term benefits, the more they might behave like that, a kind of self-fulfilling prophesy (Le Grand, 2003). If the government pushes choice, private sector delivery and commercial forms of management, the public service ethos could be expected to decline. However, bar some limited case study work (Steele, 1999), there is no evidence of this happening.

This chapter hopes to fill some of these gaps in knowledge by, first, finding out if there is a public service ethos in existence in Britain today. Secondly, we examine how and why it has changed over time. Finally, we look at whether a public service ethos does indeed foster job satisfaction as hoped for by politicians and policymakers.

Public or private?

We begin by looking at the nature of the workforce. In Britain the majority of people are employed by the private rather than public sector. The *British Social Attitudes* survey asks respondents to choose which of the following four options best represented the type of organisation they worked for:

- *Private sector firm or company, including, for example, limited companies and PLCs*

- *Nationalised industry or public corporation, including, for example, the Post Office and the BBC*

- *Other public sector employer, including, for example, Central Government, Civil Service, Government Agency, Local authority, Universities, Health Authority, NHS hospitals, NHS Trusts, GP surgeries, Police, Armed forces*

- *Charity or Voluntary sector, including, for example, charitable companies, churches, trade unions*

In 2005, two-thirds were in the private sector, three per cent in nationalised industry, 27 per cent in the rest of the public sector, and three per cent in the charity or voluntary sector. The analysis that follows combines those working in nationalised industries with those working for any other public sector employers, to represent the public sector. Those working in the charity or voluntary sector are excluded from the analysis.

As well as actually working in the public sector, it is possible to look at preferences for working in different sectors, which gives an idea of how attractive the different kinds of employment are. The survey asked:

> *Suppose you were working and could choose between different kinds of jobs. Which of the following would you personally choose?*
>
> *... working in a private business*
>
> *... working for the government or civil service*

Overall, around 51 per cent of working people would opt for a private business, compared to 23 per cent for the government or civil service, with another 24 per cent unable to decide. Naturally there is a strong correlation between the sector in which people work and the sector in which they would like to work. Some 59 per cent of those in the private sector prefer working in a private business, and only 15 per cent would prefer to work for the government or civil service. But what is revealing is that this association is weaker among those in the public sector, with only 44 per cent saying they would prefer working for the government or civil service whilst 29 per cent would prefer working in the private sector.

Is there a public service ethos?

To what extent can we identify a public service ethos? We begin by looking at how people value the importance of various components of a job. Table 5.1 shows the list of job attributes presented to respondents with the proportion saying that each attribute was "very important" to them personally in a job.

If there is such a thing as a public service ethos, we would expect to see those in the public sector attributing greater importance to "a job that allows someone to help other people" and "a job that is useful to society". We would also expect public sector respondents to value the intrinsic nature of jobs more highly, such as it being "an interesting job" and being able to "work independently".

And the expected difference is there: public sector workers are more likely to value a job that is socially useful and brings intrinsic rewards. There is also some suggestion that private sector workers are more interested in a high income, which tends to confirm the findings of other research in this area

(Crewson, 1997). However, this difference is not statistically significant with this rather small sample size.

Table 5.1 Important attributes of a job, private and public sector employees, 2005

% say "very important" to them personally …	Private sector	Public sector	Difference
… a job that is useful to society	15	32	+17
… a job that allows someone to help other people	18	27	+9
… a job that allows someone to work independently	15	22	+7
… an interesting job	46	53	+7
… job security	50	49	-1
… good opportunities for advancement	24	21	-3
… a job that allows someone to decide their times and days of work	14	11	-3
… high income	18	12	-6
Base	507	260	

Overall, the differences fit what a public service ethos should look like – public sector workers are more concerned with jobs where they can help other people and which are useful to society. Note, however, that both groups regard job security as being an important feature.

What explains the public service ethos?

There is good evidence here that something like a public service ethos actually exists. But could the difference simply be a function of the different compositions of the two sectors?

A number of socio-demographic characteristics are associated with working in the public sector. The next table shows the differences across a series of standard demographic variables: public sector employees are more likely to be older, female, trade union members, professionals and to have a degree than private sector employees. These differences all remain statistically significant once the other factors are taken into account in multivariate analysis. Because of the profile of more professional jobs in the public sector, household income is higher on average for public sector employees, despite the fact that equivalent jobs are usually worse paid. (As a result, the difference in household income disappears in multivariate analysis once the other factors are taken into account.)

Table 5.2 Composition of private and public sector employees, 2005

% of employees	Private sector	Public sector	Difference
Men	51	35	-16
Women	49	65	+16
18–34	33	20	-13
65+	19	24	+5
Professional	31	52	+21
Routine/semi-routine	37	24	-13
Degree or higher	24	44	+20
No qualifications	27	20	-7
Highest income quartile	22	27	+5
Lowest income quartile	27	19	-8
Labour supporter	41	41	0
Conservative supporter	23	24	-1
Trade union member	11	37	+26
Base	*2404*	*1158*	

Could it simply be the case that the public service ethos is nothing to do with the public sector at all, but is instead produced by these different socio-demographic characteristics? We tested for this using multivariate analysis. As shown in the appendix to this chapter, public sector employees remained significantly more likely than private sector employees to say that it is very important to them for a job to help other people and to be useful to society, even after all these other factors are taken into account. It therefore appears that there really is a measurable public service ethos.

Public service ethos under New Labour

Having established the existence of the public service ethos, the next task is to determine whether it is in decline as predicted by many commentators. As discussed earlier, many have argued that New Labour's increasing use of new management techniques within the public sector, would undermine the public service ethos. We would therefore expect public and private sector employees to have become more similar in their outlook.

It is possible to test this using questions fielded on the *British Social Attitudes* survey as part of the *International Social Survey Programme*. There are data from both 1997 and 2005, which, fortuitously, covers most of the period in which Tony Blair was in office – it was his governments, after all, that pushed the use of the private sector in public services.

Table 5.3 compares attitudes to the importance of social usefulness in a job in 1997 and 2005. As can be seen, the expectation of reduced differences between public and private sector workers is not fulfilled. In fact, quite the reverse is true, as the difference between private sector and public sector workers has actually widened since 1997. In 1997 the differences between people in the two sectors (at five and three percentage points) were not statistically significant. By 2005 these had grown to 17 and nine percentage points respectively.

Table 5.3 Importance of social usefulness in a job, private and public sector employees, 1997 and 2005

% say "very important" in a job	1997			2005		
	Private sector	Public sector	Diffe-rence	Private sector	Public sector	Diffe-rence
Useful to society	17	22	+5	15	32	+17
Allows someone to help other people	19	22	+3	18	27	+9
Base	623	282		507	260	

Note that the divergence is all down to a change in the attitudes of public sector employees – private sector employees have hardly changed their views at all. We now examine three possible reasons for this finding: a changing experience of work in the public sector, a changing composition of the public sector workforce, and a change in the nature of the young people entering the public service at the start of their careers.

Changing experience of work?

The first area to consider is people's actual experience of work. If, despite the New Labour reforms, those in the public sector are still more likely than those in the private sector to believe that their own job offers them the chance to do something useful for society or to help people, then it may help explain why we do not see the convergence we anticipated. It would not, however, explain the divergence we saw in the previous section.

One reason why public sector employees still believe their jobs to be more socially useful could be the massive expansion of the public sector under New Labour, after many years of reduction or constraint. New projects based on exciting ideas to combat public problems may have energised public sector workers and created a halo effect for those already in public sector employment.

More generally, the public sector became less of a 'dirty word' and has been valued more in its own right.

We can test this directly, because in addition to asking respondents what was important in a job, we asked them whether they agreed with the following two statements:

In my job I can help other people

My job is useful to society

As the next table shows, there are striking differences between people in the two sectors, with those in the public sector considerably more likely to say their job is useful to society and allows them to help other people. That this is the case suggests that the changes in the organisation of the public sector have yet to be fully felt 'on the ground'. However, as the table also shows, the differences between the two sectors have not changed since 1997 and thus cannot help us to explain the increase in the public service ethos.

Table 5.4 Social usefulness of own job, private and public sector employees, 1997 and 2005

% "strongly agree"	1997			2005		
	Private sector	Public sector	Diffe-rence	Private sector	Public sector	Diffe-rence
"My job is useful to society"	9	42	+33	14	45	+31
"In my job I can help other people"	11	39	+28	17	44	+27
Base	336	142		274	146	

Changing composition of the public sector?

Another possible explanation for the increase in the public service ethos relates to the composition of the public sector. If the type of people working in the public sector has changed, in terms of either their socio-demographic characteristics or the type of work they undertake, then that might account for the change.

To take the latter point first, it could be the case that people working in particular fields have distinctive views regarding work and that during the course of Labour's modernisation programme these fields moved from the public to the private sector. So, for instance, those who were previously employed by the public sector but who we might not anticipate to have had such a distinctive public service ethos (for instance, cleaners or ancillary workers) could have moved into the private sector. This would then have had the effect of increasing the relative prevalence of the public service ethos among those left in the public sector.

We can test this by looking at the proportions of the public and private sectors employed in the major areas of occupation as measured by the Standard Industrial Classification (see Appendix I to this *Report* for more details on this), and how they vary in 1997 and 2005. But Table 5.5 shows that there have not been any shifts of a size that could reasonably be expected to account for the changes we have witnessed.

Table 5.5 Composition of the workforce by industrial classification, private and public sector employees, 1997 and 2005

	Private sector			Public sector		
	1997	2005	Change	1997	2005	Change
	%	%		%	%	
Manufacturing	36	27	-9	1	2	+1
Construction	4	5	+1	4	1	-3
Wholesale, retail trade	20	19	-1	1	0	-1
Transport, storage, communications	5	8	+3	6	7	+1
Real estate, renting	9	11	+2	4	2	-2
Public admin and defence	0	1	+1	24	25	+1
Education	2	2	0	25	29	+4
Health and social work	3	5	+2	27	30	+3
Other social and personal services	4	5	+1	3	2	-1
Base	*794*	*2404*		*323*	*1158*	

Another reason for the overall change could be that the type of people working in the two sectors has changed. Perhaps socio-demographic groups with particularly distinctive views on work have changed their relative prevalence in the two sectors. To test this we need to examine whether people with particular socio-demographic characteristics have a distinctive public service ethos.

The next table shows the proportion of people in various social groups who think our two indicators of a public service ethos are "very important" in a job. Perhaps the most striking aspect of this table is how few differences there are. The only factor that was statistically significant on the question of a job being useful to society was education, with those with a degree or higher being much more likely than those with no qualifications to consider it to be "very important". On allowing someone to help other people the only factor that showed significant differences was whether people, were left wing or right wing, with those who are left wing more likely to think it very important.[1] The implications of this being that even if the composition of the public sector has changed, these factors make little or no difference to the public service ethos.

Table 5.6 Importance of social usefulness in a job, by socio-demographics, 2005

	% say "very important" for job to be useful to society	Base	% say "very important" for job to help other people	Base
18–34	25	200	22	200
65+	21	237	21	237
Degree or higher	29	269	25	269
No qualifications	17	234	19	234
Professional/managerial	23	342	22	342
Routine/semi-routine	19	247	20	247
Male	19	390	19	390
Female	22	523	23	523
Highest income quartile	22	161	21	161
Lowest income quartile	20	238	24	238
Labour supporter	23	379	21	379
Conservative supporter	19	243	25	243
Left-wing	23	314	25	314
Right-wing	20	320	18	320
Trade union member	25	150	21	150
Not trade union member	20	742	21	742

Changing entrants to the public sector?

We have one more possible explanation for the increase in the public service ethos: with the changes that New Labour has embarked upon, perhaps different types of people are being attracted to the public sector in the first place. The public service ethos might be held more by young people choosing this as a career, showing that both the environment and the cohort effects are important. Increased public spending and new opportunities may have encouraged entry by public service-motivated individuals. Ironically, because the public and private sectors are now more similar in management-style, and given that the public sector tends to pay less, it is likely to be only those really committed to the public sector who join it. Before, those with a little less public service ethos might have been tempted to join the public sector, for example because they wanted more job security. Now, for those people, the distinction is perhaps so small that they might as well join the private sector where at least they will get paid more.

A related factor might be more general changes in views about politics among younger age groups. During the last 20 years there has been a massive drop-off in interest and participation in conventional politics by young people in the forms of party membership, voting, and trust in politics; but at the same time there has been an increase in social and issue awareness, such as over the environment, which has led to more interest in non-conventional forms of political activity (Russell *et al.*, 2002). Perhaps a new idealism has fostered an interest in public sector work among some young people, perhaps as an alternative to the more 'selfish' careers in finance and management?

Table 5.7 Public service ethos, private and public sector, by age, 1997 and 2005

	1997			2005			
	Private sector	Public sector	Diffe-rence	Private sector	Public sector	Diffe-rence	Change in diffe-rence
% say "very important" that job is useful to society							
18–34	16	28	+12	19	49	+30	+18
Base	*223*	*48*		*136*	*46*		
35+	17	22	+5	13	28	+15	+10
Base	*623*	*282*		*371*	*214*		
% say "very important" that job can help other people							
18–34	15	24	+9	18	39	+21	+12
Base	*223*	*48*		*136*	*46*		
35+	19	22	+3	17	24	+7	+4
Base	*623*	*282*		*371*	*214*		

Although the numbers in our samples are rather small, we can see in Table 5.7 that young people in public and private sector jobs have diverged to a greater extent than those aged 35 and over. For instance, among those aged 18–34 in

1997, those working in the public sector were 12 percentage points more likely than those working in the private sector to think it very important that a job is useful to society, whereas amongst those aged over 35 the difference was five percentage points. By 2005, the public–private difference among the young had increased by 18 percentage points, compared to a 10 percentage point increase among the older age group. We see a similar pattern on our other question about a job that can help others: between 1997 and 2005 the differences between the public and private sector increased considerably more among the younger age group than the older one.

It is also interesting to compare younger and older age groups in terms of their experience of their own job. The next table shows considerable differences. On both questions the difference between the public and private sector among those aged between 18 and 34 has increased by more than 20 percentage points, whereas for those aged 35 and over, the difference has declined. The result is a quite startling difference between young public and private sector employees today – around two-thirds of young public sector employees now "strongly agree" that their job is useful to society and gives them the opportunity to help other people, compared with less than a fifth in the private sector who take this view.

Table 5.8 Social usefulness of own job, by private or public sector, by age, 1997 and 2005

	1997			2005			
	Private sector	Public sector	Diffe-rence	Private sector	Public sector	Diffe-erence	Change in diffe-rence
% "strongly agree" own job is useful to society							
18–34	8	36	+28	14	65	+51	+23
Base	*155*	*39*		*102*	*39*		
35+	9	42	+33	15	34	+19	-14
Base	*336*	*142*		*172*	*107*		
% "strongly agree" own job helpful to other people							
18–34	13	33	+20	19	63	+44	+24
Base	*155*	*39*		*102*	*39*		
35+	11	39	+28	16	36	+20	-8
Base	*336*	*142*		*172*	*107*		

What does it mean to have a public service ethos?

The broader context of the public service ethos

So far we have examined a rather narrow definition of public service ethos based on a desire to have a socially useful job. What does it mean to the person's broader view of work? There are other measures we can employ which are representative of something we term 'altruistic motivations' when it comes to work. For example, respondents were asked how much they agreed with the following two statements when thinking of work in general:

A job is just a way of earning money – no more

I would enjoy having a paid job even if I did not need the money

Given our conceptualisation of what a public service ethos is, namely that public sector workers are more altruistic, we would anticipate that those in the public sector would be more likely than those in the private sector to disagree with the first statement and more likely to agree with the second. Our analysis shows that this is indeed the case. Twice as many of those in the public sector strongly disagreed that a job is just a way of earning money (17 per cent compared to eight per cent), and significantly more strongly agreed that they would enjoy a job even if they did not need the money (12 per cent compared to seven per cent). And as Table 5.9 shows, the differences between public and private sector workers appears to be increasing over time.

Table 5.9 Broader public service ethos (i), private and public sector employees, 1997 and 2005

	1997			2005		
	Private sector	Public sector	Diffe-rence	Private sector	Public sector	Diffe-rence
% "strongly disagree" a job just a way to earn money	9	14	+5	8	17	+9
% "strongly agree" would enjoy job even if didn't need money	7	7	0	7	12	+5
Base	623	282		507	260	

We might also anticipate that those in the public sector would be more committed and proud to work for their organisation than those in the private sector, on the basis that doing a wider public good feeds into organisational loyalty. In addition, those in the public sector might be expected to be loyal and prepared to carry on working for less pay than elsewhere. We have three questions that allow us to assess this aspect, where people were asked the extent to which they agreed with each of the following statements:

> *I am willing to work harder than I have to in order to help the firm or organisation I work for succeed*
>
> *I am proud to be working for my firm or organisation*
>
> *I would turn down another job that offered quite a bit more pay in order to stay with this organisation*

Here we see a somewhat more mixed picture. Only on the second statement are those in the public sector more likely to strongly agree, whereas there are no differences on either of the other two statements. And, indeed, it is only on the second one that there has been any change over time, with the difference between the two sectors again increasing.

Table 5.10 Broader public service ethos (ii), private and public sector employees, 1997 and 2005

% "strongly agree" that ...	1997			2005		
	Private sector	Public sector	Diffe-rence	Private sector	Public sector	Diffe-rence
... willing to work harder than have to	13	12	-1	18	15	-3
... proud to be working for firm/organisation	10	13	+3	14	23	+9
... turn down job with more pay to stay	4	6	+2	6	3	-3
Base	336	142		274	146	

A further line of argument concerns the identities of people in the two sectors. People were asked:

> *Thinking now not just of your own workplace but more generally, how much do you feel you have in common with people who do this job, compared with other people?*
>
> *A lot more in common with them than with other people*
> *A little more in common with them than with other people*
> *No more in common with them than with other people*

Whilst this question does not specifically ask about identity with people in the same sector as the respondent, it is interesting to observe that those in the public sector seem to identify to a greater extent with people doing similar jobs to them. In the public sector 37 per cent felt they had a lot more in common with them than with other people, compared with only 24 per cent taking that view in the private sector. There seems therefore to be greater solidarity in the public sector.

In conclusion, then, we can see that working in the public sector is related to a wider set of values than purely the public service ethos of wanting to do a socially useful job. In particular, it seems to be related to a more general belief in the importance of work, a pride in the organisation and a feeling of having something in common with colleagues. How far this can stretch is a moot point – not as far as working harder than you have to or turning down a job with more pay, apparently.

What does a public service ethos mean for job satisfaction?

Do those endowed with a public service ethos have more job satisfaction? After all, if people have this wider set of values and the public sector delivers on helping them realise those, they should be more satisfied than equivalent private sector workers. They might be able to deal with the frustration of working life more effectively than someone who is just there for the money (though it is possible that people may become more dissatisfied if their expectations are higher but they fail to meet them). We asked respondents:

All in all, how satisfied are you with your main job?

Some 42 per cent of those in the public sector were very satisfied, whilst only 35 per cent of those in the private sector were.

Further, those with a particularly strong public service ethos were significantly more likely to have high job satisfaction. Table 5.11 shows the proportion of people very satisfied with their job broken down by their views on the importance of different aspects of a job. Those people who think it is "very important" that a job is useful to society were 17 percentage points more likely to be very satisfied with their job than those who did not take such a view. This difference was even higher when the importance of a job allowing someone to help other people was considered.

Table 5.11 also shows how job satisfaction is strongly related to the extent to which people believe their own job is useful to society and allows them to help other people. Those who think their job means they can be useful to society are 30 percentage points more likely to be very satisfied. And those who felt their job allowed them to help other people were 29 percentage points more likely to be very satisfied.

Table 5.11 Job satisfaction, by the public service ethos, 2005

	% "very satisfied" with their job	Base
Importance that job is useful to society		
"Very important"	55	84
Not "very important"	38	329
Difference	+17	
Importance that job allows helping other people		
"Very important"	57	91
Not "very important"	37	322
Difference	+20	
Own job is useful to society		
"Strongly agree"	64	106
Not "strongly agree"	34	302
Difference	+30	
Own job allows helping other people		
"Strongly agree"	63	109
Not "strongly agree"	34	299
Difference	+29	

To understand what is driving these differences we need to control for other potentially confounding factors. When we carry out a multivariate analysis to control for these factors, we find that having a socially useful job tends to improve it (see the appendix to this chapter for full details of this analysis). Thus the public service ethos may indeed go some way to compensate for the lower levels of remuneration and worse working conditions. This kind of compensation is at the core of the public service ethos agenda – and why it is possible to be cynical about official attempts to improve it.

Conclusions

The public service ethos is an important dimension to job motivation which can help to compensate for lower rates of pay and poorer working conditions in the public sector. It has been heralded by reformers as a key to public service performance, and many writers claim that has been neglected by the policies inspired by private sector management, such as contracting out, quasi markets and choice. The argument is that if public sector employers treat their employees as self-interested actors motivated by performance-related pay and punished by failure to meet targets, they will, in turn, behave in a strategic and egoistical fashion so eroding the public service ethos and with it the distinctive contribution of the public sector to the welfare of society at large. But these data paint a different picture: the public service ethos appears to have increased rather than withered during the New Labour years. It would seem that private sector forms of management are not necessarily incompatible with sustaining the public service ethos. The predictions of decline based on the rise of individual self-interest are not borne out by this data.

It is not easy to identify the reasons for the rise in the public service ethos, but it is clear that there is something special about the young people entering public service today. It may be that, as the public sector becomes more like the private sector, the choice of careers becomes one of values rather than, for example, job security, so that the public sector ends up attracting only those who are already committed to it. It may also be a reflection of value change among younger generations: a more issue-based cohort may be as ready to work in the public sector as to travel on an environmental gap year or to boycott certain products.

For public sector reformers, these findings do not appear to justify a roll back to a more collectivist form of public sector organisation, or suggest a rejection of the New Labour reforms – at least on public service ethos grounds. The main challenge is how to sustain these values in a period when public spending does not increase at the same rate as before. It also has to be recognised that there are limits to what a public service ethos will achieve: job security is almost as important as an interesting job, even for public sector workers, and the public service ethos will not necessarily make people work harder than they have to or turn down another job with more pay. The public service ethos cannot be expected to compensate for all sources of job dissatisfaction in the public sector. The danger is that continuing poorer working conditions and worse rates of pay will over time erode these public-minded values, particularly among new entrants.

Notes

1. Respondents were categorised as left-wing or right-wing using their score on the left–right scale (see Appendix I of this *Report* for further details).

References

Allington, N. and Morgan, P. (2003), 'Does it pay to work in the private sector? Evidence from three decades of econometric analysis', *Public Money and Management*, October: 253–262

Boyne, G. (2002), 'Public and Private Management: What's the difference?', *Journal of Management Studies*, **39(1)**: 97–122

Buelens, M. and Broeck, van den H. (2007), 'An analysis of differences in work motivation between public and private sector organizations', *Public Management Review*, **67**:65–74

Crewson, P. (1995), 'A comparative analysis of public and private sector entrant quality', *American Journal of Political Science*, **39(3)**: 628–639

Crewson, P. (1997), 'Public service motivation: building empirical evidence of incidence and effect', *Journal of Public Administration Research and Theory*, **7(4)**: 499–518

DeHart-Davis, L., Marlowe, J. and Pandey, S. (2006), 'Gender dimensions of public service motivation', *Public Administration Review*, **66**: 873–887

Houston, D. (2000), 'Public service motivation: a multivariate test', *Journal of Public Administration Research and Theory*, **10(4)**: 713–727

Jurkiewicz, C. and Brown, R. (1998), 'Generational comparisons of public employee motivation', *Review of Public Personnel Administration*, **18**: 18–37

Le Grand, J. (2003), *Motivation, Agency and Public Policy: Of Knights and Knaves, Pawns and Queens*, Oxford: Oxford University Press

Norris, P. (2003), 'Still a public service ethos? Work values, experience and job satisfaction amongst government workers', unpublished paper downloadable from www.pippanorris.com

Plant, R. (2003), 'A public service ethos and political accountability', *Parliamentary Affairs*, **56**: 560–579

Pratchett, L. and Wingfield, M. (1996), 'Petty bureaucracy and woolly minded liberalism? The changing ethos of UK local government officers', *Public Administration*, **74(4)**: 639–656

Public Administration Committee (2002), *Seventh Report, The Public Service Ethos*, London: HMSO

Public Services Productivity Panel (2002), *Making A Difference: Motivating People to Improve Performance,* London: HM Treasury

Rainey, H.G. (1982), 'Reward preferences among public and private managers: in search of the service ethic', *American Review of Public Administration*, **16**: 88–302

Rainey, H. and Bozeman, B. (2000), 'Comparing public and private organizations: empirical research and the power of the a priori', *Journal of Public Administration Research and Theory*, **10**: 447–470

Russell, A., Fieldhouse, E., Purdam, K. and Kalra, V. (2002), *Voter engagement and young people*, London: The Electoral Commission

Steele, J. (1999), *Wasted Values – Harnessing the Commitment of Public Managers*, London: Public Management Foundation

Wittmer, D. (1991), 'Serving the people or serving for pay: reward preferences among government, hybrid sector, and business managers', *Public Productivity and Management Review*, **14(4)**: 369–83

Acknowledgements

The *National Centre for Social Research* is grateful to the Economic and Social Research Council (grant number RES 501 25 5001) for the financial support which enabled us to ask the questions reported in this chapter. The views expressed are those of the authors alone.

Appendix

The multivariate analysis technique used in this chapter was ordered probit regressions. Ordered probit is needed because the dependent variable is ordinal.

Table A.1 Predictors of public service ethos

	"Very important" that job helps other people		"Very important" that job is useful to society	
	Coefficient	Standard error	Coefficient	Standard error
18–34	0.118	0.18	-0.113	0.18
65+	0.00946	0.11	0.18	0.11
Degree or higher	0.0651	0.12	-0.0276	0.12
No qualifications	0.00795	(0.12)	0.0245	0.12
Professional/managerial	-0.183*	0.10	-0.146	0.10
Routine/semi-routine	-0.164	0.11	-0.0559	0.10
Female	0.149*	0.085	0.333***	0.086
Lowest income quartile	0.0272	0.12	0.147	0.12
Highest income quartile	-0.0261	0.11	0.0412	0.11
Labour supporter	-0.0535	0.099	-0.0162	0.099
Conservative supporter	-0.0898	0.12	0.116	0.12
Left–right scale	-0.150**	0.063	-0.158**	0.063
Trade union member	0.00116	0.060	0.0278	0.060
Public sector	0.403***	0.100	0.255**	0.100
Cut 1	-2.629***	0.30	-2.370***	0.31
Cut 2	-1.806***	0.27	-1.479***	0.27
Cut 3	-0.650**	0.26	-0.348	0.26
Cut 4	0.669**	.2	1.102***	0.26
N	706		713	
Pseudo rsq	.02		.02	

* = significant at 5% level
** = significant at 1% level
*** = significant at 0.1% level

Table A.2 Predictors of job satisfaction

	Model 1		Model 2	
	Coefficient	Standard error	Coefficient	Standard error
18–34	-0.149	0.23	-0.0804	0.23
65+	0.546	0.56	0.377	0.56
Degree or higher	-0.200	0.15	-0.189	0.15
No qualifications	-0.133	0.20	-0.113	0.20
Profess/managerial	-0.237	0.16	-0.239	0.16
Routine/semi routine	-0.160	0.18	-0.180	0.17
Female	0.246**	0.12	0.192	0.12
Lowest income quartile	-0.345	0.29	-0.454	0.29
Highest income quartile	0.314**	0.14	0.316**	0.14
Trade Union member	0.228***	0.076	0.249***	0.075
Public sector	0.198	0.15	0.247*	0.15
Job useful to society	0.127*	0.076		
Job helps other people			0.197**	0.077
Cut 1	-0.61	0.42	-0.338	0.41
Cut 2	-0.102	0.41	0.158	0.42
Cut 3	0.314	0.41	0.570	0.42
Cut 4	1.623***	0.41	1.885***	0.41
Pseudo R2	.03		.04	
N	348		352	

* = significant at 5% level
** = significant at 1% level
*** = significant at 0.1% level

6 Prejudice and the workplace

Chris Creegan and Chloe Robinson[*]

The legislative and policy framework concerning equality and discrimination in Britain has undergone a major transformation in recent years. A little more than 30 years since the introduction of the Sex Discrimination Act 1975 and the Race Relations Act 1976, there is now comprehensive legislation relating to employment across six equality strands: gender, race, disability, sexual orientation, age and religion. Subsequent legislation includes the Disability Discrimination Act 1996, the Employment Equality (Sexual Orientation) Regulations 2003, the Employment Equality (Religion or Belief) Regulations 2003 and the Employment Equality (Age) Regulations 2006.

The Equality Act 2006 established the Commission for Equality and Human Rights (CEHR), renamed the Equality and Human Rights Commission in October 2007. The CEHR will promote an inclusive agenda, underlining the importance of equality for all in society, work to promote equal opportunities and tackle barriers to social and economic participation. The CEHR will cover the six strands of equality referred to above, as well as human rights. The new Commission's mission statement explains that it will be:

> ... an independent advocate for equality and human rights in Britain (which) aims to reduce inequality, eliminate discrimination, strengthen good relations between people and protect human rights.[1]

It will bring together the Disabilities Rights Commission and the Equal Opportunities Commission from October 2007, adding to their remit the areas of sexual orientation, age, and religion or belief, which are not covered by the existing Commissions. The Commission for Racial Equality will join by the end of March 2009, putting expertise on equality, diversity and human rights all in one place. The Commission will cover England, Scotland and Wales. In Scotland and Wales there will be statutory committees responsible for the work of the CEHR.

---

[*] Chris Creegan is a Research Director, Chloe Robinson is a Senior Researcher, both at the *National Centre for Social Research.*

During the development of proposals for the establishment of the CEHR, support emerged for a further Single Equality Bill to provide a coherent legislative framework for its work (Department of Communities and Local Government, 2007). In 2005, the government established the Discrimination Law Review, the terms of reference of which were to consider:

> the opportunities for creating a clearer and more streamlined equality legislation framework which produces better outcomes for those who experience disadvantage … while reflecting better regulation principles.[2]

This is therefore a key moment from which we can look backwards and forwards at questions relating to prejudice in Britain which in turn provides an indication of where we are now in relation to achieving equality.

A great deal of research exists already on the prevalence and nature of prejudice and discrimination in society. The *British Social Attitudes* survey series itself provides important information, particularly on trends over time. Chapters in *The 19th Report* and *The 20th Report* chart a decline in prejudice against ethnic minorities and homosexuals. Both chapters link this trend to rising education levels, particularly higher education, among the British population. However, neither trend has been uniformly downwards and it is now time, several years later, to update the research (Evans, 2002; Rothon and Heath, 2003).

Discrimination against disabled people was examined in detail in *The 23rd Report*. This highlighted the complex way in which respondents express prejudice:

> … whilst respondents rarely express strong 'negative' feelings about disabled people, milder 'negative' feelings are more widely held than might have been anticipated. Negative attitudes are especially pronounced in relation to people with mental health impairments. There is widespread unease among respondents at the prospect of coming into contact with people with mental health impairments, particularly in personal settings. (Rigg, 2007: 234)

A consistent theme was the positive influence of knowing a disabled person on people's attitudes towards disabled people.

Attitudes matter since prejudice fosters discrimination. The recent Discrimination Law Review report (Cabinet Office, 2007) asked why inequalities still persist and identified prejudice as a key factor. Drawing on evidence reported by Abrams and Houston (2005), it suggests that attitudes had changed partly because of the increased visibility of disadvantaged groups and because it had become increasingly unacceptable to express prejudiced views. An important distinction arose here between views expressed in public and private. The review argued that attitudes were based on stereotypes and perceived threats, cultural, physical and economic.

The 2006 *British Social Attitudes* survey asked a series of questions about prejudice, focusing on prejudice in the workplace in particular. Why focus on the workplace? Previous data from the *British Social Attitudes* survey series suggests that prejudice may actually be less in the workplace than in other more personal settings. For example, in 1996, 84 per cent of respondents said they would not mind if a person of Asian origin was appointed as their boss, while the figure was 87 per cent in the case of a boss of black or West Indian origin. This compared with only 64 per cent and 63 per cent of the public who would not mind if a person of Asian origin and of black or West Indian origin married a close relative. The 2005 survey painted a similar picture of prejudice against disabled people. For example, whereas 83 per cent said they would be "very comfortable" if someone in a wheelchair was appointed their boss, only 59 per cent thought they would take this view if the person married a close relative.

The first Fair Treatment at Work Survey revealed that a seventh of employees who worked with others said that they were aware of another person at their workplace being treated unfairly in the last two years. Of those employees who worked with others, disabled employees, gay, lesbian or bisexual employees, black employees and public sector employees were more likely to report unfair treatment of others at their workplace. By far the most common reason for this unfair treatment was long-term illness, followed by age and the way people dress, race or ethnic identity. The incidence of unfair treatment on the grounds of gender, religion and sexual orientation were lower. However, even in the case of long-term illness, less than five per cent of employees were actually aware of unfair treatment taking place in their workplace (Grainger and Fitzner, 2007).

These figures hardly suggest massive prejudice and discrimination in the workplace. But complacency would be wrong. On the one hand, apparently low levels of explicit prejudice may hide a wider problem of tacit views. As we have seen in the case of disability, the fact that respondents do not volunteer strongly negative views does not prevent the widespread existence of milder negative views that can nevertheless lead to discrimination. Moreover, given the pivotal role that economic opportunities hold in the lives of most people, any discrimination in the workplace must be considered a serious problem.

It is from this perspective that we turn to the data from the 2006 *British Social Attitudes* survey. In this our first report on the data, we wish to examine three questions. First, has there been a shift in attitudes? Is prejudice on the increase or decrease, both in society at large and in the workplace? Second, to what extent does prejudice in the workplace remain a problem? And third, what are the implications of these trends for the new and emerging legislative and policy framework?

Is prejudice increasing or decreasing?

When looking at trends over time, we are limited to those survey questions that have been asked in identical format on a number of occasions. We have only a limited set to choose from and even less that deal with the workplace, so we begin by looking at what we know about society as a whole.

The *British Social Attitudes* survey series has charted attitudes towards homosexuality for many years. These are reported in more detail in the chapter by Duncan and Phillips in this *Report* but the overall picture is one of a substantial and sustained increase in tolerance, with the proportion saying that homosexuality is "always wrong" or "mostly wrong" falling from a high point of 75 per cent in 1987 to 32 per cent in 2006 (see Figure 1.1 in the chapter by Duncan and Phillips). As discussed by Duncan and Phillips such tolerance may not extend to true approval of gay men and lesbians (as parents, for example), but it nevertheless represents a fundamental shift towards less prejudice in society.

As already mentioned, the *British Social Attitudes* survey series has also charted racial prejudice for a great many years. We asked respondents:

> *How would you describe yourself ... as very prejudiced against people of other races, a little prejudiced, or not prejudiced at all?*

Given the reluctance of many respondents to give a socially unacceptable answer, it is customary to make the assumption that "a little prejudiced" amounts to an admission of prejudice.

Figure 6.1 Racial prejudice, 1985–2006

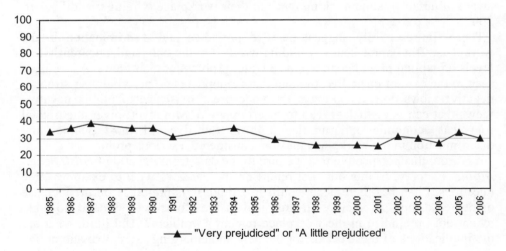

As seen in Figure 6.1, racial prejudice declined from a high point of just under two-fifths in 1987 to a low of around a quarter in 2001. However, the trend has not been without its reversals and Rothon and Heath, writing in *The 20th Report*, noticed a recent upturn (Rothon and Heath, 2003). They were right to do so. The level of racial prejudice now seems to be back to the level of the early 1990s, with 30 per cent of respondents in 2006 describing themselves as "very prejudiced" or "a little prejudiced". A similar increase in prejudice is also found in Scotland in the data from the *Scottish Social Attitudes* survey (Bromley *et al.*, 2007). Theories why this should have happened abound: the events of 9/11 are a likely candidate. Another is immigration. Rothon and Heath found no link between prejudice and levels of immigration as such, but they did find an indication that prejudice might be related to the level of media coverage of immigration (Rothon and Heath, 2003).

Nevertheless, it should still be noted that two-thirds (68 per cent) of people claim not to be prejudiced at all against people of other races and only a tiny proportion (two per cent) claim to be very prejudiced.

On racial prejudice in the workplace, the following questions were first asked on the *British Social Attitudes* survey in 1983:

> *Do you think that most white people in Britain would mind or not mind if a suitably qualified person of Asian origin were appointed as their boss?*
>
> *And you personally?*

A separate set of respondents were asked similar questions about "a suitably qualified person of black or West Indian origin".[3] As seen in the next two figures, the proportion who think that white people in general would mind "a lot" or "a little" has fallen from the mid to high 50 per cents in the 1980s to 43 per cent for an Asian boss and 41 per cent for a black boss in 2006. The proportions saying that they themselves would mind "a lot" are now down to two and three per cent respectively.

Figure 6.2 Whether white respondents think most white people would mind having an Asian or black or West Indian boss, 1983–2006

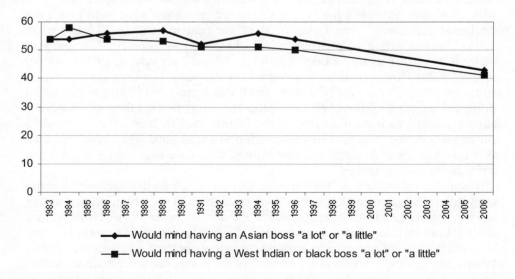

Base: White respondents

Figure 6.3 Whether white respondents themselves would mind having an Asian or black or West Indian boss, 1983–2006

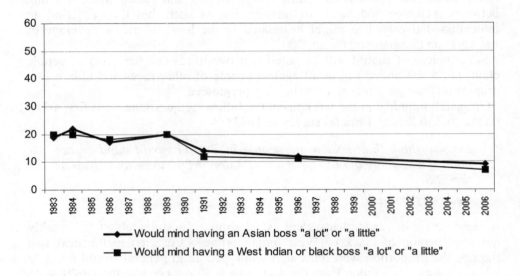

Base: White respondents

The most long-standing equal opportunities legislation in Britain concerns the position of women in the workplace. The chapter by Crompton and Lyonette in this *Report* examines the issue of gender equality in detail. They find a downward trend in prejudice against working women. So, the proportion of men who agree that "A man's job is to earn money; a woman's job is to look after the home and family", has fallen from 32 per cent in 1989 to 17 per cent in 2006. The proportion of men who think that "a pre-school child is likely to suffer if his or her mother works" has fallen from 53 per cent in 1989 to 41 per cent in 2006. However, there are some caveats: there is still a gender gap in attitudes – only 29 per cent of women think that a pre-school child would suffer if the mother works. Moreover, Crompton and Lyonette find that, while women have increased their participation in the labour market, men have not made a commensurate increase in their contribution to housework. They conclude that, as a result of their domestic responsibilities, women do not compete on equal terms in the labour market.

To sum up this review of time trends, we can conclude that the overall long-term trends in prejudice tend to be downwards, both in society in general and in the workplace. Levels of overt prejudice are now extremely low. However, we should bear in mind that this may mask higher levels of true prejudice that respondents are not prepared to disclose (and may not even be aware of). Subtle factors, such as the division of housework in the home, continue to disadvantage groups such as women. Also, the battle on prejudice is by no means won once and for all, as shown by the increase in racial prejudice, dating from around 2001.

Does prejudice in the workplace remain a problem?

In this light, we turn now to the questions available in the 2006 *British Social Attitudes* dataset which examine the extent to which prejudice does indeed remain a problem in the workplace. Respondents were asked the following questions:

> *In your workplace* how much prejudice do you think there is ...
> ... *against employees of Asian origin?*
> ... *against employees who are black?*
> ... *against employees with disabilities?*
> ... *against employees who are gay or lesbian?*

Of course, responses to these questions do not necessarily provide an indication of whether respondents were prejudiced themselves, but they do provide one indicator of the possible prevalence of prejudice. Note that they are phrased in terms of the respondent's own workplace to ensure that respondents are answering from a position of relative knowledge rather than speculating freely.

As shown in Table 6.1, perceived levels of discrimination are higher for black employees than for disabled or gay and lesbian employees, and highest of all for Asian employees. It is worth noting, however, that the "don't know" response for gay and lesbian employees is the highest of the four. This suggests a higher degree of ignorance in relation to the experiences of lesbian and gay people, and is perhaps also related to the fact that sexuality is not always obvious to other people in the way that race is. However, the differences between the groups are rather small. The overall picture is that in each case between a tenth and a fifth of employees think there is at least some prejudice in their workplace, while half to around three-fifths think there is none.

Table 6.1 Perceived levels of prejudice in the respondent's workplace

Prejudice against ...		A lot	A little	Hardly any	None	Don't know
... employees of Asian origin	%	3	15	27	51	3
... employees who are black	%	2	11	27	56	3
... employees with disabilities	%	2	10	21	61	5
... employees who are gay or lesbian	%	2	9	19	61	7

Base: 1508

Base: Employees

The 2006 survey also carried an extended version of the questions about one's boss, which we have already partially examined. In addition to asking for reactions to having a boss of Asian origin and black or West Indian origin, we asked for reactions to a boss who was younger than the respondent, who was gay or lesbian, who had a disability or long-term illness, or who was a woman.[4] In each case, the question specified that the person would be "suitably qualified". We also added a set of questions about how they thought that their colleagues would react.

Various patterns are evident from the next table. People are consistently more inclined to ascribe prejudice to their colleagues than to themselves, but the patterns are otherwise similar.[5] In both cases, people are most worried about a younger person as their boss and least worried about a woman, perhaps because having a younger boss suggests that you have been passed over for promotion.

Table 6.2 Perceived and actual views on having various types of "suitably qualified" people as one's boss

Whether respondent themselves would mind … as their boss		A lot	A little	Not mind	Base
A person of Asian origin	%	2	6	91	725
A person of black or West Indian origin	%	2	5	92	765
A younger person	%	3	13	83	765
A gay or lesbian person	%	2	5	90	754
A woman	%	1	3	94	779
A person with a disability or long-term illness	%	1	6	90	750
Whether respondent thinks colleagues would mind … as their boss					
A person of Asian origin	%	5	18	73	725
A person of black or West Indian origin	%	4	17	74	765
A younger person	%	10	25	63	765
A gay or lesbian person	%	5	13	78	754
A woman	%	3	9	86	779
A person with a disability or long-term illness	%	4	14	77	750

Base: Employees

Leaving the younger boss aside, some three-quarters or upwards of respondents do not think that their colleagues would mind having a boss from each of the groups. Around nine-tenths of respondents say they themselves would not mind. However, this still leaves around one fifth who think their colleagues *would* mind, at least a little, if their boss was of Asian origin, of black or West Indian origin, a gay man or lesbian, or a disabled person. Whether this constitutes a lot or a little prejudice may be a point for debate. However, the intention of equal opportunities legislation is to remove all discrimination, and in this context it would appear that there is still a problem here.

What are the implications for the legislative and policy framework?

From the argument above, we conclude that the CEHR will face a considerable task to realise the aspirations set out in its mission statement. But how are their efforts likely to be received? We asked:

> *Please ... say whether you think attempts to give equal opportunities to* **black people and Asians in the workplace** *have gone too far or not far enough?*

> *And whether you think attempts to give equal opportunities to* **women in the workplace** *have gone too far or not far enough?*

> *And whether you think attempts to give equal opportunities to* **people with a disability or long-term illness in the workplace** *have gone too far or not far enough?*

> *And whether you think attempts to give equal opportunities to* **gay or lesbian people in the workplace** *have gone too far or not far enough?*

Responses to these questions (presented in Table 6.3) provide a crucial indicator of the challenges ahead for the CEHR and others responsible for the promotion and enforcement of equality legislation.

Table 6.3 Views on whether equal opportunities in the workplace have gone too far or not far enough

Whether equal opportunities have gone too far for ...		Gone much too far	Gone too far	About right	Not gone far enough	Not gone nearly far enough	Don't know
... black and Asian people	%	8	28	41	16	1	5
... women	%	1	10	48	35	3	3
... people with a disability or long-term illness	%	1	5	32	52	5	6
... gay or lesbian people	%	4	14	52	15	1	13

Base: 3213

As seen in the previous table – and contrary to the impression sometimes given by the media – few people think that equal opportunities legislation has gone "much too far", the highest being the one twelfth who think this is the case for ethnic minorities. That said, there is not much appetite for more action either. Only in the case of disabled people does a majority of respondents say that efforts have "not gone far enough" or "not gone nearly far enough". In the case of ethnic minorities, women and gay or lesbian people, the majority view is firmly in the camp of the *status quo* or some roll-back.

Unfortunately, these questions about equal opportunities have not been asked before. However, similar questions – not mentioning the workplace – were asked about black people and Asians in 1994 and 2000. Over that period, the proportion who thought that equal opportunities had not gone far enough (or not nearly far enough) fell from 39 per cent to 25 per cent while the proportion who supported the *status quo* or at least some roll-back rose from 58 per cent to 71 per cent. This suggests that the trend, in the 1990s at least, was against further equal opportunities measures.

Conclusions

The picture of prejudice painted by the data is by no means a depressing one: wherever we have measures over time, the long-term trend is generally downward. However, the battle is not won. There have been reversals on racial prejudice in recent years, and pockets of prejudice against various groups undoubtedly remain across the labour market. Actual discrimination may well be even more widespread. Worryingly, the Equality and Human Rights Commission faces a climate where there is little appetite for further measures on equal opportunities (except to pursue equality for disabled people) and where there is increasing support for the *status quo* or even some roll-back. Attitudes to different groups are clearly not uniform, suggesting that despite the advantages to be gained from a single body and unified legislation in terms of a more coherent and comprehensive approach to tackling inequality, a one size fits all approach will need to be avoided.

The *British Social Attitudes* survey dataset provides a great deal of information about the respondents and their workplaces. This is only an interim report on the data, and further analysis is possible to determine what sort of workplaces are more or less prone to prejudice, what sort of people are more or less prejudiced and what sort of people are more or less likely to perceive that different types of prejudice exist. This information could be useful to policy makers seeking to target their measures and we hope to return to a fuller analysis in the future.

Notes

1. The full mission statement for the Commission for Equality and Human Rights (CEHR), which in October 2007 was renamed the Equality and Human Rights Commission, is available at http://www.cehr.org.uk/content/purpose.rhtm
2. The terms of reference of the Discrimination Law Review are available in full at http://www.womenandequalityunit.gov.uk/dlr/terms_of_ref.htm
3. Between 1983 and 1996 these questions were asked only of white respondents. In 2006 the questions were asked of all respondents, but the date for figure in Figure 6.2 is based on white respondents only for comparability.
4. The sample was divided into sub-samples so that each respondent was asked about three groups. In the case of "Asian origin" and "black or West Indian origin" the question about the respondent's own views was preceded by the question about "most white people in Britain" and followed by the question about colleagues. In the other cases the sequence was first a question about colleagues and then a question about the respondent themselves – no equivalent of the "most white people in Britain" question was asked for these groups.
5. Comparing Table 6.2 with Figures 6.2 and 6.3, we can see that they are also more likely to ascribe racial prejudice to "most white people in Britain" than to their own colleagues.

References

Abrams, D. and Houston, D. (2005), *Equalities, Diversity and Prejudice in Britain: 2005 National Survey*, London: Equalities Review

Bromley, C., Curtice, J. and Given, L. (2007, forthcoming), *Scottish Social Attitudes survey 2006: public attitudes to discrimination in Scotland*, Edinburgh: Scottish Executive

Cabinet Office (2007), *Fairness and Freedom: the Final Report of the Equalities Review*, London: Department of Communities and Local Government

Department of Communities and Local Government (2007), *Discrimination Law Review – A Framework for Fairness: Proposals for a Single Equality Bill for Great Britain*, London: Department of Communities and Local Government

Evans, G. (2002), 'In search of tolerance', in Park, A., Curtice, J., Thomson, K., Jarvis, L. and Bromley, C. (eds.), *British Social Attitudes: the 19th Report*, London: Sage

Grainger, H. and Fitzner, G. (2007), *Fair Treatment at Work Survey 2005: Executive Summary*, Employment Relations Series No. 63, London: Department of Trade and Industry

Rigg, J. (2007), 'Disabling attitudes? Public perspectives on disabled people' in Park, A., Curtice, J., Thomson, K., Phillips, M. and Johnson, M. (eds.), *British Social Attitudes: the 23rd Report – Perspectives on a changing society*, London: Sage

Rothon, C. and Heath, A. (2003), 'Trends in racial prejudice', in Park, A., Curtice, J., Thomson, K., Jarvis, L. and Bromley, C. (eds.), *British Social Attitudes: the 20th Report – Continuity and change over two decades*, London: Sage Publications

Acknowledgements

The *National Centre for Social Research* is grateful to the Department for Trade and Industry (now part of the Department for Business, Enterprise and Regulatory Reform) for the funding of the module of questions on which this chapter is based. Responsibility for the analysis of these data lies solely with the authors.

7 Car use and climate change: do we practise what we preach?

Stephen Stradling, Jillian Anable, Tracy Anderson and Alexandra Cronberg*

There can no longer be any doubt that every time each of us makes a choice of whether to go on a journey and what mode of transport to use, we are making a choice that affects the environment. In particular, motorised transport has both direct and indirect non-benign impacts on the environment and is thus less sustainable than other transport modes. Direct impacts include: anthropogenic (man-made) global warming through the production of greenhouse gases from the burning of fossil fuel; vehicle emissions affecting local pollution and health; vehicle noise; land use for roads and parking, railways and airports; extraction of materials for manufacture; and waste from scrapped vehicles. Indirect impacts include:

> spatial changes in activity and settlement patterns caused by rising car ownership, dispersed working arrangements and shopping and leisure trips, all of which over time reconfigure land use patterns and increase transport dependence (Potter and Bailey, 2008: 31)

To this may be added the development of markets for air-freighted 'out-of-season' vegetables; and the development of increasingly sedentary lifestyles with concomitant growth in childhood and adult obesity.

As to the direct environmental impact, the Intergovernmental Panel on Climate Change (IPCC) recently noted in its *Fourth Assessment Report* that global greenhouse gas (GHG) emissions have grown since pre-industrial times, with an increase of 70 per cent between 1970 and 2004. With current climate change mitigation policies and related sustainable development practices, global GHG emissions will continue to grow over the next few decades (IPCC, 2007). Carbon dioxide, with a lifetime of about 150 years, is the most abundant and

---

* Stephen Stradling is Professor of Transport Psychology at Napier University. Jillian Anable is Research Fellow at The Centre for Transport Policy, The Robert Gordon University. Tracy Anderson is a Research Director, Alexandra Cronberg is a Researcher, both at the *National Centre for Social Research.*

thus most important GHG and is produced by burning fossil fuels of the kind which presently power most motorised road vehicles. In the UK, 74 per cent of oil consumption is used for transport, while 98 per cent of the fuel used for transport is oil. The UK alone accounts for some 2.2 per cent of world oil consumption. 'Peak oil', when global demand exceeds known reserves, is estimated to arrive within the next 20 years (TRANSform Scotland, 2007).

The UK government has set targets to reduce GHG emissions by at least 12.5 per cent by 2012 and carbon emissions by 60 per cent by 2050 compared with baseline emissions at 1990. The complexity of achieving this policy is illustrated by the fact that responsibility is spread across a number of government departments, including the Department for Business Enterprise and Regulatory Reform (DBERR, previously the Department for Trade and Industry) responsible for energy policy, the Department for the Environment, Food and Rural Affairs (DEFRA) responsible for environmental policy, and the Department for Transport (DfT) responsible for transport policy. Transport is the only UK sector in which emissions have increased year on year since 1990. If this trend continues, other sectors will have to reduce emissions by more than 60 per cent in order to offset the growth from transport.

In a recent publication the Department for Transport noted that:

> The Government fully recognises the need to tackle the problem of CO_2 emissions, and is taking action to:
> 1. encourage more environmentally friendly means of transport;
> 2. improve the fuel efficiency of vehicles;
> 3. reduce the fossil carbon content of transport fuel; and
> 4. increase the care that people take over fuel consumption while driving. (DfT, 2007b: 2, numbering added)

The specific policy measures designed to achieve this are summarised in Figure 7.1. As noted in *The 20th Report*:

> There are two dimensions to debates about transport policy. The first concerns the *supply* side – investment in the means to allow people to travel. The second concerns the *demand* side of transport and is politically highly sensitive. (Exley and Christie, 2003: 46)

Measures 2 and 3, improving the fuel efficiency of vehicles and reducing the fossil carbon content of transport fuel, are supply-side measures, while 1 and 4, encouraging use of more sustainable forms of transport and more fuel conscious driving, are demand-side measures.

Unfortunately, as Exley and Christie further noted:

> Although marginal gains in the efficiency of engines and reductions in the environmental impact of particular vehicles have been achieved and will continue to be achieved, these benefits tend to be outweighed greatly by absolute increases in use of cars and planes. (2003: 46)

Figure 7.1 Road transport CO_2 policy measures in the UK (from DfT, 2007b)

Encouraging environmentally friendly forms of transport	Improving the fuel efficiency of vehicles	Reducing the fossil carbon content of transport fuel	Increasing the care taken over fuel consumption while driving
Fuel duty Investment in public transport Smarter Choices Demand management	Fuel duty Graduated VED CO_2-based company car tax Enhanced Capital Allowances Vehicle labelling EU-level car industry targets Support for innovation	Fuel duty differential Renewable Transport Fuel Obligations Enhanced Capital Allowances Support for innovation	Fuel duty Eco-driving in the driving test Sustainable distribution programme Act on CO_2 campaign

Others have made similar comments. The University College London Environment Institute, in a report on whether the government is on target to constrain UK greenhouse gas emissions, noted that:

> In contrast to overall UK carbon emissions, those from [the transport] sector have increased on the back of economic growth and rising prosperity and the ensuing demand for transport fuel over other types of fuel. (UCL Environment Institute, 2007: 34)

Action on transport is therefore critical if GHG targets are to be met, but it is difficult to ensure that supply-side policies really are effective unless the demand side is addressed simultaneously. The IPCC note that:

> There are multiple mitigation options in the transport sector, but their effect may be counteracted by growth in the sector. Mitigation options are faced with many barriers, such as consumer preferences ... (2007: 19)

Vlek and Steg (2007: 8) extend the point: "Unfortunately, the adoption of eco-technology (e.g., cleaner cars) may still lead to overall increases in environmental burden through sheer growth in activity volumes as well as the 'rebound effect' (Berkhout *et al.*, 2000)". Rebound effects are:

> the off-set part of a successful implementation of a more efficient technology, which compensates for some of its environmental gains or even negates them entirely by stimulating additional, unanticipated resource consumption, and/or use of the technology. (Midden *et al.*, 2007: 159)

For example, improving the fuel efficiency of vehicles or reducing the fossil carbon content of transport fuel may actually stimulate demand by increasing distances travelled. Indeed, in the worst case scenario, motorists, given more environmentally friendly cars and fuel, may feel they can thus drive more frequently, further and faster This is akin to the risk compensation or behavioural adaptation drivers show in consuming car safety benefits as performance benefits (OECD, 1990; Grayson, 1996) ('with ABS and side air bags I will be more protected from the consequences of driving less safely – and can thus drive less safely!')

The Air Quality Expert Group which advises DEFRA also has reservations about supply-side measures. They distinguish two types of damaging pollutants from burning fossil fuels in car engines, air quality pollutants and climate active pollutants, and characterise as 'win–lose' those measures that could reduce emissions from one kind but increase emissions from the other. Examples include:

- increased use of diesel in place of petrol reduces carbon dioxide emissions but increases emissions of particulate matter and nitrogen oxides

- increased use of biofuels reduces carbon dioxide emissions but may lead to increased emissions of ammonia, nitrous oxide and volatile organic compounds

- fitting particulate traps on diesel vehicles reduces particulate matter emissions, but may introduce a fuel penalty and an increase in carbon dioxide emissions. (DEFRA, 2007)

They, too, are more enthusiastic about demand-side improvements, noting that demand management/behavioural change measures where improved public transport is coupled with disincentives for private car usage will reduce emissions of both types of pollutant. Despite this logic, behavioural change is often deemed more difficult to achieve as it involves the use of policy instruments to influence millions of citizens' individual lifestyle decisions. These policies also need to ensure the new travel decisions are sustained over the long term. Both the choices and the changes need to be sustainable. What is more, transport issues are often controversial and lead to high profile public debate over issues such as fuel prices, taxes on air travel, speed cameras and road user charging. The University College London Environment Institute noted that:

> Whatever good intentions Government may have in setting out policies … the effect they have in practice depends on many factors, including compromises in Whitehall and the political mood of the country. (UCL Environment Institute, 2007: 6)

However, in October 2006, at the launch of the Stern Review on the Economics of Climate Change the then Prime Minister, Rt Hon. Tony Blair MP, said:

> There is nothing more serious, more urgent or more demanding of leadership ... the Stern Review has demolished the last remaining argument for inaction in the face of climate change ... We will not be able to explain ourselves to future generations if we fail.

This chapter examines to what extent this view was shared by the British public in 2006: what is the potential for demand-side change in the use of motorised private transport in Britain?

Car ownership and use

The chapter focuses on car use since this is by far the most common form of motorised transport. Department for Transport research suggests that people view cars, vans, lorries and aeroplanes as the transport modes that are the major contributors to climate change, and these are seen as more polluting than buses, coaches and trains (DfT, 2007c).

One problem is that the automobile is more than just a mode of transport. It promises the driver a sense of autonomy – freedom, independence and feeling in control – as well as increased mobility. These characteristics have proved seductive: future historians may well characterise the 20th century as the century of the car, during which over one billion cars were manufactured, with an estimated 700 million cars currently in motion on the streets or at rest in and on the car parks, garages, driveways and grass verges of the planet (mainly the latter as the average car spends less than an hour a day in motion: infrastructure thus has to be provided for stationary as well as moving vehicles). When they do move they deplete a planetary resource (fuel), contributing to problems of security of energy supply, and pollute (emissions), contributing to anthropogenic global warming and local health problems.

The most recent figures from the Department for Transport, based on the *National Travel Survey*, report that 72 per cent of adults in Britain hold a full driving licence, 81 per cent of men and 63 per cent of women, giving a total of around 33.7m. licensed motorists with, according to the latest DVLA figures, 28m. licensed cars on Britain's roads. There are also a large number of variously unlicensed (and uninsured) cars and drivers – some estimates suggest 1–2 million – whose driving habits may be even harder to constrain.

Only 18 per cent of *British Social Attitudes* respondents report that their household does not own a car or van, with 40 per cent owning one car, 33 per cent two cars and nine per cent three or more cars. Cars per adult in a household vary around a mean of 0.67 cars per adult, with a range from none to four. Twenty-five per cent of households report one car between two adults, 39 per cent report one car for every adult, and five per cent report more than one car for every adult in the household.[1]

The mobility afforded by a car is underlined by evidence which suggests that those with access to a car tend to make more trips of any sort than those without. Furthermore, those with two or more cars tend to make more trips on average than those with one (Ormston *et al.*, 2004). Data from the 2006 *National Travel Survey* confirm these findings, with the number of trips per year rising from an average of 775 among people in households without a car to 1052 trips per year among those with one car and 1139 trips among those with two or more cars in the household (DfT, 2007a). Thus those with access to a car enjoy enhanced access to destinations. Social exclusion is exacerbated by lack of access to a car, which amplifies pre-existing inequalities (Stradling *et al.*, 2005).

We can see from the *British Social Attitudes* data that car ownership and use varies with income and location. Almost everyone (97 per cent) of those who rate themselves as having high income has at least one car in the household, compared with 69 per cent of those who report low income. Those who live in urban areas are less likely to have access to a car, with only 59 per cent of those who describe themselves as living in a big city being in a household with at least one car. This compares with 93 per cent of those who describe themselves as living in the country, who are likely to be less well served by alternative means of transport. Those living in big cities who rate themselves as having low income are the least likely to have access to a car (43 per cent, compared to 87 per cent of those living in the country who have low income), but they may at least have good urban public transport links while the rural poor with access to neither private nor public transport will have impoverished access to services, facilities and other destinations.

The majority of respondents (69 per cent) report that they drive a car themselves from time to time. Of these, almost two-thirds (63 per cent) say they travel by car as a driver "every day or nearly every day". Table 7.1 shows that this equates to 43 per cent of adults driving every day or nearly every day. Furthermore, eight per cent of adults travel by car as a passenger every day or nearly every day. Thus, overall in 2006, at least half of adults travelled by car, as driver or passenger, every day or nearly every day.

Table 7.1 Patterns of transport use, 1993–2006

% who usually travel by each form of transport every day or nearly every day	1993	1996	1998	2000	2002	2004	2006
By car as driver	38	42	48	47	48	45	43
By car as passenger	10	9	9	10	11	10	8
By local bus	7	7	8	6	7	9	8
By train	2	3	2	2	3	1	2
Base	1460	1219	1075	1133	1148	1053	3220

A closer look at the table does, however, reveal that there may be a change in the making. When we last looked at this survey question in *The 20th Report*, Exley and Christie (2003) could see nothing except an unremittingly increasing trend of car use. Now, a few years on, we note that 2002 may have been something of a high point. The proportion who report they drive every day or nearly every day has fallen from 48 per cent to 43 per cent. Although this is not a startling decline, and may not yet translate into fewer trips, less distance travelled or reduced GHG emissions, it is statistically significant and seems to be part of a trend of several years' standing. We do not know why this is happening – are people starting to change their behaviour in response to the high levels of concern about the impact of transport on the environment, or are they driven by rising fuel costs, increasing perceived congestion, or the availability of electronic 'virtual' alternatives for workplace attendance, retail trips and face-to-face meetings (Stradling and Anable, 2008)? Or perhaps people are just becoming less willing to own up to extensive car use in an attitudinal survey setting. Even if it is only social desirability bias that lies behind the figures, it would reflect a change of social attitudes in Britain, which is of interest here. Changes in attitude typically precede changes in behaviour. We turn now to look at more direct measures of public attitudes and how these may affect efforts to reduce car use.

Attitudes to car use and the environment

If public attitudes are to play a role in reducing the demand for car transport, then at the very least it must be the case that people are (a) concerned over the effect of car transport on the environment and (b) believe that individual actions can make an impact.

Are people concerned?

We asked respondents to agree or disagree with the following statement:

> *The current level of car use has a serious effect on climate change*

We also asked the following question about motor transport:

> *Transport like cars, buses, trains and planes can affect the environment in a number of ways. How concerned are you about the effect of transport on climate change?*

As seen in the next table, the vast majority (around four-fifths) agree that car use has a serious effect on climate change and are at least fairly concerned about the effect of motor transport on the environment.[2]

Table 7.2 Concern about environmental impact of transport, drivers and non-drivers

	Drivers	Non-drivers	All
% agree the current level of car use has a serious effect on climate change	82	76	80
% very or fairly concerned about the effect of transport on climate change	84	76	81
Base	*2233*	*987*	*3220*

Interestingly, drivers are if anything more concerned than non-drivers, perhaps because they are more aware of the damage they are doing. However, beyond this point, concern does not increase with a greater amount of driving (either in terms of frequency of car use or of annual mileage) once other factors, such as sex were taken into account.[3] Hence, concern is not correlated with the size of one's car-based carbon footprint.

Should 'everyone' do something about it?

Even if people think that car use damages the environment and they are concerned about it, it does not necessarily follow that they think they should change their behaviour. Perhaps they think other people should change their behaviour, for example. We asked respondents to agree or disagree that:

> *For the sake of the environment everyone should reduce how much they use their cars*

'Everyone' here logically includes the respondent. As seen in Table 7.3, two in three people believe that car use, including their own, needs to be cut or adverse environmental consequences will ensue. Drivers and non-drivers were equally likely to support everyone cutting their car use – though those who were daily or almost daily drivers were less enthusiastic than their less frequent counterparts about reducing car use (with 61 per cent agreeing compared with 75 per cent).

Table 7.3 Attitudes to everyone cutting car use, drivers and non-drivers

For the sake of the environment everyone should reduce how much they use their cars	Drivers	Non-drivers	All
	%	%	%
Agree	66	66	66
Disagree	11	9	10
Base	*641*	*289*	*930*

Can individual actions make a difference?

So the majority are concerned about the impact of car use on the environment and believe that everyone should limit their car use. Even so, the question reported in Table 7.3 is a very general aspirational statement and people may not be inclined to act unless they think it will make a difference. To test this, we asked people to agree or disagree with the following statement:

> *Anyone who thinks that reducing their own car use will help the environment is wrong – one person doesn't make any difference*

As shown in the next table, three-fifths of respondents are optimistic about the impact of individual action in this case. Indeed drivers, that is those who would have to make the change, are more likely to be optimistic than non-drivers.

Table 7.4 Views on the efficacy of individual action to protect the environment, drivers and non-drivers

Anyone who thinks that reducing their own car use will help the environment is wrong – one person doesn't make any difference	Drivers	Non-drivers	All
	%	%	%
Agree	13	22	16
Disagree	62	51	59
Base	641	289	930

Carrots and sticks

Governments typically try to influence behaviour by making certain undesirable actions illegal or expensive, and/or rewarding desirable actions. Not surprisingly, respondents, especially the drivers, are more in favour of reward than punishment to change driving behaviour. As Table 7.5 shows, drivers are very keen on the idea of lower taxes for environmentally friendly cars (almost three-quarters support this idea). By contrast, higher taxes on motorists in general lacks any broad support, even among non-drivers (many of whom are, of course, regular car passengers).

Table 7.5 Attitudes to rewards and penalties for cutting car use to protect the environment, drivers and non-drivers

People who drive cars that are better for the environment should pay less to use the roads than people whose cars are more harmful to the environment	Drivers	Non-drivers	All
	%	%	%
Agree	72	54	66
Disagree	9	16	11
For the sake of the environment, car users should pay higher taxes	%	%	%
Agree	18	29	21
Disagree	60	43	55
Base	641	289	930

Drivers are also voters, which may explain the hold they seem to have over politicians and the reluctance to raise car-related taxes or otherwise act to constrain car use. It may seem more encouraging that almost three-quarters appear to be prepared to strike a bargain with the government – 'I'll drive a car that is better for the environment as long as I can continue driving.' However this attitude contains the potential for a 'rebound effect': 'If I drive a car that is better for the environment I can drive it more frequently/further/faster without causing any more damage to the environment than I was before. And if I drive just a little bit more often/further/faster I'll still be doing less damage than I was before.' Such thoughts may underlie the high degree of driver support for this option. So there is by no means any guarantee that such a policy would bring the desired environmental improvements. Nevertheless, we have seen that a large majority of the population, even drivers, recognise that current levels of car use are harming the environment, that they need to be reduced and that individual action in this sphere is likely to be effective. This is the group of people who are likely to be amenable by encouragement, cajoling and small-scale increases in the cost of motoring to reduce their car use. We turn now to look at whether there is a group of hard-core car users on whom these incentives are unlikely to work and who may need stronger measures.

Who supports unconstrained car use?

Since 1991, *British Social Attitudes* has asked about the extent to which people agree or disagree that:

> *People should be allowed to use their cars as much as they like, even*
> *if it causes damage to the environment*

This is a fairly strong statement and throughout much of this period about twice as many have disagreed as agreed, as shown in the next table.

Table 7.6 Attitudes towards unlimited car use, 1991–2006

People should be allowed to use their cars as much as they like, even if it causes damage to the environment	1991	1994	1997	2000	2002	2003	2004	2006
	%	%	%	%	%	%	%	%
Agree	19	17	15	20	20	22	16	23
Neither agree nor disagree	38	30	34	34	25	31	29	33
Disagree	43	48	49	42	48	41	49	39
Base	*1224*	*975*	*1080*	*972*	*989*	*972*	*872*	*930*

Those who disagree are implying they believe there should be some constraint on car use, while those that agree may be seen as supporting unconstrained car use. Despite all the media attention that the issue has had, there is a group – currently numbering just under a quarter of the adult population – that believes people should be able to use their cars as they like. There have been some variations in attitudes over time, but, if anything, this group has grown in recent years. It is also noteworthy that throughout the period large numbers of respondents have been undecided – neither agreeing nor disagreeing.

Table 7.7 Attitudes towards unlimited car use, drivers and non-drivers

People should be allowed to use their cars as much as they like, even if it causes damage to the environment	Drivers	Non-drivers	All
	%	%	%
Agree	24	19	23
Disagree	38	39	39
Base	641	289	930

Surprisingly, there is no statistically significant difference between drivers and non-drivers on this question (Table 7.7). Indeed, there are no significant differences by age, educational qualifications, living in rural or urban areas, self-reported income group or socio-economic class. We may have alighted here on an ideological divide in transport attitudes, a person characteristic that is largely independent of demographic differences.

Differences are, however, apparent by level of car use: high mileage drivers are more likely to support unlimited car use, with 35 per cent of high mileage drivers (>10,000 miles a year) agreeing with the statement compared to 15 per cent of low mileage drivers. But even so, there are many, indeed a majority (62 per cent) of high mileage drivers who do not think that people (such as them) should be allowed to use their cars as much as they like.[4]

It may well be that strong measures will be needed to get through to this group who believe – despite everything – that people should be able to use their cars as much as they like. Given the level of their car use it may be necessary to do so. But they are at least a minority, even among high mileage drivers.

Cutting down on short car journeys

As noted in *The 20th Report*, "Many journeys made by car are short ones, and most journeys of all kinds are short trips." (Exley and Christie, 2003: 50). Respondents were asked how many journeys of less than two miles they make by car in a typical week. As seen in the next table, drivers make more short journeys by car per week on average than non-drivers, though already a quarter of car drivers say they make no journeys of less than two miles by car in a typical week. One half of the non-drivers report no short trips by car in a typical week, but two-fifths do make such journeys (as a passenger), indicating that the reach of the car extends beyond drivers. Even non-drivers may show high levels of car dependence, with four per cent of non-driving adults making, on average, more than one car trip a day (eight or more a week).

Table 7.8 Number of journeys of less than two miles by car, drivers and non-drivers

How many journeys of less than two miles do you make by car in a typical week?	Drivers	Non-drivers	All
Mean	4.19	1.59	3.44
	%	%	%
None	24	49	32
One to seven	52	38	48
Eight or more	16	4	13
Base	*1995*	*834*	*2829*

Nevertheless, such short journeys may be the most amenable to modal shift towards more sustainable modes such as by bicycle, foot or bus. And given the number of short journeys, such switching would potentially make a big difference to GHG emissions (car engines are colder, and more polluting, on short journeys) and to inculcating new travel habits which may induce reconsideration of mode choices on longer trips.

As shown in Table 7.9, around one half of the non-drivers indicate they could cycle (if they had a bike), walk or travel by bus for such journeys and overall 53 per cent say they could use at least one of these modes for most of their current car journeys of less than two miles. Drivers are as likely as non-drivers to agree that they could cycle (if they had a bicycle) or walk, but only a quarter, half as many as amongst the non-drivers, say they could make their short journeys by bus. A similar differential for bus use between non-drivers and drivers was reported in *The 22nd Report* (Jones *et al.*, 2005). This pattern may be partly a function of income and location, with car ownership giving access to residential areas that buses don't reach.

Table 7.9 Making and cutting journeys of less than two miles by car, drivers and non-drivers

% agree many of the journeys of less than two miles that I now make by car I could just as easily ...	Drivers	Non- Drivers	All
... cycle, if I had a bike	49	53	50
... walk	47	54	49
... go by bus	26	54	33
Base	*1185*	*412*	*1597*

Base: all excluding those who rarely/never travel by car

Unsurprisingly, those in older age groups are a little less likely than respondents in younger age groups to agree that they could cycle, walk or use local buses as an alternative means of making these short car journeys, with 60 per cent of those aged 55 or older doing so compared with 71 per cent of those in the youngest age groups. Those in rural areas are also less likely than those in urban areas to agree that they could use more sustainable modes of transport instead of making short journeys by car. Nevertheless, 56 per cent of those living in rural areas say they could just as easily cycle, walk or take the bus, compared with 66 per cent of those in urban areas.

While, as we have seen, non-drivers make a number of their journeys of less than two miles by car, it is primarily drivers' behaviour that needs to be addressed if car use is to be significantly reduced to the levels needed to mitigate effects on the environment. As shown in the next table, almost two-fifths of drivers claim that they are not able to make many of their short journeys using any of the three alternative, more sustainable, methods of transport. However, a fifth could manage one, a further quarter could manage two and one in seven could manage all three alternative modes. This gives a total of three in five drivers pronouncing themselves able to make most of their current short car journeys other than by car. We take this as our measure of ability to cut car use on short journeys.

Table 7.10 Willingness and ability to cut car use on journeys under two miles among drivers

% agree could make car journeys under two miles by modes other than car	For the sake of the environment everyone should reduce their car use			
(Ability)	(Willingness)			
	Agree	Neither	Disagree	Total
None	18	10	6	37
Could do one	14	5	2	20
Could do two	19	5	2	26
Could do all three	12	2	1	16
Total	63	21	11	100
Base	358	119	69	571

Base: All drivers excluding those who drive rarely

Taking agreement with the proposition that "For the sake of the environment everyone should reduce their car use" as indicating *willingness* to change one's own car-use behaviour, Table 7.10 shows that drivers may be sorted into a number of subgroups:

- The largest group (45 per cent) are *willing* to reduce their car use and *able* to substitute one or more sustainable modes for short car journeys of under two miles.

- Almost a fifth (18 per cent) are *willing* to cut car use but, for whatever reason, *unable* to switch to cycling, walking or taking the bus for their current short car journeys.

- Twelve per cent are *able* but unsure if they are willing (although they might be persuadable, given that they could).

- A further 10 per cent are unsure whether they are willing but claim to be *unable* anyway.

- Five per cent are *unwilling* though *able*, and a further six per cent are *unwilling* and *unable*.

Each group poses a different challenge to those trying to influence their behaviours towards more environmentally friendly options. The first group (willing and able) are deserving of more encouragement to make the switch and, indeed, may already have started doing so. It may also be the case that encouragement will be enough for those who are able but unsure whether they are willing. The group who are willing but unable probably need supply-side measures, such as improved public transport and enhancement of walking and cycling environments, to help them. These three groups together account for three-quarters of the population, which suggests that even limited intervention could have substantial effects in this favourable climate of public opinion.

Conclusions

In this chapter we have seen that eight in ten adults are in a household with access to a car, and half travel by car as a driver or passenger every day or nearly every day. Furthermore, a large majority agree that current levels of car travel have a serious effect on climate change and are concerned about this. Drivers actually show slightly higher levels of concern than non-drivers. There is widespread support for the idea that everyone should be cutting down on their car use, and most people disagree that individual action is pointless. Two-thirds of drivers say they are willing to cut their car use and three in five would be able to shift from using the car on short journeys to cycling, walking, or taking the bus. True, there is a hard-core of around a quarter of the population who believe that everyone has the right to use their car as much as they wish, and the data is equivocal as to whether cutting car use is actually under way. But the overall climate of public opinion can nevertheless be described as favourable towards a reduction in car use.

As we enter the era of peak-oil, problems with energy security and scarcity, increased emissions fuelling anthropogenic climate change, increased road congestion and rapid growth in domestic and international aviation, we need to burn less carbon-based fuel as we go about our daily business. As the IPCC panel note:

> Changes in lifestyle and behaviour patterns can contribute to climate change mitigation ... Lifestyle changes can reduce GHG emissions. Changes in lifestyles and consumption patterns that emphasise resource conservation can contribute to developing a low-carbon economy that is both equitable and sustainable. (2007: 17)

If demand for private road transport is to be reduced, some changes in private car use will be necessary. This will require either fewer trips being made overall so the number of car journeys reduces, or a reduction in both the number and the proportion of traffic miles made by car trips, either by substituting other modes of travel, or by meeting journey purposes by travelling to nearer destinations, or by making 'virtual' trips. Even quite small changes can have big effects. We have previously estimated that were we in the UK to stick to the speed limit on 70 mph roads, it would cut carbon emissions from road transport by nearly one million tonnes of carbon per annum, and that a fully enforced 60 mph top speed limit would nearly double this reduction, giving 15 per cent or 29 per cent of the total savings expected from the transport sector by 2010, as required in the DEFRA 2006 Climate Change Programme Review (Anable *et al.*, 2006).

But transport joins up the places where people lead their lives, so reduction in use will only be achieved by car users modifying the organisation and articulation of their current patterns of life. The diagram of policy options from the DfT (Figure 7.1) illustrates that the environmental impact from transport is a product of the efficiency of the vehicles we use and how much we use them. Cutting car use, which two-thirds of car drivers in this survey support, requires car users to contemplate whether, how much, what and how to drive. At the very least, behaviour has to change in order to purchase more efficient vehicles to buy and use different fuels or fuel mixes. However, as Holden (2007) argues, growth in transport mileage and use of heavier, more powerful vehicles with energy-demanding auxiliaries (e.g. SUVs with air-conditioning) constantly counteracts reductions in fossil fuel consumption from increased efficiency, and the use of alternative fuels merely transfers energy consumption geographically from the vehicle to the production site and the distribution process and does not reduce total energy consumption. Once more efficient vehicles are purchased, it is important that their benefits are not eroded through the rebound effects of increasing frequency of use, journey distance and speed to compensate for reduced unit impact. More fundamentally, changes in behaviour can secure carbon savings in the absence of technological, supply-side changes by optimising what we already have (i.e. through driving less often, less far and less fast).

There are two stages in persuading people to change their behaviour. First, they need to see reasons to change. The more reasons, the more compelling the reasons, the more personally advantageous or salient the reasons, and the more thoroughly they think about the reasons the more likely they are to change. Second, they typically need practical support, help and advice on how to make the change in as easy and painless a way as possible and how to fit the changes into their life. Relatively small individual changes can, cumulatively, make big differences. The results presented here suggest that many car users are ready – willing and able – to cut their car use. But being willing and able is one thing – actually doing it is another. We know how attached some people are to their cars and that many will find it a serious wrench to change their behaviour. Nevertheless, the current climate of opinion clearly provides a window of opportunity for policy makers. Government needs to harness the substantial reported readiness to change by devoting more effort to demand-side measures, facilitating the availability, accessibility, attractiveness and use of more sustainable forms of transport and encouraging more fuel (and speed) conscious driving.

Notes

1. These figures are based upon the number of people aged 18 or older within each household. This may slightly overestimate the car ownership per adult where 17 year olds also make use of these vehicles.
2. DFT research, also conducted in 2006, reported precisely the same proportion of people saying that cars were a major contributor to climate change, adding to our confidence in the reliability of this figure (DfT, 2007c).
3. It looked at first sight as if frequent drivers were less concerned about the environmental impact than less frequent drivers. However, in order to explore more fully the factors associated with concern, logistic regression models were used, more details of which can be found in the appendix to this chapter. Looking at all respondents, being female, a driver, having post-school qualifications and identifying with either the Liberal Democrats or the Green Party all increased the likelihood of being concerned about the effects of transport on the environment. Age and self-rated income had no significant influence. Among drivers, no relationship was found with being a frequent driver (i.e. driving everyday or nearly every day) nor annual mileage once these other factors were taken into account.
4. Differences are also apparent by frequency of current car use and by gender. People who drive their car every day or nearly every day are somewhat more likely to support unconstrained car use than those who drove less frequently, with 29 per cent agreeing that people should be able to drive as much as they want compared with 16 per cent of other drivers. More males (27 per cent) than females (19 per cent) agree that people should be allowed to use their cars as much as they like, even if it causes damage to the environment. However, there are differences in extent and frequency of car use between males and females which may be a confounding factor. Indeed, when examined using logistic regression (more details again can be found in Table

A.2 in the appendix to this chapter), among drivers, gender and whether a frequent driver are not significant once annual mileage is taken into account. Those who drive a high annual mileage, however, continue to be more likely to support unconstrained car use.

References

Anable, J., Mitchell, P. and Layberry, R. (2006), *Getting the genie back in the bottle: limiting speed to reduce carbon emissions and accelerate the shift to low carbon vehicles*, Paper prepared for the LowCVP Road Transport Challenge, Aberdeen: The UK Energy Research Centre and Slower Speeds

Berkhout, P.H.G., Muskens, J.C. and Velthuijsen, J.W. (2000), 'Defining the rebound effect', *Energy Policy*, **28**: 425–432

DEFRA (2007), *Air Quality Expert Group Air Quality and Climate Change: A UK Perspective: Summary*, London: DEFRA

DfT (2007a), *Transport Statistics Bulletin: National Travel Survey 2006*, London: Department for Transport

DfT (2007b), *Road Transport and the EU Emissions Trading Scheme*, London: Department for Transport

DfT (2007c), *Attitudes to climate change and the impact of transport*, London: Department for Transport

Exley, S. and Christie, I. (2003), 'Stuck in our cars? Mapping transport preferences', in Park, A., Curtice, J., Thomson, K., Jarvis, L. and Bromley, C. (eds.), *British Social Attitudes: the 20th Report – Continuity and change over two decades*, London: Sage

Grayson, G. (1996), *Behavioural Adaptation: A Review of the Literature, TRL Report 254*, Crowthorne: Transport Research Laboratory

Holden, E. (2007), *Achieving Sustainable Mobility: Everyday and Leisure-time Travel in the EU*, Aldershot: Ashgate

IPCC (2007), *Climate change 2007: Mitigation: Contribution of Working group III to the Fourth Assessment Report of the Intergovernmental Panel on Climate Change*, Cambridge and New York: Cambridge University Press

Jones, P., Christodoulou, G. and Whibley, D. (2005), 'Transport: are policy makers and the public on the same track?', in Park, A., Curtice, J., Thomson, K., Bromley, C., Phillips, M. and Johnson, M. (eds.), *British Social Attitudes: the 22nd Report – Two terms of New Labour: the public's reaction*, London: Sage

Midden, C.J.H., Kaiser, F.G. and McCalley, L.T. (2007), 'Technology's Four Roles in Understanding Individuals' Conservation of Natural Resources', *Journal of Social Issues*, **63(1)**: 155–174

OECD (1990), *Behavioural Adaptations to Changes in the Road Transport System*, Paris: OECD

Ormston, R., Stradling, S.G., Rye, T., Cooper, J., Hamilton, K., York, I.O., Emmerson, P. and Vance, C. (2004), *Integrated Ticketing*, Edinburgh: Scottish Executive Social Research

Potter, S. and Bailey, I. (2008), 'Transport and the environment' in Knowles, R.D., Shaw, J. and Docherty, I. (eds.), *Transport Geographies: An Introduction*, Oxford: Blackwell

Stradling, S.G. and Anable, J. (2008), 'Individual travel patterns', in Knowles, R.D., Shaw, J. and Docherty, I., (eds.), *Transport Geographies: An Introduction*, Oxford: Blackwell

Stradling, S.G., Carreno, M., Ferguson, N., Rye, T., Halden, D., Davidson, P., Anable, J., Hope, S., Alder, B., Ryley, T. and Wigan, M. (2005), *Scottish Household Survey Analytical Topic Report: Accessibility and Transport*, Edinburgh: Scottish Executive

TRANSform Scotland (2007), *Peak Oil and transport briefing – Version 1.1*, Edinburgh: TRANSform Scotland

UCL Environment Institute (2007), *UK Greenhouse Gas Emissions – are we on target?*, Environment Policy Report Number 2007:01, London: University College London

Vlek, C. and Steg, L. (2007), 'Human Behavior and Environmental Sustainability: Problems, Driving Forces, and Research Topics', *Journal of Social Issues*, **63(1)**: 1–19

Acknowledgements

The *National Centre for Social Research* is grateful to the Department for Transport for their financial support which enabled us to ask the questions reported in this chapter, although the views expressed are those of the authors alone.

BRITISH SOCIAL ATTITUDES

Appendix

Two logistic regressions were carried out. The coefficients for categorical variables are presented compared with a baseline category.

Table A.1 Concern about effect of transport on climate change

	Adjusted Wald	Sig.	Odds ratio	Linearised s.e
Sex	16.55	0.0001		
Male			1	(baseline)
Female			1.682	0.215
Age	1.00	0.3191	1.004	0.004
Education	23.26	0.0000		
Post-school qualification			1	(baseline)
No post-school qualification			0.497	0.072
Driver	12.24	0.0006		
Frequent driver			1	(baseline)
Non-frequent driver			0.594	0.088
Self-rated income	1.12	0.3293		
High income			1	(baseline)
Middle income			1.593	0.628
Low income			0.907	0.137
Party identification	6.77	0.0000		
Conservative			1	(baseline)
Labour			0.983	0.154
Liberal Democrat			2.029	0.575
Other			0.440	0.115
None			0.611	0.113
Green			15.852	16.189

Base: 1987

Table A.2 Support for unconstrained car use among drivers

	Adjusted Wald	Sig.	Odds ratio	Linearised s.e
Sex	0.01	0.9233		
Male			1	(baseline)
Female			0.976521	0.240611
Driver	2.61	0.1085		
Frequent driver			1	(baseline)
Non-frequent driver			0.655725	0.171320
Annual mileage	5.38	0.0056		
5000 miles or less			1	(baseline)
5001 to 10,000 miles			2.214483	0.638958
More than 10,000 miles			2.516756	0.750575

Base: 585

8 Where have all the readers gone? Popular newspapers and Britain's political health

John Curtice and Ann Mair [*]

Britain's newspapers are often regarded as a blot on the country's political landscape. Two main charges are frequently levied. The first, and more traditional one, is that they have an undue influence on how people vote. The second, more recent, claim is that their negative, if not indeed increasingly cynical, coverage of politics has helped to undermine trust in politicians, and thus in turn discouraged people from voting at all.

Britain has long had a highly partisan national newspaper industry (Seymour-Ure, 1996), in contrast, for example, to the United States. Many newspapers ally themselves with one political party or the other. Thus, for example, the *Daily Mirror* has long been a consistent supporter of the Labour Party while *The Daily Telegraph* is sometimes regarded as the house journal of the Conservative Party. A newspaper's stance is most obviously revealed in its leader columns, but is certainly not confined to there. Its political outlook can also affect which stories are given prominence and how they are reported. Thus someone who regularly reads one particular newspaper is liable to be exposed to a slant on events that could be expected to encourage them to vote for one party rather than another.

Not only are British newspapers partisan, but traditionally more of them have favoured the Conservative Party rather than Labour (while since the demise of the *News Chronicle* in 1960 there has not been any newspaper at all consistently linked with the Liberals or Liberal Democrats). As a result many members of the Labour Party have long felt that the Conservative Party had an unfair advantage at election time (Miller, 1991). This concern reached its height in 1992 when in that year's election *The Sun* newspaper produced some highly unflattering coverage of Labour's election campaign and the party's leader, Neil Kinnock. When the Conservatives secured an unexpected victory, *The Sun* itself famously exclaimed "It's *The Sun* wot won it" (Harrop and Scammell, 1992).

---

[*] John Curtice is Research Consultant at the *Scottish Centre for Social Research*, part of NatCen, and Professor of Politics at Strathclyde University. Ann Mair is Computing Officer in the Social Statistics Laboratory at Strathclyde University.

Whether it actually did is in truth doubtful (Curtice and Semetko, 1994). In any event, the decline in the Conservatives' fortunes after the 1992 election, was matched by a decline in its support amongst newspapers, a number of which, including *The Sun* itself, switched their backing to Tony Blair's New Labour Party (Scammell and Harrop, 1997). Whether the newspapers' switch helped bring Labour many votes is, however, far from clear (Curtice, 1997). It was, perhaps, more obviously evidence that newspapers feared losing readers unless they switched to the horse that many of their readers were already backing (Norris *et al.*, 1999).

The first charge against newspapers is essentially a concern about their tendency to criticise one party while praising another. The second, in contrast, argues that the problem with newspapers is that they are critical of all politicians. Instead of reporting what politicians say and do, it is argued that journalists increasingly interpret politicians' words and actions, and do so through a cynical frame of reference. Thus, for example, if a chancellor introduces a tax cut, this may be reported as an attempt to bribe voters. If a prime minister pays a visit to the United States, it may well be considered an attempt to deflect public attention from political difficulties at home. Meanwhile, it is also argued that journalists increasingly exhibit an unnecessary and unhealthy interest in alleged improprieties in the financial and personal affairs of politicians, an interest that reached its height in the allegations of 'sleaze' that surrounded the 1992–1997 Conservative government. Such coverage, it is claimed, produces an increasingly cynical and alienated electorate that opts not to go to the polls at all (Patterson, 1993; Franklin, 1997; Cappella and Jamieson, 1997; Barnett, 2002; Lloyd, 2004).

Despite the obvious differences between these two sets of charges, they have one thing in common. They both assume that newspapers influence relatively large numbers of voters. For if newspapers influence their readers but their readership is small, they will inevitably influence insufficient people to make much difference to the overall outcome of an election amongst the population in general.

This, perhaps, suggests that Britain's democracy might be healthier if fewer people read newspapers. Yet it can be argued that newspapers have an important contribution to make to the health of the nation's democracy. It is often argued that a more informed electorate is better able to participate effectively in the political process, not least in deciding how to vote (Bartels, 1996; Christin *et al.*, 2002; Luskin *et al.*, 2002). While voters usually report that television, not newspapers, is their single most important source of information about politics, newspapers are able to cover political stories in greater depth than can any television news bulletin. Meanwhile, more popular newspapers can perhaps attract the attention of those with less interest in politics who are unlikely to watch a half-hour news bulletin but who do buy a popular newspaper for its human interest stories and then come across its political content, too. In short, newspapers could have an important role to play both in producing a more informed electorate and in helping politicians to reach out to those who might not otherwise pay much attention to them.

So, understanding how many people read newspapers, and who, is central to an adequate understanding of the relationship between newspapers and politics in Britain. It is indeed perhaps more fundamental than the question that is more commonly asked, that is, whether newspapers influence the political views and behaviour of their readers. In this chapter we examine the trends in newspaper readership over the last two decades. We consider both the overall incidence of newspaper readership and the kind of person who reads a newspaper. Our aim is to establish the possible implications of these for the health of Britain's democracy.

Trends in newspaper readership

Every year since the first survey in 1983, the *British Social Attitudes* survey has asked respondents about their newspaper readership. We ask:

> *Do you normally read any daily **morning** newspaper at least three days a week?*

The question thus focuses on regular rather than occasional newspaper reading. This means our question concentrates on those people for whom the character of their newspaper might plausibly make a difference to their views or behaviour. Moreover, those who say they do read a newspaper at least three times a week are subsequently asked which one they read (or if more than one, which paper they read most often). This means we can, for example, distinguish those who read more popular newspapers such as the *Daily Mail* or the *Daily Mirror* from those who read so-called 'quality' newspapers such as the *Daily Telegraph* and *The Guardian*.

Table 8.1 Trends in newspaper readership, 1983–2006

% say read morning newspaper "at least three days a week"	1983	1986	1990	1994	1998	2002	2006
All newspapers	77	73	68	61	57	54	50
Type of newspaper							
Popular	57	50	47	46	42	37	33
Quality	10	11	11	11	11	12	12
Base	*1761*	*3100*	*2797*	*3662*	*3146*	*3435*	*4290*

Table 8.1 shows the trends between 1983 and 2006 both in the proportion of people who read any kind of morning newspaper regularly, and, more specifically, in the proportion who read a popular or quality newspaper.[1] It shows a clear and dramatic picture. In 1983 just over three-quarters of the adult population in Britain regularly read a daily paper. Now that figure has fallen to just half. The decline has been continuous and relentless. Collectively Britain's

newspapers have lost a third of their readers and, instead of reaching the overwhelming majority of the population, are now regularly ignored by around half. This decline is indeed one of the more remarkable and persistent changes over the last 20 years to have been charted by the *British Social Attitudes* survey.

Not all newspapers have suffered equally, however. Readership of quality newspapers has maintained its share of around a tenth of the population. The overall decline in newspaper readership has in effect been a decline in the readership of (once) popular newspapers. In 1983 well over half said they read one of the nation's popular daily papers. Now just over one third do so. Not so much a case of '*The Sun* wot won it' as '*The Sun* wot's been binned'.

In fact, even the figures for quality newspapers are not as comforting for that section of the industry as they might initially seem. As we might anticipate, the more educational qualifications someone has, the more likely it is that they read a quality newspaper. Thus, for example, as the next table shows, in 1983 no less than half of graduates said that they regularly read a quality newspaper, while just three per cent of those without any qualifications did so. Meanwhile, since 1983, the proportion of graduates in the population has grown. They comprised just seven per cent of respondents to our 1983 survey but no less than 17 per cent in our 2006 survey. It seems that there ought, then, to have been a substantial increase in the readership of quality newspapers.

The next table shows why this has not happened. Whereas in 1983 half of graduates regularly read a quality newspaper, now just one fifth do so. There have also been smaller falls in readership of quality newspapers amongst those with higher education below degree level and those whose highest qualification is an A-level or its equivalent. In other words, quality newspapers have experienced a precipitate decline in their ability to penetrate what previously had appeared to be their 'natural' market. Looked at from that perspective the plight of quality newspapers appears to be as bad as that of their more popular counterparts.

Table 8.2 Readership of quality newspapers, by highest educational qualification, 1986, 1996 and 2006[2]

% say read quality morning newspaper "at least three days a week"	1986	1996	2006	Change 1986–2006
All	10	10	12	+2
Highest educational qualification				
Degree	50	36	20	-30
Other higher education	17	17	13	-4
A-level	18	12	11	-7
O-level	8	5	7	-1
CSE	3	3	7	+4
None	3	3	4	+1

As we have already noted, newspapers have long since had to compete with television for people's attention. Yet the advent of television predates 1983, and thus it is not immediately obvious that the decline in newspaper readership since then has been occasioned by competition from that quarter. More recently a new development in information technology, the advent of the internet, has provided yet another potential source of competition, at least for newspapers in their conventional printed form. In fact, the industry has embraced the internet by developing their own websites, using them to make available not simply an electronic version of their printed pages but also a continuous news service (thereby overcoming one of the disadvantages of newspapers as compared with the broadcast media) together with additional background material for which there is insufficient space in the printed version. But it is not clear that this development has had much impact on the reach of newspapers. When, in our most recent survey we asked those who do not read a newspaper regularly whether they consult a newspaper website at least three times a week, only three per cent said that they do.

Who has stopped reading newspapers?

So who has stopped reading a newspaper? The first question in which we are particularly interested here is whether there is any evidence that the decline in newspaper readership is a generational phenomenon. Older people may have acquired the newspaper reading habit many years ago when there were indeed fewer alternative sources of news or entertainment. But as they die out, they may be being replaced by younger people who have not acquired that same habit, perhaps indeed because of the wider range of sources of information that was available when they were growing up. If so, then perhaps the impact of technological development ranging from television to the internet has been a delayed one.

Table 8.3 enables us to consider this possibility. It shows for the years 1986, 1996 and 2006 the proportion of people in each of seven age groups who said that they regularly read a newspaper. Each of these three years is, of course, 10 years apart. At the same time, each of our age groups spans 10 years. This means that, for example, the group of people aged 18–27 in 1986 is the same group as those aged 28–37 in 1996 – and those who were 38–47 in 2006. [3] In other words, by reading diagonally across the table we can see whether those who belong to a particular generation or cohort have changed their newspaper reading habits over time. At the same time, by reading across the rows of the table, we can see whether later generations of, say, 18–27 year olds, are as likely to read newspapers as previous generations were 10 or 20 years previously. The final two columns of the table show both the age group and the cohort trends between 1986 and 2006.

Table 8.3 Newspaper readership, by age, 1986, 1996 and 2006[4]

	% say read a daily morning newspaper at least three days a week			Difference 1986–2006	
Age	1986	1996	2006	Age group	Cohort
18–27	72	51	42	-30	–
28–37	69	51	42	-27	–
38–47	75	55	42	-33	-30
48–57	75	64	52	-23	-17
58–67	79	69	62	-17	-13
68–77	71	72	63	-8	-12
78+	53	59	62	+9	(-17)
All	73	59	50	-23	

One conclusion does immediately emerge from the table. The decline in newspaper readership is not just a generational phenomenon. For example, reading diagonally, we see that those who belong to the cohort that was already aged 48–57 in 1986 (and who were aged 68–77 in 2006) were 12 percentage points less likely to be regularly reading a newspaper in 2006 than they were in 1986. However, this 12-point drop is little more than half the decline in newspaper readership amongst adults as a whole. Meanwhile, there is some evidence both that more recent generations of adults are less likely to read a newspaper regularly than their predecessors and that the decline in newspaper readership may have been stronger amongst more recent generations. Thus, for example, reading across the table, we can see that those aged 18–27 in 2006 are a full 30 percentage points less likely to read a newspaper than were those who were this age 20 years ago. Equally, the decline in newspaper readership amongst the cohort who were aged 18–27, 20 years ago (and who are now aged 38–47) has been no less than 30 percentage points. As a result there is now a twenty percentage point difference between the level of newspaper readership amongst younger groups and that amongst older ones, whereas two decades ago there was no consistent evidence of an age gap at all.

So, in part, newspapers have failed to keep older readers who once were loyal to them. But at the same time they have apparently found it more difficult to recruit and retain younger readers, perhaps because of their exposure at an early age to a wider range of media and sources of information and entertainment. This has an obvious but important implication. Even if newspapers can halt the decline in their reach amongst their older more established readers, a further decline in their level of readership amongst adults as a whole still seems inevitable in the future. Regularly reading a daily morning newspaper is, it seems, destined to become a minority pastime.

There is, however, a second question about the pattern of decline in newspaper readership that we should consider. We argued earlier that one of the ways in which newspapers might perform a useful contribution to the health of our democracy is by ensuring that those with relatively little interest in politics come across some news and information about politics even though they primarily value their newspaper for its human interest or entertainment content. But they can only perform this role if newspapers are actually read by those with relatively little interest in politics. We should thus consider whether they are – or whether the decline in newspaper readership has been particularly marked amongst those with little interest in politics.

Before doing so, however, we should dismiss one apparently obvious explanation of the decline in newspaper readership, that is, that fewer people are interested in politics. As has been demonstrated in previous *Reports* in this series (see, for example, Curtice *et al.*, 2006), there is no consistent evidence that the public has become less interested in politics. For example, in the 1986 *British Social Attitudes* survey, 29 per cent said they had "a great deal" or "quite a lot" of interest in politics, a view expressed by 31 per cent in 1996 and no less than 35 per cent in 2006. It is no more easy or difficult now to secure people's interest in matters political than it was two decades ago.

The first part of the next table shows the proportion of people who regularly read a newspaper depending on how much interest they say they have in politics. It presents this information for each of the years 1986, 1996 and 2006.

Table 8.4 Newspaper readership, by interest in politics, 1986, 1996 and 2006[5]

% say read a morning newspaper at least three days a week	Interest in politics	1986	1996	2006	Change 1986– 2006
All morning newspapers	Great deal	89	68	74	-15
	Quite a lot	74	64	60	-14
	Some	75	60	50	-25
	Not very much	68	54	34	-34
	None at all	69	46	40	-29
Quality newspapers	Great deal	31	27	29	-2
	Quite a lot	15	20	22	+7
	Some	9	8	8	-1
	Not very much	4	3	6	+2
	None at all	3	2	2	-1
Popular newspapers	Great deal	39	34	38	-1
	Quite a lot	47	39	31	-16
	Some	55	47	38	-17
	Not very much	57	48	24	-33
	None at all	58	42	32	-26

As we might expect, those who are interested in politics have always been rather more likely to say that they read a newspaper. In 1986 those who said they had a great deal of interest in politics were 20 percentage points more likely than those with no interest at all in politics to be a regular reader of a daily newspaper. Even so, the industry still captured the regular attention of over two-thirds of those with little or no interest in politics, and thus was a potential conduit through which information about politics might reach those who were least inclined to seek out such information for themselves.

Its ability to do so has, however, sharply declined. The decline in newspaper readership has been heaviest most of all amongst those with the least interest in politics. Amongst those with a great deal or quite a lot of interest in politics, the decline in newspaper readership over the last 20 years has been of the order of 15 percentage points; in contrast amongst those with little or no interest it has been of the order of 30 percentage points.

Moreover, as we can see from the second and third parts of the same table, which repeat the analysis separately for quality and popular newspapers, this decline in newspaper readership amongst those with little or no interest in politics has been occasioned entirely by a decline in popular newspaper readership amongst this group. Twenty years ago, someone with little or no interest in politics was actually more likely to read a popular newspaper than was someone *with* an interest in politics. Now they are no more likely to do so. Even the popular press is now as likely to be addressing the politically attuned, as it is those who usually tune out of politics.

A cynical readership?

We remarked at the beginning of this chapter that the press is often criticised for its apparently cynical coverage of politics, a cynicism that it is argued has helped to stimulate distrust in politicians. There is indeed no doubt that distrust of politicians has increased. For example, in 1986, 38 per cent said that they trusted governments of any party "to place the needs of the nation above the interests of their own political party", a proportion that had fallen to just 22 per cent by 1996 and is now no more than 19 per cent (for a more extended discussion see Curtice and Seyd, 2003; Bromley et al., 2004). What is less clear is whether newspapers are responsible for this change (see also Bromley and Curtice, 2004).

If indeed newspapers are making their readers increasing cynical, then we might anticipate that over time those who read newspapers should become increasingly different from those who do not in their level of cynicism about politics. Those who regularly read the diatribes of the 'Daily Scandal' should be increasingly relatively more cynical about politics. Moreover, of course, any difference between the attitudes of those who read newspapers and those who do not would be further exacerbated if dislike of the alleged cynicism of the political coverage of newspapers is one of the reasons why some people have stopped reading a newspaper.

Table 8.5 Newspaper readership, by trust in government, 1986, 1996 and 2006[6]

% say read a morning newspaper at least three days a week	1986	1996	2006	Change 1986–2006
Trusts governments to put interests of nation before party				
Almost always/most of the time	76	65	56	-20
Some of the time	73	55	47	-26
Almost never/never	68	58	53	-15

Table 8.6 Newspaper readership, by trust in politicians, 1986, 1996 and 2005[6]

% say read a morning newspaper at least three days a week	1986	1996	2005	Change 1986–2005
MPs lose touch with people pretty quickly				
Strongly agree	71	60	53	-18
Agree	73	60	50	-23
Neither agree nor disagree	75	46	50	-15
Disagree/strongly disagree	78	59	50	-28

Of these possibilities, however, there is no sign. Tables 8.5 and 8.6 show, for each of three years, how the proportion of people who read a newspaper varies according to the degree of trust and cynicism about politics. Their trust and cynicism is measured by two questions. The first is the question to which we have already referred about whether governments can be trusted to put the needs of the nation first. The second asks respondents to the survey whether they agree or disagree that "Generally speaking those we elect as MPs lose touch with people pretty quickly". If newspapers are increasingly making their readers more cynical about politics, or alternatively if dislike of newspapers' cynical coverage of politics helps explain why people are now less likely to read them, we should find that the difference in the level of newspaper readership between the more and less cynical has widened.

Of this, however, there is no consistent evidence. True, the decline in newspaper readership appears to have been greatest amongst those who do not feel that MPs lose touch with people pretty quickly (and thus may be regarded as least cynical). But at the same time it has fallen least amongst those who are least trustful of governments. Overall, how distrustful or cynical someone was about politics made relatively little difference in 1986 to the chances that they were a newspaper reader, and much the same is true now.

Conclusions

Readership of Britain's daily morning newspapers has declined sharply over the last 20 years, a decline that seems set to continue yet further. In particular, the country's so called 'popular' newspapers are now a lot less popular than they once were. But even the ability of the quality press to maintain its overall level of readership also looks unimpressive given the increase in the number of graduates in the population over the last 20 years.

It could be argued that this is healthy for Britain's democracy. It means that the ability of newspapers unfairly and unaccountably to sway the outcome of an election, as *The Sun* allegedly did in 1992, is now much diminished. It also means that fewer people are exposed to their supposedly cynical coverage of politics that discourages people from participating in politics at all.

But this seems too dismissive a picture. Popular newspapers were once a mechanism whereby information about politics could reach those with little inclination to follow political matters. Now they are increasingly unable to fulfil that role. Instead, the readership of newspapers in Britain is increasingly confined to those with an interest in politics. For years politicians have worried about the power of the press. But perhaps instead it is time for them to be concerned about its weakness.

Notes

1. Those reading a regional or local daily morning paper are included in the 'all papers' column but do not appear in either the 'popular' or 'quality' papers columns. The newspapers defined as 'quality' newspapers are: *The Daily Telegraph*, *The Times*, *The Financial Times*, *The Guardian* and *The Independent*. The newspapers defined as 'popular' are: *Daily Express*, *Daily Mail*, *Daily Mirror*, *Daily Record*, *Daily Star*, *Morning Star*, *The Sun*, *Today*.
2. The bases for Table 8.2 are as follows:

% say read quality morning newspaper "at least three days a week"	1986	1996	2006
All	3100	3662	4290
Highest educational qualification			
Degree	207	394	738
Other higher education	370	517	519
A-level	268	431	640
O-level	578	720	800
CSE	251	337	415
None	1394	1187	1091

3. Since the *British Social Attitudes* survey is not a panel study, the groups do not comprise the same *respondents*, but the respondents are drawn from the same groups in the population.

4. The bases for Table 8.3 are as follows:

Age	**% say read a daily morning newspaper at least three days a week**		
	1986	**1996**	**2006**
18–27	582	473	512
28–37	608	812	762
38–47	578	621	824
48–57	508	527	675
58–67	414	451	691
68–77	288	468	506
78+	119	253	315
All	3100	3662	4290

5. The bases for Table 8.4 are as follows:

% say read morning newspaper at least three days a week	**1986**	**1996**	**2006**
Interest in politics			
Great deal	111	338	107
Quite a lot	331	803	266
Some	491	1189	361
Not very much	421	917	224
None at all	188	414	119

6. The bases for Tables 8.5 and 8.6 are:

% say read a morning newspaper at least three days a week	**1986**	**1996**	**2006**
Trusts governments to put interests of nation before party			
Almost always/most of the time	589	259	203
Some of the time	708	615	491
Almost never/never	173	269	362
MPs lose touch with people pretty quickly			
Strongly agree	254	304	503
Agree	826	589	1714
Neither agree nor disagree	166	127	462
Disagree/strongly disagree	244	129	423

References

Barnett, S. (2002), 'Will a Crisis in Journalism Provoke a Crisis in Democracy?', *Political Quarterly*, **73**: 400–408

Bartels, L. (1996), 'Uniformed Votes: Information Effects in Presidential Elections', *American Journal of Political Science*, **40**: 194–230

Bromley, C. and Curtice, J. (2004), 'Are non-voters cynics anyway?', *Journal of Public Affairs*, **4(4)**:328–337

Bromley, C., Curtice, J. and Seyd, B. (2004), *Is Britain Facing a Crisis of Democracy?*, London: Constitution Unit

Cappella J. and Jamieson, K. (1997), *Spiral of Cynicism*, New York: Oxford University Press

Christin, T., Hug, S. and Sciariini, P. (2002), 'Interests and information in referendum voting: an analysis of Swiss voters', *European Journal of Political Research*, **41**: 759–776

Curtice, J. (1997), 'Is the Sun shining on Tony Blair? The electoral influence of British newspapers', *Harvard International Journal of Press/Politics*, **2**: 9–26

Curtice, J., Fisher, S. and Lessard-Phillips, L. (2006), 'Proportional representation and the disappearing voter', in Park, A., Curtice, J., Thomson, K., Phillips, M. and Johnson. M. (eds.), *British Social Attitues: the 23rd Report – Perspectives on a changing society*, London: Sage

Curtice, J. and Semetko, H. (1994), 'Does it matter what the papers say?', in Heath, A., Jowell, R. and Curtice, J. (eds.), *Labour's Last Chance? The 1992 Election and Beyond*, Aldershot: Dartmouth

Curtice, J. and Seyd, B. (2003), 'Is there a crisis of political participation?', in Park, A., Curtice, K., Thomson, K., Jarvis, L. and Bromley. C. (eds.), *British Social Attitudes: the 20th Report – Continuity and change over two decades*, London: Sage

Franklin, B., (1997), *Newszak and the Media*, London: Arnold

Harrop, M. and Scammell, M. (1992), 'A tabloid war', in Butler, D. and Kavanagh, D., *The British General Election of 1992*, London: Macmillan

Lloyd, J. (2004), *What the Media Do to Our Politics*, London: Constable and Robinson

Luskin, R., Fishkin, J. and Jowell, R. (2002), 'Considered Opinions: Deliberative Polling in Britain', *British Journal of Political Science*, **32**: 455–487

Miller, W. (1991), *Media and Voters: The Audience, Content, and Influence of Press and Television at the 1987 General Election*, Oxford: Oxford University Press

Norris, P., Curtice, J., Sanders, D., Scammell, M. and Semetko, H. (1999), *On Message: Communicating the Campaign*, London: Sage

Patterson, T. (1993), *Out of Order*, New York: Knopf

Scammell, M. and Harrop, M. (1997), 'The press: Labour's finest hour', in Butler, D. and Kavanagh, D., *The British General Election of 1997*, London: Macmillan

Seymour-Ure, C. (1996), *The British Press and Broadcasting since 1945*, Oxford: Blackwell

9 What makes a good citizen? Citizenship across the democratic world

Paul F Whiteley[*]

Citizenship can be defined as a set of norms, values and practices which bind society together, makes democratic government possible and helps individuals to solve collective action problems (Pattie *et al.*, 2004). These values and practices are rooted in an implicit bargain, or an invisible handshake between the individual and the state, in which citizens claim rights and protections in exchange for accepting various obligations to deliver things that the state needs if it is to be effective. Citizens may demand that the state provides a decent standard of living for all, for example, but in exchange they have to be willing to pay their taxes. If citizens demand rights without accepting obligations, the system will not be able to deliver, and problems of governance will arise. So in a real sense successful democratic government relies on this implicit bargain.

The aim of this chapter is to explore the norms, values and practices which underpin citizenship in a cross-national context using the 2004 *International Social Survey Programme* data.[1] This involves investigating the rights that individuals feel the state should provide, and also the extent to which such individuals acknowledge their obligations to act as good citizens. These relationships will be examined using data from 37 different countries,[2] involving more than fifty thousand survey respondents. In the course of the chapter we shall examine the relationship between these norms and practices, particularly the relationship between norms supporting participation and actual participation in politics. Participation is defined broadly to include a variety of activities such as protesting, attending political meetings, and contacting the media about political issues. Part of this exercise involves examining contextual variables measured at the level of the state to see how they influence participation at the level of the individual citizen.

This topic raises a number of interesting questions for comparative analysis. Is it the case, for example, that citizens are likely to demand rights while at the same time seeking to avoid their obligations, particularly in relation to political participation? Is this true in some countries but not in others, and if so why? Do

---

[*] Paul F Whiteley is Professor of Government at the University of Essex and Co-Director of the British Election Study.

some individuals say that they are willing to participate, but in practice then actually avoid getting involved? These questions explore the relationship between social norms and behaviour, particularly the issue of whether or not rhetoric about the desirability of participation translates into action on the ground. The advantage of a comparative approach is that we can explore the impact of societal factors like a country's standard of living and its level of inequality in influencing the norms and behaviours associated with participation.

Rights, obligations and the citizen

A battery of questions in the survey asked respondents to indicate how much importance they attached to various rights in a democracy.[3] Table 9.1 shows the percentage of respondents who assigned the highest score on the scale of importance to different types of rights. It shows that large percentages of citizens across all the countries expect their governments to provide economic security, to treat people equally and to protect their rights, while at the same time ensuring that ordinary people have a say in decision making. The expectations that the average citizen has of government are generally quite high.

Table 9.1 Perceptions of citizen rights in 37 countries, 2004

% say "very important" that …	
… government authorities treat everybody equally regardless of their position in society	73
… politicians take into account the views of citizens before making decisions	69
… all citizens have an adequate standard of living	69
… government authorities respect and protect the rights of minorities	59
… people be given more opportunities to participate in public decision making	55

Base: 53,913

Obligations are the other side of the coin, and the next table shows the percentage of individuals who attach the highest importance to different social obligations. Generally the table shows that perceptions of obligations are more varied than perceptions of rights. While majorities of respondents felt that citizens should always vote in elections, should never evade taxes and always obey the law, other obligations are assigned a lower priority. Effective democracy requires that governments should be accountable to their citizens, and that individuals should participate in politics and in society more generally.

However, only a minority of respondents attached the highest importance to keeping governments accountable, and only small minorities thought that participating in voluntary organisations or in political associations is most important. This is not to say that respondents felt these to be unimportant, but they were of lesser importance than obeying the law and paying taxes. At the same time a large number of people felt that one should help others who are worse off than oneself, both at home and abroad. There is a strong sense of egalitarianism in these societies.

Table 9.2 Perceptions of citizen obligations in 37 countries, 2004

% say "very important" to be a good citizen ...	
... always to obey laws and regulations	57
... never to try to evade taxes	54
... always to vote in elections	52
... to help people in your country who are worse off than yourself	41
... to keep watch on the actions of government	37
... to help people in the rest of the world who are worse off than yourself	29
... to choose products for political, ethical or environmental reasons, even if they cost a bit more	18
... to be active in social or political associations	15

Base: 53,913

One interesting question is how consistent people are in their views. Is it the case, for example, that people who think that the government should provide a minimum standard of living for its citizens also think that it should protect minority rights? Clearly, majorities of respondents supported these rights, but are they different majorities? A similar point can be made about obligations. Are the people who think citizens should vote the same people who think they should pay their taxes? This issue can be explored using factor analysis, which allows us to determine attitude consistency across the various measures. The full results of this analysis appear in the appendix to this chapter and they show that there is a single underlying scale of perceptions of rights, but three separate scales of perceptions of obligations. As regards rights, this means that individuals who think that the government should provide a minimum standard of living for all are quite likely to think that the government should also protect minorities and that people should be given a say in decision making. Respondents tend to be fairly consistent when it comes to supporting rights.

The three obligations factors relate to participation, obedience to the state and the redistribution of income and wealth, and they are described in Figure 9.1. This figure shows that respondents who think that citizens should vote in elections are also quite likely to believe that they should keep an eye on the government, and be active in politics and choose products for political or ethical reasons. The obedience to the state factor indicates that people are consistent in their replies to the questions about paying taxes and obeying the law. Thus respondents who think that citizens should never evade taxes are quite likely to think that they should obey the law. But there is no necessary consistency between the obligation to participate and the obligation to obey the state. People who think that citizens should pay their taxes are not necessarily more likely to think that they should vote. The same point can be made about the redistribution factor; those who favour redistribution at home are also likely to favour redistribution abroad, but they are not necessarily more likely to think the law should be obeyed or that individuals should participate in politics. Clearly, perceptions of obligations are rather more heterogeneous than perceptions of rights.

Figure 9.1 Citizen obligations: three constituent factors

Citizen obligations	Participate	Obey the state	Redistribute
Always to vote in elections	X		
To keep watch on the actions of government	X		
To be active in social or political associations	X		
To choose products for political, ethical or environmental reasons	X		
Never to try to evade taxes		X	
Always to obey laws and regulations		X	
To help people in your country who are worse off than yourself			X
To help people in the rest of the world who are worse off than yourself			X

Participation and the citizen

When it comes to evaluating the practices underpinning citizenship, political participation is the most important, since democracy cannot survive if people do not participate. Accordingly, we might expect a close relationship between norms and values that support participation and actual participation. The practice of participating is measured in two different ways in the survey. Firstly, we asked:

Here are some different forms of political and social action that people can take. Please indicate, for each one, whether:

you have done any of these things in the past year;

you have done it in the more distant past;

you have not done it but might do it;

or have not done it and would never, under any circumstances, do it

Previous research has shown that participation in politics is a minority activity, apart from electoral participation (Barnes and Kaase, 1979; Verba *et al.*, 1995; Clarke *et al.*, 2004), and Table 9.3 confirms this finding. Only relatively small minorities of citizens attended political meetings or joined protest demonstrations, and while sizeable minorities signed a petition or boycotted goods, the great majority did not participate in this way. Interestingly enough, a factor analysis of the items shows that a single dimension underlies the data. Thus people who sign petitions are quite likely to boycott goods for political or ethical reasons, and some of them will also have attended a protest demonstration.

Table 9.3 Political or social participation in the previous year in 37 countries, 2004

% "have done it in the past year"	
Signing a petition	21
Donated money or raised funds for a political or social activity	19
Boycotted, or deliberately bought, certain products for political, ethical or environmental reasons	16
Attended a political meeting or rally	9
Contacted, or attempted to contact, a politician or a civil servant to express your views	8
Took part in a demonstration	7
Contacted or appeared in the media to express your views	4
Joined an internet political forum or discussion group	3

Base: 53,913

The second way that participation was measured was by asking about organisational membership:

People sometimes belong to different kinds of groups or associations. For each type of group, please indicate whether you:

belong and actively participate;

belong but don't actively participate;

used to belong but do not any more;

or have never belonged to it

The next table shows that party membership and activism are very much minority activities and the most popular voluntary organisations are those connected with sports, leisure and cultural pursuits. Interestingly enough, the passive members outnumber the active members in the case of parties, church organisations, trade unions and professional groups. But this is not true for sports, leisure or cultural organisations, or other types of voluntary groups. The implication here is that weekend football players outnumber members of football supporters' clubs.

Table 9.4 Organisational belonging and active participation in 37 countries, 2004

Organisation	% belong, actively participate	% belong, don't participate
A sports, leisure or cultural group	20	9
A church or other religious organisation	15	23
Another voluntary association	11	6
A trade union, business or professional association	7	16
A political party	3	7

Base: 53,913

Cross-national patterns of attitudes and behaviour

Up to this point we have examined attitudes and participation across all of the countries together, but what cross-national patterns exist in the data? We look in turn at attitudes to the right to an adequate standard of living, the duty to vote, buying or boycotting goods for ethical or political reasons and participation in voluntary organisations.

The right to an adequate standard of living

We take attitudes to the right to an adequate standard of living as indicative of attitudes to rights in general. Figure 9.2 shows the variation in the proportion saying that this right is "very important" across the 37 countries. Interestingly enough, the Czech Republic is ranked lowest, with only 37 per cent of its citizens attaching the highest importance to everyone having an adequate standard of living. In contrast, no less than 95 per cent of Uruguayans support this idea. So there are wide variations in attitudes to rights across these countries.

Figure 9.2 Percentages who think the right to an adequate standard of living is "very important", by country, 2004

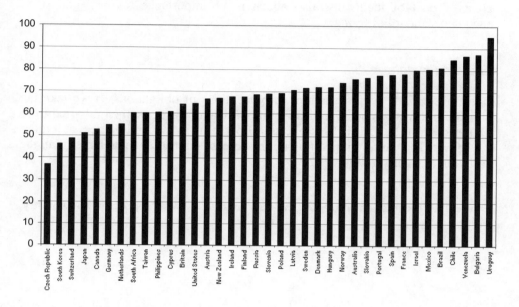

To examine this in a more rigorous fashion, we have split countries into three groups in terms of their affluence (as measured by their gross domestic product – per capita) and in terms of their inequality (as measured by the Gini coefficient).[4]

Table 9.5 Importance of the right to an adequate standard of living, by affluence and inequality of country, 2004

Standard of living (GDP per capita)	% "very important"	Base	Inequality (Gini coefficient)	% "very important"	Base
High	64	13,872	High	76	17,356
Medium	67	15,739	Medium	68	18,948
Low	74	21,092	Low	65	13,400

Table 9.5 shows that there is a negative relationship between GDP – per capita and a belief in the importance of an adequate standard of living for all, indicating that affluence reduced the demand for this right.[5] This finding fits in well with the post-materialist thesis, which argues that citizens of rich countries attach a lower importance to economic welfare, largely because they have satisfied their economic needs in this regard. In contrast, citizens of poor

countries are much more preoccupied with prosperity and economic security (Inglehart, 1997). Moreover, the table shows that citizens in countries with a great of deal of inequality also attach more importance to the right to an adequate standard of living.

The duty to vote

There are equally wide variations in perceptions of obligations. If we take the obligation to vote as being indicative of political obligations, then it varied from 21 per cent in the Czech Republic to 80 per cent in the Philippines, as Figure 9.3 shows. The variation in voting norms across countries is even larger than the variation in rights in Figure 9.2.

Figure 9.3 Percentages who think the duty to vote is "very important", by country, 2004

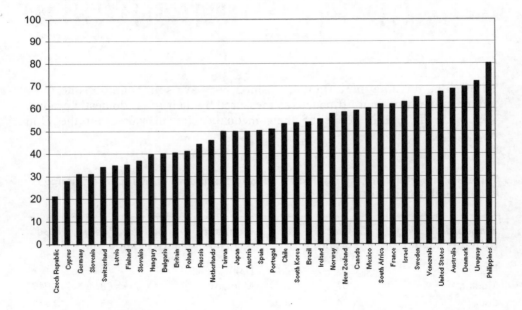

In this case, norms about voting are not linked to affluence, so it does not behave in the same way as the rights measure (Table 9.6). However, there is a significant association between inequality and voting norms.[6] This relationship is quite strong, and it suggests that inequality in society increases the importance of voting. Clearly citizens understand very well that voting allows them to promote redistribution in a democracy, so it makes sense for this obligation to be most highly valued in the most unequal societies.

Table 9.6 Importance of duty to vote, by affluence and inequality of country, 2004

Standard of living (GDP per capita)	% "very important"	Base	Inequality (Gini coefficient)	% "very important"	Base
High	52	13,872	High	62	17,356
Medium	51	15,739	Medium	50	18,948
Low	50	21,092	Low	44	13,400

Using consumer power

One of the fastest growing forms of participation is consumer participation, in which people use their buying power for political purposes. The next figure shows there are very large differences across countries. Boycotting and buycotting (as it is now called) involves less than one per cent of the population in Bulgaria and no less than 41 per cent in Switzerland.

Figure 9.4 Percentages buying or boycotting goods for ethical or political reasons, by country, 2004

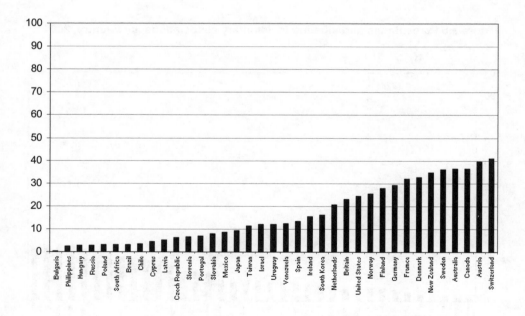

As seen in Table 9.7, there is a very strong relationship between GDP per capita and consumer participation. There is also a strong negative relationship between inequality and consumer participation.[7] It is clear that affluence promotes consumer participation, while inequality inhibits it.

Table 9.7 Percentages buying or boycotting goods for ethical or political reasons, by affluence and inequality of country, 2004

Standard of living (GDP per capita)	% participating	Base	Inequality (Gini coefficient)	% participating	Base
High	27	13,872	High	8	17,356
Medium	21	15,739	Medium	20	18,948
Low	5	21,092	Low	20	13,400

Participation in voluntary organisations

In relation to participating in voluntary organisations, Figure 9.5 again shows wide variations across the sample of countries. Bulgaria had the least number of volunteers and Canada had the most. In this case, the range goes from one per cent in the former country to 26 per cent in the latter.

Figure 9.5 Percentages participating in voluntary associations, by country, 2004[8]

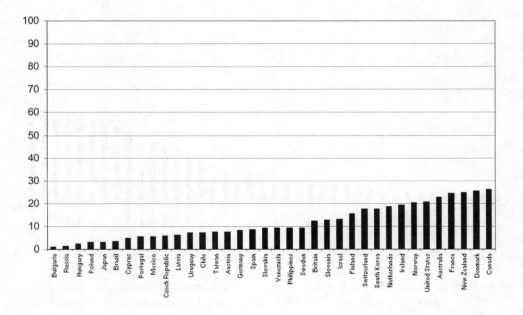

As with consumer participation, the next table shows that such voluntary activity is positively associated with affluence. This suggests that people are more willing to volunteer when they have satisfied their basic needs for economic security. The relationship with inequality appears to be slightly more complex, with the highest figures for countries of middling inequality. The important point, though, is that countries with high inequality had lower rates of volunteering, so overall volunteering is negatively associated with inequality.[9]

Table 9.8 Percentages participating in voluntary associations, by affluence and inequality of country, 2004

Standard of living (GDP per capita)	% participating	Base	Inequality (Gini coefficient)	% participating	Base
High	15	13,872	High	8	17,356
Medium	15	15,739	Medium	15	18,948
Low	5	21,092	Low	11	13,400

Rights, obligations, affluence and inequality

In summary, then, looking across Tables 9.5 to 9.8, we find that the percentage of respondents who think that a minimum standard of living is very important is significantly greater in poorer countries than it is in richer countries, but affluence has little effect on citizen's views on the importance of voting. However, a high standard of living does influence both the number of people involved in consumer participation and in voluntary organisations. These types of participation are much less common in poorer countries than in rich or moderately affluent countries. When it comes to inequality the patterns of responses are rather different. In this case citizens of very unequal countries attach much more importance to the right to a minimum standard of living and to voting than do citizens of egalitarian countries. Moreover, consumerism and voluntary activity are less likely to be found in highly unequal societies compared with their egalitarian counterparts

The evidence up to this point shows that perceptions of rights and obligations together with participation vary quite a lot across our sample of countries. But what is the relationship between these different measures? We consider this question next.

Relationships between citizen norms and citizen participation

When examining the relationship between norms and behaviour it is possible that attitudes to rights and obligations do not translate easily into actual behaviour. Thus citizens may be more willing to talk about participation than actually to get involved. This issue is explored in Table 9.9 which shows the relationship between indicators of rights and obligations and one of the indicators of participation: contact behaviour. For each dimension we use the indicator which is most strongly related to the factors identified in the appendix to this chapter. Thus contacting a politician is used as the indicator of participation. Similarly, the most important indicator of rights is the demand for citizens to be consulted by government.

Table 9.9 The relationship between participation and indicators of rights and obligations in 37 countries, 2004

	Contact with a politician or official			
% thinking activity is "very important"	Contact in previous year	Contact prior to previous year	No contact but might do	No contact and would not do
Rights – consulting citizens	76	72	71	67
Base	2,995	3,620	13,420	14,957
Obligations – vote in elections	68	60	53	48
Base	2,640	3,001	9,963	10,636
Obligations – help people worse off	31	26	28	30
Base	1,231	1,306	5,306	6,573
Obligations – obey the law	56	55	56	60
Base	2,230	2,738	10,583	13,449

The table shows that there is a positive relationship between beliefs in rights and obligations on the one hand and participation on the other. Thus 76 per cent of people who contacted a politician or official in the previous year thought that the right to be consulted was most important. But only 67 per cent of people who would never contact a politician or official thought this. The relationship is not terribly strong but it is statistically significant thus suggesting a link between perceptions of rights and participation. In the case of norms concerning voting the link is much stronger, with 68 per cent of people contacting attaching the highest importance to voting, but only 48 per cent of non-contactors doing this. Those who are most likely to contact a politician are also most likely to think that voting is very important. On the other hand the norm of helping others who are worse off than oneself appears to be unrelated to contact behaviour, and in the case of obeying the law the relationship is actually reversed, with non-contactors attaching more importance to obeying the law than contactors. Thus the overall picture is mixed, with some norms not being closely linked to actual participation. However, the key norms relating to perceptions of rights and obligations to participate *are* associated with actual participation.

Modelling citizen attitudes and citizen participation

The relationships in Table 9.9 are interesting, but they do not take into account other important variables which are known to influence political participation and civic norms. When such variables are incorporated into the analysis the relationship between norms and participation may look very different. To get a true picture of how norms relate to participation we need to develop a multivariate model that controls for many other factors than can intervene to affect the relationship between these variables. With this point in mind an important distinction exists in the literature between choice-based and structural-based approaches to explaining participation (Pattie *et al.*, 2004). Choice-based models are exemplified in their purest form by economic theory, in which the assumption is made that actors seek to maximise utility. Applied to the task of understanding civic engagement, this type of theory sees citizenship emerging from the choices which agents make, and these reflect the costs and benefits of the choice situation. Thus individuals will participate if they are engaged enough and if the returns outweigh the costs. An alternative perspective sees participation as a matter of individuals being socialised into the norms, values and practices of their families, the social groups to which they belong, and those of the wider society. In this approach, the citizen is seen as being moulded by social forces which shape their norms and behaviour. Individual choice has only a limited influence on this system of ideas, since the key determinants of attitudes and behaviour are thought to be found at the societal level. To develop a multivariate analysis of participation we consider two distinct models: one is a choice-based theory, the cognitive engagement model; and the other is a societal-based theory, the social capital model.

The cognitive engagement model

The central idea of cognitive engagement theory is that participation depends on the individual's access to information and on their ability and willingness to use it to make informed choices (Dalton and Wattenberg, 2000; Clarke *et al.*, 2004). Two developments in society help to explain the growth of interest in cognitive engagement theories of participation (Dalton, 2002). One is the growth of education, particularly higher education, which has taken place across the western world in the last few decades. Participation in higher education is particularly important to this type of theory, since it helps people to acquire, and process, large amounts of information. It provides citizens with skills for collecting and analysing information by placing it into a meaningful context. The highly educated are much more able to make sense of politics than the uneducated.

The increase in higher education is linked to the second development, the declining costs of acquiring information in print, electronic and web-based forms. The proliferation of publications and new outlets for their dissemination has greatly reduced the costs of becoming informed. Thus the growth of education, on the one hand, and the decline in the costs of acquiring and processing information, on the other, produces a process of cognitive mobilisation (Barnes and Kaase, 1979). Media consumption is a key factor in this process, since the cognitively engaged citizen will follow politics and public affairs in the media. Viewed from the perspective of normative political theory, cognitively engaged individuals are close to the Greek conceptions of the good citizen. The classical Greek citizen was an informed member of the *polis* who fully participated in politics and understood the issues and complexities of government. Cognitive mobilisation produces individuals who are interested, politically knowledgeable and understand the norms and principles of democracy. Thus the type of variables which are important in the cognitive engagement model are education, interest in politics, political efficacy, discussion of politics and, most importantly, media consumption of politics and current affairs.

In our sample across the world, just under half (47 per cent) of respondents were very or fairly interested in politics. Wide variations exist across the world, with only 21 per cent of the Taiwanese being politically interested at one end of the scale compared with 70 per cent of Americans at the other end.

Some 37 per cent said that they discussed politics often or sometimes with their friends and family. This varies from only 26 per cent in Chile to 69 per cent in Norway.

With respect to personal efficacy, respondents were asked how much they agreed with the following statement:

People like me don't have any say about what the government does

Almost half of respondents (46 per cent) agreed with this rather bleak statement, as opposed to 38 per cent who disagreed. The next figure shows an extraordinarily high variation between countries – from the lowest efficacy in Slovakia, with just 10 per cent disagreeing with the statement, to the highest in France (83 per cent).

Figure 9.6 Political efficacy (per cent who disagree they have no say in what the government does), by country, 2004

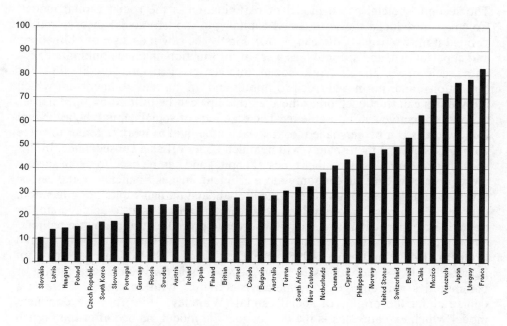

On the other hand, the next table shows that there is a healthy appetite for political news in the media. All of the indicators show that many citizens are fairly engaged with politics and current affairs. As regards media usage, the table shows that most people rely on television for their news, and the internet is a source of information for only a small minority, although this will change over time. Overall, we would expect highly educated, efficacious, interested and engaged citizens who absorb political information to be much more politically active than their counterparts.

Table 9.10 Media consumption of politics in 37 countries, 2004

		Every day	3–4 days a week	1–2 days a week	Fewer than 1–2 days a week	Never
Read newspaper	%	18	14	18	23	27
Watch television	%	45	19	14	12	9
Listen to the radio	%	23	13	13	21	30
Use the internet	%	3	3	5	14	75

Base: 52,529

The social capital model

The second, societal-based model of participation is the social capital model. Coleman introduced the term social capital into modern social theory, and he defined it in two ways (Coleman, 1990). Firstly, he saw it as a set of obligations and expectations, and secondly, as a set of information channels linking citizens with each other. In his view social interactions generate 'credit slips' of obligations and norms of reciprocation, and in an environment in which individuals can trust each other these credit slips can be utilised by third parties to solve collective action problems. The core idea of social capital theory is that if individuals can be persuaded to trust each other and to work together to solve common problems then society will be much better off as a consequence. In this sense social capital is like other types of capital and can be used to make society more productive and the economy more efficient. Just as financial capital can be invested in order to promote economic growth, and human capital, or education, can be used to raise productivity, social capital can be used to achieve similar objectives. In particular, social capital serves to promote political participation.

For most writers interpersonal trust is the key indicator of social capital (Putnam, 1993; Fukuyama, 1995; Van Deth et al., 1999). Trust is important because it allows individuals to move beyond their own immediate family or communities and engage in cooperative activities with strangers. There is a debate about the origins of social capital (Whiteley, 1999) but the dominant model which explains this is the de Tocqueville model, named after the French philosopher who studied American society in the early nineteenth century. Writing in 1832 de Tocqueville commented on the widespread growth of voluntary organisations in American society. In his view, what we now describe as social capital originates in face-to-face interactions between individuals within voluntary associations. By working together, individuals learn co-operative skills and also acquire the willingness to trust others which is at the centre of the social capital model. The type of variables which are important for the social capital model is voluntary activity in organisations, interpersonal trust and, in the case of political participation, trust in government. The former was examined in Table 9.8 and the latter are examined in Tables 9.11 and 9.12.

Table 9.11 Interpersonal trust in 37 countries, 2004

Level of trust	%
People can almost always be trusted	4
People can usually be trusted	37
You usually can't be too careful in dealing with people	42
You almost always can't be too careful in dealing with people	16

Base: 53,913

Table 9.12 Trust in government in 37 countries, 2004

Most of the time we can trust people in government to do what is right	%
Strongly agree	3
Agree	26
Neither agree nor disagree	28
Disagree	30
Strongly disagree	13

Base: 53,913

Table 9.11 shows that people are marginally less likely to trust other people than to distrust them, although there is not much difference between the two groups, with opinions being relatively evenly divided. The same point cannot be made about trusting governments, however, since as Table 9.12 shows, in this case less than a third of respondents thought that government can be trusted to do what is right, and more than four out of ten disagree with the statement in the table. In relation to political participation, we would expect people who are active in voluntary organisations, who trust other people and who trust the government, to participate more than individuals who lack these characteristics.

Figure 9.7 Cross-national variations in interpersonal trust (per cent who think people can always or usually be trusted), by country, 2004

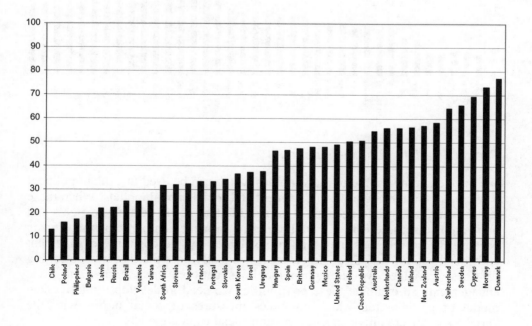

Figure 9.7 shows cross-national variations in interpersonal trust identifying the percentage of citizens who think that people can always or usually be trusted. This varies from a surprising 13 per cent of respondents in Chile to 77 per cent in Denmark, so there is a very wide range of variation in this key indicator of social capital across all of the countries.

The next figure shows cross-national variations in trust in government, that is, the percentage of respondents who agree or strongly agree with the proposition that government can be trusted to do what is right. Again we observe large variations in this measure across the sample of countries. Only nine per cent of Japanese agree with this statement compared with 58 per cent of South Africans.

Figure 9.8 Cross-national variations in trust in government (per cent who agree government can be trusted to do what is right), by country, 2004

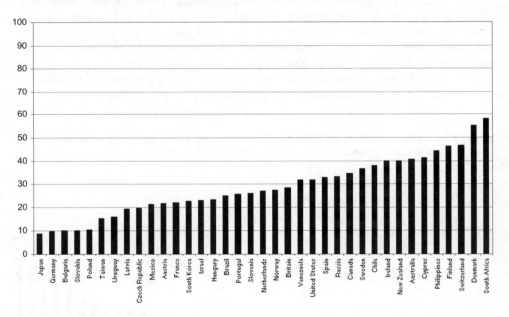

The multivariate participation model

We have examined some of the variables which can be used to explain political participation in the cognitive engagement and social capital models. When these variables are taken into account, it is possible that norms relating to rights and obligations discussed earlier have little or no influence on participation. This is because the correlations may well be explained by the cognitive engagement and social capital variables. However, it is equally possible that by controlling for these variables we strengthen the links between civic norms and civic engagement. To examine these possibilities we need to develop a multivariate model of participation which combines measures of social norms with the variables in the cognitive engagement and social capital models.

In the earlier discussion we suggested that measures of wealth and inequality in society had an important influence on participatory norms and they may very well influence actual political participation as well. To take into account simultaneously the societal- and individual-level variables, we need a multi-level regression model of political participation (Hox, 2002). This is a model which combines variables measured at the level of the individual citizen with variables measured at the state level to explain individual participation. The basic idea behind such a model is that the context in which an individual operates has a direct effect on their behaviour in addition to any attitudes or social characteristics they may posses. Thus levels of wealth and inequality in society could well influence the relationship between norms and participation, and so these indicators are incorporated into the model.

The full results of the multivariate modelling exercise are given in the appendix to this chapter, but a summary is shown in Figure 9.9.

Figure 9.9 Summary of multivariate model of participation in politics in 37 countries, 2004

	Association with propensity to participate in politics
Country-level variables	
GNP per capita	+ve
Gini coefficient	⊗
Individual-level variables	
Obligation to participate	+ve
Obligation to redistribute	-ve
Obligation to obey the state	+ve
Perceptions of rights	+ve
Voluntary activity	+ve
Trust in government	-ve
Interpersonal trust	+ve
Efficacy	+ve
Interest in politics	+ve
Discuss politics with friends	+ve
Media consumption of politics	+ve
Educational attainment	+ve
Marital status	-ve
Hours worked in average week	(-ve)
Religiosity	-ve
Age	+ve
Age squared	-ve
Gender	⊗

+ve means a higher score makes participation **more** likely
-ve means a higher score makes participation **less** likely
( ) means significant at 10% level, all others are significant at the 1% level, except gender and the Gini coefficient.
⊗ means no statistically significant association

To consider the social capital model first, a key indicator of this is voluntary activity. And indeed we find that this has a strong and positive effect on participation – it is in fact the variable with the biggest impact. If someone is a volunteer, then they are very likely to participate in politics as well. Another key indicator is interpersonal trust and this also turns out to have a positive impact on participation in the model. So the social capital model certainly has explanatory power. However, some of the relationships associated with the social capital model are surprising. The negative relationship with trust in government shows that mistrust of government helps to stimulate participation rather than the other way round. In one sense this is reassuring for democracy, since democratic accountability means that citizens should be willing to distrust the government to some extent.

The cognitive engagement model also plays a role. The second most important variable in the model is, in fact, discussion of politics, indicating that talking about politics and being active are closely related. Interest in politics, media consumption and educational attainment are all important predictors of participation, all of which would be predicted by the cognitive engagement model.

But even when these two models are taken into account, the obligation to participate and the obligation to redistribute both have a rather similar impact on participation except in opposite directions. Thus individuals who feel an obligation to participate will do so, whereas individuals who feel that government should redistribute are less likely to get involved. The obligation to obey the state has a positive impact on participation, but it is much weaker than the impact of the other obligation measures.[10]

The demographic measures show that being married, being religious and (possibly) long hours of work all inhibit participation while gender has no effect. Age has a positive impact but at a declining rate of importance as individuals get older.[11]

The aggregate- or country-level model appears at the top of the figure and the estimates confirm that a country's wealth has a positive impact on its citizens' willingness to get involved in politics. Thus individuals are more likely to participate in richer countries than they are in poorer countries, even when civic engagement and social capital variables are taken into account. So the results found in Tables 9.5 to 9.8 are not an artefact of ignoring additional variables in the analysis. The magnitude of the effect of wealth can be seen by means of a calculation. If we compare two countries, one with a GDP per capita $10,000 higher than the other, the political participation of the average citizen will be about 16 per cent higher in the former country than in the latter.

On the other hand, and contrary to our earlier findings, the multivariate analysis shows that inequality, as measured by the Gini coefficient, has no significant effect on individual participation once all the other variables are taken into account. While affluence has an independent effect in explaining political participation, inequality does not.

The aggregate level variables explain two-thirds of the aggregate variation in participation across these countries, which indicates how important economic factors are in understanding political participation.

Conclusions

Citizenship involves balancing the rights and obligations of the individual. This chapter shows that individuals across a wide variety of countries strongly support rights of various kinds, particularly the right to a minimum standard of living and the right to be treated equally. It also shows that rights are not out of balance with obligations, since there is widespread support for the rule of law and for taxation, and a majority of respondents feel that every citizen has a duty to vote. This is relatively reassuring for democracy.

A second important finding is that the norms and values associated with perceptions of rights and obligations contribute directly to promoting political participation, and this is fundamentally important to promoting democracy and a healthy civil society. Only one aspect of perceptions of obligations, which relates to redistribution, does not have a positive impact on participation. Aside from that, norms that citizens should obey the state and that they should get involved in politics support actual participation in these societies.

A third important finding is that the wealth of a country has a direct impact on the level of participation of its citizens; if people live in an affluent state this stimulates their participation. While inequality may influence particular forms of involvement, it does not influence overall participation.

To test the robustness of these findings we controlled for variables associated with the cognitive engagement and social capital models of political participation. These models do not, of course, exhaust the possible factors which explain participation, but they represent two important strands of theory which have been present in the literature for many years. One strand stresses the importance of individual decision making and the other the importance of socialisation processes in influencing the individual's participation. Our findings remain unchanged after controlling for these models.

The findings imply that as countries become more affluent and educated, participation is likely to grow more important. This does not, of course, mean that all types of participation will increase, and in fact there is good evidence to suggest that voting turnout has declined across the western world over recent decades (Wattenberg, 2000). But voluntary activity and consumer participation are likely to grow in importance as societies become richer. On the whole these findings suggest that civil society in these democracies is reasonably healthy and enough people are engaged to ensure that democracy will be sustained in the future.

Notes

1. See Appendix I in this *Report* for an explanation of the *International Social Survey Programme*.
2. The countries are: Australia, Austria, Brazil, Britain, Bulgaria, Canada, Chile, Cyprus, the Czech Republic, Denmark, Finland, France, Germany, Hungary, Ireland, Israel, Japan, Latvia, Mexico, the Netherlands, New Zealand, Norway, Philippines, Poland, Portugal, Russia, Slovakia, Slovenia, South Africa, South Korea, Spain, Sweden, Switzerland, Taiwan, the United States, Uruguay and Venezuela.
3. The answers were given as a seven-point scale where 1 was labelled "not at all important" and 7 was labelled "very important. The analysis in this chapter focuses on those respondents who assigned a 7 to the various rights and obligations.
4. The Gini coefficient is a measure of income inequality based on the Lorenz curve. It plots the relationship between the fraction of individuals found at different points of the income distribution and the fraction of total income they earn. An equal distribution of incomes is represented by a 45-degree straight line Lorenz curve. As the actual distribution of income in a country deviates from equality, so the Gini coefficient increases in value.

   The countries are classified as follows:

   GDP per capita ($1000s) – (source: World Bank). In Tables 9.5–9.8 high GDP per capita countries all had incomes above $25,000 per annum; medium GDP per capita countries had incomes above $10,000 and below $25,000, and low GDP per capita countries had incomes below $10,000 per annum.

   Low income countries were the Phillippines, Bulgaria, South Africa, Russia, Brazil, Latvia, Uruguay, Venezuela, Chile, Slovakia, Poland, Mexico, Hungary and the Czech Republic.

   Medium income countries were South Korea, Slovenia, Portugal, Cyprus, New Zealand, Israel, Spain, Australia, Canada, Germany and France.

   High income countries were Finland, Austria, the Netherlands, Britain, Sweden, Ireland, Japan, Denmark, the United States, Switzerland and Norway.

   Gini coefficient – (source: World Bank) In Tables 9.5–9.8 low inequality countries had Gini coefficients of 30 or less, medium inequality countries had a coefficient of between 31 and 38, and high inequality countries had a coefficient larger than 38.

   The low inequality countries are Hungary, Denmark, Japan, Sweden, the Czech Republic, Slovakia, Norway, Finland, Germany, Slovenia and Austria.

   The medium inequality countries were Poland, South Korea, Bulgaria, Latvia, Spain, the Netherlands, France, Canada, Switzerland, Australia, Israel, Ireland, Britain and New Zealand.

   The high inequality countries were Portugal, the United States, Uruguay, Russia, Philippines, Venezuela, Mexico, Chile, Brazil and South Africa.
5. The correlation between attitudes to the right to an adequate standard of living and GDP per capita is -0.31.
6. The correlation between the Gini coefficient and voting norms was +0.41 in the set of countries.

7. The correlation between GDP per capita and consumer participation is +0.75. The correlation between inequality and consumer participation is 0.49.
8. South Africa is omitted from this figure as the data for voluntary organisations for that country are missing.
9. The correlation between GDP per capita and volunteering was +0.62 and between the Gini coefficient and volunteering -0.22.
10. We are here making the key assumption that norms influence behaviour. It is, of course, possible that the relationship runs the other way round: actual contact with politics helps to foster a belief that such behaviour is correct, or there could be an interaction between the two. However, cross-sectional data of the type used in this analysis cannot be used to identify this type of two-way causation, so we shall assume that the predominant relationship is one of beliefs leading to behaviour.
11. Age is incorporated into the equation with a quadratic specification, that is, by including the age variable squared. The positive coefficient on the age variable means that age stimulates participation, while the negative coefficient on the age-squared variable means that this positive effect declines in importance as people get older.

References

Barnes, S. and Kaase, M. (1979), *Political Action*, London: Sage

Clarke, H.D., Sanders, D., Stewart, M. and Whiteley, P. (2004), *Political Choice in Britain*, Oxford: Oxford University Press

Coleman, J.S. (1990), *Foundations of Social Theory*, Cambridge, Massachusetts: The Belknap Press of Harvard University Press

Dalton, R.J. (2002), *Citizen Politics*, New York: Seven Bridges Press

Dalton, R.J. and Wattenberg, M.P. (eds.) (2000), *Parties without Partisans: Political Change in Advanced Industrial Democracies*, Oxford: Oxford University Press

Fukuyama, F. (1995), *Trust: The Social Virtues and the Creation of Prosperity*, London: Hamish Hamilton

Hox, J. (2002), *Multilevel Analysis*, Mahwah, NJ: Lawrence Erlbaum Associates

Inglehart, R.J. (1997), *Modernization and Postmodernization*, Princeton, NJ: Princeton University Press

Pattie, C., Seyd, P. and Whiteley, P. (2004), *Citizenship in Britain: Values, Participation and Democracy*, Cambridge: Cambridge University Press

Putnam, R.D. (1993), *Making Democracy Work: Civic Traditions in Modern Italy*, Princeton, NJ: Princeton University Press

Van Deth, J., Marraffi, M., Newton, K. and Whiteley, P. (eds.) (1999), *Social Capital and European Democracy*, London: Routledge

Verba, S., Schlozman, K.L. and Brady, H. (1995), *Voice and Equality: Civic Voluntarism in American Politics*, Cambridge, Massachusetts: Harvard University Press

Wattenberg, M.J. (2000), 'The Decline of Party Mobilisation', in Dalton, R.J. and Wattenberg, M.P. (eds.), *Parties without Partisans: Political Change in Advanced Industrial Democracies*, Oxford: Oxford University Press

Whiteley, P. (1999), 'The Origins of Social Capital', in Van Deth, J., Marraffi, M., Newton, K. and Whiteley, P. (eds.), *Social Capital and European Democracy*, London: Routledge

Acknowledgements

The *National Centre for Social Research* is grateful to the Economic and Social Research Council (grant number RES-501-25-5001) for their financial support which enabled us to ask the *International Social Survey Programme* questions reported in this chapter.

Appendix

The scaling and measurement of the variables

The results of the factor analysis for the rights, obligations and participation scales appear below. In each case the factor model was based on a principal components analysis and we show the varimax rotated factor loadings, together with the Eigenvalues and explained variances.

Tabel A.1 Items in rights scale

	Loadings
All citizens have an adequate standard of living	0.73
Government protects the rights of minorities	0.72
Government treats everyone equally regardless of their position in society	0.78
Politicians take into account the views of citizens before making decisions	0.78
People be given more opportunities to participate in public decision-making	0.70
Eigenvalue	2.75
Percentage of variance explained	55.0

Table A.2 Items in obligation scales

	Participation loadings	Obey state loadings	Redistribute loadings
Always to vote in elections	0.60		
To keep watch on the actions of government	0.71		
To be active in social or political associations	0.75		
To choose products for political, ethical or environmental reasons	0.61		
Never to try to evade taxes		0.82	
Always to obey laws and regulations		0.83	
To help people in your country who are worse off than yourself			0.84
To help people in the rest of the world who are worse off than yourself			0.88
Eigenvalue	1.89	1.69	1.66
Percentage of variance explained	23.6	21.1	20.8

Table A.3 Items in political participation scale

	Loadings
Signing a petition	0.67
Donating money or raised funds for a political or social activity	0.66
Boycotted or bought products for political or ethical reasons	0.68
Attended a political meeting or rally	0.68
Contacted a politician or official to express a view	0.72
Taken part in a demonstration	0.64
Contacted the media to express a view	0.70
Joined an internet political forum or discussion group	0.58
Eigenvalue	3.55
Percentage of variance explained	44.3

Table A.4 Items in voluntary activity scale

	Loadings
A political party	0.48
A trade union, business or professional association	0.59
A church or other religious organisation	0.54
A sports, leisure or cultural group	0.71
Another voluntary association	0.70
Eigenvalue	1.86
Percentage of variance explained	37.2

Multi-level regression model

The analysis is most efficiently done by using all of the indicators in the factor analyses to create scales which represent the various concepts in the models. Thus the dependent variable is the political participation scale constructed from the factor analysis discussed earlier and set out in the appendix. We are trying to explain variations in all of the different types of participation measures which appear in Table 9.3, since they all contribute to the political participation scale. Similarly all of the items in Table 9.1 contribute towards the rights scale, and the items identified in Table 9.2 contribute to the three obligations scales.

The independent variables are:

- **GNP per capita ($1000s)** – (source: World Bank)
- **Gini coefficient** – (source: World Bank)
- **Rights** – factor scores from variables listed in the items in rights scale table
- **Obligation to participate scale** – factor scores from variables listed in the items in obligation scales table
- **Obligation to redistribute** – factor scores from variables listed in the items in obligations scales table
- **Obligation to obey state** – factor scores variables listed in the items in obligations scales table
- **Voluntary activity scale** – factor scores from variables listed in the items in voluntary activity scale table
- **Trust in government** – sum of responses to two statements:
  'Most of the time we can trust people in government to do what is right'
  'Most politicians are in politics only for what they can get out of it personally'
  (coded so that a high score denotes high trust).

- **Intepersonal trust** – sum of responses to two statements:
  'How often do you think that people would try to take advantage of you if they got the chance and how often would they try to be fair?'
  'Generally speaking, would you say that people can be trusted or that you can't be too careful in dealing with people'
  (coded so that a high score denotes high levels of trust)
- **Efficacy scale** – sum of responses to three statements:
  'People like me don't have any say about what the government does'
  'I don't think the government cares much what people like me think'
  'I think most people in (Britain) are better informed about politics and government than I am'
  (coded so that a high score denotes high levels of efficacy).
- **Interest in politics** – responses to:
  'How interested would you say you personally are in politics'
  (coded so that a high score denotes high levels of interest).
- **Discuss politics** – responses to:
  'When you get together with your friends, relatives or fellow workers, how often do you discuss politics'
  (coded so that a high score denotes high levels of discussion).
- **Media consumption of politics** – sum of responses from Table 9.10
  (coded so that a high score denotes high levels of media consumption).
- **Educational attainment** – highest educational level achieved
- **Age**
- **Gender**
- **Marital status**
- **Hours worked in the average week**
- **Religiosity**

Note that all missing values in the multivariate models are recoded to their mean values to avoid sampling bias created by listwise deletion of missing values.

The coefficients are standardised so they vary from -1.0 to +1.0 and their magnitude indicates how important they are as predictors of participation.

Table A.5 The multivariate model of participation

Aggregate-level model	Coefficient
GNP per capita in 2002 ($10,000s)	0.10**
Gini coefficient	0.03
R-squared	0.67
Individual-level model	
Obligation to participate scale	0.08**
Obligation to redistribute scale	-0.09**
Obligation to obey the state scale	0.04**
Perceptions of rights	0.03**
Voluntary activity scale	0.32**
Trust in government	-0.02**
Interpersonal trust	0.04**
Efficacy scale	0.08**
Interest in politics	0.12**
Discuss politics with friends	0.15**
Media consumption of politics	0.10**
Educational attainment	0.10**
Marital status	-0.02**
Hours worked in average week	-0.01(*)
Religiosity	-0.03**
Age	0.07**
Age squared	-0.19**
Gender	0.00
R-squared	0.43

Standardised coefficients
** = significant at the 1% level
(*) = significant at the 10% level

10 The role of government: public values and party politics

Robert Johns and Stephen Padgett[*]

The last decade has seen shifts in the policy positions of the main British parties in relation to welfare, the role of government and the market economy. The polarisation of the 1980s has been superseded by progressive re-convergence, as New Labour accommodated some of Mrs Thatcher's liberal thinking, whilst Conservative leaders from Major to Cameron have renounced their predecessor's instinctive hostility to welfare. The parties now share a broad conception of a streamlined welfare state geared to cost-effectiveness, selective benefits (that is, with qualifying conditions) rather than universal ones, individual responsibility and incentives to exit welfare in favour of work. Labour has also retreated from old orthodoxies in relation to government intervention in the economy, whilst the Conservatives are less aggressively oriented towards the free market. At the same time, observers have noted changes in public opinion towards the welfare state. Labour partisans show less support for the redistribution of income and a greater readiness to accept incentives to reduce welfare dependency. For their part, Conservatives have become less averse to taxation to support welfare (Curtice and Fisher, 2003; Sefton, 2003; Taylor-Gooby, 2004). This chapter assesses whether there has been a deep-seated change in Britain's core ideological values, perhaps as a consequence of changes in party discourse, and examines how this has affected public opinion about welfare, government intervention and the market economy.

The distinction between values and opinions is rooted in a long-standing theoretical literature. Opinions are the preferences that people have in relation to specific issues, and may change with transient political circumstances. 'Core' beliefs or values are enduring and persistent orientations to general political principles. Since people have limited information with which to form opinions about complex issues, they can use values as shortcuts to simplify their choices (Feldman, 1988; Zaller, 1991, 1992; Alvarez and Brehm, 2002). Political issues are therefore reduced to opposing value orientations about government

---

[*] Robert Johns is Lecturer in Politics at Strathclyde University. Stephen Padgett is Professor of Politics at Strathclyde University.

intervention in the economy (Downs, 1957), or the desirability of equality (Rokeach, 1973). These values thus serve to constrain policy opinions, imparting a broad consistency across related issues. Consequently, people's opinions on issues such as income redistribution, the welfare state and tax have tended in the past to relate to one another in quite predictable ways (Heath *et al.*, 1991).

From this perspective, changing opinions about issues such as welfare may be explained by shifts in underlying core ideological values. We may simply be seeing a shift to the right, away from the values of equality and government intervention that informed support for the post-war welfare state. Alternatively, changing opinions may be indicative of a more general *decline* of left–right ideology and a corresponding weakening of the role that core ideological values play in shaping people's opinions.

This chapter begins by showing the trends in Labour and Conservative manifestos on welfare, government intervention and the market economy since 1983. We then examine trends in beliefs and values among the general public, using *British Social Attitudes* data. In so doing we aim to establish whether there is evidence of a shift to the right. We also assess whether there has been a decline in the *intensity* with which citizens adhere to values, in order to see whether there is any evidence of ideological weakening over time.

The chapter then examines the *internal* consistency of an individual's belief systems, in order to assess whether the constraining effects of core values have weakened over time. We also examine the relationship between values and political partisanship. Values, it has been argued, are formed by the socialising effects of society's institutions. In particular, citizens' values may depend on the articulation of values in the party system (Knutsen and Scarbrough, 1995). Political parties influence the way citizens perceive policy issues (McQuail and Windahl, 1981: 493–494), and serve as agents in transforming social conflict into political divisions (Przeworski and Sprague, 1986: 7–8; Bartolini and Mair, 1990; De Graaf *et al.*, 2001: 2–3). If party cues on particular political values diminish, we would expect ideological constraints on opinion to weaken, resulting in increasing fragmentation and inconsistency in public opinion.

Finally, the chapter investigates the relationship between the packaging of welfare issues in the party system and the trends that we have found in public opinion and in individual belief systems.

Party values: welfare, government and the market

In the introduction to this chapter, we suggested that the character of core values in a society, and their impact on citizens' opinions, may depend on the articulation of these values by political parties. So we begin by outlining the changing messages that the Labour and Conservative Parties have conveyed to voters since 1983. We use data from the Manifesto Research Group which has analysed and mapped UK election programmes over time using 56 policy categories (Budge *et al.*, 2001; Klingemann *et al.*, 2006). Whilst manifestos may not be the most effective way of communicating with voters, they provide a means of quantifying the message, and we assume that they are representative of other forms of discourse.

We begin by showing where parties are located on a summary left–right scale, and how this has changed over time. A party's position on the scale is calculated from its manifesto's emphasis on a basket of 13 policy positions associated with the right, and then subtracting the emphasis on a similar basket of policies associated with the left. Positive scores therefore indicate that a party is oriented towards the right; negative scores show an orientation to the left (Budge and Klingemann, 2001: 21). As we can see from Figure 10.1, the 1980s appear as a decade of unprecedented polarisation, with a gulf of 68 percentage points between the parties on the left–right scale. 1983 was the apotheosis of old Labour, with manifesto commitments to employment creation, economic intervention and welfare expansion. In sharp contrast, the Conservatives, at the height of the Thatcher era, emphasised a reduced role for the government in the economy, the expansion of property ownership and more incentives for individual achievement. By the end of the decade, however, the gap had begun to narrow, with the emergence – hesitant at first – of New Labour, and the gradual moderation of Thatcherite Conservatism. This trend gathered momentum in the 1990s, so that by 2001 the parties were separated by a mere nine percentage points on the left–right scale.

Figure 10.1 Party movements on left–right scale

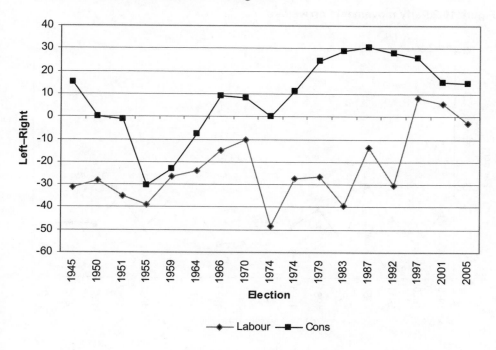

The pattern of convergence shows a striking asymmetry since the 1980s, with Labour conceding considerably more ground than the Conservatives. Labour made a 45-point shift to the right between 1983 and 2001, three times the Conservatives shift of 15 points in the opposite direction. Moreover, Labour has travelled further from its roots than its rival. The Conservative position in the early 21st century is on a par with where the party stood in 1945, whilst Labour occupy uncharted ideological territory.

Next we turn to the manifesto coverage of three specific policy categories: *government intervention* (economic planning, control and regulation); the *market economy* (free enterprise, economic orthodoxy and incentives); and *welfare* (welfare state expansion and social justice). This produces a more nuanced view of the dynamics of ideological convergence. Thus, convergence on the role of government in the economy is the result of *Labour* relinquishing its traditional interventionist position. Having occupied 12 per cent of Labour's 1983 manifesto, it hardly figured at all in 2001 and was negligible in 2005. A similar picture of retreat from core values is evident in the decline in *Conservative* emphasis on the market economy, from 18 per cent in 1987 to less than five per cent in 2001, with only a slight rebound in 2005.

However, the dynamics of convergence on welfare and social justice are quite different. Here, convergence is the result of both parties shifting position. Labour reduced its emphasis on welfare and social justice by around six per cent between 1983 and 2005, whilst the Conservatives increased their attention to these issues by a similar margin.

Figure 10.2 Party movements on welfare

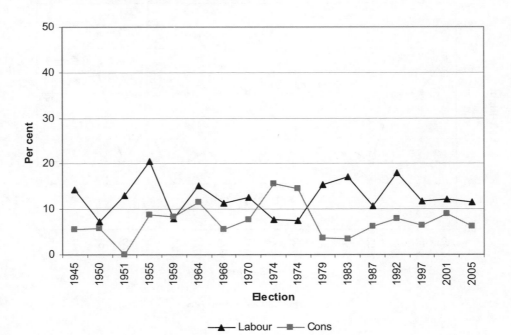

This analysis of party manifestos shows two contrasting dynamics of convergence. Government intervention and the market economy – once defining issues in left–right ideology – have disappeared from political discourse almost without trace. Welfare and social justice, on the other hand, retain a presence in political discourse, but are no longer the focus of partisan ideological conflict.

Ideological convergence between the main parties is not, of course, new. As we can see from Figure 10.1, it was the dominant trend of the 'Butskellite' consensus of the late 1950s and early 1960s. In this era, however, political values and behaviour were firmly rooted in the social structure. Without strong foundations in the class structure, it might be argued, citizens' values are more dependent on supportive party discourse. In the remainder of this chapter, we ask whether the waning of ideological differences in the party system is reflected in a weakening of core values in citizens' belief systems.

Values and public opinion

Earlier we suggested that citizens' opinions about the role of government and welfare are informed by underlying value orientations, and that the persistence of these core values may depend on their articulation in the party system. If this is the case, the previous discussion suggests we should expect to see two contrasting trends in public opinion – a decline in support for government intervention and the market economy, with support for welfare and social justice remaining more robust. So we turn now to examine whether the disappearing difference between New Labour and the Conservatives is reflected in a weakening of left–right and welfare values in British society, and if so, what the implications might be for public opinion.

Core values

We begin to answer this question by examining overall trends in left–right value orientations and welfare values. Value standpoints can only be observed indirectly, so we derive them from a set of relevant agree–disagree items designed to capture both left–right and welfare value dimensions (see Heath *et al.*, 1991). Left–right value orientations are captured by five questions relating to equality, income redistribution and class relations. People were asked how much they agreed or disagreed with the following statements:

> *Ordinary working people do not get their fair share of the nation's wealth*
>
> *There is one law for the rich and one for the poor*
>
> *Government should redistribute income from the better-off to those who are less well off*
>
> *Management will always try to get the better of employees if it gets the chance*
>
> *Big business benefits owners at the expense of workers*

BRITISH SOCIAL ATTITUDES

Table 10.1 shows the proportion of people who "agree" or "strongly agree" with the statements over the two decades from 1986 to 2006. It suggests a substantial proportion of people share a perception of social injustice in society and, by inference at least, have a positive orientation towards the core value of equality.[1] The most striking observation from Table 10.1 is the stability in left–right values between 1986 and 2002. On all five of these indicators, support is relatively stable, with little year-to-year fluctuation. Despite the reduced emphasis of New Labour on the principle of equality, perceptions of social injustice and support for income redistribution declined only marginally between the mid-1980s and 2002. Since then, however, there has been a steep plunge both in perceptions of social injustice and in support for income redistribution. We are left with the impression that this abrupt shift in popular beliefs may be a delayed reaction to the waning of equality in party discourse.

Table 10.1 Left–right values, 1986–2006

% agree	1986	1990	1994	1998	2002	2006
Ordinary people do not get fair share of wealth	66	65	n/a	64	63	55
One law for rich, one for poor	59	67	69	64	61	55
Management will always try to get better of employees if gets chance	52	61	63	60	60	52
Big business benefits owners at expense of workers	54	52	60	54	57	51
Government should redistribute income	43	49	51	39	39	34
Base	*1321*	*2430*	*2929*	*2531*	*2900*	*3748*

n/a = not asked

We investigate welfare values focusing on support for redistributive measures providing social security for the less well off rather than services like health-care which confer benefits more widely and might attract self-interested support. We captured welfare values by using a set of six agree–disagree items designed for this purpose:

The welfare state encourages people to stop helping each other

The government should spend more money on welfare benefits for the poor, even if it leads to higher taxes

Around here, most unemployed people could find a job if they really wanted one

Many people who get social security don't really deserve any help

Most people on the dole are fiddling in one way or another

If welfare benefits weren't so generous, people would learn to stand on their own two feet

Table 10.2 shows a steep decline in support for welfare values. Over the last two decades, people have become less supportive of benefits for the poor, less sympathetic to welfare recipients and more critical of welfare dependency. The timing of the decline in support for welfare values, however, differs from that of the decline in support for the core values of the left. Whilst support for core left values held up relatively well until 2002, the decline in core welfare values set in some time previously, in the 1990s. This finding accords with those of Curtice and Fisher (2003), who found a steep decline in support for welfare occurring around the time Labour came to power in 1997. Welfare values, it may be concluded, are less resilient than left–right values, and perhaps are more dependent on supportive cues from party discourse.

Table 10.2 Welfare values, 1987–2006

	1987	1991	1995	1999	2002	2006
% disagree						
Welfare state encourages people to stop helping each other	37	42	35	31	30	29
Most unemployed people could find a job if they wanted	42	41	38	20	15	11
Many people who get social security don't deserve help	45	47	43	40	31	32
Most people on dole are fiddling	39	39	37	28	28	29
If welfare benefits weren't so generous people would learn to stand on own two feet	45	50	44	34	30	25
% agree						
Government should spend more on welfare benefits	55	58	50	40	44	35
Base	*1281*	*2481*	*3135*	*2450*	*2900*	*3748*

Policy opinions

How do these core left–right orientations and welfare values relate to public opinion about specific socio-economic issues? We address this by examining responses to a number of questions about policy issues that traditionally divide left and right. We begin with the following questions, which require respondents to cast judgement on a number of 'traditional' left-wing policy matters:

> *On the whole do you think it should or should not be the government's responsibility to provide a job for everyone who wants one?*
>
> *[Definitely should be/Probably should be/Probably should not be/ Definitely should not be]*
>
> *Please show whether you would like to see <u>more</u> or <u>less</u> government spending [...]. Remember that if you say "much more", it might require a tax increase to pay for it ... Unemployment benefits*
>
> *[Spend much more/Spend more/Spend the same as now/Spend less/ Spend much less]*
>
> *Here are some things the government might do for the economy. Please show which actions you are in favour of and which you are against ... Support for declining industries to protect jobs*
>
> *[Strongly in favour of/In favour of/Neither in favour of nor against/ Against/Strongly against]*

Is the decline in the core values of the left that we saw in the previous section of the chapter reflected in a shift in opinion on specific policy issues? There is some evidence of a linkage between values and opinions.

Table 10.3 Policy opinions on 'core left' issues, 1985–2006

	1985	1990	1996	2002	2006
% agree government responsibility to provide jobs	68	60	65	71	52
% in favour of more government spending on unemployment benefits	40	36	33	n/a	16
% in favour of government support for declining industries to protect jobs	48	59	62	n/a	57
Base	*1530*	*1197–2430*	*989–3085*	*1911*	*932*

n/a = not asked

The first two lines in the previous table relate to government responsibility for employment and social security. On the one hand, the downward trend in the perception that government should be responsible for jobs dates from 2002, coinciding with the decline in core left values. Meanwhile, the longer-term decline in support for increased government spending on unemployment benefits coincides with the erosion of support for welfare values. On the other hand, the third line shows no attrition at all in support for government intervention to help declining industries. So, despite the erosion of core left values, and notwithstanding New Labour's retreat from interventionism since 1983, popular support for intervention to support declining industries to protect jobs is as strong at the turn of the millennium as it was in 1990.

We turn now to see whether there is any evidence of a shift to the right in policy opinions. To address this, we asked respondents for their views on two key right-wing policy areas:

> *Here are some things the government might do for the economy. Please show which actions you are in favour of and which you are against ... Less government regulation of business*
>
> *[Strongly in favour of/In favour of/Neither in favour of nor against/ Against/Strongly against]*
>
> *Private enterprise is the best way to solve Britain's economic problems*
>
> *[Strongly agree/Agree/Neither agree nor disagree/Disagree/Strongly disagree]*

Even at its height in 1986, support for private enterprise as the answer to Britain's economic problems fell short of a majority (Table 10.4). Thereafter, it declined steeply until 1996, recovering only marginally in the 2000s. The trend corresponds closely with the decline in Conservative Party emphasis on the market economy observed earlier in the chapter.

Table 10.4 Policy opinions on 'core right' issues, 1985–2006

	1985 (1986)	1990 (1991)	1996	2001	2005 (2006)
% in favour of less government regulation of business	53	42	40	n/a	(40)
% agree private enterprise best way to solve economic problems	(44)	(35)	24	29[+]	28[+]
Base	*1316–1530*	*1197–2702*	*989–3085*	*1947*	*932–3190*

n/a = not asked
[+]Data from British Election Study, 2001/2005

Support for the de-regulation of business is somewhat more stable, but follows a similar trend. Overall we can conclude that the decline in support for the core values of the left has *not* been accompanied by an attitudinal shift in favour of the market economy and private enterprise.

At the aggregate level, then, our results are not inconsistent with the view that core values 'frame' the way people see issues. Shifting opinions towards government responsibility for jobs and the jobless, social security and its recipients may be taken to reflect the weakening of the core values of the left, and this may be attributable to New Labour's retreat from traditional values. Before drawing any firm conclusions, however, about the linkage between values and opinions we need to investigate the relationship at the individual level, and it is to this that we now turn.

The coherence of individual belief systems

In this section we build up measures of an individual's core values, and explore trends in the internal consistency of these values. In so doing, we use the indicators of left–right and welfare values described earlier in relation to Tables 10.1 and 10.2. This time, however, we are interested in respondents' overall scores across all the questions that make up the value scale. Responses to each statement are scored from 1 (the most left-wing/pro-welfare position) to 5 (the most right-wing/anti-welfare position). We derive respondents' overall positions on each dimension by summing their scores and dividing by the number of items answered, such that the overall value positions range along the same 1 to 5 scale.[2] Further details about these value scales and their scoring can be found in Appendix I of this Report.

The first two columns in Table 10.5 show the overall scores for our two value dimensions, and how these have changed over time. These summary measures reproduce the patterns that we saw with individual items in Table 10.1. With the left–right scale, there is relative stability between 1987 and 2002, followed by a noticeable shift to the right since 2002. However, since scores can vary between 1 and 5, the 2006 average of 2.66 is still somewhat to the left of the theoretical central value of 3. Meanwhile, on the welfare scale there has been an earlier and more pronounced shift away from welfarist values, leaving the 2006 mean of 3.17 slightly to the right of the centre

The third and fourth columns provide a measure of the internal consistency of each value dimension by showing its mean inter-item correlation. Details of this correlation can be found in the appendix to this chapter but, for now, it will suffice to say that the higher this figure the greater the degree of internal consistency. These data show some evidence of a decline in the internal consistency of left–right values. So changes in government policy and party discourse appear to have led to a slight weakening in the coherence of left–right thinking in the electorate. In contrast, there is only limited and apparently trendless fluctuation in the internal consistency of welfarist values (which from the outset hung together less closely than left–right item responses). One possible explanation for this difference is that welfarist values have never been as prominent in public discourse as left–right arguments, and so have been less affected by changes in that context.

Table 10.5 Left–right and welfarist value scores, and internal consistency, 1987–2006

	Average score		Mean inter-item correlation		Bases	
	Left–right	Welfarist	Left–right	Welfarist	*Left–right*	*Welfarist*
1987	2.50	2.85	0.57	0.37	*2392*	*1239*
1991	2.52	2.75	0.43	0.39	*2586*	*2397*
1995	2.50	3.10	0.52	0.41	*3083*	*3081*
1999	2.56	3.08	0.49	0.35	*2434*	*2436*
2002	2.50	3.12	0.50	0.35	*2858*	*2872*
2006	2.66	3.17	0.47	0.35	*3720*	*2805*
Difference 1987–2006	+0.16	+0.32	-0.10	-0.02		

Table 10.6 provides two additional time-series of relevance to our task. The first two columns show the standard deviation of scores on each value dimension, which indicates the dispersion of respondents along the scale. This allows us to gauge whether respondents have, like the parties, tended to converge on the centre-ground. These columns show a discernible decline in the standard deviation of scores on both value dimensions. This does not necessarily imply a convergence on some putative centre-ground: as we saw earlier the mean score on left–right remains towards the left-wing pole of the dimension, while the mean welfarism score is now slightly to the right. Here the point is simply that the average respondent has moved towards those mean scores; put another way, fewer respondents are now very left- or right-wing, and fewer are very pro- or anti-welfare. These trends are clearly in line with developments in the party system and the role of ideology therein.

The final column in the table provides the correlation between left–right and welfarism value scores. This indicates how closely left–right and welfarist values are linked together in empirical practice. Despite the clear theoretical links between left–right and welfarism values, these are unlikely to hang together in respondents' belief systems unless socialising agents – especially political parties – articulate those links. In the mid-1980s, there was a moderate correlation between scores on the two value scales; by the mid-2000s, knowing a respondent's left–right position had become of negligible use in predicting her welfarism score, and *vice versa*. Our earlier evidence from party manifestos provides a plausible explanation: the parties are no longer providing ideological cues linking the two dimensions.

Table 10.6 Internal consistency of left–right and welfarist values, 1987–2006

	Standard deviation of value scores					
	Left–right	Base	Welfarist	Base	Correlation of left–right and welfarism	Base
1987	0.87	2392	0.77	1239	0.25	1234
1991	0.73	2586	0.75	2397	0.18	2373
1995	0.78	3083	0.76	3081	0.20	3068
1999	0.76	2434	0.67	2436	0.14	2429
2002	0.77	2858	0.68	2872	0.11	2849
2006	0.74	3720	0.62	2805	0.10	2800
Difference 1987–2006	-0.13		-0.15		-0.15	

Value constraints on individual opinions

Having considered the internal consistency of people's values, we now look at the extent to which these values constrain their policy opinions on issues such as welfare, government and the market. Evidence of declining constraint would tally with the evidence presented thus far, which has suggested that rather fewer respondents now than in the past have clear and cohesive left–right or welfarist ideological positions. To test this hypothesis, we draw on a wide variety of questions from the *International Social Survey Programme* (*ISSP*) 'Role of Government' module (more details about ISSP can be found in Appendix I of this Report). These questions were included in the *British Social Attitudes* questionnaire in 1990, 1996 and 2006, years which provide reasonably full coverage of the period under study here. The method used to gauge constraint is simple: we correlate people's value scores with their responses to a number of questions about the role and responsibilities of government. Table 10.7 reports the results.

There is quite a lot of information in the table, which can obscure trends rather, so we include rows showing the average correlation for each set of questions in a given year and each core value. Two key messages stand out. Firstly, with a few exceptions, the correlation between values and policy opinions is not very strong, suggesting that values do not exert a particularly powerful constraining influence over policy opinions.[3] Second, the main story is one of declining constraint. The differences are minimal between 1990 and 1996, but more marked between 1996 and 2006. This is partly, perhaps, because the latter is a longer time period, but also probably because, as we observed earlier, that period saw the most noticeable ideological convergence in the British party system.

Table 10.7 Correlations between value positions and policy opinions, 1990, 1996 and 2006 [4]

	Left–right			Welfarism		
	1990	**1996**	**2006**	**1990**	**1996**	**2006**
Government responsibility …						
… to provide a job for everyone who wants one	0.47	0.40	0.28	0.21	0.15	0.05
… to reduce income differentials	0.52	0.60	0.50	0.26	0.24	0.18
… to improve the standard of living of the unemployed	0.39	0.31	0.28	0.46	0.47	0.42
Average	0.46	0.44	0.35	0.31	0.29	0.22
Government should spend more …						
… on old-age pensions	0.32	0.33	0.20	0.13	0.11	0.05
… on unemployment benefits	0.36	0.30	0.23	0.50	0.54	0.53
Average	0.34	0.32	0.22	0.32	0.33	0.29
Support for government to …						
… cut spending	0.00	0.01	0.08	n/a	0.20	0.17
… create jobs	0.16	0.23	0.18	n/a	0.16	0.19
… cut regulation on business	0.14	0.11	0.07	n/a	0.13	0.13
… support declining industry	0.35	0.35	0.23	n/a	0.07	0.02
Average	0.22	0.23	0.16		0.12	0.11

n/a = not asked

Core values and partisanship

In this section we explore the relationship between core values and partisanship. This latter variable can be defined in attitudinal terms, as party identification, or in behavioural terms, as vote choice in an election. We consider both of these in turn. However, before reporting our results, we should make some comment about causal direction in the relationship between values and partisanship. Some voters will derive their partisanship from their values: that is, they support a party because it shares their core beliefs. Others may adopt the values articulated by their chosen party. Initially, we remain agnostic about causality, and simply report the bivariate relationship between values and party identification. Later, when analysing voting behaviour, we take party choice as the dependent variable, and measure the impact of value orientations on it independent of a range of control variables.

To begin with we use the first part of the standard *British Social Attitudes* party identification question, which is included in every survey and therefore lends itself to this kind of time-series. People are asked "*Do you think of yourself as a supporter of a particular political party?*" Those answering "yes" are then asked "*Which party is that?*"[5] The first data column of Table 10.8 contains the percentages of respondents in each year who define themselves as a party supporter. We then separate those respondents reporting Conservative or Labour support, and measure their mean scores on the two value scales outlined in the previous section. We also report the party differentials in these mean scores.

Table 10.8 Mean value scores on left–right and welfarism scales among Conservative and Labour supporters, 1987–2006 [6]

	% identifiers	Left–right			Welfarism		
		Con	Lab	diff.	Con	Lab	diff.
1987	49	3.18	1.82	1.36	3.24	2.31	0.93
1991	47	3.06	2.09	0.97	3.14	2.36	0.78
1995	43	3.00	1.95	1.05	3.26	2.58	0.68
1999	39	3.04	2.21	0.83	3.34	2.88	0.46
2002	36	3.06	2.18	0.88	3.35	2.97	0.38
2006	34	3.08	2.38	0.70	3.38	2.97	0.41
Difference 1987–2006	-15	-0.10	+0.56	-0.66	+0.14	+0.66	-0.52

A number of patterns of change are clear in Table 10.8. First, the gap between Labour and Conservative supporters on both value dimensions has narrowed appreciably. Second, this narrowing is driven largely by Labour identifiers: they have shifted towards the centre, while Conservative identifiers have remained fairly static. This asymmetry matches the trends in manifesto data reported earlier, with convergence in party discourse being the result mainly of Labour shifting their ideological ground. Third, while on left–right values Conservative supporters have shifted a little towards the centre, on welfarism they have moved slightly in the opposite direction. Here, then, convergence is the result entirely of a particularly pronounced anti-welfarist shift among Labour identifiers. This again tallies with the manifesto data, which showed both parties talking less about left–right issues, but the Conservatives actually saying more about those welfare issues that Labour was seeking to downplay. Conceivably, the Conservative Party's more positive outlook on welfare has held its supporters closer to the centre-ground than might otherwise have been the case.

We cannot determine whether these shifts are the result of parties following their identifiers or *vice versa*. However, it is notable that these changes occurred over a period during which the proportion of party supporters among the public fell, from around a half to a third of people. Sanders (1999) shows that a party's core supporters tend to be more ideologically extreme than its residual sympathisers. Other things remaining the same, then, we would expect a marked decline in the number of supporters to be accompanied by ideological *polarisation* of supporters. The fact that convergence is observed even among a dwindling band of diehard partisans makes the trend still more striking.

With both voters and parties converging on the centre-ground, the *potential* for core values to influence voting behaviour is reduced. We cannot, however, conclude that the *actual* influence of values has weakened without investigating whether, at the beginning of our time period, that potential for influence was realised. Next, then, we report two analyses estimating the impact of left–right and welfarist values on party choice at the two elections at either end of our time period, 1987 and 2005.[7] These are logistic regression analyses, which allow us to identify those factors that best predict whether a respondent voted for Labour or the Conservatives in those elections. A brief explanation of the logistic regression method, and the full results from those analyses, are included in the appendix to this chapter.

To identify the effect of core values, we need to take account of (or 'control for') those variables that might influence core values *and* vote choice. For example, working-class voters may be more likely to be left-wing and pro-welfare, and are also more likely to vote Labour. In that case, part of the apparent relationship between values and vote reflects a link between values and social class. By using logistic regression to control for class, and other such causally prior variables, we can estimate the independent impact of values on party choice. Here, we control for the following variables: age, sex, ethnicity, region, newspaper readership, housing tenure, subjective social class and trade union membership. The results show that, even controlling for all these other variables, both left–right and welfarist values had a significant impact on vote choice in both elections. However, there are important differences between the two types of value and the two elections. These are best illustrated in two graphs.

The lines in each graph in Figure 10.3 show the increasing probability of voting Conservative among respondents as they move closer to the right-wing and anti-welfarist poles of those value dimensions. For example, in 1987, the probability of someone who scored 1 on the left–right scale (the most left-wing score possible) voting Conservative was around 0.1, indicating – not surprisingly – a very low likelihood. Conversely, someone with a left–right score of 5 (the most right-wing score possible) was 1.0, indicating a near certainty that this person would vote Conservative.

In each graph, the line for 1987 has a noticeably steeper slope than the line for 2005, indicating that values were a more powerful predictor in the earlier election year. This result tallies with the earlier findings presented in this chapter. For example, in 1987 the probability of a person with a score of 3 on the left–right scale voting Conservative was around 0.8; in 2005 it was under 0.5.

Comparing across the graphs shows that the slopes are somewhat steeper in the left–right graph, which indicates that those values exert rather more influence over vote choice than welfarism. However, that difference seems to have narrowed over time. This too is in line with earlier findings that partisan ideological conflict was always based more on the left–right dimension, and that convergence on those values has been the most prominent change over the period studied here.

Figure 10.3 Probability of voting Conservative versus Labour by value scores, 1987 and 2005: a) left–right; b) welfarism

Figure 10.3a Left–right

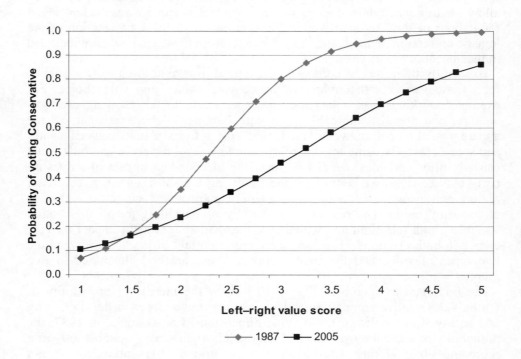

Figure 10.3b Welfarism

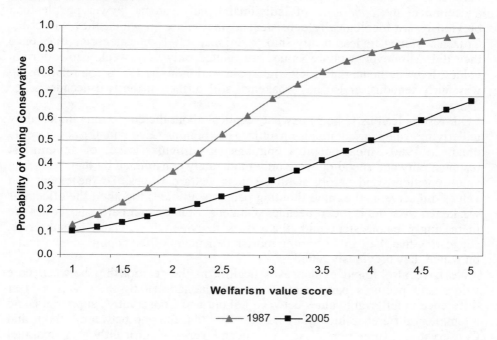

Conclusions

The purpose of this chapter was to establish whether changes in public opinion about the role of government and the welfare state reflect more deep-seated changes in core values in British society. We suggested that changing opinions might simply reflect a rightward shift in ideological values, or they might be indicative of a more general relaxation of the constraints that values impose on opinions. Such a weakening in the relationship between values and opinions, we suggested, might be attributable to changes in party discourse, and the way that the main parties 'package' the issues.

Aggregate data shows declining support for social justice, equality and welfare – the core values of the left – and a corresponding shift in opinions about government responsibility for employment, and support for the unemployed. Decline has not, however, been uniform. The erosion of support for welfare values dates from the early 1990s, whereas most of the attrition in support for egalitarian values has occurred in the last five years. Nor is the decline in support for the values of the left matched by an increase in support for the values associated with the right. Endorsement of private enterprise and support for the de-regulation of business declined for a decade from 1986, and although it stabilised thereafter it showed no signs of significant recovery. Rather than suggesting a value shift from left to right, the evidence suggests a general decline in attachment to core ideological values.

Parallel to the erosion of aggregate support for core left–right values, we found a decline in the *coherence* of individual belief systems. Fewer people than previously are ideologically consistent in the values to which they subscribe. Citizens' values fit less neatly into traditional left–right categories than once they did. Moreover, welfare values are related only very weakly to left–right values. Even at the height of left–right polarisation in the 1980s, the relationship was fairly tenuous, and it has weakened still further in the two decades since then.

Our results lead us to be somewhat sceptical about the constraints imposed by underlying value orientations on citizens' opinions. Even in the supposedly polarised 1980s, most people's opinions on particular issues of government responsibility and spending were only moderately constrained by their left–right value positions, and hardly at all by their welfare values. To the extent that values did serve as the 'glue' holding people's attitudes together, the effect has weakened over the last two decades. Citizens' opinions on particular issues are increasingly inconsistent with the values to which they claim to subscribe, suggesting that they are becoming more independent of the cognitive 'shortcuts' on which they previously relied.

We have also found evidence of decline in the relationship between core values and people's party preferences. In the late 1980s there was a clear difference in left–right values between Labour and Conservative supporters, and a (smaller) difference in welfare values. By 2006 the gap between Labour and Conservative supporters had narrowed very significantly. A parallel development is the weakening influence of left–right values on voting behaviour. In 2005, a person's values were a significantly less powerful predictor of whether they would vote Labour or Conservative than they were in 1987.

What evidence is there to suggest that the changes in the structure of the public's belief systems are related to changes taking place in party discourse? Most of the evidence, it has to be said, comes from the observation of parallel trends in values and opinions, on the one hand, and party discourse. on the other. Thus, the decline in support for the core values of the left coincides closely with New Labour's retreat from traditional discourse. Similarly, the decline in the constraints imposed by left–right values on citizens' opinions on particular issues coincides with the ideological convergence in party discourse. Causal relations, however, can only be inferred from the chronological coincidence of trends and are difficult to verify empirically.

Shifts in the left–right value orientations of Labour and Conservative partisans also fit closely with the *direction* of change in party discourse. Programmatic convergence between the parties was largely the result of Labour's shift to the right. Similarly, convergence in the left–right value orientation of party supporters was the result of Labour partisans shifting to the right whilst the values of Conservative supporters remained largely unchanged. Once again, however, causality is difficult to verify. We are not able to determine whether these parallels are the result of partisans following their parties or *vice versa*.

It is also important to note that the changes we have found could reflect wider social developments than party discourse alone. Perhaps, with the spread of education and the proliferation of the media, citizens may be acquiring the cognitive resources to form opinions independently of underlying value orientations.

Why does it matter if people's attachment to core values is declining, if their values are becoming less consistent and imposing weaker constraints on their opinions? It matters, first, because of the effect it has on relations between voters and parties. Core values play an important role in voter–party allegiances, and have been a key instrument in party strategies for mobilising voters. Citizens with weak attachments to values and highly differentiated palates of opinions become increasingly difficult to satisfy. Parties have to pay more attention to designing mixed policy packages, and in so doing they lose their distinctive character. A perception that there is no difference between the parties is one of the main drivers of voter alienation from, or apathy towards, political parties. A second reason why core values matter is that they also serve to orientate public policy, helping to define policy problems, prescribing solutions and providing standards against which policies are evaluated. In short, values help to organise democracy, and any weakening in their popular currency undermines the democratic process. We have seen how electoral competition drives parties to renounce traditional left–right values, and have provided some evidence that this has contributed to the weakening of values in the electorate. As Labour and the Conservatives gear-up for the post-Blair era, a central question will be whether they can reconstitute core values to reconnect with their voters and orientate public policy.

Notes

1. Table 10.1 also shows that the endorsement of the principle of equality does not translate directly into support for the redistribution of income, as shown by the comparatively low proportion of people who agree with the statement "government should redistribute income from the better-off to those who are less well off". There is a wide and consistent gap between recognising injustice and inequality in British society and endorsing measures to tackle it. However, the *trend* in support for income redistribution between 1986 and 2006 runs strikingly parallel to the decline in support for the *values* of equality. There is no sign of this relationship weakening over time. Indeed, statistical analysis shows that the relationship is stronger between 1996 and 2006 than it was in the previous decade.
2. To be assigned an overall value position, respondents have to answer three or more of the items from that list; otherwise their value positions are coded as missing.
3. It is notable that the few very strong correlations involve policy items that are more or less identical to items included in the value batteries – for example, a person's score on the welfare scale (which includes statements about unemployment benefits) and their beliefs about whether government should be responsible for improving the standard of living of the unemployed.

4. Bases for Table 10.7 are as follows:

Government responsibility ...	Left–right			Welfarism		
	1990	1996	2006	1990	1996	2006
... to provide a job for everyone who wants one	1137	922	849	1131	922	849
... to reduce income differentials	1133	902	856	1125	902	856
... to improve the standard of living of the unemployed	1184	909	831	1177	909	832
Government should spend more ...						
... on old-age pensions	1186	950	883	1192	951	884
... on unemployment benefits	1151	915	849	1157	915	850
Support for government to ...						
... cut spending	1159	933	845	n/a	934	845
... create jobs	1168	947	867	n/a	947	868
... cut regulation on business	1156	933	809	n/a	934	809
... support declining industry	1172	945	860	n/a	946	861

n/a = not asked

5. This differs importantly from the traditional British Election Study question, which presumes an identification in asking "Generally speaking, do you think of yourself as Conservative, Labour, Liberal (Democrat), or what?" Not surprisingly, the *British Social Attitudes* approach yields much higher reported non-identification than the BES question.
6. Bases for Table 10.8 are as follows:

	% identifiers	Left–right		Welfarism	
		Con	Lab	Con	Lab
1987	1401	609	391	315	190
1991	1410	605	482	571	433
1995	1593	474	696	475	698
1999	1236	330	485	330	484
2002	1254	359	529	363	532
2006	1498	494	575	384	416

7. The left–right and welfarist value batteries are not available for the 1983 election.

References

Alvarez, R.M. and Brehm, J. (2002), *Hard Choices, Easy Answers: Values, Information and American Public Opinion*, Princeton, NJ: Princeton University Press

Bartolini, S. and Mair, P. (1990), *Identity, Competition, and Electoral Availability: The Stability of European Electorates, 1885–1985*, Cambridge: Cambridge University Press

Budge, I. and Klingemann, H-D. (2001), 'Finally! Comparative Over-Time Mapping of Party Policy Movement', in Budge, I., Klingemann, H-D., Volkens, A., Bara, J. and Tanenbaum, E., *Mapping Policy Preferences, Estimates for Parties, Electors and Governments 1945–1998*, Oxford: Oxford University Press

Budge, I., Klingemann, H-D., Volkens, A., Bara, J. and Tanenbaum, E. (2001), *Mapping Policy Preferences, Estimates for Parties, Electors and Governments 1945–1998*, Oxford: Oxford University Press

Curtice, J and Fisher, S. (2003), 'The power to persuade? A tale of two Prime Ministers', in Park, A., Curtice, J., Thomson, K., Jarvis, L. and Bromley, C. (eds.), *British Social Attitudes: the 20th Report – Continuity and change over two decades*, London: Sage

De Graaf, N.D, Heath, A. and Need, A (2001), 'Declining Cleavages and Political Choices: the interplay of social and political factors in the Netherlands,' *Electoral Studies*, **20**: 1-15

Downs, A. (1957), *An Economic Theory of Democracy*, New York: Harper and Row

Feldman, S. (1988), 'Structure and Consistency in Public Opinion: the Role of Core Beliefs and Values', *American Journal of Political Science*, **32**: 416-440

Heath, A., Evans, G., Lalljee, M., Martin, J. and Witherspoon, S. (1991), *The Measurement of Core Beliefs and Values*, CREST Working Paper, No. 2

Klingemann, H-D. Volkens, A., Bara, J., Budge, I. and McDonald, M. (2006), *Mapping Policy Preferences II; Estimates for Parties, Electors and Governments in Central and Eastern Europe, European Union and OECD 1990–2003*, Oxford: Oxford University Press

Knutsen, O. and Scarbrough, E. (1995), 'Cleavage Politics', in van Deth, J. and Scarbrough, E., *The Impact of Values*, Oxford: Oxford University Press

McQuail, D. and Windahl, S. (1981), *Communication Models for the Study of Mass Communication*, London: Longman

Przeworski, A. and Sprague, J. (1986), *Paper Stones: a History of Electoral Socialism*, Chicago: University of Chicago Press

Rokeach, M. (1973), *The Nature of Human Values*, New York: Free Press

Sanders, D. (1999), 'The impact of left–right ideology', in Evans, G. and Norris, P. (eds.), *Critical Elections: British Parties and Voters in Long-Term Perspective*, London: Sage

Sefton, T. (2003), 'What we want from the welfare state', in Park, A., Curtice, J., Thomson, K., Jarvis, L. and Bromley, C. (eds.), *British Social Attitudes: the 20th Report – Continuity and change over two decades*, London: Sage

Taylor-Gooby, P. (2004), 'The work-centred welfare state', in Park, A., Curtice, J., Thomson, K., Bromley, C. and Phillips, M. (eds.), *British Social Attitudes: the 21st Report*, London: Sage

Zaller, J. (1991), 'Information, Values and Opinions', *American Political Science Review*, **85**: 1215–1237

Zaller, J. (1992), *The Nature and Origins of Mass Opinion*, Princeton, NJ: Princeton University Press

Acknowledgements

The *National Centre for Social Research* is grateful to the Economic and Social Research Council for their financial support (grant number RES-501-25-5001) which enabled us to ask the *International Social Survey Programme* questions reported in this chapter. We are also grateful to the Department for Work and Pensions for their financial support which enabled us to ask some of the questions reported in this chapter. Responsibility for the analysis of these data lies solely with the authors.

Appendix

The inter-item correlation is a summary measure of the extent to which attitudes indicative of that core value tend to hang together. Alpha, probably the most commonly used coefficient of internal consistency, is based on the mean inter-item correlation, but is also a function of the number of items in the scale. Since our left–right and welfarism batteries are of uneven length, alpha is not directly comparable, whereas the mean inter-item correlation is.

The multivariate analysis technique used is logistic regression, about which more details can be found in Appendix I of this Report. The tables below report the logistic coefficients (Bs), their standard errors, Wald statistics testing that the coefficients are significantly different from zero, and the exponents of the logistic coefficients, which are the odds ratios. (For example, the odds of voting Conservative are 2.29 times greater among those reading Conservative tabloids, other things remaining the same.)

Table A.1 Voted Conservative rather than Labour in 1987 election

	Coefficient	Standard error	Wald statistic	Odds ratio
Region				
South	.073	.285	.066	1.076
Midlands	-.252	.301	.702	.777
North	-.865	.279	9.654	.421
Scotland	-.388	.371	1.093	.678
Wales	-1.457	.409	12.715	.233
Newspaper readership				
Labour tabloid	-.893	.215	17.264	.410
Conservative tabloid	.829	.177	21.848	2.291
Labour broadsheet	-.560	.323	3.003	.571
Conservative broadsheet	1.452	.403	12.950	4.271
Ethnicity	2.026	.418	23.479	7.582
Home owner	.863	.164	27.667	2.370
Trade union member	-.362	.157	5.326	.696
Social class				
Middle class	-.092	.223	.169	.912
Working class	-.673	.163	17.045	.510
Sex	-.323	.153	4.433	.724
Age	.001	.004	.017	1.001
Left–right value scale	2.011	.126	254.991	7.468
Welfare value scale	1.325	.102	168.412	3.763
N	2110			
R^2	0.73			

Table A.2 Voted Conservative rather than Labour in 2005 election

	Coefficient	Standard error	Wald statistic	Odds ratio
Region				
South	.442	.289	2.336	1.556
Midlands	.317	.311	1.044	1.374
North	-.336	.298	1.271	.715
Scotland	-.474	.387	1.504	.622
Wales	-.939	.414	5.157	.391
Newspaper readership				
Labour tabloid	-1.625	.392	17.148	.197
Conservative tabloid	.869	.158	30.367	2.384
Labour broadsheet	-1.248	.667	3.500	.287
Conservative broadsheet	1.127	.251	20.137	3.085
Ethnicity	1.101	.321	11.738	3.007
Home owner	.950	.193	24.370	2.587
Trade union member	-.344	.144	5.702	.709
Social class				
Middle class	.418	.274	2.336	1.519
Working class	-.952	.323	8.704	.386
Sex	-.180	.142	1.604	.836
Age	.019	.004	18.984	1.019
Left–right value scale	1.030	.107	93.074	2.800
Welfare value scale	.757	.113	45.213	2.132
N	1327			
R^2	0.44			

11 Trends in sympathy for the poor

*Peter Taylor-Gooby and Rose Martin**

In March 1999, Prime Minister Tony Blair pledged to halve child poverty by 2010 and eradicate it by 2020 (Townsend and Kennedy, 2004). These targets are ambitious; poverty in the United Kingdom increased rapidly during the 1980s and early 1990s to the highest level in western Europe. It has since fallen, but not fast enough to meet the targets, and more strenuous policies, involving more public spending, will be required if they are to be achieved (Centre for Economic Performance, 2007; Sharma and Hirsch, 2007). While the trend to rising inequalities in income of the 1980s and 1990s has slowed, inequality (as measured by the Gini coefficient) "has fluctuated slightly since 1994/95, but has shown evidence of a marginal rise … since 2004/05", according to official data (Department for Work and Pensions, 2007: 6). One long term study, which uses a broader definition of inequality, concludes that "Britain is moving back towards levels of inequality in poverty and wealth last seen more than 40 years ago" (Joseph Rowntree Foundation, 2007; see Dorling *et al.*, 2007). These trends raise obvious questions about the feasibility of redistributing from the better off to the poor.

The *British Social Attitudes* survey series has charted attitudes to poverty and inequality since it was established nearly a quarter of a century ago. In this chapter we analyse the factors that influence attitudes to the poor, and to poverty policy, and how they have changed over time. We consider whether people *are* committed to improving the living conditions of poorer groups, or whether values have shifted towards a greater acceptance of inequality, incentives and competition, in line with the general trajectory of recent market-centred policies pursued under both Conservative and Labour governments. These findings are important, as they affect the extent to which people support the kinds of government policies necessary to reduce poverty. Certainly, if we find there to have been a shift away from sympathy for the poor, this might help

---

* Peter Taylor-Gooby is Professor of Social Policy and Rose Martin is a Research Associate, both in the School of Social Policy, Sociology and Social Research at the University of Kent.

explain the unwillingness of government to claim credit more emphatically for
its policies in this field (Piachaud, 1999; Sefton, 2005).

We also consider how any shifts in attitudes to government policies for the
poor might be explained, examining perceptions of the poor, beliefs about
policy and social values. Perhaps, for instance, concern about poverty and
inequality reflects the extent to which people increasingly feel better off? Or
does it result from a belief that poverty is less prevalent, meaning people are
less aware of a need to address the problem? Alternatively, people may believe
that government intervention is increasingly ineffective or counter-productive,
or perhaps there has been an underlying shift in values which undermines
support for welfare for the poor. In concluding, we consider how these various
explanatory factors might interact with one another, and whether this helps
explain any change we find in how people think about the responsibility of
government to help the poor.

Changing contexts

British society has changed rapidly during the past quarter century, with a
number of developments influencing patterns of poverty and inequality. First
and most obviously, society has got both richer and more unequal. GDP per
head roughly doubled between 1981 and 2005 (Office for National Statistics
(ONS), 2007a: Figure 5.1). Within the general rise in living standards, some
groups have done better than others. Real disposable household income has
risen by about 60 per cent on average, but that of the top 10 per cent has grown
faster, by just under 80 per cent, whereas for the bottom 10 per cent the increase
is much lower, at just over 40 per cent (*ibid.*: Figure 5.11). The big increase in
inequality took place during the 1980s, followed by greater stability in relative
incomes during the 1990s and a moderate trend towards greater equality during
the early 2000s. However, in 2006, inequality again started to increase (ONS,
2007b). Two factors are identified by the ONS as contributing to these changes.
Most significant are shifts in the pattern of earnings. Incomes rose much faster
for the better paid, particularly in the early period. The next most important
reason is cuts in direct taxes for the better paid (ONS, 2007a).

These trends are paralleled by patterns of poverty among households with
children, which also rose sharply during the 1980s, but started to fall back from
the late 1990s. The number of those in relative poverty, taking into account
changes in average living standards and housing costs, fell by 2.4 million
between 1996/97 and 2004/05, including a cut by one fifth in child poverty and
by a third among pensioners.[1]

Over the same period, there have been substantial policy shifts on
unemployment, poverty and social benefits. The main thrust of policy from the
mid-1980s to the early 1990s, under Conservative governments, was to cut back
social benefits and strengthen the requirement on claimants to pursue work
actively, culminating in 1996 with the introduction of Jobseeker's Allowance
(JSA), conditional on pursuing employment opportunities, formalised through
the JSA Jobseeker's Agreement. The background assumption was that

government should limit its interventions in the labour market and, over time, that wealth would trickle down from rich to poor. The commitment to policies encouraging paid work has continued since the election of a reforming Labour government in 1997, but has been softened by the introduction of more positive enabling policies, through targeted benefits and tax credits which support the incomes of low-paid working families and pensioners and contribute to childcare costs and are based on families' income. The introduction of a minimum wage also helps those in employment at the bottom of the labour market. The New Deal programmes have provided further assistance in getting targeted groups (especially young people and single parents, with some help for disabled people, older unemployed people and partners of unemployed people) into paid work. The introduction of a 'Single Gateway' scheme for all claimants of working age, and of individual case-management, which confronts those claiming benefits with the available job and training opportunities and strengthens the personal pressures to move from benefits to paid work, has further strengthened incentives. Overall, these policies are designed to meet the needs of most of the unemployed (which may include the poor) while continuing to reinforce incentives to work and provide for oneself. They do not address the growth of inequality at the top end of the income spectrum.

Such policies, which improve the position of families with children and low-paid workers, have been combined with a 'make-work-pay' strategy which allows the benefits available to single people who are not in work to fall relative to the incomes of the rest of the population. This continues a trend established in the 1980s under which the incomes of single unemployed people have fallen sharply in relative terms and are likely to continue to do so (New Policy Institute, 2007).

The policy shift of the 1980s and 1990s under Conservative and Labour governments is often summed up as a transition from a passive to an active social policy (Organisation for Economic Co-operation and Development, 2005). This forms part of a larger pattern of restructuring. Recent developments in the massive expansion of global economic activity and the constraints on the capacity of governments to control key features of their national economies have contributed to a general re-orientation from the collective to the individual, reflected in the abandonment of neo-Keynesian economic policies by most western governments (McNamara, 1998).

How might public opinion have responded to the trend towards greater inequality, and to an emphasis in government policy on individual responsibility? Has the rise in inequality led to increased concern about the poor and those in need? Or has the increased emphasis on individual, rather than collective, responsibility led to an unwillingness to support policies that aim to improve the position of the poor? It is to this issue that we now turn.

Poverty, inequality and government policy

Over the years, the *British Social Attitudes* survey series has included a number of key questions about attitudes to poverty and inequality, and what the government should do about them. A consistent time-series, with some gaps, can be constructed back to 1987. The questions cover views on the *size* of the income gap between better and worse off, issues of *fairness*, and whether government should be *responsible* for tackling poverty (see, for example, Sefton's chapter in *The 22ⁿᵈ Report*, 2005: 4). These will allow us to see how perceptions of poverty and inequality have changed, as well as the extent to which people think the government should be doing something about these issues.

We begin by considering two questions that ask about the size of the gap between rich and poor, and the extent to which "ordinary people" get their fair share of Britain's wealth:

> *Thinking of income levels generally in Britain today, would you say that the **gap** between those with high incomes and those with low incomes is too large, about right, or, too small?*

> *Ordinary working people do not get their fair share of the nation's wealth*
> *[Agree/disagree 5-point scale]*

The first two lines in Table 11.1 show that a large majority, about 80 per cent, think that the income gap is too large, with a slight decline in the last few years. When the question raises the issue of *fairness* (second row) there is a lower but still strong level of support for the view that inequality is prevalent, again declining in recent years (around two-thirds falling to 55 per cent).

The last three rows of the table show responses to a number of questions that ask, directly and indirectly, about the role of government in reducing inequality:

> *It is the responsibility of the government to reduce the differences in income between people with high incomes and those with low incomes*
> *[Agree/disagree 5-point scale]*

> *The government should spend more money on welfare benefits for the poor, even if it leads to higher taxes*
> *[Agree/disagree 5-point scale]*

> *Government should redistribute income from the better-off to those who are less well off*
> *[Agree/disagree 5-point scale]*

As Table 11.1 shows, the level of support for government intervention falls as the degree of explicit intervention increases. For instance, support for government redistributing income from the better off to the poorer stands at just over a third, despite concern about the gap between those with high and low incomes. A similar proportion feel government should spend more upon the poor. A slightly higher proportion agree with the less explicitly redistributive statement that it is government's responsibility to reduce income differences. In recent years (roughly speaking, since the mid-1990s) the decline in support for policies of higher spending on the poor becomes more marked, with a further fall between 2002 and 2004. In summary, there is a strong indication that that people are becoming less concerned about inequality and poverty and less likely to think government should do something about them. It is also clear that support for government intervention declines when the degree of interventionism is spelt out.

Table 11.1 Concerns about inequality and enthusiasm for government policies, 1987–2006

	1987	1991	1995	1999	2002	2004	2006
% say gap between high and low incomes is "too large"	79	79	87	81	82	73	76
Base	*2847*	*1445*	*1234*	*2091*	*1148*	*2146*	*2170*
% agree ...							
... ordinary people don't get their fair share of the nation's wealth	64	67	66	60	63	53	55
Base	*2493*	*2702*	*3135*	*2450*	*2900*	*2609*	*3748*
... govt. responsible for reducing differences in income	62	64	n/a	65	n/a	43	n/a
Base	*1212*	*1224*	*n/a*	*804*	*n/a*	*1737*	*n/a*
... govt. should spend more on welfare benefits for the poor	55	58	49	40	44	36	35
Base	*1281*	*2481*	*3135*	*2450*	*2900*	*2609*	*2822*
... govt. should redistribute income from the better off to those who are less well off	45	41	47	36	39	32	34
Base	*2493*	*2702*	*3135*	*2450*	*2900*	*2609*	*3748*

n/a = not asked

The pattern of declining sympathy for the poor is reinforced by analysis of the 'welfarism' scale (more details of which can be found in the appendix to this chapter). This scale provides a general measure of support for state welfare provision to tackle poverty. Here we use a simplified but robust version of the standard scale to enable us to take our analysis back to the late 1980s. The scale includes variables which measure attitudes to the impact of the welfare state on poverty, incentives and living standards, whether claimants are lazy and whether benefit abuse is widespread. It assesses orientation towards the poor and is often used as a general measure of sympathy towards them.

As Table 11.2 shows, sympathy for the poor remained roughly constant during the late 1980s and rose by 1994, but has fallen back since then, so that the proportion who are unsympathetic on this overall measure now outnumbers those who are sympathetic.

Table 11.2 Welfare scale, 1987–2006

Welfare scale	1987	1989	1994	2000	2006
	%	%	%	%	%
Very unsympathetic	5	5	4	7	6
Slightly unsympathetic	35	35	32	45	50
Slightly sympathetic	43	44	47	41	39
Very sympathetic	17	16	17	7	4
Net sympathy	20	20	28	-4	-13
Base	1246	1273	2823	2878	2718

People's general orientation to the poor and to what government should do for them has shifted in recent years. The pattern of attitudes to poverty and to government policies to tackle it might be explained in a number of ways. We suggest here that the factors underpinning people's attitudes can be divided into three broad categories: *perceptions* about what the world is like (for example, the extent to which people recognise poverty as an issue in society); the *beliefs* people hold about how social processes work (for example, their understanding of benefit levels and how these relate to people's willingness to work); and the *social values* that direct people's orientation to what ought to be done (for example, the basic judgements that influence people's orientation to the poor and the priority they attach to dealing with poverty). The assumption is that attitudes may be affected by new information becoming available to a person (perceptions), by rational mental processes leading to different conclusions (beliefs) or by the normative assumptions that guide action (social values). Of course, these different areas interact in complex ways, since everyday thinking is not pursued in watertight compartments. So we now consider each explanation separately and then try to disentangle some of the interactions.

Perceptions

We begin by considering people's perceptions of a range of issues of relevance to poverty, and government policies that attempt to tackle it. Perhaps, for instance, people have become less aware of poverty within British society, so they think that there is less need to address the issue.[2] Alternatively, they may perceive benefits as having improved and so feel that poverty is already being dealt with. Perceptions of social changes may also interact with an individual's own position. People may feel better off themselves and, self-interestedly, be less inclined to support provision for the poor. After all, from this perspective they will think of themselves as less likely to be on the receiving end of state welfare.

Levels of poverty

One explanation for a fall in support for government policies aimed at tackling poverty is a shift in perceptions as to how many people are poor. If there are fewer poor people, less needs to be done for them overall. Equally, the risk that one might become poor oneself diminishes. Three questions are relevant to this issue:

> *Some people say there is very little **real** poverty in Britain today. Others say there is quite a lot. Which come closest to **your** view, that there is very little real poverty in Britain, or, that there is quite a lot?*

> *Over the last ten years, do you think that poverty in Britain has been increasing, decreasing or staying at about the same level?*

> *And over the **next** ten years, do you think that poverty in Britain will increase, decrease, or, stay at about the same level?*

The first rows in Table 11.3 show that during the late 1980s around half thought poverty had increased over the previous decade, rising to around two-thirds in 1994. Thereafter the perception that poverty had increased declines, this view being held by around a third in 2006, with just under a quarter thinking poverty had decreased. When we turn to respondents' perceptions of current levels of poverty (the middle rows of Table 11.3) the proportion who thought poverty was prevalent increased up to the mid-1990s (peaking at 71 per cent in 1994) and afterwards fell back, with just over a half taking this view in 2006. Finally, perceptions about future levels of poverty show that over four in ten think poverty will increase in the future, while about a third think it is likely to remain roughly constant, despite well-publicised government policy objectives aimed at tackling poverty, and the evidence that poverty has pursued a general downward trend (apart from some fluctuations) from the late 1990s.

Table 11.3 Perceptions of poverty, 1986–2006

	1986	1989	1994	2000	2003	2006
Over the last 10 years …	%	%	%	%	%	%
Poverty has increased	51	50	67	36	35	32
Poverty has decreased	15	16	6	20	19	23
Poverty has stayed the same	30	31	24	38	39	39
Perceived levels of poverty in Britain today	%	%	%	%	%	%
Very little	41	34	28	35	41	45
Quite a lot	55	63	71	62	55	52
Over the next 10 years …	%	%	%	%	%	%
Poverty will increase	44	44	54	41	46	44
Poverty will decrease	12	16	10	18	13	16
Poverty will stay the same	36	34	32	35	33	35
Base	*1548*	*1516*	*1167*	*3426*	*3272*	*3240*

These findings suggest that changing perceptions of poverty could help explain shifts in attitudes towards government policy on poverty. In general, perceptions of the level of poverty within society started high in the 1980s and remained high until the mid-1990s. After that date they started to decline, around the same time that attitudes towards government policy began to shift. Expectations about future poverty levels show much less fluctuation.

Welfare benefits

A second area of relevant perceptions concerns welfare benefits and, in particular, who people would prioritise for extra help and their perceptions as to the levels of benefits enjoyed by different groups.

In 2005, we asked respondents about their support for extra spending on various types of benefits: retirement pensions, child benefits, benefits for the unemployed, benefits for disabled people and benefits for single parents:

> *Thinking now only of the government's spending on **social benefits** like those on the card. Which of these items would be your highest priority for extra spending? And which next?*

Table 11.4 suggests that, from the mid-1990s, there has been a small but steady increase in support for more expenditure on pensions and child benefits, the first and third most popular targets for extra spending. Meanwhile, any desire for extra spending on the unemployed has dwindled to an extremely low level, now standing at one in fourteen, down from one in three in 1986. The other categories have seen broadly consistent levels of support.

Table 11.4 First or second priority for extra spending, 1986–2005

% choosing as 1st /2nd priority for extra spending	1986	1989	1994	1996	2000	2003	2005
Retirement pensions	64	67	64	71	74	78	80
Benefits for disabled people	58	60	57	55	61	55	52
Child benefits	23	30	34	30	33	38	39
Benefits for single parents	18	16	14	13	18	15	15
Benefits for the unemployed	33	25	26	26	12	10	7
Base	3100	3029	1167	3620	3426	3272	3193

Percentages sum to over 100 as the figures combine first and second priorities for extra spending

A comparison of these views with the real trajectory of the two types of benefit is interesting. Out-of-work benefits for those with children have, broadly speaking, matched or risen faster than increases in average earnings. However, compared to earnings, Jobseeker's Allowance and Income Support have been falling for those without children. So, compared to the rest of society, the childless unemployed are more likely now to be on a low income. Conversely, pensioners' real incomes have increased over the period (New Policy Institute, 2007).

A partial explanation for the decline in support for increased spending on the unemployed is a growing belief that unemployment benefits are too high and discourage the unemployed from seeking work (see Table 11.9 later in this chapter). This is important because, if people think the benefits available to the poor enable them to command higher standards of living than they used to, this may contribute to declining support for government intervention.

To examine this issue in more detail our 2005 survey asked:

> *Think of a couple living together without children who are both unemployed. Their only income comes from state benefits. Would you say that they have more than enough to live on, have enough to live on, are hard up, or, are really poor?*

> *Now think about a pensioner couple living together. Their only income comes from the state pension and other benefits specially for pensioners. Would you say that they have more than enough to live on, have enough to live on, are hard up, or, are really poor?*

Similar questions were asked in 1986 and 1998, allowing us to examine changing perceptions of benefit levels over time.[3] The responses are shown in

Table 11.5 and suggest that many people think that benefit levels for the unemployed have improved in real terms. In 1986, for instance, nearly six in ten people thought an unemployed couple living on benefits was poor (which we define as being "hard up" or "really poor"); by 2005 this applied to just under four in ten. A higher proportion, nearly seven in ten, would see a pensioner couple in this situation as poor, though this figure has also declined somewhat since 1986 (when eight in ten took this view). It seems, therefore, that people's perceptions of the living standards enjoyed by those on benefits have changed over the last two decades, and that benefit levels are now seen as being more generous than they were in the mid-1980s and mid-1990s.

Table 11.5 Perceptions of benefit levels, 1986, 1998 and 2005

	1986	1998	2005
Unemployed couple	%	%	%
Hard up	47	45	35
Really poor	12	11	4
Pensioner couple	%	%	%
Hard up	51	56	59
Really poor	19	17	9
Base	*1548*	*3146*	*3210*

Table 11.5 also shows that people tend to think of a basic rate pensioner couple as being poorer than an unemployed couple living on state benefits. However, this perception is largely reversed when we provide people with more information about the reality of income levels for these two groups. This backs up our earlier observation that people have an unrealistic view of benefit and pension levels. We asked:

> *Now thinking again of that couple living together without children who are both unemployed. After rent, their income is £88 a week. Would you say that they have more than enough to live on, have enough to live on, are hard up, or, are really poor?*

> *And thinking again about that pensioner couple living together. After rent, their income is £171 a week. Would you say that they have more than enough to live on, have enough to live on, are hard up, or, are really poor?*

Once the income levels of these two groups is made clear, the proportion who think the unemployed couple are poor increases markedly, while the proportion thinking this of the pensioner couple decreases. Now over half (56 per cent) take the view that the unemployed couple are "hard up", while 13 per cent say they are "really poor". The equivalent figures for the pensioner couple are 27 and two per cent respectively.

These findings show that support for more spending on benefits for the unemployed is at a very low level, with pensioners being by far the most popular nomination for additional spending. These changes occurred during the mid- to late 1990s, around the point at which people's views about government policies towards the poor also changed. However, the finding should be considered alongside the fact that people's perceptions of benefit levels for different groups are hazy, and are perhaps 'clouded' by beliefs about who does and does not 'deserve' state help. Here, too, there is evidence that people's views about the generosity of benefit levels changed between the late 1990s and 2005.

Self-interest

We now move on to focus on people's perceptions of their own income. We asked respondents to describe their household's standard of living as follows:

Which of the phrases on this card would you say comes closest to your feelings about your household's income these days?

Here we find some cautious optimism (see Table 11.6). The largest group, those who describe themselves as "coping", has remained roughly stable, at about half the sample, since 1986. Meanwhile, the group who see themselves as "living comfortably" has increased, with a sharp rise in the late 1990s to two-fifths. The proportion who find life "difficult" or "very difficult" has correspondingly shrunk from a quarter to a seventh.

Table 11.6 Perceptions of respondent's own household income, 1986–2006

Feelings about own household's present income	1986	1990	1994	1998	2002	2006
	%	%	%	%	%	%
Living comfortably	24	25	29	37	39	41
Coping	49	51	49	46	45	45
Finding it difficult	18	17	15	12	13	10
Finding it very difficult	8	7	6	4	3	4
Base	3100	2797	1167	3146	1148	1093

Changes in perceptions about one's own circumstances follow the general pattern we found when looking at perceptions of poverty, where there was a notable *reduction* during the second half of the 1990s in the proportion of people who thought poverty was increasing (the point at which the proportion of people who said they themselves were "living comfortably" increased). This suggests that people's perceptions of poverty, and their willingness to contemplate measures to help counter poverty, might be influenced by their own circumstances.

So far we have examined a variety of examples of the ways in which people's perceptions might influence their views about government policies aimed at tackling poverty and inequality. We have seen that people are now less aware of poverty than they were, that there is considerable confusion over the level of benefits to which unemployed people are already entitled, and that people's perceptions of their own living standards have improved. In most cases, the key changes occurred during the mid- to late 1990s, at very much the same point that attitudes towards government policy in this area began to change. This strengthens the case for believing that perceptions might help explain attitudes towards government interventions to reduce poverty, and we shall return to this issue in the second half of this chapter.

Beliefs and understanding of poverty

We turn now to examine the second area we identified as possibly helping explain levels of support for government policies aimed at tackling poverty: people's *beliefs* about poverty and the poor. Here we are interested in people's understanding of what constitutes poverty, as well as in their views about the impact of benefits on the behaviour of the poor, or the extent to which welfare rules promote fraud.

Defining poverty

How do we define poverty? After all, if poverty is defined more severely than it once was, the numbers included among 'the poor' will fall, and less will seem to be required to address the problem. There is indeed some evidence of a shift in how poverty is understood. The *British Social Attitudes* survey has a long-running series of three separate questions about the meaning of poverty:

> *Would you say that someone in Britain was or was not in poverty ...*
>
> *... if they had enough to buy the things they really needed, but not enough to buy the things most people take for granted?*
>
> *... if they had enough to eat and live, but not enough to buy other things they needed?*
>
> *... if they had not got enough to eat and live without getting into debt?*
>
> *[Was in poverty/Was not]*

These questions reflect academic debates about relative, minimum standards and absolute destitution conceptions of poverty. The first uses a relative definition, defining poverty in terms of ability to share in the normal standard of living. The second describes a minimum standard of subsistence, while the third refers to absolute want, when people are not even able to command the minimum level of necessities. Studies such as 'Breadline Britain' (see, for example, Gordon *et al.*, 2005) have shown that perceptions of what people understand by the 'things people need' may have changed over the years as living standards (for the majority) improve (Hills, 2001). The data available from *British Social Attitudes* do not allow us to address these issues directly, because the questions do not investigate what is understood as constituting "the things most people take for granted". It must also be borne in mind when interpreting these findings that the level of resources referred to by these questions may well have shifted over time, so that even an absolute level of want (in the third question) may be used to refer to command over more goods in later years, because people tend to think of more things as necessities. Nonetheless, the figures give us a broad indication of overall perspectives on poverty.

The great majority of people adopt the very basic definition of poverty in the third row of Table 11.7, with a slight fall from the mid-1990s from about 95 to 89 per cent. Round about half (rather higher in the early and mid-period up to 2000) accept the minimum subsistence definition of the second row (enough to "eat and live" but no more). Roughly a quarter (rising in the 1990s, falling somewhat more recently to 22 per cent) assent to the relative definition in the first row, which understands poverty as lack of sufficient income to "buy the things most people take for granted".

Table 11.7 Definitions of poverty, 1986–2006

% say in poverty if ...	1986	1989	1994	2000	2003	2006
... enough to buy things really needed, but not things most people take for granted	25	25	28	27	19	22
... enough to eat and live, but not for other things needed	55	60	60	59	47	50
... not enough to eat and live without getting into debt	95	95	90	93	90	89
Base	*1548*	*1516*	*1167*	*3426*	*3272*	*3240*

These findings suggest most people are strict in their understanding of poverty. The shifts we have found are not large and may indicate a slightly greater generosity towards the poor in the period of highest poverty in the mid-1990s. If anything, conceptions of poverty appear to have got rather harsher since the beginning of the period covered. People are slightly less likely to describe someone who gets into debt to meet basic needs as poor. Similarly, they are less likely to describe those who can "eat and live" but not afford other things they need as poor. While the minority counting those who can't afford "the things most people take for granted" as poor increased during the early and mid-1990s, it had fallen back to the level of the mid-1980s by the most recent survey. In general, however, there is little indication that changing understanding of what counts as poverty is sufficiently strong to serve as a major influence on shifts in attitudes to policy.

We turn now to examine people's beliefs about the *reasons* behind poverty. We asked:

> *Why do you think there are people who live in need? Of the four views on this card, which **one** comes closest to your own?*
>
> *Because they have been unlucky*
> *Because of laziness or lack of willpower*
> *Because of injustice in our society*
> *It's an inevitable part of modern life*

The view that poverty is inevitable in modern life remains the most widely and consistently held, endorsed by about a third (see Table 11.8). However, the proportion thinking that poverty is due to laziness or lack of willpower, and is thus a personal responsibility, has risen from 19 per cent in 1986 to 27 per cent two decades later.

Table 11.8 Views on the explanation for poverty, 1986–2006

Why do people live in need?	1986	1989	1994	2000	2003	2004	2006
	%	%	%	%	%	%	%
Unlucky	11	11	15	15	13	16	10
Laziness/lack of willpower	19	19	15	23	28	21	27
Injustice in society	25	29	29	21	19	16	21
Inevitable in modern life	37	34	33	34	32	38	34
Base	*1548*	*1516*	*1167*	*3426*	*3272*	*2146*	*3240*

Beliefs about the impact of benefits on the poor

We focus now on people's beliefs about the poor, their behaviour and the way they respond to incentives. The impact of government policies on the poor has long been a focus of controversy. The less eligibility principle in the 1834 Poor Law aimed to make claiming a last resort for the truly destitute; more recently, the distinction between 'undeserving' and 'deserving' poor has been prominent. Charles Murray's argument for a 'dependency culture' proposed that welfare benefits could easily lead to dependency on the state, while in the present day, concern is directed at 'inactive' recipients. Our questions allow us to contrast the idea that claimants are often fraudulent with the view that people are failing to get benefits to which they are entitled:

> *Large numbers of people these days **falsely** claim benefits.*
>
> *Large numbers of people who are eligible for benefits these days **fail** to claim them*
>
> *[Agree/disagree 4-point scale]*

The first two rows of Table 11.9 show that most people believe *both* that there is a great deal of fraudulent claiming and that many people fail to get benefits to which they are entitled. From our first measure in 1986, as incomes have improved and unemployment and poverty rates fallen, the belief that false claiming is prevalent has strengthened, while rather fewer people believe that many people fail to claim benefits.

Table 11.9 Beliefs about how unemployed people behave, 1986–2006

% agree that	1986	1990	1994	1998	2002	2006
Large numbers falsely claim benefits	70	69	72	83	81	84
Large numbers of those eligible for benefits fail to claim	83	83	79	79	80	77
Benefits for unemployed people are …	%	%	%	%	%	%
… too low and cause hardship	46	50	53	29	29	23
… too high and discourage them from finding jobs	35	29	24	46	47	54
Base	*3100*	*2979*	*3469*	*3146*	*3435*	*3240*

We also wanted to understand people's beliefs about how benefits impact upon work incentives. We asked:

> *Opinions differ about the level of benefits for unemployed people. Which of these two statements comes closest to your own view: benefits for unemployed people are **too low** and cause hardship, or, benefits for unemployed people are **too high** and discourage them from finding jobs?*

This shows (rows three and four of Table 11.9) that the proportions thinking benefits are too low and cause hardship has fallen since the mid-1990s. This reflects the trends we saw earlier in perceptions of poverty, and in the level of unemployment benefits and pensions discussed earlier, and is at odds with the fact that childless unemployment benefit claimants have seen a fall in their real income (compared with earnings) in the last 10 years (New Policy Institute, 2007). The proportion expressing concern that benefits have a disincentive effect because they are too high now exceeds 50 per cent, for the first time in the history of the survey.

We began this section by showing that people's beliefs about what constitutes poverty are fairly strict, and appear to have got slightly stricter over the last two decades. At the same time, we have seen that an increasing number of people see poverty as reflecting lack of willpower (although a larger proportion take the view that it is simply an inevitable feature of modern life). Meanwhile, when we examine people's beliefs about the impact of the benefit system on the poor, there is clearly a strong concern about false claims and about perverse incentives among the public, although the parallel concern about failure to claim among those entitled remains high. The rise in numbers believing that many people claim benefits fraudulently only becomes noticeable in the post-1997 period, as does the rise in the view that unemployment benefits are too high and discourage recipients from finding work. As was the case with the perceptions we examined earlier, the timing of these changes in people's beliefs, and the fact that these largely coincide with changing attitudes towards government policy, suggests that beliefs of this sort might be important drivers of people's views about the desirability of government intervention to reduce inequality. We shall return to this issue in the second half of this chapter.

Social values and the poor

We turn now to examine what we have defined as "social values", the values which influence people's overall orientation to the poor. Our concern here is to see whether these have changed, as this might help explain why the needs of the poor are seen as less important and may help explain a diminished concern about poverty and declining support for poverty policies.

Earlier, in Tables 11.1 and 11.2, we saw how general orientations to the poor and to government policies to meet their needs have changed over recent years. Indeed, the scale that forms the basis of Table 11.2 indicates that underlying values in this area have shifted. However, for our purposes, this scale is not an ideal measure of social values, because some of the statements that make it up relate to perceptions or beliefs as well as value orientations. Examples include the statements "around here, most unemployed people could find a job if they really wanted one", and "most people on the dole are fiddling in one way or another" (see the appendix to this chapter for further details of the composition of the welfare scale). Such statements are typically used to express value orientation, but could also indicate beliefs about the state of the local job market or perceptions of behaviour. For this reason, we will take as our measure of social values people's response to a single statement which seems least likely to be contaminated by other factors: the view that "government should redistribute income from the better off to those who are less well off". As the last row of Table 11.1 shows, since the 1980s and early 1990s there has been a decline in the proportion of people agreeing with this statement, from over 40 per cent in the period until 1995 to a proportion hovering in the low 30s since the millennium.

Examining trends in support for the poor

As Tables 11.1 and 11.2 show, public sympathy for the poor and support for government spending on benefits to meet their needs has fallen in recent years. This is despite a government commitment to eliminate poverty and a complex array of policies which have improved the position of some groups, notably families with children, low-paid workers and pensioners.

The questions discussed so far have charted shifts in perceptions, beliefs and social values relevant to the puzzle that, while people still tend to see poverty and inequality as major issues, nearly as much as they did in the late 1980s, they are much less inclined to support government interventions designed to tackle these issues. The responses show a common general pattern:

- People tend to perceive poverty as being at a lower level now than in the recent past.

- There has been a fall in support for the unemployed compared to other groups of benefit recipients.

- Popular beliefs about what counts as poverty are strict and have not changed greatly during the period.

- Increasing proportions of people describe their own living standards as being "comfortable".

- People are now rather more inclined to believe that many people falsely claim benefits.

- They are also more inclined to believe that the availability of benefits damages work incentives and undermines the willingness of claimants to pursue opportunities.

- Social values associated with sympathy for the poor have become weaker, especially since the mid-1990s.

There are a substantial number of factors here that might contribute to explanations as to why concern for the poor and support for government policies to address these issues has declined. Since the factors interact with one another, the pattern is extremely complex. We now seek to make some progress in understanding which are *most* important. This can help us understand how views might shift in the future. To put it crudely, if the explanation is mainly to do with changing *perceptions*, the implication is that changes in levels of poverty may generate different attitudes to poverty among the public, once it is aware of them. However, if shifts in *social values* are largely responsible, the changing social context and new, more competitive and individualist, social milieu is likely to play a greater part and the changes we have seen are unlikely to be reversed. Finally, if it is changing *beliefs* about how the poor respond to welfare, then we are in a middle position, since such ideas are likely to be influenced by perceptions and values.

We begin our analysis by selecting particular questions to represent our three areas of interest: perceptions, beliefs and values. We also select a question to best represent people's attitudes to policy in this area. These are shown in Table 11.10. Our choice of variables is to some extent limited by the range of questions asked in different years in the survey; the questions shown in the table are chosen because they represent views expressed in the survey in the relevant area and because they are available for the appropriate years to support the analysis. We now focus upon three particular years: 1994, 2000 and 2006.

The table summarises the change that has taken place over time in our key questions. The first row in the table shows the proportion of people in each year who think government should spend more upon welfare benefits for the poor, even if this leads to higher taxes. This confirms the pattern we saw earlier in Table 11.1, one of a decline in support for this form of spending, from 55 per cent in 1987 to 35 per cent in 2006. The other rows show the percentage of people with particular perceptions, beliefs and social values. As remarked upon earlier in this chapter, this shows a fall in the proportion who take the view that poverty is at a high level and that government should redistribute income, and an increase in the proportion who have sceptical views about benefits and benefit recipients.

Table 11.10 Summary: support for more welfare state spending, perceptions, beliefs and values, 1994, 2000 and 2006 [4]

	1994	2000	2006
Policy: % agree government should spend more on welfare for poor	50	40	35
Perception: % think level of poverty is currently high	71	62	52
Belief: % agree large numbers falsely claim benefits	69	77	84
Value: % agree government should redistribute from better off to less well off	51	39	34

Why might views about these issues change over time, and to what extent are these changes related to one another? Perhaps, for example, the decline in support for government spending reflects the fact that fewer people now think there is a high level of poverty in modern Britain. To address this we need to look at how people's views about welfare spending relate to their perceptions, beliefs and values, and whether this relationship has changed over time. The results are shown in Table 11.11.

Table 11.11 Support for more welfare state spending, by perceptions, beliefs and values, 1994, 2000 and 2006 [5]

% agree government should spend more on welfare for poor	1994	2000	2006	Change 1994–2006
All	50	40	35	-15
Perception: level of poverty is currently high	58	44	44	-14
Belief: large numbers falsely claim benefits	44	35	33	-11
Value: government should redistribute from better off to less well off	64	57	56	-8

A number of key points emerge from the table. Firstly, people's perceptions and values are clearly related to their policy preferences, in very much the direction that we would expect. For instance, people who think there is a high level of poverty are more likely than average to think government should spend more on the poor (44 per cent in 2006, compared to 35 per cent among the population as a whole). A similar point can be made about those who think government should redistribute income from the better off to the less well off. In contrast, people's beliefs about benefit claiming are less clearly related to their views about spending on the poor. Secondly, support for more government spending on the poor has fallen among all the groups shown in the table. For example, in 1994, well over half (58 per cent) of those who thought there was a lot of poverty in Britain thought government should spend more on welfare for the poor. Now only 44 per cent take this view. Similarly, support for more spending on the poor has fallen among those who think that government should redistribute income from the better off to the less well off, as it has among those who believe that false claiming is rife. Clearly, this means that we cannot explain falling support for spending on the poor by the fact that fewer people now think poverty to be prevalent, or support redistribution, or because more believe that false claiming is extensive; among all these groups support for more spending has fallen. These answers raise interesting and important issues, especially for a government that has set itself targets for the reduction of poverty. Why is it that people who think poverty levels are currently high are much less reluctant now to endorse government policies that might tackle this issue?

Of course, we must not forget that people's views about government policy, as well as their perceptions, beliefs and values, might be shaped by social characteristics such as their age, class and education. Previous studies (for example, Hills, in *The 18th Report*, 2001 and Sefton, in *The 22nd Report*, 2005) have shown demographic factors to be very important in explaining people's views about government policy. We know that the last two decades have been marked by substantial social changes in some of these demographic characteristics. For instance, the proportion of non-manual workers, especially more senior and intermediate non-manual workers, has increased, and the proportion of manual workers has fallen. Education has expanded rapidly; the proportion of the population with two or more A-levels increased by 40 per cent between 1993/94 and 2004/05, and the proportion on degree courses went up by 170 per cent between 1980/81 and 2004/05 (ONS, 2007a: Table 3.10 and Figure 3.14). Political support has also changed. These social shifts could help explain some of the changes we have seen in perceptions, beliefs and values. For example, if unsympathetic welfare values or the belief that benefits damage incentives are highest among non-manual workers, then the increasing proportion of non-manual workers in the population might help explain the shifts in perceptions, beliefs and values that we have seen.

We turn now to examine the relative importance of the various factors – the socio-demographic on the one hand and the subjective (perceptions, beliefs and values) on the other – that might influence views about government policy. Our interest here is twofold. Firstly, we want to see which of these factors are the most important in explaining people's attitudes towards spending on the poor. To do this we use multivariate regression analysis which allows us to identify the *independent* influence of different factors upon attitudes towards government policy (further details of multivariate analysis can be found in the Appendix to this *Report*). Secondly, we want to ascertain the extent to which these factors help explain any of the changes over time we have seen in support for more spending on the poor. In order to do this, we have pooled together data from 1994, 2000 and 2006 to see whether there are differences between the various years once all the variables in the model are taken into account.

The full models are given in Table A.2 in the appendix to this chapter. Figure 11.1 gives a summary of the socio-demographic variables which significantly predict people's views about government spending on the poor, as measured by their response to our 'policy' measure – that is, the statement "government should spend more on welfare benefits for the poor" (outlined in Table 11.1 earlier). This analysis confirms that there has been a significant decline in sympathy for spending on the poor over time, even when the other characteristics included in the model are taken into account. We cannot explain changing attitudes towards government policy simply by reference to changes in the education, income or class structure in contemporary Britain, or changes in party support.

The relationships shown in Figure 11.1 between the various characteristics and support for spending are intuitively convincing: it is the old, those on low incomes, the more educated (weakly) and Labour voters who favour more spending on the poor, while the converse groups tend to be more strongly opposed to this. Once these factors are taken into account, social class membership makes little difference to a person's views. The rejection of spending on the poor by those who identify with the Conservative Party is rather stronger in its impact than the other variables, the next strongest being support among the bottom fifth of the income distribution.

These findings are robust. Other models were examined in which individual variables were omitted and showed very similar patterns of results. The fact that the statistics for the variables representing the 2000 and 2006 surveys remain roughly constant when different combinations of socio-demographic and political support variables are included or omitted suggests that it is not variations over time in particular social factors that explain the trend towards declining support.

Figure 11.1 Summary of findings from regression models predicting levels of support for more spending on the poor, socio-demographic variables only

Year of survey	Support for increased spending fell between 1994 and 2000 and fell further by 2006
Age	Younger people (under 35) less supportive than middle-aged (35 to 54) of increased spending, older people (55 plus) more supportive
Income	Those in the bottom fifth are most supportive of increased spending, and those in the next fifth somewhat supportive
Education	Those with degree level education are slightly more supportive than those with no qualifications, while education below degree level appears to make no difference
Social class	Not significantly linked to support for increased spending, once income and education are taken into account
Political party support	Labour identifiers more supportive of increased spending than Liberal Democrat or minority party identifiers, while Conservative identifiers are strongly less supportive

Having established the overall socio-demographic pattern of support for the poor, we move on to consider the part played by the subjective perceptions, beliefs and social values we considered earlier in this chapter. These are important both because it may be possible for government to influence perceptions and, to some extent, beliefs and values, and because government policy platforms are likely to be influenced themselves by the subjective orientation of the electors to whom they must appeal. Objective socio-demographic factors are, of course, much more difficult to influence, at least in the short term.

The part played by subjective factors is analysed through a regression model that includes the variables outlined in Table 11.11, that is, those selected to represent the most salient aspects of people's perceptions, beliefs and values, as well as indicators of the year of interview, to enable us to examine change over time.

The model is shown in the chapter appendix (Table A.2). It shows that, once subjective factors are taken into account, the coefficient for 2006 is somewhat reduced. In other words, it seems that changes in the sorts of subjective factors explored earlier in this chapter help explain some of the recent decline in support for government welfare spending on the poor. The rest of the model enables us to explore the relative importance of perceptions, beliefs and values. These indicate that it is values that are most important, and that perceptions of poverty and beliefs about the behaviour of the poor play a lesser role in explaining people's views on policy. Further analysis using different combinations of the subjective variables indicates that the coefficients are relatively stable, showing that separate areas of subjective orientation are identified by the questions.

What message do these findings have for government? From the point of view of a government that wishes to promote anti-poverty policy and may be concerned about a continued decline in sympathy for pro-poor spending, these results may have both an encouraging and a discouraging side. They suggest that the decline in support for such spending cannot simply be explained by socio-demographic changes – greater inequality, rising living standards for the mass of the population, population ageing, changes in class structure or in level of education. Clearly, subjective factors play an important role. These are factors that government may be able to influence and to which, in any case, government must respond if it is to retain electoral support. The problem is that it is not so much perceptions of the level of poverty, or even beliefs about the extent of false benefit claiming (both areas that might possibly be influenced by information) that appear to matter most. Rather, it is social values about the moral obligation of government to redistribute that seem to have the most impact – and these values are much harder to change. This raises a dilemma for a government committed to achieving sharp reductions in poverty, when such a policy appears to run counter to the direction of social values.

Conclusions

This chapter has examined attitudes to poverty and inequality during a time of rapid social change. Attitudes to poverty and inequality themselves have not changed greatly during the past two decades. Most people continue to believe that the income gap between those with high and those with low incomes is too large (Table 11.1) – poverty continues to be seen as a bad thing by most people. However, views on what government should *do* to address the issues have shifted markedly. A smaller proportion want direct interventions to reduce inequality or improve the position of the poor. These shifts in views on poverty policies have taken place for the most part during the last decade or slightly earlier, a period during which new government approaches have contributed to a substantial reduction in poverty for families with children, low-paid workers and pensioners, but not for unemployed people without children, and when ambitious targets have been set for future poverty reductions.

A number of factors are relevant to attitudes to poverty and to support for spending on the poor. Socio-demographic factors and political party support clearly play a role. The analysis in this chapter shows that these are important factors in relation to government poverty policies in general. Older people, those on lower incomes, Labour Party supporters and, to some extent, those with highest levels of education are most strongly sympathetic to the poor, while Conservative supporters in particular, younger people and, more weakly, those who are better off, tend not to support spending on this group. These findings are intuitively plausible and in line with previous work. However, these factors do not appear to explain the change in attitudes to poverty and poverty policy in recent years. This chapter analyses the role played by more subjective factors in influencing attitudes to poverty and policies designed to mitigate it. The relevance of this approach is that the socio-demographic factors shift slowly and it is these subjective factors that are, in principle, available for government policy makers to work on in seeking to gain support from the mass of the population for policies designed to abolish poverty. Moreover, these factors influence public response to policy and must be taken seriously by a political party that wishes to retain power.

We identify three kinds of subjective factor as being relevant to attitudes in this area: *perceptions* of what the world is like, *beliefs* about the impact of policies, produced as a result of people's thinking about the area, and the *social values* that direct their judgements. Applying this simple framework and using the variables available from the survey to measure factors in each area, the *British Social Attitudes* survey shows that more people now perceive poverty to have fallen than did two decades ago, that benefits are seen to have improved, that there are large shifts in beliefs about the impact of benefits on work incentives, and that pro-welfare and pre-redistribution values have declined among the general public. There is little indication that any shift in the (part-perceptual, part-belief) understanding of poverty, from the absolute view that it is about the capacity to purchase the necessities of life to the relative notion that it is about inequality or the extent to which the living standard of the poor differs markedly from the average, makes a strong contribution. Of course, it is likely that people's ideas about what constitutes the necessities of life have expanded at a time of generally rising standards of consumption.

The survey data shows that perceptions, beliefs and values have all shifted in line with attitudes to poverty and poverty policy. Examining these aspects further offers a useful way to examine changes across the period and to consider the opportunities for policy makers to engage with shifts in attitudes. The pooled regression analysis for the years 1994, 2000 and 2006 shows that all these factors have an important bearing on attitudes to spending on the poor and on the decline in support in recent years. The strongest predictors appear to be the social values that support a governmental role in redistribution. Perceptions of poverty and beliefs about false claiming play a lesser role.

On the face of it, government faces a problem in promoting a principled commitment to the sharp reduction and eventual abolition of poverty during a climate of public attitudes in which support for spending on the poor is in decline. Values are hard to shift and the reluctance of government ministers to stress the redistributive aspects of policy in public indicate the difficulties. However, this is an area which offers opportunities to counter the shift in attitudes against the poor. Perceptions of poverty, which might be influenced by attempts to raise public awareness of poorer groups with whom people might not come into everyday contact, and beliefs about false benefit claims, to which attempts to reduce scrounging and benefit fraud are relevant, also play a role.

Most people recognise poverty as a social issue, but are increasingly unwilling to support government policies to address it. This fact provides a simple explanation of why the current government does not trumpet its anti-poverty commitments more loudly. However, the analysis in this chapter (of public attitudes, and of the roles played by socio-demographic factors and by perceptions of poverty, beliefs about the impact of relevant policies and social values) indicates that there are areas where government might seek to shift the dominant current in public ideas towards the direction of its policies.

Notes

1. Department for Work and Pensions Press Release: "New figures show good progress on poverty – Hutton", 9th March 2006.
2. On a similar note, recent research suggests that long-term economic stability in the UK has led to a change in public attitudes to poverty (Castell and Thompson, 2007)
3. The questions in 2005 were worded slightly differently than those asked in 1986 and 1998, in order to be clearer about the fictional couples' situation. In 1986 and 1998 we asked: "Think about a married couple without children living only on unemployment benefit. Would you say that they are … really poor, hard up, have enough to live on, or have more than enough to live on". The equivalent question about pensioners asked: "And what about a married couple living only on the state pension. Would you say that they are …". It is possible that these differences in wording account for some of the changes we have found between 1998 and 2005. However, it should be noted that the change over this period is more pronounced in relation to the couple on unemployment benefits than it is in relation to the pensioner couple, suggesting that wording differences alone cannot account for the change over time we have found.

4. Bases for Table 11.10 are as follows:

	1994	2000	2006
Policy: % agree government should spend more on welfare for poor	2929	2980	2822
Perception: % think level of poverty is currently high	1167	3426	3240
Belief: % agree large numbers falsely claim benefits	3469	3426	3240
Value: % agree government should redistribute from better off to less well off	2929	2980	3748

5. Bases for Table 11.11 are as follows:

% agree government should spend more on welfare for poor	**1994**	**2000**	**2006**	**Change 1994–2006**
All	2929	2980	2822	
Perception: level of poverty is currently high	721	1851	1443	
Belief: large numbers falsely claim benefits	2127	2297	2333	
Value: government should redistribute from better off to less well off	1499	1188	907	

References

Castell, S. and Thompson, J. (2007), *Understanding attitudes to poverty in the UK: Getting the public's attention*, Joseph Rowntree Foundation, available at http://www.jrf.org.uk/bookshop/details.asp?pubID=860

Centre for Economic Performance (2007), 'Blair's economic legacy', *Centrepiece*, **12 (1)**, Summer

Dorling, D., Rigby, J., Wheeler, B., Ballas, D., Thomas, B., Fahmy, E., Gordon, D. and Lupton, R. (2007), *Poverty, Wealth and Place in Britain 1968 to 2005*, Bristol: Policy Press

Department for Work and Pensions (2007), *Households below Average Income 1994/5–2005/6 available at* http://www.dwp.gov.uk/asd/hbai.asp

Gordon, D., Pantazis, C. and Levitas, R. (2005), *Poverty and Social Exclusion in Britain: the Millennium Survey*, Bristol: Policy Press

Hills, J. (2001), 'Poverty and social security: What rights? Whose responsibilities?', in Park, A., Curtice, J., Thomson, K., Jarvis, L., and Bromley, C. (eds.), *British Social Attitudes, the 18th Report – Public policy, social ties*, London: Sage

Joseph Rowntree Foundation (2007), *Poverty and Wealth across Britain 1968 to 2005*, available at *http://www.jrf.org.uk/knowledge/findings/housing/2077.asp*

McNamara, K. (1998), *The Currency of Ideas: Monetary Politics in the European Union*, Cornell UP, London: Ithaca

New Policy Institute (2007), *Out-of-work benefit levels*, available at http://www.poverty.org.uk/06/index.shtml

Office for National Statistics (2007a), *Social Trends no 37*, Basingstoke: Palgrave Macmillan

Office for National Statistics (2007b), *Income Inequality*, available at http://www.statistics.gov.uk/cci/nugget_print.asp?ID=332

Organisation for Economic Co-operation and Development (2005), *Extending Opportunities: How active social policy can benefit us all*, Paris: OECD

Piachaud, D. (1999), Wealth by Stealth, Guardian, 1st September

Sefton, T. (2005) 'Give and take: attitudes to redistribution', 'in Park, A., Curtice, J., Thomson, K., Bromley, C., Phillips, M. and Johnson, M. (eds.) *British Social Attitudes, the 22nd Report – Two terms of New Labour: the public's reaction*, London: Sage

Sharma, N. and Hirsch, D. (2007), *It doesn't happen here: The reality of child poverty in the UK*, London: Barnardos, available at http://www.barnardos.org.uk/poverty_full_report_07.pdf

Townsend, I. and Kennedy, S. (2004), *Poverty: Measures and Targets*, House of Commons Library research paper 4/23, London: House of Commons Library, available at http://www.parliament.uk/commons/lib/research/rp2004/rp04-023.pdf

Acknowledgements

The *National Centre for Social Research* is grateful to the Department for Work and Pensions for their financial support which enabled us to ask the questions reported in this chapter, although the views expressed are those of the authors alone.

Appendix

Welfare scale

The scale is based on six questions:

The government should spend more money on welfare benefits for the poor, even if it leads to higher taxes

Around here, most unemployed people could find a job if they really wanted one

Many people who get social security don't really deserve any help

Most people on the dole are fiddling in one way or another

If welfare benefits weren't so generous people would learn to stand on their own two feet

The welfare state encourages people to stop helping each other

The scale is constructed by adding the scores for the six questions listed above. The mean score offers a measure of general sympathy towards welfare, ranging from 1 to 5, with higher values indicating greater sympathy. The four categories "very unsympathetic" to "very sympathetic" in Table 11.2 are derived by dividing this possible range into quarters. Where the mean score falls in the bottom quarter of the range, the respondent is rated as "very unsympathetic", where it falls in the next quarter, the respondent is described as "slightly unsympathetic", and so on.

The Cronbach's Alpha for the scale is shown in Table A.1.

Table A.1 Welfarism scale, 1987–2006

Welfarism scale	1987	1989	1994	2000	2006
	%	%	%	%	%
Cronbach's alpha	0.79	0.79	0.81	0.78	0.76
Standard deviation	0.798	0.789	0.772	0.731	0.685
Variance	0.636	0.622	0.595	0.534	0.469
Base	1246	1273	2823	2878	2718

Regression models

Table A.2 shows the results of the OLS linear regression analyses referred to in the text. The analyses are based on pooled data from the 1994, 2000 and 2006 surveys. These years are chosen because they each include data for the relevant variables of interest, and cover the period since the mid-1990s when attitudes appear to have shifted (as explored in Table 11.1). The dependent variable is the statement "the government should spend more on welfare for the poor" (see Tables 11.1 and 11.10). The question takes the form of a 5-point scale, where a value of 1 indicates strong disagreement, and a value of 5 indicates strong agreement. Consequently, a positive coefficient in the next table denotes higher support for the statement, while a negative one denotes lower support. For each variable, the category in brackets is the reference category. Further details about the analysis are available from the authors on request.

Table A.2 Levels of support for more government spending on welfare for the poor and socio-demographic and subjective variables, 1994, 2000 and 2006

		Standardised coefficients		
		Year only	Socio-demographic variables only	Subjective variables only
Year	(1994)			
	2000	-.11**	-.12**	-.10**
	2006	-.13**	-.15**	-.07**
Socio-demographic factors				
Age	18–34		-.09**	
	(35–54)			
	55+		.08**	
Income	Lowest quintile		.14**	
	Second lowest		.06**	
	Mid		.01	
	Second highest		-.01	
	(Highest)			
Party support	Conservative		-.16**	
	Labour		.10**	
	(Liberal Democrat, other party)			
Education	Higher		.04*	
	A-level		.01	
	O-level		-.02	
	(No qualifications)			
Social class	(Manual)			
	Non-manual		.00	
Subjective factors				
Perception	High levels of poverty in Britain today		-	.16**
	(Do not perceive high levels of poverty)			
Social values	Agree govt. should redistribute income		-	.26**
	(Do not agree with statement)			
Beliefs	Agree many people claim falsely		-	-.12**
	(Do not agree with statement)			
R squared		.015	.12	.14

* = significant at 5% level; ** = significant at 1% level

Appendix I
Technical details of the survey

In 2006, the sample for the *British Social Attitudes* survey was split into four sections: versions A, B C and D each made up a quarter of the sample. Depending on the number of versions in which it was included, each 'module' of questions was thus asked either of the full sample (4,291 respondents) or of a random quarter, half or three-quarters of the sample.

The structure of the questionnaire is shown at the beginning of Appendix III.

Sample design

The *British Social Attitudes* survey is designed to yield a representative sample of adults aged 18 or over. Since 1993, the sampling frame for the survey has been the Postcode Address File (PAF), a list of addresses (or postal delivery points) compiled by the Post Office.[1]

For practical reasons, the sample is confined to those living in private households. People living in institutions (though not in private households at such institutions) are excluded, as are households whose addresses were not on the PAF.

The sampling method involved a multi-stage design, with three separate stages of selection.

Selection of sectors

At the first stage, postcode sectors were selected systematically from a list of all postal sectors in Great Britain. Before selection, any sectors with fewer than 500 addresses were identified and grouped together with an adjacent sector; in Scotland all sectors north of the Caledonian Canal were excluded (because of the prohibitive costs of interviewing there). Sectors were then stratified on the basis of:

- 37 sub-regions
- population density with variable banding used, in order to create three equal-sized strata per sub-region
- ranking by percentage of homes that were owner-occupied.

Two hundred and ninety-six postcode sectors were selected, with probability proportional to the number of addresses in each sector.

Selection of addresses

Thirty addresses were selected in each of the 296 sectors. The issued sample was therefore 296 x 30 = 8,880 addresses, selected by starting from a random point on the list of addresses for each sector, and choosing each address at a fixed interval. The fixed interval was calculated for each sector in order to generate the correct number of addresses.

The Multiple-Occupancy Indicator (MOI) available through PAF was used when selecting addresses in Scotland. The MOI shows the number of accommodation spaces sharing one address. Thus, if the MOI indicates more than one accommodation space at a given address, the chances of the given address being selected from the list of addresses would increase so that it matched the total number of accommodation spaces. The MOI is largely irrelevant in England and Wales, as separate dwelling units generally appear as separate entries on PAF. In Scotland, tenements with many flats tend to appear as one entry on PAF. However, even in Scotland, the vast majority of MOIs had a value of one. The remainder, which ranged between three and 13, were incorporated into the weighting procedures (described below).

Selection of individuals

Interviewers called at each address selected from PAF and listed all those eligible for inclusion in the *British Social Attitudes* sample – that is, all persons currently aged 18 or over and resident at the selected address. The interviewer then selected one respondent using a computer-generated random selection procedure. Where there were two or more 'dwelling units' at the selected address, interviewers first had to select one dwelling unit using the same random procedure. They then followed the same procedure to select a person for interview within the selected dwelling unit.

Weighting

The *British Social Attitudes* survey has previously only been weighted to correct for the unequal selection of addresses, dwelling units (DU) and individuals. However, falling response in recent years prompted the introduction of non-response weights. This weighting was carried out in 2006; in addition to the selection weights, a set of weights were generated to correct for any biases due to differential non-response. The final sample was then calibrated to match the population in terms of age, sex and region.

Selection weights

Selection weights are required because not all the units covered in the survey had the same probability of selection. The weighting reflects the relative selection probabilities of the individual at the three main stages of selection: address, DU and individual. First, because addresses in Scotland were selected using the MOI, weights were needed to compensate for the greater probability of an address with an MOI of more than one being selected, compared to an address with an MOI of one. (This stage was omitted for the English and Welsh data.) Secondly, data were weighted to compensate for the fact that a DU at an address that contained a large number of DUs was less likely to be selected for inclusion in the survey than a DU at an address that contained fewer DUs. (We use this procedure because in most cases where the MOI is greater than one, the two stages will cancel each other out, resulting in more efficient weights.) Thirdly, data were weighted to compensate for the lower selection probabilities of adults living in large households, compared with those in small households.

At each stage the selection weights were trimmed to avoid a small number of very high or very low weights in the sample; such weights would inflate standard errors, reducing the precision of the survey estimates and causing the weighted sample to be less efficient. Less than one per cent of the sample was trimmed at each stage.

Non-response model

It is known that certain subgroups in the population are more likely to respond to surveys than others. These groups can end up over-represented in the sample, which can bias the survey estimates. Where information is available about non-responding households, the response behaviour of the sample members can be modelled and the results used to generate a non-response weight. This non-response weight is intended to reduce bias in the sample resulting from differential response to the survey.

The data was modelled using logistic regression, with the dependent variable indicating whether or not the selected individual responded to the survey. Ineligible households[2] were not included in the non-response modelling. A number of area level and interviewer observation variables were used to model response. Not all the variables examined were retained for the final model: variables not strongly related to a household's propensity to respond were dropped from the analysis.

The variables found to be related to response were Government Office Region (GOR), population density (population in private households divided by area in hectares) and whether there were entry barriers to the selected address. The model shows that the propensity for a household to respond increases if it is located in a low-density area. Response is lower at addresses where there are physical barriers to entry, such as entry systems and door staff. Response is lower if the household is located in London, the South West and or the West Midlands. The full model is given in Table A.1 below.

Table A.1 The final non-response model

Variable	B	S.E.	Wald	df	Sig.	Odds
Population density	0.00	0.00	7.1	1	0.008	0.99
Government Office Region			70.8	10	0.000	
East Midlands	-0.02	0.13	0.0	1	0.896	0.98
East of England	0.03	0.12	0.0	1	0.825	1.03
London	-0.77	0.12	38.4	1	0.000	0.47
North East	-0.04	0.15	0.1	1	0.789	0.96
North West	-0.07	0.11	0.3	1	0.559	0.94
Scotland	-0.06	0.12	0.3	1	0.600	0.94
South East	-0.09	0.11	0.6	1	0.429	0.92
South West	-0.32	0.12	7.2	1	0.007	0.73
Wales	0.00	0.14	0.0	1	0.981	1.00
West Midlands	-0.26	0.12	4.7	1	0.030	0.77
Yorkshire & Humber					*(baseline)*	
Any barriers to entry			29.7	1	0.000	
No barriers	0.44	0.08	29.7	1	0.000	1.56
One or more barriers to entry					*(baseline)*	
Constant	0.67	0.12	31.5	1	0.000	1.95

Notes:
1. The response is 1 = individual responding to the survey, 0 = non response
2. Only variables that are significant at the 0.05 level are included in the model
3. The model R^2 is 0.026 (Cox and Snell)
4. **B** is the estimate coefficient with standard error **S.E.**
5. The **Wald**-test measures the impact of the categorical variable on the model with the appropriate number of degrees of freedom **df**. If the test is significant (**sig.** < 0.05) then the categorical variable is considered to be 'significantly associated' with the response variable and therefore included in the model

The non-response weight is calculated as the inverse of the predicted response probabilities saved from the logistic regression model. The non-response weight was then combined with the selection weights to create the final non-response weight. The top and bottom one per cent of the weight were trimmed before the weight was scaled to the achieved sample size (resulting in the weight being standardised around an average of one).

Calibration weighting

The final stage of the weighting was to adjust the final non-response weight so that the weighted respondent sample matched the population in terms of age, sex and region. Only adults aged 18 and over are eligible to take part in the survey, therefore the data have been weighted to the British population aged 18+ based on the 2006 mid-year population estimates from the Office for National Statistics/General Register Office for Scotland.

The survey data were weighted to the marginal age/sex and GOR distributions using raking-ratio (or rim) weighting. As a result, the weighted data should exactly match the population across these three dimensions. This is shown in Table A.2.

Table A.2 Weighted and unweighted sample distribution, by GOR, age and sex

Government Office Region	Population	Unweighted respondents	Respondents weighted by selection weight only	Respondents weighted by un-calibrated non-response weight	Respondents weighted by final weight
	%	%	%	%	%
East Midlands	7.4	7.6	7.5	7.1	7.4
East of England	9.4	10.3	10.5	9.9	9.4
London	12.9	7.5	7.6	10.0	12.9
North East	4.4	4.6	4.5	4.3	4.4
North West	11.6	13.4	13.1	12.6	11.6
Scotland	8.8	9.1	8.8	8.7	8.8
South East	13.9	15.0	15.3	14.9	13.9
South West	8.8	8.7	8.5	8.9	8.8
West Midlands	9.1	8.8	9.2	9.4	9.1
Yorks. and Humber	8.6	9.7	9.5	9.0	8.6
Wales	5.1	5.5	5.5	5.2	5.1

table continued on next page

Age and sex	Population	Unweighted respondents	Respondents weighted by selection weight only	Respondents weighted by un-calibrated non-response weight	Respondents weighted by final weight
	%	%	%	%	%
M 18–24	5.9	3.5	5.2	5.2	5.9
M 25–34	8.4	6.8	6.9	7.1	8.4
M 35–44	9.7	9.5	9.4	9.4	9.7
M 45–54	8.1	7.2	8.0	7.9	8.1
M 55–59	4.1	3.9	3.9	3.8	4.1
M 60–64	3.2	3.7	3.6	3.6	3.2
M 65+	8.8	10.1	9.1	9.1	8.8
F 18–24	5.7	4.6	5.8	5.8	5.7
F 25–34	8.4	9.1	8.6	8.7	8.4
F 35–44	9.9	10.4	10.2	10.2	9.9
F 45–54	8.3	8.9	10.1	10.1	8.3
F 55–59	4.2	5.1	5.0	5.0	4.2
F 60–64	3.4	4.3	4.2	4.2	3.4
F 65+	11.7	13.0	10.1	10.0	11.7
Total	45,731,021	4,290	4,290	4,290	4,290

The calibration weight is the final non-response weight to be used in the analysis of the 2006 survey; this weight has been scaled to the responding sample size. The range of the weights is given in Table A.3.

Table A.3 Range of weights

	N	Minimum	Mean	Maximum
DU and person selection weight	4,290	0.18	1.00	2.19
Un-calibrated non-response weight	4,290	0.51	1.00	2.23
Final calibrated non-response weight	4,290	0.39	1.00	3.47

Effective sample size

The effect of the sample design on the precision of survey estimates is indicated by the effective sample size (neff). The effective sample size measures the size of an (unweighted) simple random sample that would achieve the same precision (standard error) as the design being implemented. If the effective sample size is close to the actual sample size then we have an efficient design with a good level of precision. The lower the effective sample size is, the lower the level of precision. The efficiency of a sample is given by the ratio of the effective sample size to the actual sample size. Samples that select one person per household tend to have lower efficiency than samples that select all household members. The final calibrated non-response weights have an effective sample size (neff) of 3,534 and efficiency of 82 per cent.

All the percentages presented in this Report are based on weighted data.

Questionnaire versions

Each address in each sector (sampling point) was allocated to either the A, B, C or D portion of the sample. If one serial number was version A, the next was version B, the third version C and the fourth version D. Thus, each interviewer was allocated seven or eight cases from each of versions A, B, C and D. There were 2,220 issued addresses for each version.

Fieldwork

Interviewing was mainly carried out between June and September 2006, with a small number of interviews taking place in October and November.

Table A.4 Response rate on *British Social Attitudes*, 2006

	Number	%
Addresses issued	8,880	
Vacant, derelict and other out of scope	965	
In scope	7,915	100.0
Interview achieved	4,291	54.2
Interview not achieved	3,624	45.8
Refused[1]	2,796	35.3
Non-contacted[2]	487	6.2
Other non-response	341	4.3

1 'Refused' comprises refusals before selection of an individual at the address, refusals to the office, refusal by the selected person, 'proxy' refusals (on behalf of the selected respondent) and broken appointments after which the selected person could not be recontacted

2 'Non-contacted' comprises households where no one was contacted and those where the selected person could not be contacted

Fieldwork was conducted by interviewers drawn from the *National Centre for Social Research*'s regular panel and conducted using face-to-face computer-assisted interviewing.[3] Interviewers attended a one-day briefing conference to familiarise them with the selection procedures and questionnaires.

The mean interview length was 64 minutes for version A of the questionnaire, 63 minutes for version B, 64 minutes for version C and 49 minutes for version D.[4] Interviewers achieved an overall response rate of 54 per cent. Details are shown in Table A.4.

As in earlier rounds of the series, the respondent was asked to fill in a self-completion questionnaire which, whenever possible, was collected by the interviewer. Otherwise, the respondent was asked to post it to the *National Centre for Social Research*. If necessary, up to three postal reminders were sent to obtain the self-completion supplement.

A total of 542 respondents (13 per cent of those interviewed) did not return their self-completion questionnaire. Version A of the self-completion questionnaire was returned by 89 per cent of respondents to the face-to-face interview, version B by 86 per cent, version C by 88 per cent and version D by 88 per cent. As in previous rounds, we judged that it was not necessary to apply additional weights to correct for non-response.

Advance letter

Interviewers were supplied with letters describing the purpose of the survey and the coverage of the questionnaire, which they posted to sampled addresses before making any calls.[5]

Analysis variables

A number of standard analyses have been used in the tables that appear in this Report. The analysis groups requiring further definition are set out below. For further details see Stafford and Thomson (2006).

Region

The dataset is classified by the 12 Government Office Regions.

Standard Occupational Classification

Respondents are classified according to their own occupation, not that of the 'head of household'. Each respondent was asked about their current or last job, so that all respondents except those who had never worked were coded. Additionally, all job details were collected for all spouses and partners in work.

With the 2001 survey, we began coding occupation to the new Standard Occupational Classification 2000 (SOC 2000) instead of the Standard

Occupational Classification 1990 (SOC 90). The main socio-economic grouping based on SOC 2000 is the National Statistics Socio-Economic Classification (NS-SEC). However, to maintain time-series, some analysis has continued to use the older schemes based on SOC 90 – Registrar General's Social Class, Socio-Economic Group and the Goldthorpe schema.

National Statistics Socio-Economic Classification (NS-SEC)

The combination of SOC 2000 and employment status for current or last job generates the following NS-SEC analytic classes:

- Employers in large organisations, higher managerial and professional
- Lower professional and managerial; higher technical and supervisory
- Intermediate occupations
- Small employers and own account workers
- Lower supervisory and technical occupations
- Semi-routine occupations
- Routine occupations

The remaining respondents are grouped as "never had a job" or "not classifiable". For some analyses, it may be more appropriate to classify respondents according to their current socio-economic status, which takes into account only their present economic position. In this case, in addition to the seven classes listed above, the remaining respondents not currently in paid work fall into one of the following categories: "not classifiable", "retired", "looking after the home", "unemployed" or "others not in paid occupations".

Registrar General's Social Class

As with NS-SEC, each respondent's Social Class is based on his or her current or last occupation. The combination of SOC 90 with employment status for current or last job generates the following six Social Classes:

I	Professional etc. occupations	
II	Managerial and technical occupations	'Non-manual'
III (Non-manual)	Skilled occupations	
III (Manual)	Skilled occupations	
IV	Partly skilled occupations	'Manual'
V	Unskilled occupations	

They are usually collapsed into four groups: I & II, III Non-manual, III Manual, and IV & V.

Socio-Economic Group

As with NS-SEC, each respondent's Socio-Economic Group (SEG) is based on his or her current or last occupation. SEG aims to bring together people with jobs of similar social and economic status, and is derived from a combination of employment status and occupation. The full SEG classification identifies 18 categories, but these are usually condensed into six groups:

- Professionals, employers and managers
- Intermediate non-manual workers
- Junior non-manual workers
- Skilled manual workers
- Semi-skilled manual workers
- Unskilled manual workers

As with NS-SEC, the remaining respondents are grouped as "never had a job" or "not classifiable".

Goldthorpe schema

The Goldthorpe schema classifies occupations by their 'general comparability', considering such factors as sources and levels of income, economic security, promotion prospects, and level of job autonomy and authority. The Goldthorpe schema was derived from the SOC 90 codes combined with employment status. Two versions of the schema are coded: the full schema has 11 categories; the 'compressed schema' combines these into the five classes shown below.

- Salariat (professional and managerial)
- Routine non-manual workers (office and sales)
- Petty bourgeoisie (the self-employed, including farmers, with and without employees)
- Manual foremen and supervisors
- Working class (skilled, semi-skilled and unskilled manual workers, personal service and agricultural workers)

There is a residual category comprising those who have never had a job or who gave insufficient information for classification purposes.

Industry

All respondents whose occupation could be coded were allocated a Standard Industrial Classification 2003 (SIC 03). Two-digit class codes are used. As with Social Class, SIC may be generated on the basis of the respondent's current occupation only, or on his or her most recently classifiable occupation.

Party identification

Respondents can be classified as identifying with a particular political party on one of three counts: if they consider themselves supporters of that party, as closer to it than to others, or as more likely to support it in the event of a general election (responses are derived from Qs. 237–239). The three groups are generally described respectively as *partisans*, *sympathisers* and *residual identifiers*. In combination, the three groups are referred to as 'identifiers'.

Attitude scales

Since 1986, the *British Social Attitudes* surveys have included two attitude scales which aim to measure where respondents stand on certain underlying value dimensions – left–right and libertarian–authoritarian.[6] Since 1987 (except 1990), a similar scale on 'welfarism' has been asked. Some of the items in the welfarism scale were changed in 2000–2001. The current version of the scale is listed below.

A useful way of summarising the information from a number of questions of this sort is to construct an additive index (DeVellis, 1991; Spector, 1992). This approach rests on the assumption that there is an underlying – 'latent' – attitudinal dimension which characterises the answers to all the questions within each scale. If so, scores on the index are likely to be a more reliable indication of the underlying attitude than the answers to any one question.

Each of these scales consists of a number of statements to which the respondent is invited to "agree strongly", "agree", "neither agree nor disagree", "disagree" or "disagree strongly".

The items are:

Left–right scale

Government should redistribute income from the better off to those who are less well off. *[Redistrb]*

Big business benefits owners at the expense of workers. *[BigBusnN]*

Ordinary working people do not get their fair share of the nation's wealth. *[Wealth]*[7]

There is one law for the rich and one for the poor. *[RichLaw]*

Management will always try to get the better of employees if it gets the chance. *[Indust4]*

Libertarian–authoritarian scale

Young people today don't have enough respect for traditional British values. *[TradVals]*

People who break the law should be given stiffer sentences. *[StifSent]*

For some crimes, the death penalty is the most appropriate sentence. *[DeathApp]*

Schools should teach children to obey authority. *[Obey]*

The law should always be obeyed, even if a particular law is wrong. *[WrongLaw]*

Censorship of films and magazines is necessary to uphold moral standards. *[Censor]*

Welfarism scale

The welfare state encourages people to stop helping each other. *[WelfHelp]*

The government should spend more money on welfare benefits for the poor, even if it leads to higher taxes. *[MoreWelf]*

Around here, most unemployed people could find a job if they really wanted one. *[UnempJob]*

Many people who get social security don't really deserve any help. *[SocHelp]*

Most people on the dole are fiddling in one way or another. *[DoleFidl]*

If welfare benefits weren't so generous, people would learn to stand on their own two feet. *[WelfFeet]*

Cutting welfare benefits would damage too many people's lives. *[DamLives]*

The creation of the welfare state is one of Britain's proudest achievements. *[ProudWlf]*

The indices for the three scales are formed by scoring the leftmost, most libertarian or most pro-welfare position as 1 and the rightmost, most authoritarian or most anti-welfarist position as 5. The "neither agree nor disagree" option is scored as 3. The scores to all the questions in each scale are added and then divided by the number of items in the scale, giving indices ranging from 1 (leftmost, most libertarian, most pro-welfare) to 5 (rightmost, most authoritarian, most anti-welfare). The scores on the three indices have been placed on the dataset.[8]

The scales have been tested for reliability (as measured by Cronbach's alpha). The Cronbach's alpha (unstandardised items) for the scales in 2006 are 0.82 for the left–right scale, 0.79 for the 'welfarism' scale and 0.73 for the libertarian–authoritarian scale. This level of reliability can be considered "very good" for the left–right scale and "respectable" for the libertarian–authoritarian and welfarism scales (DeVellis, 1991: 85).

Other analysis variables

These are taken directly from the questionnaire and to that extent are self-explanatory. The principal ones are:

Sex (Q. 40)
Age (Q. 41)
Household income (Q. 1108)
Economic position (Q. 706)
Religion (Q. 866)
Highest educational qualification obtained (Qs. 999–1000)
Marital status (Q. 134–135)
Benefits received (Qs. 1063–1101)

Sampling errors

No sample precisely reflects the characteristics of the population it represents, because of both sampling and non-sampling errors. If a sample were designed as a random sample (if every adult had an equal and independent chance of inclusion in the sample) then we could calculate the sampling error of any percentage, *p*, using the formula:

$$s.e.\ (p) = \sqrt{\frac{p(100 - p)}{n}}$$

where *n* is the number of respondents on which the percentage is based. Once the sampling error had been calculated, it would be a straightforward exercise to calculate a confidence interval for the true population percentage. For example, a 95 per cent confidence interval would be given by the formula:

$$p \pm 1.96 \times s.e.\ (p)$$

Clearly, for a simple random sample (srs), the sampling error depends only on the values of *p* and *n*. However, simple random sampling is almost never used in practice because of its inefficiency in terms of time and cost.

As noted above, the *British Social Attitudes* sample, like that drawn for most large-scale surveys, was clustered according to a stratified multi-stage design into 286 postcode sectors (or combinations of sectors). With a complex design like this, the sampling error of a percentage giving a particular response is not simply a function of the number of respondents in the sample and the size of the percentage; it also depends on how that percentage response is spread within and between sample points.

The complex design may be assessed relative to simple random sampling by calculating a range of design factors (DEFTs) associated with it, where:

$$DEFT = \sqrt{\frac{\text{Variance of estimator with complex design, sample size n}}{\text{Variance of estimator with srs design, sample size n}}}$$

and represents the multiplying factor to be applied to the simple random sampling error to produce its complex equivalent. A design factor of one means that the complex sample has achieved the same precision as a simple random sample of the same size. A design factor greater than one means the complex sample is less precise than its simple random sample equivalent. If the DEFT for a particular characteristic is known, a 95 per cent confidence interval for a percentage may be calculated using the formula:

$$p \pm 1.96 \text{ x complex sampling error (p)}$$

$$= p \pm 1.96 \text{ x DEFT x } \sqrt{\frac{p(100 - p)}{n}}$$

Calculations of sampling errors and design effects were made using the statistical analysis package STATA.

Table A.5 gives examples of the confidence intervals and DEFTs calculated for a range of different questions. Most background variables were fielded on the whole sample, whereas many attitudinal variables were asked only of a half or quarter of the sample; some were asked on the interview questionnaire and some on the self-completion supplement. The table shows that most of the questions asked of all sample members have a confidence interval of around plus or minus two to three per cent of the survey percentage. This means that we can be 95 per cent certain that the true population percentage is within two to three per cent (in either direction) of the percentage we report.

Variables with much larger variation are, as might be expected, those closely related to the geographic location of the respondent (for example, whether they live in a big city, a small town or a village). Here, the variation may be as large as five or six per cent either way around the percentage found on the survey. Consequently, the design effects calculated for these variables in a clustered sample will be greater than the design effects calculated for variables less strongly associated with area. Also, sampling errors for percentages based only on respondents to just one of the versions of the questionnaire, or on subgroups within the sample, are larger than they would have been had the questions been asked of everyone.

Table A.5 Complex standard errors and confidence intervals of selected variables

	% (p)	Complex standard error of p	95% confidence interval	DEFT	Base
Classification variables					
Q226	**Party identification (full sample)**				
Conservative	25.3	0.9	23.6–27.1	1.34	*4290*
Labour	32.8	1.0	30.9–34.8	1.40	*4290*
Liberal Democrat	11.9	0.6	10.7–13.1	1.20	*4290*
Q655	**Housing tenure (full sample)**				
Owns	70.9	1.2	68.5–73.3	1.76	*4290*
Rents from local authority	10.4	0.8	8.6–11.9	1.67	*4290*
Rents privately/HA	16.9	1.0	15.0–18.8	1.67	*4290*
Q866	**Religion (full sample)**				
No religion	45.8	1.1	43.6–47.9	1.45	*4290*
Church of England	22.2	0.8	20.7–23.7	1.21	*4290*
Roman Catholic	9.0	0.5	8.0–10.1	1.23	*4290*
Q934	**Age of completing continuous full-time education (full sample)**				
16 or under	51.9	1.1	49.7–54.2	1.48	*4290*
17 or 18	18.9	0.7	17.5–20.4	1.22	*4290*
19 or over	24.4	1.0	22.4–26.5	1.60	*4290*
Q219	**Home internet access (full sample)**				
Yes	64.7	0.9	63.0–66.5	1.21	*4290*
No	35.2	0.9	33.5–37.0	1.21	*4290*
Q856	**Urban or rural residence (full sample)**				
A big city	9.4	1.0	7.4–11.4	2.28	*4290*
The suburbs of outskirts of a big city	22.9	1.5	20.0–25.8	2.27	*4290*
A small city/town	47.9	2.1	43.8–52.0	2.72	*4290*
Country village	16.1	1.5	13.2–19.1	2.67	*4290*
Farm/home in the country	2.6	0.5	1.7–3.5	1.88	*4290*
Attitudinal variables (face-to-face interview)					
Q246	**Benefits for the unemployed are … (3/4 sample)**				
… too low	22.7	1.0	20.9–24.6	1.30	*3240*
… too high	54.4	1.1	52.2–56.6	1.27	*3240*
Q377	**NHS should be only available to those with lower incomes (1/2 sample)**				
Support a lot	10.3	0.8	8.8–11.8	1.17	*2143*
Support a little	13.5	0.8	11.9–15.1	1.07	*2143*
Oppose a little	14.7	0.8	13.1–16.4	1.08	*2143*
Oppose a lot	59.0	1.2	56.6–61.5	1.17	*2143*

table continued on next page

	% (p)	Complex standard error of p	95% confidence interval	DEFT	Base

Q311   Concern that building roads could damage countryside (3/4 sample)

Very concerned	24.5	0.9	22.7–26.3	1.22	*3220*
Fairly concerned	49.7	1.1	47.6–51.8	1.21	*3220*
Not very concerned	19.9	0.8	18.2–21.5	1.17	*3220*
Not at all concerned	5.4	0.5	4.5–6.3	1.15	*3220*

Q292   Household income (1/4 sample)

Living comfortably on present income	40.7	1.7	37.5–44.0	1.11	*1093*
Coping on present income	45.3	1.5	42.4–48.0	0.99	*1093*
Finding it difficult on present income	10.1	1.0	8.1–12.1	1.10	*1093*
Finding it very difficult on present income	3.8	0.7	2.4–5.3	1.25	*1093*

Q736   Would vote for Great Britain to join the Euro (1/4 sample)

Yes	25.7	1.6	22.5–29.0	1.23	*1077*
No	68.4	1.8	64.8–71.9	1.37	*1077*

Attitudinal variables (self-completion)

A21a   Government should redistribute income from the better off to those who
B46a   are less well off (full sample)

C43a	Agree strongly	7.4	0.5	6.4–8.3	1.13	*3748*
D42a	Agree	26.2	0.9	24.4–28.1	1.30	*3748*
	Neither agree nor disagree	26.9	0.8	25.2–28.6	1.13	*3748*
	Disagree	31.0	0.9	29.2–32.8	1.18	*3748*
	Disagree strongly	7.0	0.4	6.2–7.8	1.01	*3748*

A17a   Trade unions have too much power (3/4 sample)

C18a	Far too much power	8.7	1.0	6.8–10.6	1.80	*2818*
D18a	Too much power	22.3	1.5	19.4–23.5	1.87	*2818*
	Right amount of power	48.7	2.1	44.4–53.0	2.29	*2818*
	Too little power	16.4	1.6	13.3–19.5	2.24	*2818*
	Far too little power	2.8	0.3	1.7–3.8	1.72	*2818*

C27   How often married couples agree about sharing housework (1/2 sample)
D27

Several times a week	6.2	0.8	4.7–7.7	1.14	*1147*
Several times a month	8.9	0.9	7.2–10.7	1.11	*1147*
Several times a year	10.1	1.0	8.2–12.0	1.15	*1147*
Rarely	35.5	1.5	32.6–38.5	1.12	*1147*
Never	42.2	1.6	31.0–37.3	1.19	*1147*

B10   Level of interest in politics (1/4 sample)

Very interested	9.9	1.0	8.0–11.9	1.00	*930*
Fairly interested	28.1	1.6	25.0–31.3	1.07	*930*
Somewhat interested	27.4	1.8	23.9–30.9	1.22	*930*
Not very interested	22.5	1.5	19.5–25.5	1.11	*930*
Not at all interested	9.8	1.1	7.8–11.9	1.08	*930*

Analysis techniques

Regression

Regression analysis aims to summarise the relationship between a 'dependent' variable and one or more 'independent' variables. It shows how well we can estimate a respondent's score on the dependent variable from knowledge of their scores on the independent variables. It is often undertaken to support a claim that the phenomena measured by the independent variables *cause* the phenomenon measured by the dependent variable. However, the causal ordering, if any, between the variables cannot be verified or falsified by the technique. Causality can only be inferred through special experimental designs or through assumptions made by the analyst.

All regression analysis assumes that the relationship between the dependent and each of the independent variables takes a particular form. In *linear regression*, it is assumed that the relationship can be adequately summarised by a straight line. This means that a one percentage point increase in the value of an independent variable is assumed to have the same impact on the value of the dependent variable on average, irrespective of the previous values of those variables.

Strictly speaking the technique assumes that both the dependent and the independent variables are measured on an interval level scale, although it may sometimes still be applied even where this is not the case. For example, one can use an ordinal variable (e.g. a Likert scale) as a *dependent* variable if one is willing to assume that there is an underlying interval level scale and the difference between the observed ordinal scale and the underlying interval scale is due to random measurement error. Often the answers to a number of Likert-type questions are averaged to give a dependent variable that is more like a continuous variable. Categorical or nominal data can be used as *independent* variables by converting them into dummy or binary variables; these are variables where the only valid scores are 0 and 1, with 1 signifying membership of a particular category and 0 otherwise.

The assumptions of linear regression cause particular difficulties where the *dependent* variable is binary. The assumption that the relationship between the dependent and the independent variables is a straight line means that it can produce estimated values for the dependent variable of less than 0 or greater than 1. In this case it may be more appropriate to assume that the relationship between the dependent and the independent variables takes the form of an S-curve, where the impact on the dependent variable of a one-point increase in an independent variable becomes progressively less the closer the value of the dependent variable approaches 0 or 1. *Logistic regression* is an alternative form of regression which fits such an S-curve rather than a straight line. The technique can also be adapted to analyse multinomial non-interval level dependent variables, that is, variables which classify respondents into more than two categories.

The two statistical scores most commonly reported from the results of regression analyses are:

A measure of variance explained: This summarises how well all the independent variables combined can account for the variation in respondent's scores in the dependent variable. The higher the measure, the more accurately we are able in general to estimate the correct value of each respondent's score on the dependent variable from knowledge of their scores on the independent variables.

A parameter estimate: This shows how much the dependent variable will change on average, given a one-unit change in the independent variable (while holding all other independent variables in the model constant). The parameter estimate has a positive sign if an increase in the value of the independent variable results in an increase in the value of the dependent variable. It has a negative sign if an increase in the value of the independent variable results in a decrease in the value of the dependent variable. If the parameter estimates are standardised, it is possible to compare the relative impact of different independent variables; those variables with the largest standardised estimates can be said to have the biggest impact on the value of the dependent variable.

Regression also tests for the statistical significance of parameter estimates. A parameter estimate is said to be significant at the five per cent level if the range of the values encompassed by its 95 per cent confidence interval (see also section on sampling errors) are either all positive or all negative. This means that there is less than a five per cent chance that the association we have found between the dependent variable and the independent variable is simply the result of sampling error and does not reflect a relationship that actually exists in the general population.

Factor analysis

Factor analysis is a statistical technique which aims to identify whether there are one or more apparent sources of commonality to the answers given by respondents to a set of questions. It ascertains the smallest number of *factors* (or dimensions) which can most economically summarise all of the variation found in the set of questions being analysed. Factors are established where respondents who give a particular answer to one question in the set, tend to give the same answer as each other to one or more of the other questions in the set. The technique is most useful when a relatively small number of factors are able to account for a relatively large proportion of the variance in all of the questions in the set.

The technique produces a *factor loading* for each question (or variable) on each factor. Where questions have a high loading on the same factor, then it will be the case that respondents who give a particular answer to one of these questions tend to give a similar answer to the other questions. The technique is most commonly used in attitudinal research to try to identify the underlying ideological dimensions which apparently structure attitudes towards the subject in question.

International Social Survey Programme

The *International Social Survey Programme* (*ISSP*) is run by a group of research organisations, each of which undertakes to field annually an agreed module of questions on a chosen topic area. Since 1985, an *International Social Survey Programme* module has been included in one of the *British Social Attitudes* self-completion questionnaires. Each module is chosen for repetition at intervals to allow comparisons both between countries (membership is currently standing at over 40) and over time. In 2006, the chosen subject was Role of Government, and the module was carried on the B version of the self-completion questionnaire (Qs. 2.1–2.22).

Notes

1. Until 1991 all *British Social Attitudes* samples were drawn from the Electoral Register (ER). However, following concern that this sampling frame might be deficient in its coverage of certain population subgroups, a 'splicing' experiment was conducted in 1991. We are grateful to the Market Research Development Fund for contributing towards the costs of this experiment. Its purpose was to investigate whether a switch to PAF would disrupt the time-series – for instance, by lowering response rates or affecting the distribution of responses to particular questions. In the event, it was concluded that the change from ER to PAF was unlikely to affect time trends in any noticeable ways, and that no adjustment factors were necessary. Since significant differences in efficiency exist between PAF and ER, and because we considered it untenable to continue to use a frame that is known to be biased, we decided to adopt PAF as the sampling frame for future *British Social Attitudes* surveys. For details of the PAF/ER 'splicing' experiment, see Lynn and Taylor (1995).
2. This includes households not containing any adults aged 18 and over, vacant dwelling units, derelict dwelling units, non-resident addresses and other deadwood.
3. In 1993 it was decided to mount a split-sample experiment designed to test the applicability of Computer-Assisted Personal Interviewing (CAPI) to the *British Social Attitudes* survey series. CAPI has been used increasingly over the past decade as an alternative to traditional interviewing techniques. As the name implies, CAPI involves the use of lap-top computers during the interview, with interviewers entering responses directly into the computer. One of the advantages of CAPI is that it significantly reduces both the amount of time spent on data processing and the number of coding and editing errors. There was, however, concern that a different interviewing technique might alter the distribution of responses and so affect the year-on-year consistency of *British Social Attitudes* data.

   Following the experiment, it was decided to change over to CAPI completely in 1994 (the self-completion questionnaire still being administered in the conventional way). The results of the experiment are discussed in *The 11ᵗʰ Report* (Lynn and Purdon, 1994).

4. Interview times recorded as less than 20 minutes were excluded, as these timings were likely to be errors.
5. An experiment was conducted on the 1991 *British Social Attitudes* survey (Jowell *et al.*, 1992) which showed that sending advance letters to sampled addresses before fieldwork begins has very little impact on response rates. However, interviewers do find that an advance letter helps them to introduce the survey on the doorstep, and a majority of respondents have said that they preferred some advance notice. For these reasons, advance letters have been used on the *British Social Attitudes* surveys since 1991.
6. Because of methodological experiments on scale development, the exact items detailed in this section have not been asked on all versions of the questionnaire each year.
7. In 1994 only, this item was replaced by: Ordinary people get their fair share of the nation's wealth. *[Wealth1]*
8. In constructing the scale, a decision had to be taken on how to treat missing values ('Don't knows,' 'Refused' and 'Not answered'). Respondents who had more than two missing values on the left–right scale and more than three missing values on the libertarian–authoritarian and welfarism scale were excluded from that scale. For respondents with just a few missing values, 'Don't knows' were recoded to the midpoint of the scale and 'Refused' or 'Not answered' were recoded to the scale mean for that respondent on their valid items.

References

DeVellis, R.F. (1991), 'Scale development: theory and applications', *Applied Social Research Methods Series*, **26**, Newbury Park: Sage

Jowell, R., Brook, L., Prior, G. and Taylor, B. (1992), *British Social Attitudes: The 9th Report*, Aldershot: Dartmouth

Lynn, P. and Purdon, S. (1994), 'Time-series and lap-tops: the change to computer-assisted interviewing', in Jowell, R., Curtice, J., Brook, L. and Ahrendt, D. (eds.), *British Social Attitudes: the 11th Report*, Aldershot: Dartmouth

Lynn, P. and Taylor, B. (1995), 'On the bias and variance of samples of individuals: a comparison of the Electoral Registers and Postcode Address File as sampling frames', *The Statistician*, **44**: 173–194

Spector, P.E. (1992), 'Summated rating scale construction: an introduction', *Quantitative Applications in the Social Sciences*, **82**, Newbury Park: Sage

Stafford, R. and Thomson, K. (2006), *British Social Attitudes and Young People's Social Attitudes surveys 2003*: Technical Report, London: National Centre for Social Research

Appendix II
Notes on the tabulations in chapters

1. Figures in the tables are from the 2006 *British Social Attitudes* survey unless otherwise indicated.
2. Tables are percentaged as indicated by the percentage signs.
3. In tables, '*' indicates less than 0.5 per cent but greater than zero, and '–' indicates zero.
4. When findings based on the responses of fewer than 100 respondents are reported in the text, reference is made to the small base size.
5. Percentages equal to or greater than 0.5 have been rounded up (e.g. 0.5 per cent = one per cent; 36.5 per cent = 37 per cent).
6. In many tables the proportions of respondents answering "Don't know" or not giving an answer are not shown. This, together with the effects of rounding and weighting, means that percentages will not always add to 100 per cent.
7. The self-completion questionnaire was not completed by all respondents to the main questionnaire (see Appendix I). Percentage responses to the self-completion questionnaire are based on all those who completed it.
8. The bases shown in the tables (the number of respondents who answered the question) are printed in small italics. The bases are unweighted, unless otherwise stated.

Appendix III
The questionnaires

As explained in Appendix I, four different versions of the questionnaire (A, B, C and D) were administered, each with its own self-completion supplement. The diagram that follows shows the structure of the questionnaires and the topics covered (not all of which are reported on in this volume).

The four interview questionnaires reproduced on the following pages are derived from the Blaise computer program in which they were written. For ease of reference, each item has been allocated a question number. Gaps in the numbering system indicate items that are essential components of the Blaise program but which are not themselves questions, and so have been omitted. In addition, we have removed the keying codes and inserted instead the percentage distribution of answers to each question. We have also included the SPSS variable name, in square brackets, at each question. Above the questions we have included filter instructions. A filter instruction should be considered as staying in force until the next filter instruction. Percentages for the core questions are based on the total weighted sample, while those for questions in versions A, B, C or D are based on the appropriate weighted sub-samples.

The four versions of the self-completion questionnaire follow. We begin by reproducing version A of the interview questionnaire in full; then those parts of versions B, C and D that differ.

The percentage distributions do not necessarily add up to 100 because of weighting and rounding, or for one or more of the following reasons:

(i)   Some sub-questions are filtered – that is, they are asked of only a proportion of respondents. In these cases the percentages add up (approximately) to the proportions who were asked them. Where, however, a series of questions is filtered, we have indicated the reduced weighted base (for example, all employees), and have derived percentages from that base.

(ii)   At a few questions, respondents were invited to give more than one answer and so percentages may add to well over 100 per cent. These are clearly marked by interviewer instructions on the questionnaires.

As reported in Appendix I, the 2006 *British Social Attitudes* self-completion questionnaire was not completed by 13 per cent of respondents who were successfully interviewed. The answers in the supplement have been percentaged on the base of those respondents who returned it. This means that the distribution of responses to questions asked in earlier years are comparable with those given in Appendix III of all earlier reports in this series except in *The 1984 Report*, where the percentages for the self-completion questionnaire need to be recalculated if comparisons are to be made.

BRITISH SOCIAL ATTITUDES: 2006 SURVEY

| Version A (quarter of sample) | Version B (quarter of sample) | Version C (quarter of sample) | Version D (quarter of sample) |

Face-to-face questionnaires

Household grid, newspaper readership and party identification			
Public spending and social security		Public spending and social security	—
Transport		—	Transport
	New families		
Health	—	—	Health
—	Cohabitation		
Education			—
Job details			
Employment relations	Politics	Employment relations	
National identity			—
Classification			

Self-completion questionnaires

	ISSP (Role of government)		
Public spending and social security		Public spending and social security	—
Transport		—	Transport
	New families		
Health	—	—	Health
—	Cohabitation		
Education			—
Employment relations	Politics	Employment relations	
Standard scales			

BRITISH SOCIAL ATTITUDES 2006

FACE-TO-FACE QUESTIONNAIRE

Contents

Introduction

Q1   **ASK ALL**   N=4290
        [Serial] **(NOT ON SCREEN)**
        Serial Number
        Range: 180001 ... 189999

Q17 [GOR2] **(NOT ON SCREEN)**   N=4290
  %   Government office region 2003 version
  4.4   North East
 11.6   North West
  8.6   Yorkshire and Humberside
  7.4   East Midlands
  9.1   West Midlands
  8.7   SW
  9.5   Eastern
  4.8   Inner London
  8.0   Outer London
 13.9   South East
  5.1   Wales
  8.8   Scotland

Q28 [ABCDVer] **(NOT ON SCREEN)**
  %   A, B, C or D?
 25.4   A
 25.1   B
 24.7   C
 24.8   D

Q29 [Country] **(NOT ON SCREEN)**
  %   England, Scotland or Wales?
 86.1   England
  8.8   Scotland
  5.1   Wales

Household grid

Q38 **ASK ALL**   N=4290
        [Househld]
        (You have just been telling me about the adults that
        live here. Thinking now of **everyone** living in this
        household, **including children**:)

        Including yourself, how many people live here
        regularly as members of this **household**?

        CHECK INTERVIEWER MANUAL FOR DEFINITION OF HOUSEHOLD
        IF NECESSARY.
        NOTE THAT THIS MAY BE **DIFFERENT** TO THE DWELLING UNIT
        YOU ENUMERATED FOR THE SELECTION.

        IF YOU DISCOVER THAT YOU WERE GIVEN THE WRONG
        INFORMATION FOR THE RESPONDENT SELECTION ON THE ARF:
        *DO **NOT** REDO THE ARF SELECTION PRODECURE
        *DO ENTER THE CORRECT INFORMATION HERE
        *DO USE <CTRL + M> TO MAKE A NOTE OF WHAT HAPPENED.
        Median: 2 people

Q39 **FOR EACH PERSON AT** [Household]   N=4290
        [Name]
        FOR RESPONDENT: (Can I just check, what is your first
        name?)
        PLEASE TYPE IN THE FIRST NAME (OR INITIALS) OF
        RESPONDENT
        FOR OTHER HOUSEHOLD MEMBERS: PLEASE TYPE IN THE FIRST
        NAME (OR INITIALS) OF PERSON NUMBER (number)
        Open Question (Maximum of 10 characters)

Q40 [RSex] *(Figures refer to respondent)*   N=4290
  %   PLEASE CODE SEX OF (name)
 48.3   Male
 51.7   Female

Q41 [RAge]
(Figures refer to second person in household)   N=4290
FOR RESPONDENT IF ONE PERSON IN HOUSEHOLD: I would now like to ask you a few details about yourself. What was your **age** last birthday?
FOR RESPONDENT IF SEVERAL PEOPLE IN HOUSEHOLD: I would like to ask you a few details about each person in your household. Starting with yourself, what was your **age** last birthday?
FOR OTHER PEOPLE IN HOUSEHOLD: What was *(name's)* age last birthday?
FOR 97+, CODE 97.
Median: 46 years
%
0.0   (Don't know)
0.0   (Refusal)

FOR PEOPLE IN THE HOUSEHOLD OTHER THAN RESPONDENT
N=4290

Q48 [Rel3] *(Figures refer to second person in household)*
%   PLEASE ENTER RELATIONSHIP OF *(name)* TO RESPONDENT
62.7   Partner/ spouse/ cohabitee
6.5   Son/ daughter (inc step/adopted)
0.2   Grandson/ daughter (inc step/adopted)
6.2   Parent/ parent-in-law
0.2   Grand-parent
2.4   Brother/ sister (inc. in-law)
0.5   Other relative
3.3   Other non-relative
0.0   (Don't know)
0.0   (Refusal)

Q134   [MarStat5]   N=4290
CARD A1
Can I just check, which of these applies to you at present?
Please choose the first on the list that applies
%
54.0   Married
0.1   In civil partnership
11.2   Living with a partner
2.4   Separated (after being married)
5.6   Divorced
6.8   Widowed
19.8   Single (never married)
0.0   (Don't know)
0.0   (Refusal)

Q137   **IF 'Living with a partner' AT [MarStat5]**   N=4290
[LegStat2]
CARD A2
And what is your legal marital status?
%
0.1   Married
0.7   In civil partnership
0.4   Separated (after being married)
2.3   Divorced
0.2   Widowed
7.4   Single (never married)
0.1   (Other (WRITE IN))
-    (Don't know)
0.1   (Refusal)

Q153-   CARD A3   N=4290
Q160   Can I just check which, if any, of these types of relatives do you yourself have alive at the moment.
Please include adoptive and step relatives.
PROBE: Which others?
DO NOT INCLUDE FOSTER RELATIVES
CODE ALL THAT APPLY
Multicoded (Maximum of 8 codes)
%
47.7   Father   [RelFath]
57.0   Mother   [RelMoth]
61.8   Brother   [RelBroth]
59.6   Sister   [RelSist]
51.2   Son   [RelSon]
52.2   Daughter   [RelDaug]
21.4   Grandchild (daughter's child)   [RelGrChD]
18.9   Grandchild (son's child)   [RelGrChS]
2.0   None of these   [RelNone3]
-    (Don't Know)
0.1   (Refusal/Not answered)

Q170   **ASK ALL WITH 'Grandchild' IN [RelGrChD] or [RelGrChS]**
[GChild16]   N=1240
Do you have any grandchildren aged under 16?
%
84.4   Yes
15.3   No
0.0   (Don't know)
0.2   (Refusal)

Q171 **[GChild16]**
IF 'Yes' AT [GChild16]   N=1240
Thinking of your grandchildren aged under 16, are they all living together with both their parents?
%
58.2 Yes
26.1 No
0.1 (Don't know)
0.3 (Refusal)

Q172 **[GChWhich]**
IF 'No' AT [GChBothP]   N=1240
These grandchildren who are not living with both their parents, are they your son's children, your daughter's children or both?
%
10.3 Son's children
13.4 Daughter's children
2.4 Both
- (Don't know)
0.4 (Refusal)

Q173 **[StepCh]**
VERSIONS B, C AND D: ASK ALL WITH 'daughter' OR 'son' AT [RElat3]   N=2224
Can I just check, do you have any step-children?
THIS IS RESPONDENT'S DEFINITION OF STEP CHILDREN, RATHER THAN A LEGAL DEFINITION
%
10.1 Yes
89.8 No
- (Don't know)
0.2 (Refusal)

Q673 **[REconAct] (NOT ON SCREEN)**
ASK ALL   N=4290
CARD A4
Which of these descriptions applied to what you were doing last week, that is the seven days ending last Sunday?
PROBE: Which others? CODE ALL THAT APPLY
Priority coded
%
4.2 In full-time education (not paid for by employer, including on vacation)
0.3 On government training/ employment programme
56.9 In paid work (or away temporarily) for at least 10 hours in week
0.5 Waiting to take up paid work already accepted
1.9 Unemployed and registered at a JobCentre or JobCentre Plus
1.0 Unemployed, **not** registered, but actively looking for a job (of at least 10 hrs a week)
0.8 Unemployed, wanting a job (of at least 10 hrs a week) but **not** actively looking for a job
3.7 Permanently sick or disabled
21.7 Wholly retired from work
8.1 Looking after the home
0.9 (Doing something else) (WRITE IN)
- (Don't know)
0.1 (Refusal)

Q674 **[RLastJob]**
ASK ALL THOSE WHO ARE NOT WORKING OR WAITING TO TAKE UP WORK (I.E. 'in full-time education', 'on government training scheme', 'unemployed', 'permanently sick or disabled', 'wholly retired from work', 'looking after the home' OR 'doing something else' AT [REconAct]   N=1829
How long ago did you last have a paid job of at least 10 hours a week?
GOVERNMENT PROGRAMS/SCHEMES DO NOT COUNT AS 'PAID JOBS'.
%
15.9 Within past 12 months
19.0 Over 1, up to 5 years ago
15.2 Over 5, up to 10 years ago
24.9 Over 10, up to 20 years ago
16.4 Over 20 years ago
8.3 Never had a paid job of 10+ hours a week
0.1 (Don't know)
0.2 (Refusal)

ASK ALL 'married', 'in civil partnership' OR 'living with a partner' AT [MarStat5]

Q1001 [SEconAct]   (NOT ON SCREEN)   N=2807
CARD A4
Which of these descriptions applied to what your (husband/wife/partner) was doing last week, that is the seven days ending last Sunday?
PROBE: Which others? CODE ALL THAT APPLY
Priority coded
%
1.0 In full-time education (not paid for by employer, including on vacation)
0.0 On government training/ employment programme
62.1 In paid work (or away temporarily) for at least 10 hours in week
0.6 Waiting to take up paid work already accepted
1.2 Unemployed and registered at a JobCentre or JobCentre Plus
0.9 Unemployed, **not** registered, but actively looking for a job (of at least 10 hrs a week)
0.5 Unemployed, wanting a job (of at least 10 hrs a week) but **not** actively looking for a job
2.5 Permanently sick or disabled
20.8 Wholly retired from work
9.7 Looking after the home
0.5 (Doing something else) (WRITE IN)
0.1 (Don't know)
0.1 (Refusal)

ASK ALL THOSE WHOSE SPOUSE/PARTNER IS NOT WORKING OR WAITING TO TAKE UP WORK (I.E. 'in full-time education', 'on government training scheme', 'unemployed', 'permanently sick or disabled', 'wholly retired from work', 'looking after the home' OR 'doing something else' AT [SEconAct])

Q1002 [SLastJob]   N=1043
How long ago did your (wife/husband/partner) last have a paid job of at least 10 hours a week?
GOVERNMENT PROGRAMS/SCHEMES DO NOT COUNT AS 'PAID JOBS'.
%
12.9 Within past 12 months
21.1 Over 1, up to 5 years ago
16.8 Over 5, up to 10 years ago
27.6 Over 10, up to 20 years ago
15.3 Over 20 years ago
5.3 Never had a paid job of 10+ hours a week
0.7 (Don't know)
0.3 (Refusal)

Newspaper readership and internet

Q207 **ASK ALL**
[Readpap]
Do you normally read any daily **morning** newspaper at least 3 times a week?   N=4290

	%
Yes	50.0
No	50.0
(Don't know)	-
(Refusal)	-

Q208 **IF 'yes' AT [Readpap]**
[WhPaper]
Which one do you normally read?
IF MORE THAN ONE: Which one do you read **most** frequently?   N=4290

	%
(Scottish) Daily Express	3.0
(Scottish) Daily Mail	10.1
Daily Mirror (/Scottish Mirror)	5.4
Daily Star	1.4
The Sun	11.6
Daily Record	1.3
Daily Telegraph	3.8
Financial Times	0.5
The Guardian	2.8
The Independent	1.4
The Times	3.6
Morning Star	0.1
Other Irish/Northern Irish/Scottish regional or local **daily morning** paper (WRITE IN)	4.3
Other (WRITE IN)	0.6
EDIT ONLY: MORE THAN ONE PAPER READ WITH EQUAL FREQUENCY	0.1
(Don't know)	-
(Refusal)	0.1

Q213 **IF 'no' AT [ReadPap]**
[InterPap]
Can I just check, do you read a newspaper on the internet at least 3 times a week?
EXCLUDE BBC WEBSITE.   N=4290

	%
Yes	3.0
No	46.6
(Don't know)	0.1
(Refusal)	0.3

Q214 **IF 'yes' AT [InterPap]**
[WhintPap]
Which one?   N=4290

	%
(Scottish) Daily Express	0.1
(Scottish) Daily Mail	0.1
Daily Mirror (/Scottish Mirror)	0.0
Daily Star	-
The Sun	0.1
Daily Record	0.0
Daily Telegraph	0.3
Financial Times	0.1
The Guardian	0.7
The Independent	0.1
The Times	0.3
Morning Star	-
Other Irish/Northern Irish/Scottish regional or local **daily morning** paper (WRITE IN)	0.4
Other (WRITE IN)	0.8
EDIT ONLY: MORE THAN ONE PAPER READ WITH EQUAL FREQUENCY	-
(Don't know)	-
(Refusal)	0.4

Q219 ASK ALL
[Internet]
Does anyone have access to the internet or World Wide Web from this address?   N=4290

Q220 IF 'Yes' AT [Internt]
[BroadBnd]
Do you have a **broadband** connection to the internet?   N=4290

Q221 ASK ALL
[WWWUse]
Do you yourself ever use the internet or World Wide Web for any reason (other than your work)?   N=4290

	[Internet]	[BroadBnd]	[WWWUse]
	%	%	%
Yes	64.7	51.4	63.7
No	35.2	12.9	36.2
(Don't Know)	-	0.4	-
(Refusal/Not answered)	0.0	0.0	0.0

Q222 IF 'Yes' AT [WWWUse]
[WWWHrsWk]
How many **hours** a week on average do you spend using the Internet or World Wide Web (other than for your work)?   N=4290
INTERVIEWER: ROUND UP TO NEAREST HOUR
Median: 3 hours

%
0.3 (Don't know)
0.1 (Refusal)

Party identification

Q223 ASK ALL
[SupParty]
Generally speaking, do you think of yourself as a supporter of any one political party?   N=4290

Q224 IF 'no' OR DON'T KNOW AT [SupParty]
[ClosePty]
Do you think of yourself as a little closer to one political party than to the others?   N=4290

	[SupParty]	[ClosePty]
	%	%
Yes	34.2	23.7
No	65.7	42.0
(Don't Know)	0.1	0.1
(Refusal/Not answered)	0.0	0.1

IF 'Yes' AT [SupParty] OR 'yes', 'no' OR DON'T KNOW AT [ClosePty]

Q226 [Partyid1] (NOT ON SCREEN)   N=4290
IF 'Yes' AT [SupParty] OR AT [ClosePty]: Which one?
IF 'no' OR DON'T KNOW AT [SupParty] OR AT [ClosePty]: If there were a general election tomorrow, which political party do you think you would be most likely to support?
DO NOT PROMPT

%
25.3 Conservative
32.8 Labour
11.9 Liberal Democrat
1.5 Scottish National Party
0.4 Plaid Cymru
0.1 Other party
1.7 Other answer
15.2 None
0.7 UK Independence Party (UKIP)/Veritas
1.3 British National Party (BNP) / National Front
0.4 RESPECT/ Scottish Socialist Party (SSP)/ Socialist Party
2.4 Green Party
4.4 (Don't Know)
1.8 (Refusal)

Public spending and social welfare (mainly versions A, B and C)

VERSIONS A, B AND C: ASK ALL   N=3228

Q236   [Spend1] *
        CARD B1
        Here are some items of government spending.
        Which of them, if any, would be your highest priority
        for **extra** spending?
        Please read through the whole list before deciding.
        ENTER ONE CODE ONLY FOR HIGHEST PRIORITY

        IF NOT 'none', DON'T KNOW OR REFUSAL AT [Spend1]
                                                N=3228
Q237   [Spend2] *
        CARD B1 AGAIN
        And which next?
        ENTER ONE CODE ONLY FOR NEXT HIGHEST

| | [Spend1] | [Spend2] |
	%	%
Education	27.4	32.9
Defence	2.3	3.7
Health	46.9	27.9
Housing	4.1	7.9
Public transport	4.4	6.4
Roads	2.1	3.0
Police and prisons	6.7	9.9
Social security benefits	2.0	2.9
Help for industry	1.6	2.4
Overseas aid	1.4	1.7
(None of these)	0.6	0.4
(Don't Know)	0.4	0.0
(Refusal/Not answered)	0.0	-

IF PARTY GIVEN AT [PartyID1]
                                N=4290
Q233   [Idstrng]
        Would you call yourself very strong (party), fairly
        strong, or not very strong?

        %
        5.4   Very strong (party)
        24.7   Fairly strong
        46.3   Not very strong
        4.6   (Don't know)
        3.7   (Refusal)

VERSION B: ASK ALL
                                N=1077
Q234   [Politics]
        How much interest do you generally have in what is
        going on in politics
        ...READ OUT ...

        %
        10.0   ... a great deal,
        24.4   quite a lot,
        33.7   some,
        20.6   not very much,
        11.4   or, none at all?
        -       (Don't know)
        -       (Refusal)

VERSIONS A, B AND C: ASK ALL

Q238   [SocSpnd1] *   N=3228
CARD B2
Some people think that there should be more government spending on social security, while other people disagree. For each of the groups I read out please say whether you would like to see **more** or **less** government spending on them than now. Bear in mind that if you want more spending, this would probably mean that you would have to pay more taxes. If you want less spending, this would probably mean paying less taxes.
Firstly, ...READ OUT...
... benefits for unemployed people: would you like to see more or less government spending than now?

Q239   [SocSpnd2] *   N=3228
CARD B2 AGAIN
(Would you like to see more or less government spending than now on ...)
... benefits for disabled people who cannot work?

Q240   [SocSpnd3] *   N=3228
CARD B2 AGAIN
(Would you like to see more or less government spending than now on ...)
... benefits for parents who work on very low incomes?

	[SocSpnd1]	[SocSpnd2]	[SocSpnd3]
	%	%	%
Spend much more	2.0	8.8	8.4
Spend more	13.7	53.0	57.6
Spend the same as now	36.1	31.2	27.0
Spend less	36.7	2.9	3.9
Spend much less	8.1	0.4	0.3
(Don't Know)	3.3	3.6	2.8
(Refusal/Not answered)	0.1	0.0	0.1

Q241   [SocSpnd4] *   N=3228
CARD B2 AGAIN
(Would you like to see more or less government spending than now on ...)
... benefits for single parents?

Q242   [SocSpnd5] *   N=3228
CARD B2 AGAIN
(Would you like to see more or less government spending than now on ...)
... benefits for retired people?

Q243   [SocSpnd6] *   N=3228
CARD B2 AGAIN
(Would you like to see more or less government spending than now on ...)
... benefits for people who care for those who are sick or disabled?

	[SocSpnd4]	[SocSpnd5]	[SocSpnd6]
	%	%	%
Spend much more	5.0	17.6	22.3
Spend more	32.8	54.6	59.5
Spend the same as now	39.3	23.9	15.2
Spend less	15.9	2.1	0.8
Spend much less	3.3	0.1	0.1
(Don't Know)	3.7	1.7	2.1
(Refusal/Not answered)	0.0	0.0	0.0

Q244   [FalseClm] *   N=3228
I will read two statements. For each one please say whether you agree or disagree. Firstly...
Large numbers of people these days **falsely** claim benefits.
IF AGREE OR DISAGREE: Strongly or slightly?

Q245   [FailClm] *   N=3228
(And do you agree or disagree that...)
Large numbers of people who are eligible for benefits these days **fail** to claim them.
IF AGREE OR DISAGREE: Strongly or slightly?

	[FalseClm]	[FailClm]
	%	%
Agree strongly	55.7	32.0
Agree slightly	27.8	44.8
Disagree slightly	8.6	13.7
Disagree strongly	4.0	2.7
(Don't Know)	3.9	6.7
(Refusal/Not answered)	-	0.0

Q246 [Dole]   N=3228
Opinions differ about the level of benefits for
unemployed people.
Which of these two statements comes closest to your
own view
...READ OUT...
%
22.7 ...benefits for unemployed people are **too low** and
cause hardship,
54.4 or, benefits for unemployed people are **too high** and
discourage them from finding jobs?
16.4 (Neither)
0.1 BOTH: UNEMPLOYMENT BENEFIT CAUSES HARDSHIP BUT CAN'T
BE HIGHER OR THERE WOULD BE NO INCENTIVE TO WORK
0.4 BOTH: UNEMPLOYMENT BENEFIT CAUSES HARDSHIP TO SOME,
WHILE OTHERS DO WELL OUT OF IT
0.4 ABOUT RIGHT/IN BETWEEN
1.9 Other answer (WRITE IN)
3.8 (Don't know)
- (Refusal)

Q249 [TaxSpend]   N=3228
CARD B3
Suppose the government had to choose between the three
options on this card. Which do you think it should
choose?
%
5.7 Reduce taxes and spend **less** on health, education and
social benefits
43.5 Keep taxes and spending on these services at the **same**
level as now
46.4 Increase taxes and spend **more** on health, education and
social benefits
3.5 (None)
0.9 (Don't know)
0.0 (Refusal)

VERSIONS A, B AND C: ASK ALL
Q250 [MtUnmar1] *   N=3228
Imagine an unmarried couple who split up. They have a
child at primary school who remains with the mother.
Do you think that the father should always be made to
make maintenance payments to support the child?

Q251 [MtUnmar2] *   N=3228
If he **does** make the maintenance payments for the
child, should the amount depend on his income, or not?

Q252 [MtUnmar3] *   N=3228
Do you think the amount of maintenance should depend
on the **mother's** income, or not?

	[MtUnmar1]	[MtUnmar2]	[MtUnmar3]
	%	%	%
Yes	88.1	89.3	73.6
No	10.5	10.0	24.9
(Don't Know)	1.4	0.6	1.4
(Refusal/Not answered)	0.0	-	-

Q253 [MtUnmar4] *   N=3228
Suppose the mother now marries someone else. Should
the child's natural father go on paying maintenance
for the child, should he stop or should it depend on
the step-father's income?

Q254 [MtUnmar5] *   N=3228
Suppose instead the mother does not marry, but the
father has another child with someone else. Should he
go on paying maintenance for the first child, should
he stop or should it depend on his income?

	[MtUnmar4]	[MtUnmar5]
	%	%
Continue	53.3	74.8
Stop	8.7	1.4
Depends	36.6	23.1
(Don't know)	1.3	0.7
(Refusal/Not answered)	-	-

Q255 [MuchPov]   N=3228
Some people say there is very little **real** poverty in
Britain today. Others say there is quite a lot.
Which come closest to **your** view ... READ OUT ...
%
45.2 ... that there is very little real poverty in Britain,
51.6 or, that there is quite a lot?
3.2 (Don't know)
- (Refusal)

Q256 [PastPov]
Over the last ten years, do you think that poverty in Britain has been increasing, decreasing or staying at about the same level?

N=3228

%
Increasing 32.2
Decreasing 22.7
Staying at same level 39.1
(Don't know) 6.0
(Refusal) -

Q257 [FuturPov]
And over the **next** ten years, do you think that poverty in Britain will
... READ OUT ...

N=3228

%
... increase, 43.7
decrease, 15.7
or, stay at about the same level? 34.9
(Don't know) 5.7
(Refusal) -

Q258 [Poverty1]
Would you say that someone in Britain **was** or **was not** in poverty if....
... they had enough to buy the things they really needed, but not enough to buy the things most people take for granted?

N=3228

%
Was in poverty 21.8
Was not 75.9
(Don't know) 2.3
(Refusal) -

Q259 [Poverty2]
(Would you say someone in Britain **was** or **was not** in poverty ...)
... if they had enough to eat and live, but not enough to buy other things they needed?

N=3228

%
Was in poverty 49.8
Was not 47.7
(Don't know) 2.5
(Refusal) -

Q260 [Poverty3]
(Would you say someone in Britain **was** or **was not** in poverty ...) ... if they had not got enough to eat and live without getting into debt?

N=3228

%
Was in poverty 89.0
Was not 9.8
(Don't know) 1.2
(Refusal) 0.0

Q261 [WhyNeed]
CARD B4
Why do you think there are people who live in need? Of the four views on this card, which **one** comes closest to your own?
CODE ONE ONLY

N=3228

%
Because they have been unlucky 10.1
Because of laziness or lack of willpower 27.0
Because of injustice in our society 20.5
It's an inevitable part of modern life 34.4
(None of these) 5.3
(Don't know) 2.6
(Refusal) 0.1

Q262 [PovEver]
CARD B5
Looking back over your life, how often have there been times in your life when you think you have lived in poverty by the standards of that time? Please choose a phrase from this card.

N=3228

%
Never 57.1
Rarely 16.6
Occasionally 18.4
Often 6.2
Most of the time 1.6
(Don't know) 0.1
(Refusal) -

Q263 **IF NOT 'Never' AT [PovEver]**
[PovChAd]
And was this ... READ OUT ...

N=3228

%
... as a child, 13.8
or, as an adult? 18.3
(Both) 10.7
(Don't know) -
(Refusal) 0.1

Q264 **VERSIONS A, B AND C: ASK ALL**
[SpChild1] *
CARD B6/B7   N=3228
Which of the groups on this card, if any, would be
your highest priority for extra government spending on
children?
ENTER ONE CODE ONLY FOR HIGHEST PRIORITY

IF NOT 'none of these', 'Don't know' or 'Not answered'
AT [SpChild1]
Q265 [SpChild2] *   N=3228
CARD B6/B7 AGAIN
And which would be your next highest priority?
ENTER ONE CODE ONLY FOR NEXT HIGHEST

	[SpChild1] %	[SpChild2] %
Children from low-income families	33.0	18.1
Children from single parent families	4.8	10.2
Children with disabilities	38.0	25.2
Children with disabled parents	12.5	28.2
Children living in overcrowded accommodation	5.4	9.0
Children who have been permanently excluded from school	1.5	2.7
Children whose first language is not English (or Welsh)	0.8	1.3
None of these	3.1	0.9
(Don't Know)	0.8	0.4
(Refusal/Not answered)	0.0	-

Q266 **VERSIONS A, B AND C: ASK ALL**
[SpDisab1] *
CARD B8   N=3228
Which of these areas, if any, would be your highest
priority for extra government spending on disabled
people in general?
ENTER ONE CODE ONLY FOR HIGHEST PRIORITY

IF NOT 'none of these', 'Don't know' or 'Not answered'
AT [SpDisab1]
Q267 [SpDisab2] *   N=3228
CARD B8 AGAIN
And which would be your next highest priority?
ENTER ONE CODE ONLY FOR NEXT HIGHEST

	[SpDisab1] %	[SpDisab2] %
Financial support for the parents of disabled children	23.7	19.2
Support for disabled children at school	16.2	19.6
Improving disabled people's access to goods and services	8.3	10.8
Personal and social care for disabled people	23.8	18.5
Benefits for disabled adults	4.7	8.5
Encouraging employers to recruit more disabled adults	17.4	14.6
Grants to improve disabled people's access to buildings	2.7	5.0
None of these	1.7	0.6
(Don't Know)	1.4	0.1
(Refusal/Not answered)	0.1	-

VERSIONS A, B AND C: ASK ALL   N=3228

Q268 [SpDisCh1]
CARD B9
And which of these areas, if any, would be your
highest priority for extra government spending on
disabled children and disabled young people?
ENTER ONE CODE ONLY FOR HIGHEST PRIORITY

**IF NOT 'none of these', 'Don't know' or 'Not answered'
AT [SpDisCh1]**

Q269 [SpDisCh2]   N=3228
CARD B9 AGAIN
And which would be your next highest priority?
ENTER ONE CODE ONLY FOR NEXT HIGHEST

	[SpDisCh1]	[SpDisCh2]
	%	%
Pre-school / Nursery education	11.2	6.4
Primary school education	15.6	13.0
Secondary school education	12.8	17.1
Financial support for parents	13.5	17.8
Health and care services	30.3	19.4
Career advice and support	10.2	15.5
Leisure facilities	3.2	6.5
None of these	1.8	0.7
(Don't Know)	1.3	0.4
(Refusal/Not answered)	0.0	-

VERSIONS A, B AND C: ASK ALL   N=3228

Q270 [DisBenef]
CARD B10
Please tell me whether you think the following
statement is true or false. If you don't know just say
so.
In general, disabled adults are more likely to have to
rely on state benefits than non-disabled adults?
FOR 'DON'T KNOW' CODE CTRL + K

	%
Definitely true	38.1
Probably true	47.6
Probably false	4.5
Definitely false	0.9
(Don't know)	9.0
(Refusal)	-

[Pen2FW]   N=3228
CARD B11
Imagine an unmarried couple who split up. They have a
child at primary school who remains with the mother.
The father has been judged to have sufficient income
to pay maintenance. If he **doesn't** pay it, which, if
any, of these do you think should
happen?
PROBE: Which others?
CODE ALL THAT APPLY

Q271- Multicoded (Maximum of 8 codes)
Q278

	%	
No action should be taken	0.9	[MPenNon2]
He should have the money deducted from his earnings	79.9	[MPenMoD2]
He should be encouraged to pay the money, but it should not be deducted from his earnings	20.9	[MPenMoE2]
He should be 'named & shamed' (meaning his name & photo would appear in a local newspaper)	9.9	[MPenNSh2]
His access to the child should be stopped	15.5	[MPenAcc2]
He should be sent to prison	5.0	[MPenPri2]
His driving licence should be withdrawn	4.6	[MPenDri2]
His passport should be withdrawn	8.3	[MPenPas2]
Other answer (WRITE IN)	2.0	[MPenOth2]
(Don't Know)	0.6	
(Refusal/Not answered)	0.0	

VERSIONS A AND B: ASK ALL   N=2166

Q290 [IncomGap]
Thinking of income levels generally in Britain today,
would you say that the **gap** between those with high
incomes and those with low incomes is ...READ OUT...

	%
... too large,	75.9
about right,	18.2
or, too small?	1.9
(Don't know)	4.0
(Refusal)	-

Q291 [SRInc] N=2166
Among which group would you place yourself ...READ OUT...
%
5.5 ... high income,
58.2 middle income,
35.6 or, low income?
0.5 (Don't know)
0.2 (Refusal)

VERSION A: ASK ALL
Q292 [HIncDiff] N=1089
CARD B12
Which of the phrases on this card would you say comes closest to your feelings about your household's income these days?
%
40.7 Living comfortably on present income
46.0 Coping on present income
10.1 Finding it difficult on present income
3.8 Finding it very difficult on present income
- (Other answer (WRITE IN))
- (Don't know)
- (Refusal)

VERSION B: ASK ALL
Q293 [HIncDif2] N=1077
CARD B12
Which of the phrases on this card would you say comes closest to your feelings about your household's income these days?
%
9.2 Living very comfortably on present income
41.7 Living comfortably on present income
37.0 Coping on present income
9.2 Finding it difficult on present income
2.4 Finding it very difficult on present income
0.3 (Other answer (WRITE IN))
0.1 (Don't know)
0.1 (Refusal)

VERSIONS A, B AND C: ASK ALL 'Wholly retired from work' AT [REconAct]
Q296 [RetirAg2] N=678
At what age did you retire from work?
NEVER WORKED, CODE: 00
Median: 60 years
%
0.2 (Don't know)
0.7 (Refusal)

IF [RetirAg2] > 0 OR 'Don't know' OR 'Refused' AT [RetirAg2]
Q297 [RRetPlcy] N=678
Did you have to retire because of your employer's policy on retirement age?
%
14.9 Yes
82.6 No
- Left work before retirement
0.6 (Don't know)
0.7 (Refusal)

IF 'No' AT [RRetPlcy]
Q298- [RWhyRet] N=678
Q304 CARD B12/B13
Why did you retire?
Please choose a phrase from this card.
CODE AS MANY AS APPLY.
Multicoded (Maximum of 7 codes)
%
21.2 I left because of ill health [RRetIll]
9.2 I left to look after someone else [RRetCare]
5.1 I left because my husband/wife/partner retired [RRetPrtn]
5.2 It was made attractive to me to retire early [RRetPack]
7.6 I lost my job/I was made redundant/
11.4 My firm closed down [RRetLJob]
31.0 I just wanted to retire [RRetWant]
7.1 Other answer (WRITE IN) [RRetOth]
- (Don't know)
1.3 (Refusal/Not answered)

Transport (versions A, B and D)

VERSIONS A, B AND D: ASK ALL

Q308 [TRFPB6U] *
CARD C1
Now thinking about traffic and transport problems, how serious a problem **for you** is congestion on motorways?
N=3228

Q309 [TRFPB9U] *
CARD C1 AGAIN
(And how serious a problem **for you** is ...)
traffic congestion in towns and cities?
N=3228

Q310 [TrfPb10u] *
CARD C1 AGAIN
(And how serious a problem **for you** are ...)
exhaust fumes from traffic in towns and cities?
N=3228

	[TRFPB6U]	[TRFPB9U]	[TrfPb10u]
	%	%	%
A very serious problem	11.7	19.5	22.8
A serious problem	20.7	34.0	37.2
Not a very serious problem	33.9	30.7	25.6
Not a problem at all	32.9	15.6	13.9
(Don't Know)	0.7	0.2	0.4
(Refusal/Not answered)	0.1	0.1	-

Q311 [TrfConc1] *
CARD C2
Transport like cars, buses, trains and planes can affect the environment in a number of ways.
How **concerned** are you about damage to the countryside from building roads?
N=3228

Q312 [TrfConc2] *
CARD C2 AGAIN
And how **concerned** are you about the effect of transport on climate change?
N=3228

Q313 [TrfConc3] *
CARD C2 AGAIN
And how **concerned** are you about exhaust fumes from traffic?
N=3228

	[TrfConc1]	[TrfConc2]	[TrfConc3]
	%	%	%
Very concerned	24.5	35.6	38.2
Fairly concerned	49.7	45.8	43.8
Not very concerned	19.9	13.2	13.2
Not at all concerned	5.4	4.4	4.3
(Don't Know)	0.6	0.9	0.5
(Refusal/Not answered)	-	0.0	-

Q314 [DRIVE]
May I just check, do you yourself drive a car at all these days?
N=3228

	%
Yes	68.7
No	31.3
(Don't know)	-
(Refusal)	-

IF 'Yes' AT [Drive]

Q315 [DRIVMIL]
CARD C3
How many miles have you personally driven in the last 12 months?
N=3228

	%
3,000 miles or less	20.2
3,001 to 5,000 miles	11.9
5,001 to 7,000 miles	10.3
7,001 to 10,000 miles	10.7
10,001 miles or more	15.2
(Don't know)	0.2
(Refusal)	-

VERSIONS A, B AND D: ASK ALL

Q316 [CarNum]
How many, if any, cars or vans does your household own or have the regular use of?
median: 1 car or van
N=3228

	%
(Don't know)	-
(Refusal)	0.1

	[TRAVEL1]	[TRAVEL2]	[TRAVEL3]	[TRAVEL4a]
	%	%	%	%
Every day or nearly every day	43.0	8.1	8.4	2.1
2-5 days a week	18.0	25.7	11.7	2.4
Once a week	5.1	25.0	8.1	3.0
Less often but at least once a month	1.4	14.9	10.3	14.1
Less often than that	0.8	12.8	12.9	35.3
Never nowadays	0.5	13.5	48.4	43.0
(Don't Know)	0.0	-	0.0	0.1
(Refusal/ Not answered)	-	-	-	-

Q317 **[MainDri]** **IF 'Yes' AT [Drive] AND [CarNum] <> 0** N=3228
Are you the main driver of (this vehicle/either of these vehicles/any of these vehicles)?
By main driver we mean the person who does the most mileage in the vehicle over a year.
%
58.7 Yes
9.4 No
- (Don't know)
0.1 (Refusal)

VERSIONS A, B AND D: ASK ALL

Q318 **[Bikeown]** N=3228
Do you own, or have access to, a bicycle that is in good enough condition for riding?
(INTERVIEWER: code yes even if respondent says they have one but that they wouldn't use it
%
40.0 Yes
60.0 No
- (Don't know)
- (Refusal)

IF 'Yes' AT [Drive]

Q319 **[TRAVEL1]** *
CARD C4 N=3228
How often nowadays do you **usually** travel ...by car as a driver?

VERSIONS A, B AND D: ASK ALL

Q320 **[TRAVEL2]** *
CARD C4 (AGAIN) N=3228
(How often nowadays do you **usually**) ...travel by car as a passenger?

Q321 **[TRAVEL3]** *
CARD C4 AGAIN N=3228
(How often nowadays do you **usually**) ...travel by local bus?

Q322 **[TRAVEL4a]** *
CARD C4 AGAIN N=3228
(How often nowadays do you **usually**) ...travel by train (not including underground, tram or light rail)?

Q323 **[AirTrvl]** N=3228
And how many trips did you make by plane during the last 12 months? Please count the outward and return flight and any transfers as one trip.
INTERVIEWER WRITE IN ANSWER
ACCEPT BEST ESTIMATE IF NECESSARY
CODE 'NONE' AS 0
Median: 1 trip.
%
- (Don't know)
0.0 (Refusal)

Q324 **[CliCar]** *
CARD C5 N=3228
Please tell me how much you agree or disagree with each of these statements:
The current level of **car use** has a serious effect on climate change.

Q325 **[CliPlane]** *
CARD C5 AGAIN N=3228
(Please tell me how much you agree or disagree with this statement)
The current level of **air travel** has a serious effect on climate change.

	[CliCar]	[CliPlane]
	%	%
Agree strongly	28.2	29.7
Agree	51.6	44.0
Neither agree nor disagree	13.2	17.0
Disagree	4.6	5.6
Disagree strongly	0.9	0.6
(Don't Know)	1.5	3.1
(Refusal/Not answered)	-	-

VERSIONS A, B AND D: ASK ALL IN WORK OR STUDY (I.E. 'In full time education', 'On government training' OR 'in paid work' AT [REconAct])

Q326 [JnyWrk]   N=1963
CARD C6
What is the main form of transport you normally use for your journey to (work/the place where you study)?
INTERVIEWER: by main form of transport we mean the form used for the longest distance

	%
Walk	12.9
Car - driver	55.9
Car - passenger	5.4
Train	4.5
Bicycle (pedal)	4.1
Bus	8.0
Underground or metro	2.7
Light railway or tram	0.4
Motorcycle, moped or scooter	0.9
Other (WRITE IN)	1.4
((Works/Studies) at home)	3.5
(Don't know)	0.1
(Refusal)	0.3

VERSIONS A, B AND D: ASK ALL

Q329 [JnyShop]   N=3228
CARD C6 (AGAIN)
(and) what is the main form of transport you normally use to get to local shops and services?
INTERVIEWER: by main form of transport we mean the form used for the longest distance

	%
Walk	38.1
Car - driver	42.6
Car - passenger	9.5
Train	0.1
Bicycle (pedal)	1.7
Bus	6.2
Underground or metro	0.1
Light railway or tram	0.2
Motorcycle, moped or scooter	0.4
Other (WRITE IN)	0.3
(Never go to shops or services)	0.8
(Don't know)	-
(Refusal)	0.0

VERSIONS A, B AND D: ASK ALL

Q332-   CARD C7   N=3228
Q338
Which, if any, of the difficulties listed on this card do you usually experience when travelling to...
...the place where you do your main food shopping?
CODE ALL THAT APPLY
Multicoded (Maximum of 7 codes)

	%	
Too far away	7.7	[AccFFar]
Public transport difficulties, eg. no or poor public transport	9.5	[AccFPub]
Traffic congestion	11.1	[AccFCong]
Parking problems - availability or cost	10.0	[AccFPark]
Too expensive to get there	1.5	[AccFExp]
Personal disability	3.5	[AccFDisb]
Some other difficulty (WRITE IN)	1.5	[AccFOth]
Don't have any difficulties	65.7	[AccFNone]
(Don't know)	0.2	
(Refusal)	0.0	

VERSIONS A, B AND D: ASK ALL

Q341-
Q347   CARD C7 AGAIN   N=3228
(Which, if any, of the difficulties listed on this card do you usually experience when travelling to...)
..your doctor's surgery?
CODE ALL THAT APPLY
Multicoded (Maximum of 7 codes)

%		
4.0	Too far away	[AccDFar]
3.6	Public transport difficulties, eg no or poor public transport	[AccDPub]
4.2	Traffic congestion	[AccDCong]
10.0	Parking problems - availability or cost	[AccDPark]
0.4	Too expensive to get there	[AccDExp]
2.1	Personal disability	[AccDDisb]
0.5	Some other difficulty (WRITE IN)	[AccDOth]
79.1	Don't have any difficulties	[AccDNone]
0.2	(Don't know)	
-	(Refusal)	

VERSIONS A, B AND D: ASK ALL

Q350-
Q356   CARD C7 AGAIN   N=3228
(Which, if any, of the difficulties listed on this card do you usually experience when travelling to...)
...your nearest NHS hospital?
INTERVIEWER: if respondent queries, we mean the nearest hospital regardless of what services are or are not offered there.
CODE ALL THAT APPLY
Multicoded (Maximum of 7 codes)

%		
10.2	Too far away	[AccHFar]
10.0	Public transport difficulties, eg no or poor public transport	[AccHPub]
11.2	Traffic congestion	[AccHCong]
30.6	Parking problems - availability or cost	[AccHPark]
2.2	Too expensive to get there	[AccHExp]
2.2	Personal disability	[AccHDisb]
0.6	Some other difficulty (WRITE IN)	[AccHOth]
51.6	Don't have any difficulties	[AccHNone]
0.7	(Don't know)	
0.0	(Refusal)	

VERSIONS A, B AND D: ASK ALL

Q359-
Q365   CARD C7 AGAIN   N=3228
(Which, if any, of the difficulties listed on this card do you usually experience when travelling to...)
...(work/the place where you study)?
CODE ALL THAT APPLY
Multicoded (Maximum of 7 codes)

%		
5.0	Too far away	[AccWFar]
6.7	Public transport difficulties, eg no or poor public transport	[AccWPub]
15.0	Traffic congestion	[AccWCong]
3.9	Parking problems - availability or cost	[AccWPark]
2.8	Too expensive to get there	[AccWExp]
0.1	Personal disability	[AccWDisb]
0.4	Some other difficulty (WRITE IN)	[AccWOth]
36.5	Don't have any difficulties	[AccWNone]
0.1	(Don't know)	
0.1	(Refusal)	

Health (versions A and D)

VERSIONS A AND D: ASK ALL

Q368 **[NHSSat]** *
CARD D1   N=2151
All in all, how satisfied or dissatisfied would you
say you are with the way in which the National Health
Service runs nowadays?
Choose a phrase from this card.

Q369 **[GPSat]** *
CARD D1 AGAIN   N=2151
From your own experience, or from what you have heard,
please say how satisfied or dissatisfied you are with
the way in which each of these parts of the National
Health Service runs nowadays:
First, local doctors or GPs?

Q370 **[DentSat]** *
CARD D1 AGAIN   N=2151
(And how satisfied or dissatisfied are you with the
NHS as regards...)
... National Health Service dentists?

Q371 **[InpatSat]** *
CARD D1 AGAIN   N=2151
(And how satisfied or dissatisfied are you with the
NHS as regards...)
... being in hospital as an **in**-patient?

Q372 **[OutpaSat]** *
CARD D1 AGAIN   N=2151
(And how satisfied or dissatisfied are you with the
NHS as regards...)
... attending hospital as an **out**-patient?

Q373 **[AESat]** *
CARD D1 AGAIN   N=2151
(And how satisfied or dissatisfied are you with the
NHS as regards...)
... Accident and Emergency departments?

Q374 **[NDirSat]** *
CARD D1 AGAIN   N=2151
(And how satisfied or dissatisfied are you with the
NHS as regards...)
... (NHS Direct/NHS 24), the telephone or internet
advice service?

Q375 **[MentSat]** *
CARD D1 AGAIN   N=2151
Now from your own experience, **or from what you have
heard**, please say how satisfied or dissatisfied you
are with ...
... NHS services for people with mental health
problems?

Q376 **[CYPSat]** *
CARD D1 AGAIN   N=2151
Now from your own experience, **or from what you have
heard**, please say how satisfied or dissatisfied you
are with ...
... NHS services for children and young people?

	[NHSSat]	[GPSat]	[DentSat]
	%	%	%
Very satisfied	10.4	29.5	14.8
Quite satisfied	38.6	46.2	27.6
Neither satisfied nor dissatisfied	16.4	10.1	16.1
Quite dissatisfied	21.6	10.6	16.5
Very dissatisfied	12.2	3.2	20.5
(Don't Know)	0.9	0.4	4.4
(Refusal/Not answered)	-	-	0.1

	[InpatSat]	[OutpaSat]	[AESat]
	%	%	%
Very satisfied	14.2	14.2	14.9
Quite satisfied	31.9	43.2	31.0
Neither satisfied nor dissatisfied	23.8	20.5	21.9
Quite dissatisfied	13.3	12.0	14.8
Very dissatisfied	5.8	5.1	8.8
(Don't Know)	10.9	5.0	8.5
(Refusal/Not answered)	-	-	-

	[NDirSat]	[MentSat]	[CYPSat]
	%	%	%
Very satisfied	9.9	2.8	10.4
Quite satisfied	20.6	12.7	39.5
Neither satisfied nor dissatisfied	33.5	35.4	26.2
Quite dissatisfied	5.6	14.9	6.9
Very dissatisfied	4.1	8.4	1.9
(Don't Know)	26.2	25.8	15.2
(Refusal/Not answered)	-	-	-

Q377 [NHSLimit] N=2151

It has been suggested that the National Health Service should be available **only to those with lower incomes.** This would mean that contributions and taxes could be lower and most people would then take out medical insurance or pay for health care.

Do you support or oppose this idea?

IF 'SUPPORT' OR 'OPPOSE': A lot or little?

%	
10.3	Support a lot
13.5	Support a little
14.7	Oppose a little
59.0	Oppose a lot
2.4	(Don't know)
-	(Refusal)

Q378 [OutPat1] * N=2151

CARD D2

Now suppose you had a back problem and your GP referred you to a hospital out-patients' department. From what you know or have heard, please say whether you think...

...you would get an appointment within three months?

Q379 [OutPat2] * N=2151

CARD D2 AGAIN

(And please say whether you think ...)

...when you arrived, the doctor would see you within half an hour of your appointment time?

Q380 [OutPat3] * N=2151

CARD D2 AGAIN

(And please say whether you think ...)

...if you wanted to complain about the treatment you received, you would be able to without any fuss or bother?

	[OutPat1]	[OutPat2]	[OutPat3]
	%	%	%
Definitely would	11.3	9.1	14.1
Probably would	38.6	36.7	44.1
Probably would not	33.5	35.1	25.0
Definitely would not	12.8	16.5	9.6
(Don't Know)	3.7	2.5	7.3
(Refusal/Not answered)	-	-	-

Q381 [SRHealth] N=2151

How is your health in general for someone of your age? Would you say that it is ... READ OUT ...

%	
37.3	...very good,
42.8	fairly good,
14.0	fair,
4.8	bad,
0.9	or, very bad?
0.0	(Don't know)
0.0	(Refusal)

Q382 [PrDepres] N=2151

Suppose an employee applied for a promotion. He has had repeated periods off work because of depression but this has been under control for a year or so through medication. Do you think he would be ... READ OUT ...

%	
12.8	...just as likely as anyone else to be promoted,
48.5	slightly less likely to be promoted,
36.3	or, much less likely to be promoted?
2.4	(Don't know)
0.0	(Refusal)

Q383 [ShdDep]   N=2151
CARD D3
And what do you think **should** happen? Should his
medical history make a difference or not?
%
10.5 Definitely should
31.0 Probably should
32.6 Probably should not
21.9 Definitely should not
1.9   EDIT ONLY: Depends on the job / type of work / depends
      on whether it would affect his / her job
0.3   (Other (PLEASE WRITE IN))
1.6   (Don't know)
0.0   (Refusal)

VERSIONS A AND D: ASK ALL
Q386 [PrSchiz]   N=2151
And now think about someone who has had repeated
periods off work because of schizophrenia but this has
been under control for a year or so through
medication. Do you think he would be ... READ OUT ...
%
5.9   ... just as likely as anyone else to be promoted,
32.4 slightly less likely to be promoted,
59.1 or, much less likely to be promoted?
2.6   (Don't know)
-     (Refusal)

Q387 [ShdSchiz]   N=2151
CARD D3 AGAIN
And what do you think **should** happen? Should his
medical history make a difference or not?
%
16.0 Definitely should
35.2 Probably should
31.2 Probably should not
13.4 Definitely should not
1.5   EDIT ONLY: Depends on the job / type of work / depends
      on whether it would affect his / her job
0.1   (Other (PLEASE WRITE IN))
2.5   (Don't know)
-     (Refusal)

Q390 [PrDiab]   N=2151
And now think about someone who has had repeated
periods off work because of diabetes but this has been
under control for a year or so through medication. Do
you think he would be ... READ OUT ...
%
53.8 ... just as likely as anyone else to be promoted,
37.4 slightly less likely to be promoted,
6.9   or, much less likely to be promoted?
1.8   (Don't know)
-     (Refusal)

Q391 [ShdDiab]   N=2151
CARD D3 AGAIN
And what do you think **should** happen? Should his
medical history make a difference or not?
%
9.3   Definitely should
17.8 Probably should
33.2 Probably should not
37.7 Definitely should not
0.9   EDIT ONLY: Depends on the job / type of work / depends
      on whether it would affect his / her job
-     (Other (PLEASE WRITE IN))
1.2   (Don't know)
-     (Refusal)

Q394 [MentProb]   N=2151
Have you, a member of your family or a close friend
ever sought medical help for a mental health problem?
%
33.8 Yes
66.1 No
0.1   (Don't know)
-     (Refusal)

Q395   [DprHelp]
CARD D4   N=2151
Suppose you developed serious depression and wanted to
seek help. Who would you turn to **first** for help?
Please take your answer from this card

%
58.1   NHS doctor/ GP
3.2   Private counsellor or psychotherapist
34.5   A friend/ someone in my family
1.1   A helpline, such as NHS Direct or the Samaritans
1.9   Someone else
0.1   (This would never happen to me)
0.7   (I would not seek help)
0.3   (Don't know)
-    (Refusal)

New families (versions B, C and D)

VERSIONS B, C AND D: ASK ALL

Q398   [SChPar]
CARD E1   N=3201
Now some questions about people's families and
friends.
I would like you to think about a family where the
parents separated some time ago. The children are all
under 12 years old and now live with their mother and
her new partner. Do you think that these children
could be brought up just as well by their
mother and her partner as they could be by their
mother and father?

%
36.1   Definitely could
41.6   Probably could
10.0   Probably could not
4.7   Definitely could not
6.1   (SPONTANEOUS: It depends)
1.4   (Don't know)
0.0   (Refusal)

Q399   [SChMon]   N=3201
Still thinking about the same family, where the
parents separated some time ago, and the children now
live with their mother and her partner. The children's
mother and her partner don't have very much money, and
are worried that the children are being
spoilt by their father, because he regularly buys them
expensive gifts and pays for outings that the
children's mother and her partner cannot afford. Which
of these statements comes closest to your view about
this situation ...READ OUT...

%
29.5   ...the father should be allowed to spend what he likes
      on his children,
62.9   or, the children's mother and her partner should have
      the right to insist that the children's father spends
      money on things the children need, rather than
      expensive gifts?
6.1   (SPONTANEOUS: Neither)
1.5   (Don't know)
0.0   (Refusal)

Q400 [SChWhoL]
CARD E2   N=3201
If a couple with children divorce, who do you think
the children should normally live with for most of the
time?
They should spend equal time with both parents
They should live with the parent who is best able to
look after them
%
18.2 They should spend equal time with both parents
56.8 They should live with the parent who is best able to
      look after them
0.2   The father
23.2 The mother
1.5   (Don't know)
0.1   (Refusal)

Q401 [SChSay]
CARD E3   N=3201
Now imagine a 9 year old child whose parents are
divorcing. How much say should a child of this age
have over who they will live with after the divorce?
%
14.0 A great deal
30.1 Quite a lot
40.1 Some
9.9   Not much
4.6   None at all
1.2   (Don't know)
0.0   (Refusal)

VERSIONS B, C AND D: ASK ALL 'Separated', 'Divorced',
'Widowed', OR 'Single' AT [Marstat5]

Q402 [LAT]   N=1116
Can I check, are you currently in a relationship but
not living with your partner?
INTERVIEWER: THIS IS RESPONDENT'S DEFINITION OF
RELATIONSHIP
%
24.5 Yes
74.8 No
0.2   (Don't know)
0.5   (Refusal)

VERSIONS B, C AND D: ASK ALL CURRENTLY IN A
RELATIONSHIP BUT NOT LIVING WITH PARTNER (I.E. 'Yes'
AT [LAT])

Q403 [LATlen]   N=281
About how long have you and your partner been together
as a couple?
INTERVIEWER: ROUND UP/DOWN TO NEAREST YEAR
IF LESS THAN SIX MONTHS, ENTER 0
%
Median: 2 years
-     (Don't know)
3.2   (Refusal)

Q404- [LATwhy]   N=281
Q415   CARD E4
Here are some reasons why a couple might not live
together. Which of these, if any, apply to you and
your partner?
PROBE: What others?
CODE ALL THAT APPLY
Multicoded (Maximum of 12 codes)
40.4 We are not ready to live together / too early
      in our relationship   [LATWErly]
11.2 My partner has a job elsewhere   [LATWPJob]
7.7   My partner is studying elsewhere   [LATWPStd]
1.8   I prefer not to live with my partner (though
      (s)he wants to live with me)   [LATWIPrf]
7.1   My partner prefers not to live with me (though
      I want to live with him/her)   [LATWPPrf]
3.8   Because of my or my partner's children   [LATWChld]
23.3 We can't afford to live together   [LATWAfrd]
14.2 We both want to keep our own homes   [LATWHome]
4.7   We have other responsibilities (e.g. caring
      for an elderly relative)   [LATWResp]
5.0   We are waiting until we get married   [LATWMard]
13.9 We just don't want to live together   [LATWNotw]
3.3   Other reason (WRITE IN)   [LATWOth]
0.5   (SPONTANEOUS: None of these)   [LATWNone]
3.9   (Don't know)
      (Refusal)

Q418 [LATlive]
CARD E5   N=281

Regardless of what you think might happen in the
future, would you like to live with your partner?

%
42.2 Definitely would
36.8 Probably would
7.4   Probably would not
6.8   Definitely would not
3.0   (Don't know)
3.8   (Refusal)

Q419- [LATdo]
Q425 CARD E6   N=281

Here are some activities that partners sometimes do
together. Which, if any, do you and your partner often
do together?
CODE ALL THAT APPLY
Multicoded (Maximum of 7 codes)

%
54.9 Go on holiday together   [LATDoHol]
53.0 See relatives together   [LATDoRel]
74.8 See friends together   [LATDoFr]
72.6 Spend weekends together   [LATDoWke]
36.8 Do weekly food shopping together   [LATDoFod]
58.1 Go to the cinema together   [LATDoCin]
81.0 Go out to eat or for a drink together   [LATDoDrk]
2.8   None of these   [LATDoNon]
-     (SPONTANEOUS: All of these)
3.0   (Refusal)

VERSIONS B, C AND D: ASK ALL
Q426 [RelIndl]
CARD E7   N=3201

Which of the statements on this card comes closest to
your view?

%
62.0 Relationships are much stronger when both partners
      have the independence to follow their own careers and
      friendships
27.6 OR partners who have too much independence from each
      other put their relationship at risk
6.9   (SPONTANEOUS: both)
3.5   (Don't know)
0.0   (Refusal)

Q427 [SpDSing]
CARD E8   N=3201

These days it's possible for women to get pregnant by
paying a clinic and using sperm from a donor. I'm
going to read out two scenarios about different
people. For each, assume that they can afford to pay
for the treatment and bring up the child without
relying on benefits.
First, do you think that a single woman who lives
alone, who wants to have a child, should be allowed to
have this treatment?

%
28.9 Definitely should
32.4 Probably should
15.9 Probably should not
20.3 Definitely should not
2.4   (Don't know)
0.1   (Refusal)

Q428 [SpDCoup]
CARD E8 AGAIN   N=3201

And what about a man and woman who live together as a
couple, and who want to have a child, but the man
can't have children. Should the woman be allowed to
have this treatment?
(IF NECESSARY REPEAT: Assume they can afford to pay
for the treatment and bring up the child without
relying on benefits.)

%
59.6 Definitely should
30.8 Probably should
3.6   Probably should not
4.3   Definitely should not
1.6   (Don't know)
0.0   (Refusal)

Q429 [FrFamSc]   N=3201
CARD E9
Some people feel that having close friends is more important than having close ties with their family. Others disagree. Where would you put yourself on this scale between these two positions?

%
   More important to have close friends
4.5
8.4 ...
38.7 ...
23.8 ...
24.2 More important to have close ties with family
0.3 (Don't know)
- (Refusal)

Q430 [CloseFr]   N=3201
Leaving aside your (wife/husband/partner) or anyone in your family, do you have a particularly close friend you can share your private feelings and concerns with?
IF HAS CLOSE FRIENDS BUT CANNOT CHOOSE ONE WHO IS PARTICULARLY CLOSE, CODE 2

%
33.8 Yes (one)
40.8 Yes - more than one
25.4 No
0.1 (Don't know)
- (Refusal)

Q431 [ClFrSupp]   N=3201
IF 'Yes...' AT [CloseFr]
(Has this close friend/have any of these close friends) ever helped or supported you when you were facing a difficult problem in your life?

%
62.5 Yes
8.6 No
3.4 (SPONTANEOUS: Respondent has never faced a difficult problem)
- (Don't know)
0.1 (Refusal)

Cohabitation (versions B, C and D)

VERSIONS B, C AND D: ASK ALL
Q432 [CohbShd1] *   N=3201
CARD F1
I'd now like you to imagine an unmarried couple with no children who have been living together for ten years. Say their relationship ends.
Do you think the woman **should** or **should not** have the same rights to claim for financial support from the man as she would if they had been married?

Q433 [CohbShd8] *   N=3201
CARD F2
What if the couple had been living together for two years and had a young child. The couple had agreed that the woman should give up her job when the child was born but hoped that she would take up part time work when the child started school. Say their relationship ends. The child now lives mainly with the mother and the father pays child support.
Do you think the woman **should** or **should not** have the same rights to claim for financial provision for herself from the man as she would if they had been married?

Q434 [CohbShd9] *   N=3201
CARD F3
Imagine an unmarried couple who have lived together for 20 years and have three children. The woman had reduced her working to part-time when the first child was born but gave up work entirely after the second child was born in order to care for the family and home. The man has supported the family financially throughout and also owns the family home. The youngest child recently left home and the couple's relationship has now broken down. The woman has no income and poor job prospects.
Should she have a claim for financial provision from her partner?

Q435   [CohbSh10] *   N=3201
CARD F4
Now imagine a married couple with no children who have been married for two years. One of them has a much higher income than the other and owns the family home. Say their relationship ends.
Do you think the less well-off person **should** or **should not** have a claim for financial provision from the better-off person?

Q436   [CohbSh11] *   N=3201
CARD F5
Say that the same couple were not married, but have lived together for two years.
Do you think the less well-off person **should** or **should not** have a claim for financial provision from the better-off person?

Q437   [CohbSh12] *   N=3201
CARD F6
Imagine an unmarried couple without children who have been living together for two years in a house bought in the man's name three years ago, before their relationship began. Say the man died without making a will.
Do you think the woman **should** or **should not** have the same financial rights regarding his property as she would if she had been married to the man?

Q438   [CohbSh13] *   N=3201
CARD F7
Imagine a married couple who have been together for ten years. One partner had a well-paid job which required frequent moves to new locations at short notice. The other partner had taken up employment whenever possible, albeit lower paid, but had not had a settled career. Say their relationship breaks down.
Do you think the lower-paid partner **should** or **should not** have a claim for financial provision from the other partner?

Q439   [CohbSh14] *   N=3201
CARD F8
Say the same couple were not married, but had lived together for ten years.
Do you think the lower-paid partner **should** or **should not** have a claim for financial provision from the other partner in these circumstances?

Q440   [CohbSh15] *   N=3201
CARD F9
Imagine another couple who have been married for ten years who have no children. While they were together one partner worked unpaid to help build up the other partner's business. The family home is owned by the partner who runs the business, and the partner who worked unpaid does not have any property or income of their own. The couple's relationship has broken down.
Should the partner who worked unpaid have a claim for financial provision from the other partner?

Q441   [CohbSh16] *   N=3201
CARD F10
Say that the same couple were not married, but had lived together for ten years.
Should the partner who worked unpaid have a claim for financial provision from the other partner?

	[CohbShd1]	[CohbShd8]	[CohbShd9]	[CohbShd10]
	%	%	%	%
Definitely should	30.9	35.4	58.0	23.2
Probably should	30.7	39.1	31.1	38.5
Probably should not	20.6	15.5	5.4	24.8
Definitely should not	14.5	6.4	3.0	10.1
(Don't Know)	3.2	3.5	2.5	3.4
(Refusal/	0.1	0.1	0.1	0.0
Not answered)				

	[CohbSh11]	[CohbSh12]	[CohbSh13]
	%	%	%
Definitely should	10.9	28.3	37.0
Probably should	26.9	37.9	44.7
Probably should not	37.3	21.3	11.5
Definitely should not	21.9	8.7	3.5
(Don't Know)	2.9	3.8	3.2
(Refusal/	0.0	0.0	0.0
Not answered)			

	[CohbSh14]	[CohbSh15]	[CohbSh16]
	%	%	%
Definitely should	24.4	68.5	54.2
Probably should	44.9	24.8	33.4
Probably should not	20.4	3.6	7.4
Definitely should not	7.1	1.0	2.5
(Don't Know)	3.0	2.0	2.3
(Refusal/Not answered)	0.1	0.1	0.1

Q442 [PoolInc]
CARD F11
Imagine an unmarried couple living together with young children. Both the man and woman work part-time, but he earns more. They share the childcare between them. Which of the options on this card do you think is the best way for them to organise their money as a couple?

%	
14.2	They pool **some** of their income, with each giving the **same** amount, and keep the rest of their income separate
16.6	They pool **some** of their income, with the man giving **more**, and keep the rest of their income separate
7.0	They keep their incomes **separate** and deal with bills when they come in, with each paying the **same** amount
6.1	They keep their incomes **separate** and deal with bills when they come in, with the man paying **more**
52.9	They pool **all** their income together
0.6	Some other arrangement (WRITE IN)
0.2	EDIT ONLY: Both pool an equal proportion of income
0.1	EDIT ONLY: The couple should decide
2.2	(Don't know)
0.1	(Refusal)

N=3201

Education (versions A, B and C)

VERSIONS A, B AND C: ASK ALL

Q445 [Graffiti] *   N=3228
CARD G1
Please use this card to say how common or uncommon each of the following things is **in your area**.
Graffiti on walls or buildings?

Q446 [TeenOnSt] *   N=3228
CARD G1 AGAIN
(How common or uncommon is this **in your area**?)
Teenagers hanging around on the streets?

Q447 [Drunks] *   N=3228
CARD G1 AGAIN
(How common or uncommon is this **in your area**?)
Drunks or tramps on the streets?

Q448 [Vandals] *   N=3228
CARD G1 AGAIN
(How common or uncommon is this **in your area**?)
Vandalism and deliberate damage to property?

	[Graffiti]	[TeenOnSt]	[Drunks]	[Vandals]
	%	%	%	%
Very common	10.7	28.3	7.6	12.7
Fairly common	21.8	36.6	14.5	25.7
Not very common	47.1	25.0	43.5	44.3
Not at all common	20.2	9.9	33.9	17.0
(Don't Know)	0.3	0.2	0.6	0.4
(Refusal/	-	-	-	-
Not answered)				

Q449 [YPTime]　　　　　　　　　　　　　　　　N=3228
CARD G2
Please say whether you agree or disagree with the
following statement.
Young people in this area do not have enough
constructive things to do in their spare time.
%
28.7　Agree strongly
35.9　Agree
14.6　Neither agree nor disagree
16.7　Disagree
2.3　Disagree strongly
1.8　(Don't know)
-　(Refusal)

Q450 [EdSpndlc]　　　　　　　　　　　　　　　N=3228
CARD G3
Now some questions about education.
Which of the groups on this card, if any, would be
your highest priority for **extra** government spending on
education?
%
9.4　Nursery or pre-school children
18.7　Primary school children
26.8　Secondary school children
28.3　Children with special educational needs
10.3　Students at universities
3.8　Students in further education
1.3　(None of these)
1.2　(Don't know)
0.1　(Refusal)

**IF NOT 'None of these', 'Don't know' OR 'Refusal' AT
[EdSpndlc]**
Q451 [EdSpnd2c]　　　　　　　　　　　　　　　N=3228
CARD G3 AGAIN
And which is your next highest priority?
%
9.4　Nursery or pre-school children
21.1　Primary school children
23.0　Secondary school children
22.2　Children with special educational needs
11.0　Students at universities
9.7　Students in further education
0.6　(None of these)
0.2　(Don't know)
2.6　(Refusal)

VERSIONS A, B AND C: ASK ALL
Q452 [ChoicePS] *　　　　　　　　　　　　　　N=3228
From what you know or have heard, do you think parents
in your area have enough choice about which **primary
school** their children attend, or would you like to see
more choice?
IF MORE: A bit more or a lot more?

Q453 [ChoiceSS] *　　　　　　　　　　　　　　N=3228
And do you think parents in your area have enough
choice about which **secondary school** their children
attend, or would you like to see more choice?
IF MORE: A bit more or a lot more?

	[ChoicePS]	[ChoiceSS]
	%	%
Enough choice	48.5	43.0
A bit more choice	20.0	23.4
A lot more choice	14.4	17.1
(Don't Know)	17.0	16.5
(Refusal/Not answered)	0.1	0.1

Q454 [WorkChil]　　　　　　　　　　　　　　　N=3228
Can I just check, do you ever work with children,
either in a paid job or as a volunteer?
%
23.7　Yes
76.0　No
0.1　(Don't know)
0.1　(Refusal)

Q455 [ESTerm] *　　　　　　　　　　　　　　　N=3228
CARD G4
It has been suggested that school buildings and
equipment could be used to provide a number of
services for local communities. A range of staff would
provide the services, not necessarily teachers. Some
people support this because they think schools
should make their facilities available to everyone.
Other people oppose it because they think that schools
should concentrate on supporting and educating the
school's pupils.
For each of the following please say whether you
support or oppose schools offering these services....
...all-day childcare, available from 8am to 6pm,
during term time?

	[ESTerm]	[ESHoli]	[ESHelp]	[ESSport]
	%	%	%	%
Strongly support	18.9	17.5	24.0	32.7
Support	51.6	53.2	62.4	56.8
Neither support nor oppose	11.5	12.8	7.4	4.7
Oppose	14.0	12.8	4.1	4.4
Strongly oppose	2.6	2.4	0.7	0.6
(Don't Know)	1.3	1.2	1.2	0.8
(Refusal/Not answered)	0.1	0.1	0.1	0.1

	[ESArt]	[ESComp]	[ESCours]
	%	%	%
Strongly support	22.9	23.1	28.4
Support	62.1	56.8	60.9
Neither support nor oppose	8.5	8.3	5.4
Oppose	5.0	9.5	4.1
Strongly oppose	0.4	1.2	0.4
(Don't Know)	1.0	1.0	0.7
(Refusal/Not answered)	0.1	0.1	0.1

Q456   [ESHoli] *   N=3228
CARD G4 AGAIN
(Please say whether you support or oppose schools offering these services...)
..all-day childcare, available from 8am to 6pm, during school holidays?

Q457   [ESHelp] *   N=3228
CARD G4 AGAIN
(Please say whether you support or oppose schools offering these services...)
..help and advice for parents?

Q458   [ESSport] *   N=3228
CARD G4 AGAIN
(Please say whether you support or oppose schools offering these services...)
..the use of sports facilities?

Q459   [ESArt] *   N=3228
CARD G4 AGAIN
(Please say whether you support or oppose schools offering these services...)
..arts activities?

Q460   [ESComp] *   N=3228
CARD G4 AGAIN
(Please say whether you support or oppose schools offering these services...)
..the use of computer facilities, such as internet access?

Q461   [ESCours] *   N=3228
CARD G4 AGAIN
(Please say whether you support or oppose schools offering these services...)
..courses for adults?

Q462   [ChildHH]
(derived from HH grid)   N=3228

	%
Doesn't live with own child 5-16	81.2
Lives with own child 5-16	18.8

ASK ALL WHO LIVE WITH OWN CHILD AGED 5 TO 16 (I.E. 'Lives with own child 5-16' AT [ChildHH])

Q463   [ESUsTerm] *   N=606
CARD G5
Imagine a school near you started offering such services for the local community. How likely do you think you would be to...
..use all-day childcare, available from 8am to 6pm, during term time?

Q464   [ESUsHoli] *   N=606
CARD G5 AGAIN
(How likely do you think you would be to...)
..use all-day childcare, available from 8am to 6pm, during school holidays?

Q465 [ESUsHelp] * N=606
CARD G5 AGAIN
(How likely do you think you would be to...)
..use help and advice services for parents?

	[ESUsTerm]	[ESUsHoli]	[ESUsHelp]
	%	%	%
Very likely	15.0	14.9	12.1
Quite likely	17.0	22.2	40.1
Not very likely	23.6	20.9	26.8
Not at all likely	42.4	40.4	19.9
(Don't Know)	1.6	1.2	0.6
(Refusal/Not answered)	0.4	0.4	0.4

VERSIONS A, B AND C: ASK ALL

Q466 [SchBusi] * N=3228
CARD G6
It has been proposed that different groups and organisations get more involved with schools. Some people support this because they think it will help schools to improve. Other people oppose it because they don't think schools should be influenced by such groups. For each of these groups please tell me whether you support or oppose them getting more involved with schools...
..businesses?

Q467 [SchChu] * N=3228
CARD G6 AGAIN
(Please tell me whether you support or oppose the following getting more involved with schools...)
..churches or faith organisations?

Q468 [SchChar] * N=3228
CARD G6 AGAIN
(Please tell me whether you support or oppose the following getting more involved with schools...)
..charities?

Q469 [SchUni] * N=3228
CARD G6 AGAIN
(Please tell me whether you support or oppose the following getting more involved with schools...)
..universities?

Q470 [SchCoun] * N=3228
CARD G6 AGAIN
(Please tell me whether you support or oppose the following getting more involved with schools...)
..local councils?

Q471 [SchPar] * N=3228
CARD G6 AGAIN
(Please tell me whether you support or oppose the following getting more involved with schools...)
..organisations set up by parents?
INTERVIEWER: If asked, this does NOT just mean Parent Teacher Associations (PTAs)

	[SchBusi]	[SchChu]	[SchChar]
	%	%	%
Strongly support	13.6	7.9	8.0
Support	52.5	37.5	53.4
Neither support nor oppose	13.6	23.9	20.2
Oppose	15.3	22.1	14.4
Strongly oppose	3.3	7.2	2.2
(Don't Know)	1.6	1.3	1.7
(Refusal/Not answered)	0.1	0.1	0.1

	[SchUni]	[SchCoun]	[SchPar]
	%	%	%
Strongly support	19.7	10.1	13.5
Support	60.5	49.0	62.8
Neither support nor oppose	11.1	20.4	13.9
Oppose	6.1	15.2	7.2
Strongly oppose	1.0	3.8	1.1
(Don't Know)	1.6	1.4	1.4
(Refusal/Not answered)	0.1	0.1	0.1

Q472 [VocVAcad] N=3228
In the long-run, which do you think gives people more opportunities and choice in life ... READ OUT ...

	%
..having good practical skills and training,	49.8
or, having good academic results?	16.1
(Mixture/depends)	33.5
(Don't know)	0.5
(Refusal)	0.1

Q473   [HEdOpp]   N=3228
CARD G7
Do you feel that opportunities for young people in Britain to go on to **higher education** - to a university or college - should be increased or reduced, or are they at about the right level now?
IF INCREASED OR REDUCED: a lot or a little?

%	
17.6	Increased a lot
21.3	Increased a little
46.3	About right
10.6	Reduced a little
2.2	Reduced a lot
2.0	(Don't know)
-	(Refusal)

Q474   [NumPop] *   N=3228
CARD G8
Thinking now about the numeracy skills of people in Britain, that is how good they are with numbers and at doing basic calculations. In general, how would you describe the numeracy skills of...
..the population as a whole?

Q475   [NumScLIT] *   N=3228
CARD G8 AGAIN
(In general, how would you describe the numeracy skills of...)
..school leavers today?

Q476   [NumScLP] *   N=3228
CARD G8 AGAIN
(In general, how would you describe the numeracy skills of...)
..school leavers 10 years ago?

	[NumPop]	[NumScLIT]	[NumScLP]
	%	%	%
Very good	1.8	2.3	4.3
Good	20.5	19.9	35.1
Fair	45.2	38.4	39.0
Poor	23.8	27.6	12.3
Very poor	5.1	6.6	1.8
(Don't Know)	3.5	5.2	7.4
(Refusal/Not answered)	0.0	-	-

Q477   [AbPreAm]   N=3228
Now I would like to ask a couple of questions about child abuse.
IF IT BECOMES CLEAR THAT IT WOULD DISTRESS THE RESPONDENT TO COMPLETE THIS SECTION, ENTER CTRL + R HERE TO SKIP THIS SECTION.
Press 1 and <Enter> to continue.

%	
99.2	
0.1	(Don't know)
0.7	(Refusal)

VERSIONS A, B AND C: IF NOT REFUSAL AT [AbPreAm]

Q478   [AbTell]   N=3228
CARD G9
Thinking about a 10 year old child, how easy or difficult do you think it is to tell whether a child of that age is suffering abuse or neglect?

%	
3.2	Very easy
18.3	Fairly easy
18.0	Neither easy nor difficult
42.7	Fairly difficult
12.9	Very difficult
3.9	(Don't know)
0.9	(Refusal)

Q479   [AbConfDo]   N=3228
CARD G10
Now imagine your neighbours had a 10 year old child who you were **certain** was being really seriously abused or neglected. How confident are you that you would know what to do?

%	
27.6	Very confident
42.1	Quite confident
23.9	Not very confident
4.8	Not at all confident
0.8	(Don't know)
0.9	(Refusal)

Q480- [AbWhatDo]
Q488   N=3228
What, if anything, do you think you would do?
DO NOT PROMPT
CODE FROM ANSWER OPTIONS
PROBE: Anything else?
Multicoded (Maximum of 9 codes)

%
11.9   Speak to the parents   [AbWSPar]
6.5   Speak to the child   [AbWSChld]
44.0   Report it to the police   [AbWPolic]
58.6   Report it to the social services   [AbWSocs]
5.9   Tell a doctor/GP   [AbWDoc]
1.9   Tell someone from a church/religious group [AbWRelig]
7.2   Tell a teacher   [AbWTeach]
16.8   Report it to a children's charity,
       eg NSPCC, Childline   [AbWChrty]
4.7   Other (WRITE IN)   [AbWOth]
1.4   Would not do anything   [AbWNone]
5.1   Seek advice (e.g. C.A.B., community group,
       friend etc)   [AbWAdvce]
2.5   (Don't know)
0.9   (Refusal)

Employment

Employment relations (mainly versions A, C and D)

ASK ALL THOSE WHO ARE NOT WORKING (I.E. 'in full-time
education', 'on government training scheme', 'waiting
to take up work, 'unemployed', 'permanently sick or
disabled', 'wholly retired from work', 'looking after
the home' OR 'doing something else' AT [REconAct])

Q492   [NPwork10]   N=1850
In the seven days ending last Sunday, did you have any
paid work of less than 10 hours a week?
%
5.7   Yes
94.1   No
-      (Don't know)
0.2   (Refusal)

VERSIONS A, C AND D: ASK ALL EMPLOYEES IN CURRENT/LAST
JOB ('employee' OR DON'T KNOW AT [REmplyee])
Q493   [WorkHome]   N=1545
Do you ever do any work at home for your employer?
%
33.4   Yes
66.1   No
0.1   (Don't know)
0.3   (Refusal)

IF 'Yes' AT [WorkHome]
Q494   [WHomComp]   N=1545
Do you ever use a computer at home to do this work?
%
29.2   Yes
4.2   No
-      (Don't know)
0.4   (Refusal)

Q495   **IF 'Yes' AT [WHOmComp]**   N=1545
        [WHComTyp]
        CARD H2
        Which of the options on this card best describes the
        computer you use to do this work?
        IF SEVERAL COMPUTERS: Please think about the computer
        you use most often
        %
15.8   Computer owned by myself or my household, bought
        without contribution from my employer
1.4   Computer owned by myself, bought **with** a contribution
        from my employer
3.7   Computer owned by my employer and permanently located
        in my home while I am in my current job
7.7   Computer owned by my employer which I bring home from
        time to time
0.6   Other (PLEASE SPECIFY)
-       (None of these)
-       (Don't know)
0.4   (Refusal)

**VERSIONS A, C AND D: ASK ALL EMPLOYEES IN CURRENT/LAST
JOB ('employee' OR DON'T KNOW AT [REmployee])**   N=1545

Q498   [JobSat3]
        CARD H3
        All in all, how satisfied are you with your main job?
        %
36.3   Very satisfied
42.5   Satisfied
11.2   Neither satisfied nor dissatisfied
7.9   Dissatisfied
2.0   Very dissatisfied
0.1   (Don't know)
0.2   (Refusal)

Q501   [EmploydT]
        For how long have you been continuously employed by
        your present employer? (MONTHS)
        MEDIAN: 60 months
        %
0.2   (Don't know)
0.2   (Not answered)

Q502   [WageNow]   N=1545
        How would you describe the wages or salary you are
        paid for the job you do - on the low side, reasonable,
        or on the high side?
        IF LOW: Very low or a bit low?
        %
8.9   Very low
21.9   A bit low
59.8   Reasonable
9.0   On the high side
0.2   Other answer (WRITE IN)
0.1   (Don't know)
0.2   (Refusal)

Q505   [PayGap]   N=1545
        CARD H4
        Thinking of the **highest** and the **lowest** paid people at
        your place of work, how would you describe the **gap**
        between their pay, as far as you know?
        Please choose a phrase from this card.
        %
16.5   Much too big a gap
28.6   Too big
45.1   About right
3.0   Too small
0.2   Much too small a gap
-       OTHER ANSWERS
6.3   (Don't know)
0.3   (Refusal)

Q506   [WageXpct]   N=1545
        If you stay in this job, would you expect your wages
        or salary over the coming year to ...READ OUT...
        %
21.9   ... rise by **more** than the cost of living,
48.1   rise by the **same** as the cost of living,
18.6   rise by **less** than the cost of living,
8.2   or, **not** to rise at all?
1.5   (Will not stay in job)
1.5   (Don't know)
0.2   (Refusal)

Q507 **IF 'not to rise at all' AT [WageXpct]**
[WageDrop]   N=1545
Would you expect your wages or salary to stay the
same, or in fact to go down?
%
7.7 Stay the same
0.4 Go down
0.1 (Don't know)
1.7 (Refusal)

**VERSIONS A, C AND D: ASK ALL EMPLOYEES IN CURRENT/LAST
JOB ('employee' OR DON'T KNOW AT [REmplyee])**
Q508 [NumEmp]   N=1545
Over the coming year do you expect your workplace to
be ...READ OUT...
%
26.0 ... increasing its number of employees,
16.4 reducing its number of employees,
55.2 or, will the number of employees stay about the same?
0.5 Other answer(WRITE IN)
1.7 (Don't know)
0.3 (Refusal)

Q511 [Leavejob]   N=1545
Thinking now about your own job.
How likely or unlikely is it that you will leave this
employer over the next year for any reason?
Is it ...READ OUT...
%
11.2 ... very likely,
15.4 quite likely,
32.5 not very likely,
39.8 or, not at all likely?
0.8 (Don't know)
0.2 (Refusal)

Q512- CARD H5
Q520   Why do you think you will leave? Please choose a   N=1545
       phrase from this card or tell me what other reason
       there is.
       PROBE: Which others?
       CODE ALL THAT APPLY
       Multicoded (Maximum of 9 codes)
%
1.4   Firm will close down   [WhyGo1]
2.6   I will be declared redundant   [WhyGo2]
1.7   I will reach normal retirement age   [WhyGo3]
0.8   My contract of employment will expire   [WhyGo4]
0.7   I will take early retirement   [WhyGo5]
13.8 I will decide to leave and work for another   [WhyGo6]
        employer
3.4   I will decide to leave and work for myself,   [WhyGo7]
        as self-employed
1.1   I will leave to look after home/children/   [WhyGo10]
        relative
0.5   RETURN TO EDUCATION   [WhyGo11]
5.4   Other answer(WRITE IN)   [WhyGo8]
0.8   (Don't know)
0.2   (Refusal)

**VERSIONS A, C AND D: ASK ALL EMPLOYEES IN CURRENT/LAST
JOB ('employee' OR DON'T KNOW AT [REmplyee])**
Q533   [WpUnion3]   N=1545
       At your place of work are there any unions or staff
       associations?
       IF ASKED: A union or staff association is any
       independent organisation that represents the interests
       of people at work.
       IF YES, PROBE FOR UNION OR STAFF ASSOCIATION. CODE
       FIRST TO APPLY.
%
46.0 Yes : trade union(s)
5.6   Yes : staff association
45.8 No, none
2.4   (Don't know)
0.2   (Refusal)

IF 'Yes : trade union(s)' OR 'Yes : staff association' IN [WpUnion3]   N=1545

Q534 [UnionRec]
Does management recognise (these unions/this staff association) for the purposes of negotiating pay and conditions of employment?

%
46.3 Yes
3.7 No
1.6 (Don't know)
2.6 (Refusal)

Q535 [WPUnioW3]   N=1545
On the whole, do you think (these unions do their/this staff association does its) job well or not?

%
30.9 Yes
15.0 No
5.6 (Don't know)
2.7 (Refusal)

Q536 [TUElig]   N=1545
Are people doing your job eligible to join a union or staff association at your workplace?
IF ASKED: A union or staff association is any independent organisation that represents the interests of people at work.
IF YES, PROBE FOR UNION OR STAFF ASSOCIATION. CODE FIRST TO APPLY.

%
42.6 Yes : trade union(s)
5.2 Yes : staff association
2.8 No
0.9 (Don't know)
2.6 (Refusal)

VERSIONS A, C AND D: ASK ALL   N=3213

Q537 [TUMstImp]
CARD H6
Listed on this card are a number of things that trade unions or staff associations can do. Which, if any, do you think should be the **most important** thing they should try to do?

%
5.0 Reduce pay differences in the workplace
9.5 Promote equality for women or for ethnic and other minority groups
29.6 Represent individual employees in dealing with their employer about problems at work
13.2 Protect existing employees' jobs
23.6 Improve working conditions across the workplace
11.0 Improve pay for all employees
2.3 Have an input into the running of the business
2.8 (None of these)
2.8 (Don't know)
0.1 (Refusal)

VERSIONS A, C AND D: ASK ALL EMPLOYEES IN CURRENT/LAST JOB ('employee' OR DON'T KNOW AT [REmplyee])   N=1545

Q538 [IndRel]
In general how would you describe relations between management and other employees at your workplace ...
READ OUT ....

%
30.5 ... very good,
50.6 quite good,
14.1 not very good,
3.5 or, not at all good?
1.1 (Don't know)
0.2 (Refusal)

Q539 [SayJob]   N=1545
Suppose there was going to be some decision made at your place of work that changed the way you do your job. Do you think that **you personally** would have any say in the decision about the change, or not?
IF 'DEPENDS': Code as 'Don't know' <CTRL+K+Enter>

%
52.6 Yes
43.7 No
3.5 (Don't know)
0.2 (Refusal)

Q540 **IF 'Yes' AT [MuchSay]**
How much say or chance to influence the decision do you think you would have ... READ OUT ... N=1545
%
12.5 ..a great deal,
22.6 quite a lot,
17.2 or, just a little?
0.3 (Don't know)
3.7 (Refusal)

VERSIONS A, C AND D: ASK ALL EMPLOYEES IN CURRENT/LAST JOB ('employee' OR DON'T KNOW AT [REmplyee])

Q541 **[PrefHr2]**
Thinking about the number of hours you work including regular overtime, would you prefer a job where you worked ... READ OUT ... N=1545
%
5.8 ..more hours per week,
28.8 fewer hours per week,
64.9 or, are you happy with the number of hours you work at present?
0.3 (Don't know)
0.2 (Refusal)

Q542 **IF 'fewer hours' AT [EarnHr2]**
Would you still prefer to work fewer hours, if it meant earning less money as a result? N=1545
%
7.3 Yes
19.3 No
2.0 It depends
0.1 (Don't know)
0.5 (Refusal)

Q543 **ASK ALL [DisNew3]**
Do you have any long-term illness, health problems or disability. By long-term we mean that it can be expected to last for a year or more? N=4290
%
28.2 Yes
71.6 No
0.0 (Don't know)
0.1 (Refusal)

VERSIONS C AND D: ASK ALL EMPLOYEES IN CURRENT/LAST JOB ('employee' OR DON'T KNOW AT [REmplyee])

Q544- CARD H7 N=1036
Q547 And now some more questions about your job.
Say you had to take a day off work, with little notice, for family or personal reasons. In general, which of the things on this card would you do to cover the lost time?
PROBE: Which others?
CODE ALL THAT APPLY
Multicoded (Maximum of 4 codes)
%
46.7 Use holiday or flexi hours [LTHoli]
10.1 Put in extra effort within normal working hours [LTEffort]
26.1 Work extra hours afterwards [LTExtrHr]
21.3 Take unpaid leave [LTUnpaid]
16.6 None of these [LTNone]
0.4 (Don't know)
0.6 (Refusal)

Q553 **[LoseMony]**
And if you took time off work for family or personal reasons would you... READ OUT ... N=1036
%
18.0 ..usually lose money as a result,
11.8 sometimes lose money,
66.3 or, not usually lose money as a result?
2.3 (Varies too much to say)
1.0 (Don't know)
0.6 (Refusal)

Q554 [UpLadder]
CARD H8
N=1036
I'd like you to think about how people in your kind of job move up the ladder at your workplace - for example, by getting themselves promoted. Do you agree or disagree that people who want to do this usually have to put in long hours?

%
9.9 Agree strongly
28.3 Agree
15.2 Neither agree nor disagree
33.0 Disagree
4.3 Disagree strongly
4.4 (No-one moves up ladder/gets promoted)
2.8 (It depends)
1.4 (Don't know)
0.6 (Refusal)

Q555 [ImpLaddr]
CARD H9
N=1036
Speaking for yourself, how important is it that you move up the career ladder at work?

%
16.6 Very important
29.1 Fairly important
36.0 Not very important
17.3 Not important at all
0.5 (Don't know)
0.6 (Refusal)

Q556 [LongHrs2] *
CARD H10
N=1036
How much do you agree or disagree with these statements:
People in my kind of job are expected to work longer hours these days than they used to

Q557 [JobCaree] *
CARD H10 AGAIN
N=1036
(How much do you agree or disagree with this statement:)
I see my present job as part of a career

Q558 [CareeHap] *
CARD H10 AGAIN
N=1036
(How much do you agree or disagree with this statement:)
I am happy with the way my career has gone so far

Q559 [CareePat] *
CARD H10 AGAIN
N=1036
(How much do you agree or disagree with this statement:)
My partner's career takes priority over my own

	[LongHrs2]	[JobCaree]	[CareeHap]	[CareePat]
	%	%	%	%
Agree strongly	14.7	17.1	15.8	5.1
Agree	31.1	41.2	55.3	11.0
Neither agree nor disagree	20.5	14.6	14.5	17.6
Disagree	29.5	19.9	11.4	30.7
Disagree strongly	3.0	6.6	2.3	7.0
(Don't Know)	0.5	0.1	0.1	0.7
(Refusal)/	0.6	0.6	0.6	0.7
Not answered				0.3

VERSIONS A, C AND D: ASK ALL EMPLOYEES IN CURRENT/LAST JOB ('employee' OR DON'T KNOW AT [REmplyee])

Q560 [WkAcWWW]
N=1545
At your workplace, do you have access to the internet or World Wide Web?

%
65.8 Yes
33.6 No
0.2 (Don't know)
0.4 (Refusal)

Q561 [WkWWWHrw]
IF 'Yes' AT [WkAcWWW]
N=1545
At your workplace, how many hours a week on average do you spend using the internet or World Wide Web, including e-mail, **for your work**?
INTERVIEWER: ROUND UP TO NEAREST HOUR
IF ASKED: Do not include intranet.
Median: 4 hours

%
0.3 (Don't know)
0.4 (Refusal)

Q562　[WkWWWHrP]　　　N=1545
At your workplace, how many hours a week on average do you spend using the internet or World Wide Web, including e-mail, **for your own personal use?**
INTERVIEWER: ROUND UP TO NEAREST HOUR
IF ASKED: Do not include intranet.
Median: 1 hour
%
0.3　(Don't know)
0.4　(Refusal)

IF >0 AT [WkWWWHrP]
Q563-　CARD H7/H11　　　N=1545
Q578　At your workplace, for which of the following do you use the internet or World Wide Web **for your own personal use?**
PROBE: Which others?
Multicoded (Maximum of 16 codes)
%
10.5　Shopping　　　[WkWPShop]
0.4　Chat rooms　　　[WkWPChat]
22.3　E-mail　　　[WkWPEmai]
17.9　News and current affairs　　　[WkWPNews]
8.7　Training, education and learning　　　[WkWPEduc]
16.8　Travel and weather information　　　[WkWPTrav]
3.1　Keeping in touch with groups I belong to　　　[WkWPGrp]
13.5　General information　　　[WkWPInfo]
13.2　Banking and bill-paying　　　[WkWPBank]
1.5　Downloading music　　　[WkWPMusi]
8.8　Sports information　　　[WkWPSpor]
2.2　Games　　　[WkWPGame]
5.1　Job search　　　[WkWPJobs]
6.2　Accessing local/central government
　　information/services　　　[WkWPGovt]
1.3　Trade union activities　　　[WkWPPTU]
0.4　Other (PLEASE SPECIFY)　　　[WkWPOth]
　　(None of these)
0.2　(Don't know)
0.4　(Refusal)

VERSIONS A, C AND D: ASK ALL

Q597　**[MonInter] ***　　　N=3213
CARD H8/H12
I am going to read out a list of activities that an employer may want to routinely monitor in the workplace. This could be done either electronically or manually. For each item, please say whether you think that employers **should** or **should not**
have the right to routinely ...
... monitor internet usage?

Q598　**[MonEmail] ***　　　N=3213
CARD H8/H12 AGAIN
(And do you think that employers **should** or **should not** have the right to routinely ...)
... monitor e-mail?

Q599　**[MonTele] ***　　　N=3213
CARD H8/H12 AGAIN
(And do you think that employers **should** or **should not** have the right to routinely ...)
... monitor telephone calls?

Q600　**[MonVideo] ***　　　N=3213
CARD H8/H12 AGAIN
(And do you think that employers **should** or **should not** have the right to routinely ...)
... use video surveillance to monitor employees?

Q601　**[MonDrugs] ***　　　N=3213
CARD H8/H12 AGAIN
(And do you think that employers **should** or **should not** have the right to routinely ...)
... test employees for drugs and alcohol?

Q602　**[MonBelon] ***　　　N=3213
CARD H8/H12 AGAIN
(And do you think that employers **should** or **should not** have the right to routinely ...)
... search employees' personal belongings when entering or leaving the workplace?

Q603 [MonitLaw] *   N=3213
CARD H8/H12 AGAIN
Should employers be required by law to inform
employees what, if any, activities they are routinely
monitoring?

	[MonInter]	[MonEmail]	[MonTele]	[MonVideo]
	%	%	%	%
Definitely should	44.5	29.5	21.9	9.7
Probably should	38.2	35.5	37.9	25.3
Probably should **not**	8.7	20.0	23.8	33.6
Definitely should **not**	4.5	11.1	14.7	28.9
(Don't Know)	4.0	3.9	1.6	2.3
(Refusal/ Not answered)	0.1	0.1	0.1	0.1

	[MonDrugs]	[MonBelon]	[MonitLaw]
	%	%	%
Definitely should	31.9	10.7	74.6
Probably should	39.2	28.1	19.3
Probably should **not**	18.5	31.9	3.2
Definitely should **not**	8.2	26.4	1.6
(Don't Know)	2.1	2.7	1.1
(Refusal/Not answered)	0.1	0.1	0.1

**VERSIONS A, C AND D: ASK ALL EMPLOYEES IN CURRENT/LAST
JOB ('employee' OR DON'T KNOW AT [REmplyee])**   N=1545

Q604 [WorkGend]
Thinking now of the people at your place of work who
do a similar job to yours.
Are they ... READ OUT ....
%
15.7   ...only men,
24.1   mainly men,
26.3   mainly women,
7.8   only women,
24.8   or are there similar numbers of men and women?
0.7   (Don't know)
0.5   (Refusal)

Q605 [WorkEthn]   N=1545
Still thinking of the people at your place of work who
do a similar job to yours.
Are they ... READ OUT ...
%
33.7   ... only from a white ethnic group,
45.1   mainly from a white ethnic group,
2.1   mainly from a non-white ethnic group,
0.7   only from a non-white ethnic group,
17.1   or are there similar numbers of people from white and
       non-white ethnic groups?
0.8   (Don't know)
0.5   (Refusal)

Q606 [WorkAged]   N=1545
(Still thinking of the people at your place of work
who do a similar job to yours.)
Are they ... READ OUT ...
%
3.7   ... mainly aged under 25,
52.1   mainly between the ages of 25 and 49,
4.8   mainly aged 50 and over,
38.1   or is there a mixture of people from different age
       groups?
0.8   (Don't know)
0.5   (Refusal)

VERSIONS A, C AND D: ASK ALL   N=3213

Q607 [PrejNow]
Do you think there is generally more racial prejudice
in Britain now than there was 5 years ago, less, or
about the same amount?
%
35.2   More now
14.6   Less now
29.1   About the same
0.5   Other (WRITE IN)
2.5   (Don't know)
0.1   (Refusal)

Q610 [PrejFut]　　　　　　　　　　N=3213
Do you think there will be more, less, or about the same amount of racial prejudice in Britain in 5 years time compared with now?
%
59.1　More in 5 years
12.9　Less
23.2　About the same
1.0　Other (WRITE IN)
3.6　(Don't know)
0.1　(Refusal)

Q613 [SRPrej]　　　　　　　　　　N=3213
How would you describe yourself ... READ OUT ...
... as very prejudiced against people of other races,
%
2.2　a little prejudiced,
28.3
67.9　or, not prejudiced at all?
0.8　Other (WRITE IN)
0.7　(Don't know)
0.2　(Refusal)

Q616 [EqOpWBlk] *　　　　　　　　N=3213
CARD H9/H13
Please use this card to say whether you think attempts to give equal opportunities to **black people and Asians in the workplace** have gone too far or not gone far enough?

Q617 [EqOpWWmn] *　　　　　　　　N=3213
CARD H9/H13 AGAIN
And, whether you think attempts to give equal opportunities to **women in the workplace** have gone too far or not gone far enough?

Q618 [EqOpWDis] *　　　　　　　　N=3213
CARD H9/H13 AGAIN
And, whether you think attempts to give equal opportunities to **people with a disability or a long-term illness in the workplace** have gone too far or not gone far enough?

Q619 [EqOpWGay] *　　　　　　　　N=3213
CARD H9/H13 AGAIN
And, whether you think attempts to give equal opportunities to **gay or lesbian people in the workplace** have gone too far or not gone far enough?

	[EqOpWBlk]	[EqOpWWmn]	[EqOpWDis]	[EqOpWGay]
	%	%	%	%
Gone much too far	7.8	1.4	0.7	4.3
Gone too far	28.3	9.7	5.0	14.1
About right	41.2	48.2	31.6	51.6
Not gone far enough	16.3	35.1	52.0	15.4
Not gone nearly far enough	1.1	2.5	4.9	1.1
(Don't Know)	5.1	2.9	5.6	13.2
(Refusal/ Not answered)	0.1	0.2	0.2	0.3

VERSIONS A, C AND D: ASK ALL EMPLOYEES IN CURRENT/LAST JOB ('employee' OR DON'T KNOW AT [REmployee])

Q620 [PrejWAs] *　　　　　　　　N=1545
CARD H10/H14
In your workplace how much prejudice do you think there is against employees of Asian origin? Please take your answer from this card.

Q621 [PrejWBlk] *　　　　　　　　N=1545
H10/H14 AGAIN
In your workplace how much prejudice do you think there is against employees who are black? (Please take your answer from this card)

Q622 [PrejWDis] *　　　　　　　　N=1545
H10/H14 AGAIN
In your workplace how much prejudice do you think there is against employees with disabilities? (Please take your answer from this card)

Q623 [PrejWGay] *　　　　　　　　N=1545
H10/H14 AGAIN
In your workplace how much prejudice do you think there is against employees who are gay or lesbian? (Please take your answer from this card)

	[PrejWAs]	[PrejWBlk]	[PrejWDis]	[PrejWGay]
	%	%	%	%
A lot	3.5	2.0	2.5	2.4
A little	14.6	11.4	10.3	8.8
Hardly any	27.5	27.0	20.9	19.4
None	50.8	55.9	60.7	61.3
(Don't Know)	3.1	3.2	5.0	7.4
(Refusal)/ Not answered	0.5	0.5	0.5	0.5

Q625   VERSIONS A, C AND D: ASK ALL
[EmpRand]   N=3213
Random number for OBossAs etc
Range: 1 ... 4

Q627   VERSIONS A, C AND D: ASK ALL IN RANDOM GROUPS 1 AND 2
[OBossAs]   N=1550
Do you think **most** white people in Britain would mind or not mind if a suitably qualified person of **Asian** origin were appointed as their boss?
IF 'WOULD MIND': A lot or a little?

%	
12.7	Mind a lot
29.5	Mind a little
52.0	Not mind
0.2	Other answer (PLEASE SPECIFY)
1.6	EDIT ONLY: Depends if person is suitably qualified / experienced
3.7	(Don't know)
0.2	(Refusal)

Q630   VERSIONS A, C AND D: ASK ALL IN RANDOM GROUPS 1 AND 2 WHO CONSIDER THEMSELVES WHITE (at [RaceOri1])   N=1389
[OBossAsA]
%   Derived from [OBossAsA] limited to [RaceOri2] = 'white'

%	
11.5	Mind a lot
28.8	Mind a little
52.9	Not mind
1.7	Other answer (PLEASE SPECIFY)
0.2	EDIT ONLY: Depends if person is suitably qualified / experienced
3.6	(Don't know)
1.2	(Refusal)

Q631   VERSIONS A, C AND D: ASK ALL IN RANDOM GROUPS 1 AND 2
[SBossAsA]   N=1550
And you personally? Would you mind or not mind?
IF 'WOULD MIND': A lot or a little?

%	
3.3	Mind a lot
6.4	Mind a little
87.8	Not mind
0.2	Other answer (PLEASE SPECIFY)
0.1	EDIT ONLY: Depends if person is suitably qualified / experienced
0.9	(Don't know)
1.2	(Refusal)

Q634   VERSIONS A, C AND D: ASK ALL IN RANDOM GROUPS 1 AND 2 WHO CONSIDER THEMSELVES WHITE (at [RaceOri1])   N=1389
[SBossAs]
%   derived from [SBossAsA] limited to [RaceOri2] = 'white'

%	
3.3	Mind a lot
6.4	Mind a little
87.8	Not mind
0.2	Other answer (PLEASE SPECIFY)
0.1	EDIT ONLY: Depends if person is suitably qualified / experienced
0.9	(Don't know)
1.2	(Refusal)

Q635   VERSIONS A, C AND D: ASK ALL EMPLOYEES IN CURRENT/LAST JOB ('employee' OR DON'T KNOW AT [REmployee]) IN RANDOM GROUPS 1 AND 2   N=737
[CBossAsA]
And your colleagues? Would they mind or not mind?
IF 'WOULD MIND': A lot or a little?

%	
4.7	Mind a lot
17.6	Mind a little
	Not mind
0.2	Other answer (PLEASE SPECIFY)
0.2	EDIT ONLY: Depends if person is suitably qualified / experienced
-	EDIT ONLY: Does not have any colleagues
0.2	EDIT ONLY: It varies for different colleagues
3.8	(Don't know)
0.4	(Refusal)

Q638 [OBossWIA]

VERSIONS A, C AND D: ASK ALL IN RANDOM GROUPS 2 AND 4   N=1589

Do you think **most** white people in Britain would mind or not mind if a suitably qualified person of **Black or West Indian** origin were appointed as their boss?

IF 'WOULD MIND': A lot or a little?

%
9.9 Mind a lot
31.1 Mind a little
53.3 Not mind
0.8 Other answer (PLEASE SPECIFY)
0.1 EDIT ONLY: Depends if person is suitably qualified / experienced
4.6 (Don't know)
0.2 (Refusal)

Q641 [SBossWI]

VERSIONS A, C AND D: ASK ALL IN RANDOM GROUPS 2 AND 4 WHO CONSIDER THEMSELVES WHITE (at [RaceOri])   N=1447

derived from [OBossWIA] limited to [RaceOri2] = 'white'

%
8.9 Mind a lot
30.7 Mind a little
54.2 Not mind
0.9 Other answer (PLEASE SPECIFY)
0.1 EDIT ONLY: Depends if person is suitably qualified / experienced
4.1 (Don't know)
1.2 (Refusal)

Q642 [SBossWI]

VERSIONS A, C AND D: ASK ALL IN RANDOM GROUPS 2 AND 4   N=1589

And you personally? Would you mind or not mind?

IF 'WOULD MIND': A lot or a little?

%
2.2 Mind a lot
5.5 Mind a little
90.5 Not mind
0.4 Other answer (PLEASE SPECIFY)
0.1 EDIT ONLY: Depends if person is suitably qualified / experienced
1.1 (Don't know)
0.2 (Refusal)

Q645 [SBossWI]

VERSIONS A, C AND D: ASK ALL IN RANDOM GROUPS 2 AND 4 WHO CONSIDER THEMSELVES WHITE (at [RaceOri])   N=1447

derived from [SBossWIA] limited to [RaceOri2] = 'white'

%
2.4 Mind a lot
5.8 Mind a little
89.1 Not mind
0.4 Other answer (PLEASE SPECIFY)
0.2 EDIT ONLY: Depends if person is suitably qualified / experienced
0.9 (Don't know)
1.2 (Refusal)

Q646 [CBossWI]

VERSIONS A, C AND D: ASK ALL EMPLOYEES IN CURRENT/LAST JOB ('employee' OR DON'T KNOW AT [REmployee]) IN RANDOM GROUPS 2 AND 4   N=757

And your colleagues? Would they mind or not mind?

IF 'WOULD MIND': A lot or a little?

%
3.5 Mind a lot
17.4 Mind a little
74.2 Not mind
0.2 Other answer (PLEASE SPECIFY)
- EDIT ONLY: Depends if person is suitably qualified / experienced
0.1 EDIT ONLY: Does not have any colleagues
0.1 EDIT ONLY: It varies for different colleagues
3.7 (Don't know)
0.8 (Refusal)

VERSIONS A, C AND D: ASK ALL EMPLOYEES IN CURRENT/LAST JOB ('employee' OR DON'T KNOW AT [REmplyee]) IN RANDOM GROUPS 1 AND 3

Q649 [CBossAge]   N=788
Do you think your colleagues would mind or not mind if
a suitably qualified person aged younger than them
were appointed as their boss?
IF 'WOULD MIND': A lot or a little?

%	
9.9	Mind a lot
25.1	Mind a little
62.6	Not mind
0.7	Other answer (PLEASE SPECIFY)
0.3	EDIT ONLY: Depends if person is suitably qualified / experienced
0.1	EDIT ONLY: Does not have any colleagues
0.2	EDIT ONLY: It varies for different colleagues
1.0	(Don't know)
-	(Refusal)

Q652 [SBossAge]   N=788
And you personally? Would you mind or not mind?
IF 'WOULD MIND': A lot or a little?

%	
3.2	Mind a lot
13.3	Mind a little
82.8	Not mind
0.3	Other answer (PLEASE SPECIFY)
0.2	EDIT ONLY: Depends if person is suitably qualified / experienced
0.3	(Don't know)
-	(Refusal)

VERSIONS A, C AND D: ASK ALL EMPLOYEES IN CURRENT/LAST JOB ('employee' OR DON'T KNOW AT [REmplyee]) IN RANDOM GROUPS 2 AND 3

Q655 [CBossGay]   N=777
Do you think your colleagues would mind or not mind if
a suitably qualified person who is gay or lesbian were
appointed as their boss?
IF 'WOULD MIND': A lot or a little?

%	
4.9	Mind a lot
12.9	Mind a little
77.5	Not mind
0.3	Other answer (PLEASE SPECIFY)
-	EDIT ONLY: Depends if person is suitably qualified / experienced
0.1	EDIT ONLY: Does not have any colleagues
0.1	EDIT ONLY: It varies for different colleagues
3.6	(Don't know)
0.5	(Refusal)

Q658 [SBossGay]   N=777
And you personally? Would you mind or not mind?
IF 'WOULD MIND': A lot or a little?

%	
2.0	Mind a lot
5.4	Mind a little
90.4	Not mind
0.2	Other answer (PLEASE SPECIFY)
-	EDIT ONLY: Depends if person is suitably qualified / experienced
1.5	(Don't know)
0.4	(Refusal)

VERSIONS A, C AND D: ASK ALL EMPLOYEES IN CURRENT/LAST JOB ('employee' OR DON'T KNOW AT [REmplyee]) IN RANDOM GROUPS 1 AND 4

Q661 [CBossDis]   N=768
Do you think your colleagues would mind or not mind if a suitably qualified person with a disability or long-term illness were appointed as their boss?
IF 'WOULD MIND': A lot or a little?
%
3.7 Mind a lot
13.9 Mind a little
77.2 Not mind
0.2 Other answer (PLEASE SPECIFY)
0.2 EDIT ONLY: Depends if person is suitably qualified / experienced
0.1 EDIT ONLY: Does not have any colleagues
-    EDIT ONLY: It varies for different colleagues
0.6 EDIT ONLY: Job could not be done by disabled person
2.5 (Don't know)
0.4 (Refusal)

Q664 [SBossDis]   N=768
And you personally? Would you mind or not mind?
IF 'WOULD MIND': A lot or a little?
%
1.3 Mind a lot
6.0 Mind a little
90.1 Not mind
1.1 Other answer (PLEASE SPECIFY)
-    EDIT ONLY: Depends if person is suitably qualified / experienced
0.4 EDIT ONLY: Job could not be done by disabled person
0.8 (Don't know)
0.4 (Refusal)

VERSIONS A, C AND D: ASK ALL EMPLOYEES IN CURRENT/LAST JOB ('employee' OR DON'T KNOW AT [REmplyee]) IN RANDOM GROUPS 3 AND 4

Q667 [CBossWom]   N=808
Do you think your colleagues would mind or not mind if a suitably qualified woman were appointed as their boss?
IF 'WOULD MIND': A lot or a little?
%
2.9 Mind a lot
8.9 Mind a little
86.0 Not mind
1.0 Other answer (PLEASE SPECIFY)
-    EDIT ONLY: Depends if person is suitably qualified / experienced
0.3 EDIT ONLY: Does not have any colleagues
0.1 EDIT ONLY: It varies for different colleagues
0.5 (Don't know)
0.3 (Refusal)

Q670 [SBossWom]   N=808
And you personally? Would you mind or not mind?
IF 'WOULD MIND': A lot or a little?
%
1.3 Mind a lot
3.3 Mind a little
94.4 Not mind
0.1 Other answer (PLEASE SPECIFY)
-    EDIT ONLY: Depends if person is suitably qualified / experienced
0.5 (Don't know)
0.3 (Refusal)

Respondent's job details

ASK ALL WHO HAVE EVER HAD A JOB ('paid work' OR 'waiting to take up a job' AT [REconAct] OR NOT 'never had a paid job' AT [RLastJob])

Q675 [Title] **NOT ON DATAFILE** N=4137
Now I want to ask you about your (present/last/future) job.
PRESENT JOB: What is your job?
PAST JOB: What was your job?
FUTURE JOB: What will that job be?
PROBE IF NECESSARY: What (is/was) the name or title of the job?
Open Question (Maximum of 80 characters)

Q676 [Typewk] **NOT ON DATAFILE** N=4137
What kind of work (do/did/will) you do most of the time?
IF RELEVANT: What materials/machinery (do/did/will) you use?
Open Question (Maximum of 80 characters)

Q677 [Train] **NOT ON DATAFILE** N=4137
What training or qualifications (are/were) needed for that job?
Open Question (Maximum of 80 characters)

Q678 [Remplyee] **NOT ON DATAFILE** N=4137
In yourp (main) job (are you/ were you/ will you be)
... READ OUT ...
%
87.3 ... an employee,
12.4 or self-employed?
0.1 (Don't know)
0.2 (Refusal)

Q680 [RSuperv] N=4137
In your job, (do/did/will) you have any formal responsibility for supervising the work of other (employees/people)?
DO NOT INCLUDE PEOPLE WHO ONLY SUPERVISE:
- CHILDREN, E.G. TEACHERS, NANNIES, CHILDMINDERS
- ANIMALS
- SECURITY OR BUILDINGS, E.G. CARETAKERS, SECURITY GUARDS
%
39.0 Yes
60.8 No
0.0 (Don't know)
0.2 (Refusal)

Q681 **IF 'yes' AT [Superv]** N=4137
[RMany]
How many?
%
Median: 6 (of those supervising any)
0.3 (Don't know)
0.2 (Refusal)

ASK ALL EMPLOYEES IN CURRENT/LAST JOB ('employee' OR DON'T KNOW AT [EmployA])

Q683 [ROcSect2] N=3625
CARD H1
Which of the types of organisation on this card (do you work/did you work/will you be working) for?
%
63.7 PRIVATE SECTOR FIRM OR COMPANY Including, for example, limited companies and PLCs
3.0 NATIONALISED INDUSTRY OR PUBLIC CORPORATION Including, for example, the Post Office and the BBC
29.0 OTHER PUBLIC SECTOR EMPLOYER
Incl eg: - Central govt/ Civil Service/ Govt Agency
- Local authority/ Local Educ Auth (INCL 'OPTED OUT' SCHOOLS)
- Universities
- Health Authority / NHS hospitals / NHS Trusts/ GP surgeries
- Police / Armed forces
3.0 CHARITY/ VOLUNTARY SECTOR Including, for example, charitable companies, churches, trade unions
0.7 Other answer (WRITE IN)
0.1 (Don't know)
0.4 (Refusal)

Q686   **ASK ALL WHO HAVE EVER HAD A JOB ('paid work' OR 'waiting to take up a job' AT [REconAct] OR NOT 'never had a paid job' AT [RLastJob]**
[EmpMake] NOT ON DATAFILE   N=4137
IF EMPLOYEE: What (does/did) your employer make or do at the place where you (will) usually work(ed) from?
IF SELF-EMPLOYED: What (do/did/will) you make or do at the place where you (will) usually work(ed) from?
Open Question (Maximum of 80 characters)

Q688   **ASK ALL SELF-EMPLOYED IN CURRENT/LAST JOB ('self-employed' AT [REmploye]**
[SEmpNum]   N=512
In your work or business, (do/did/will) you have any employees, or not?
IF YES: How many?
IF 'NO EMPLOYEES', CODE 0.
FOR 500+ EMPLOYEES, CODE 500.
NOTE: FAMILY MEMBERS MAY BE EMPLOYEES ONLY IF THEY RECEIVE A REGULAR WAGE OR SALARY.
Median: 0 employees
%
1.2   (Don't know)
0.3   (Refusal)

Q693   [SNumEmp]   N=367
(derived from [SEmpNum]) - does R have any employees?
%
31.5   Yes
65.6   No
0.4   (Don't know)
2.4   (Refusal)

Q694   **ASK ALL IN PAID WORK (AT [REconAct])**
[WkJbTim]   N=2445
In your present job, are you working ... READ OUT ...
RESPONDENT'S OWN DEFINITION
%
77.8   ... full-time,
21.6   or, part-time?
0.2   (Don't know)
0.4   (Refusal)

Q697   **ASK ALL IN PAID WORK (AT [REconAct])**
[WkJbHrsI]   N=2443
How many hours do you normally work a week in your main job - including any paid or unpaid overtime?
ROUND TO NEAREST HOUR.
IF RESPONDENT CANNOT ANSWER, ASK ABOUT LAST WEEK.
IF RESPONDENT DOES NOT KNOW EXACTLY, ACCEPT AN ESTIMATE.
FOR 95+ HOURS, CODE 95.
FOR 'VARIES TOO MUCH TO SAY', CODE 96.
MEDIAN: 40 hours
%
0.3   (Varies too much to say)
0.4   (Don't know)
0.3   (Refusal)

Q698   **ASK ALL CURRENT EMPLOYEES ('paid work' at [REconAct] and 'employee' OR DON'T KNOW AT [REmplyee]**
[EdJbHrsX]   N=2083
What are your **basic** or **contractual hours** each week in your main job - **excluding** any paid and unpaid overtime?
ROUND TO NEAREST HOUR.
IF RESPONDENT CANNOT ANSWER, ASK ABOUT LAST WEEK.
IF RESPONDENT DOES NOT KNOW EXACTLY, ACCEPT AN ESTIMATE.
FOR 95+ HOURS, CODE 95.
FOR 'VARIES TOO MUCH TO SAY', CODE 96.
MEDIAN: 37 hours
%
2.0   (Varies too much to say)
1.3   (Don't know)
0.3   (Refusal)

Q699   **ASK ALL WHO HAVE EVER WORKED BUT ARE NOT CURRENTLY WORKING ('waiting to take up work' AT [REconAct] OR NOT 'never worked' AT [RLastJob]**
[ExPrtFul]   N=1700
(Is/Was/Will) the job (be) ... READ OUT ...
%
67.8   ... full-time - that is, 30 or more hours per week,
31.6   or, part-time?
0.1   (Don't know)
0.5   (Refusal)

Q700
ASK ALL CURRENT EMPLOYEES ('paid work' at [REconAct]
AND 'employee' OR DON'T KNOW AT [REmployee])
[EJbHrCaI] (NOT ON SCREEN)   N=2083
Respondent's working time including overtime -
categorised - current employees
Derived from [REconAct], [REmplyee] and [WkJbHrsI]

%
4.9   10-15 hours a week
10.2 16-23 hours a week
4.9   24-29 hours a week
79.1 30 or more hours a week
0.2   (Don't know)
0.4   (Refusal)

Q701
[EJbHrCaX] (NOT ON SCREEN)   N=2083
Respondent's working time excluding overtime -
categorised - current employees
Derived from [REconAct], [REmplyee] and [EJbHrsX]

%
4.4   10-15 hours a week
10.4 16-23 hours a week
5.0   24-29 hours a week
74.4 30 or more hours a week
1.5   (Don't know)
0.4   (Refusal)

Q702
ASK ALL CURRENT SELF-EMPLOYED ('paid work' at
[REconAct] AND 'self-employed' AT [REmplyee])
[SJbHrCaI] (NOT ON SCREEN)   N=367
Respondent's working time including overtime -
categorised - current self-employed
Derived from [REconAct], [REmplyee] and [WkJbHrsI].

%
7.9   10-15 hours a week
6.4   16-23 hours a week
4.0   24-29 hours a week
77.7 30 or more hours a week
0.9   (Varies too much to say)
0.7   (Don't know)
2.4   (Refusal)

Q703
ASK ALL WHO HAVE EVER WORKED ('paid work' OR 'waiting
to take up a job' AT [REconAct] OR NOT 'never had a
paid job' AT [RLastJob])
[RPartFul] (NOT ON SCREEN)   N=4137
Full-time/part-time status - all respondents who have
ever worked
Derived from [REconAct], [WkJbTim] and [ExPrtFul]

%
73.9 Full-time (30+ hours)
25.7 Part-time (10-29 hours)?
0.2   (Don't know)
0.2   (Refusal)

ASK ALL
Q720
[UnionSA]   N=4290
(May I just check) are you now a member of a trade
union or staff association?
PROBE AS NECESSARY AND CODE FIRST TO APPLY

%
17.2 Yes, trade union
3.1   Yes, staff association
79.6 No
0.1   (Don't know)
0.1   (Refusal)

Q721
IF 'no' OR DON'T KNOW AT [UnionSA]
[TUSAEver]   N=4290
Have you ever been a member of a trade union or staff
association?
PROBE AS NECESSARY AND CODE FIRST TO APPLY

%
23.4 Yes, trade union
2.5   Yes, staff association
53.6 No
0.1   (Don't know)
0.1   (Refusal)

Q722
VERSION B: ASK ALL 'married', 'in civil partnership'
OR 'living as married' AT [Marstat5]
[SUnionSA]   N=674
Is your (wife/husband/partner) now a member of a trade
union or staff association?
PROBE AS NECESSARY AND CODE FIRST TO APPLY

%
17.7 Yes: trade union
4.0   Yes: staff association
74.4 No
3.2   (Don't know)
0.7   (Refusal)

Politics (version B)

VERSION B: ASK ALL

Q734 [Monarchy]   N=1077

How important or unimportant do you think it is for
Britain to continue to have a monarchy

... READ OUT ....

%	
27.1	..very important,
35.4	quite important,
23.2	not very important,
5.4	not at all important,
7.0	or, do you think the monarchy should be abolished?
1.7	(Don't know)
0.1	(Refusal)

Q735 [ECPolicy]   N=1077
CARD J1

Do you think Britain's long-term policy should be...
READ OUT ....

%	
15.2	... to leave the European Union,
35.8	to stay in the EU and try to **reduce** the EU's powers,
26.6	to leave things as they are,
9.2	to stay in the EU and try to **increase** the EU's powers,
4.3	or, to work for the formation of a single European government?
8.9	(Don't know)
0.2	(Refusal)

Q736 [EuroRef]   N=1077

And if there were a referendum on whether Britain
should **join the single European currency, the Euro**,
how do you think you would vote? Would you vote to
join the Euro, or not to join the Euro?
IF 'would not vote', PROBE: If you did vote, how would
you vote?
IF RESPONDENT INSISTS THEY WOULD NOT VOTE, CODE DON'T
KNOW

%	
25.7	To join the Euro
68.4	Not to join the Euro
5.8	(Don't know)
0.1	(Refusal)

Q737 [GovTrust]   N=1077
CARD J2

How much do you trust British governments of any party
to place the needs of the nation above the interests
of their own political party?
Please choose a phrase from this card.

%	
1.4	Just about always
17.5	Most of the time
45.6	Only some of the time
33.6	Almost never
1.9	(Don't know)
-	(Refusal)

Q738 [MPsTrust]   N=1077
CARD J2 AGAIN

And how much do you trust politicians of any party in
Britain to tell the truth when they are in a tight
corner?

%	
0.6	Just about always
6.5	Most of the time
34.8	Only some of the time
57.1	Almost never
1.0	(Don't know)
-	(Refusal)

Q739 [SocTrust]   N=1077

Generally speaking, would you say that most people can
be trusted, or that you can't be too careful in
dealing with people?

%	
41.1	Most people can be trusted
57.5	Can't be too careful in dealing with people
1.3	(Don't know)
-	(Refusal)

Q740 [NIreland]   N=1077

Do you think the long-term policy for Northern Ireland
should be for it ... READ OUT ...

%	
34.0	..to remain part of the United Kingdom
38.8	or, to unify with the rest of Ireland?
0.2	NORTHERN IRELAND SHOULD BE AN INDEPENDENT STATE
-	NORTHERN IRELAND SHOULD BE SPLIT UP INTO TWO
5.0	IT SHOULD BE UP TO THE IRISH TO DECIDE
3.1	Other answer (WRITE IN)
18.6	(Don't know)
0.2	(Refusal)

VERSION B: ASK ALL

Q743 [EngParl2]
CARD J3   N=1077

With all the changes going on in the way the different parts of Great Britain are run, which of the following do you think would be best for England ...READ OUT...

%
53.6 ...for England to be governed as it is now, with laws made by the UK parliament,

17.4 for each region of England to have its own elected assembly that makes decisions about the region's economy, planning and housing,

22.0 or, for England as a whole to have its own new parliament with law-making powers?

3.4 (None of these)
3.6 (Don't know)
- (Refusal)

National identity (versions A, B and C)

Q744 VERSIONS A, B AND C: ASK ALL
[WhrBrn]
CARD K1   N=3228

Please tell me where you were born?

%
74.2 England
9.2 Scotland
4.6 Wales
0.6 Northern Ireland
0.8 Republic of Ireland
10.6 Other
- (Don't know)
0.1 (Refusal)

Q745 VERSIONS A, B AND C: ASK ALL BORN IN BRITAIN (I.E. 'England', 'Scotland' OR 'Wales' AT [WhrBrn]
[NatIdB]
CARD K2/K3/K4   N=2842

INTERVIEWER: PLEASE DOUBLE-CHECK RESPONDENT IS REFERRING TO CORRECT SHOWCARD

Which, if any, of the following best describes how you see yourself?

%
22.1 (English/Scottish/Welsh) not British
17.5 More (English/Scottish/Welsh) than British
42.8 Equally (English/Scottish/Welsh) and British
7.3 More British than (English/Scottish/Welsh)
6.4 British not (English/Scottish/Welsh)
3.1 Other description (WRITE IN)
0.7 (None of these)
0.1 (Don't know)
0.1 (Refusal)

Q748 IF '(English/Scottish/Welsh) not British' OR 'More (English/Scottish/Welsh) than British' AT [NatIdB] N=2842
[Intro1]
CARD K5
I am going to read out a list of reasons people sometimes give for saying that they see themselves as (English not British/more English than British/equally English and British than English/British not English/Scottish not British/more Scottish than British/equally Scottish and British/more British than Scottish/British not Scottish/Welsh not British/more Welsh than British/equally Welsh and British/more British than Welsh/British not Welsh).
Using this card, please say how much you agree or disagree with each one as a reason why you see yourself as (English not British/more English than British/equally English and British/British not English/Scottish not British/more Scottish than British/equally Scottish and British/more British than Scottish/British not Scottish/Welsh not British/more Welsh than British/equally Welsh and British/more British than Welsh/British not Welsh).
Press 1 and <Enter> to continue.

Q749 [RDistEmp] * N=2842
CARD K5 AGAIN
I feel uncomfortable about the idea of being British because I want to distance myself from the British Empire and all it stood for.

Q750 IF 'England' AT [WhrBrn] AND 'English not British' OR 'More English than British' AT [NatIdB] N=2842
[RDPEng] *
CARD K5 AGAIN
(And how much do you agree or disagree that)
In having to be British, English people too often downplay being English, and I think that's wrong.

Q751 IF 'Scotland' OR 'Wales' AT [WhrBrn] AND '(Scottish/Welsh) not British' OR 'More (Scottish/Welsh) than British' AT [NatIdB] N=2842
[BrConfEn] *
CARD K5 AGAIN
(And how much do you agree or disagree that)
Being British is too often confused with being English and people don't always realise that there is a difference between Britain and England.

VERSIONS A, B AND C: ASK ALL BORN IN BRITAIN (I.E. 'England', 'Scotland' OR 'Wales' AT [WhrBrn]): IF '(English/Scottish/Welsh) not British' OR 'More (English/Scottish/Welsh) than British' AT [NatIdB]

Q752 [RIdHist] * N=2842
CARD K5 AGAIN
(And how much do you agree or disagree that)
I identify with (English/Scottish/Welsh) history, traditions and culture.

Q753 [REdLawC] * N=2842
CARD K5 AGAIN
(And how much do you agree or disagree that)
The values of (English/Scottish/Welsh) education, (English law/Scottish Law/the law) and (English/Scottish/Welsh) community spirit are important to me.

Q754 [RBrnthr] * N=2842
CARD K5 AGAIN
(And how much do you agree or disagree that)
I was born in (England/Scotland/Wales) and if you're born in (England/Scotland/Wales) you feel (English/Scottish/Welsh).

Q755 [RDevol] * N=2842
CARD K5 AGAIN
(And how much do you agree or disagree that)
IF RESP BORN IN ENGLAND: I feel more English now that Scotland has its own Parliament and Wales its National Assembly.
IF RESP BORN IN SCOTLAND: I feel more Scottish now that Scotland has its own Parliament.
IF RESP BORN IN WALES: I feel more Welsh now that Wales has its National Assembly.

	[RDistEmp] %	[RDPEng] %	[BrConfEn] %	[RIdHist] %
Strongly agree	1.1	4.6	3.4	12.3
Agree	3.7	14.1	4.3	20.7
Neither agree nor disagree	6.5	5.5	0.5	4.2
Disagree	18.6	4.8	0.8	1.8
Strongly disagree	9.0	0.9	0.1	0.3
(Don't Know)	0.6	0.6	0.0	0.4
(Refusal/ Not answered)	0.1	0.1	0.1	0.1

	[REdLawC] %	[RBrnthr] %	[RDevol] %
Strongly agree	13.8	16.4	5.2
Agree	20.7	18.6	7.9
Neither agree nor disagree	3.9	2.4	13.2
Disagree	0.9	1.9	10.9
Strongly disagree	0.1	0.1	2.0
(Don't Know)	0.4	0.2	0.4
(Refusal/Not answered)	0.1	0.1	0.1

VERSIONS A, B AND C: ASK ALL BORN IN BRITAIN (I.E. 'England', 'Scotland' OR 'Wales' AT [WhrBrn]): IF 'Equally (English/Scottish/Welsh) and British' AT [NatIdB]

Q756 [Intro2]   N=2842
CARD K5
I am going to read out a list of reasons people
sometimes give for saying they see themselves as
equally (English/Scottish/Welsh) and British. Using
this card, please say how much you agree or disagree
with each one as a reason why you see yourself as
equally (English/Scottish/Welsh) and British.
Press 1 and <Enter> to continue.

Q757 [REqlPrd] *   N=2842
You can be equally proud of being British and of being
(English/Scottish/Welsh); it's not a matter of
choosing between them.

Q758 [REqlPart] *   N=2842
CARD K5 AGAIN
(And how much do you agree or disagree that)
It is important to me to recognise that
(England/Scotland/Wales) is an equal partner with the
other countries in the United Kingdom.

Q759 [RappBr] *   N=2842
CARD K5 AGAIN
(And how much do you agree or disagree that)
Sometimes it is more appropriate to say you are
British and sometimes it is more appropriate to say
you are (English/Scottish/Welsh).

Q760 [RimpHist] *   N=2842
CARD K5 AGAIN
(And how much do you agree or disagree that)
Britain has an important history in which
(England/Scotland/Wales) played a significant part.

Q761 [RDevol2] *   N=2842
CARD K5 AGAIN
(And how much do you agree or disagree that)
I feel (English/Scottish/Welsh) as well as British now
that (Scotland has its own Parliament) (and) (Wales
(has) its National Assembly).

IF 'Equally (English/Scottish/Welsh) and British' AT [NatIdB] AND 'England' AT [WhrBrn]

Q762 [RNoDiff]   N=2842
CARD K5 AGAIN
(And how much do you agree or disagree that)
There is no real difference between 'English' and
'British'.

	[REqlPrd] %	[REqlPart] %	[RappBr] %
Strongly agree	57.0	11.0	4.9
Agree	14.7	25.8	20.1
Neither agree nor disagree	25.3	4.2	10.8
Disagree	2.2	1.2	6.6
Strongly disagree	0.6	0.4	0.3
(Don't Know)	0.2	0.3	0.3
(Refusal/Not answered)	0.1	0.1	0.1

VERSIONS A, B AND C: ASK ALL BORN IN BRITAIN (I.E. 'England', 'Scotland' OR 'Wales' AT [WhrBrn]): IF 'More British than (English/Scottish/Welsh)' OR 'British not (English/Scottish/Welsh)' AT [NatidB]
N=2842

Q763 [Intro3]
CARD K5
I am going to read out a list of reasons people sometimes give for saying they see themselves as (English not British/more English than British/equally English and British/more British than English/British not English/Scottish not British/more Scottish than British/equally Scottish and British/more British than Scottish/British not Scottish/Welsh not British/more Welsh than British/equally Welsh and British/more British than Welsh/British not Welsh). Using this card, please say how much you agree or disagree with each one as a reason why you see yourself as (English not British/more English than British/equally English and British/more British than English/British not English/Scottish not British/more Scottish than British/equally Scottish and British/more British than Scottish/British not Scottish/Welsh not British/more Welsh than British/equally Welsh and British/more British than Welsh/British not Welsh).
Press 1 and <Enter> to continue.

Q764 [RAllUK] *
Being British is important to me because all parts of the United Kingdom are included.
N=2842

Q765 [RPastAch] *
CARD K5 AGAIN
(And how much do you agree or disagree that)
I think we should celebrate the past achievements of Great Britain.
N=2842

Q766 [REthMin] *
CARD K5 AGAIN
(And how much do you agree or disagree that)
Being British brings us together because it includes ethnic minorities and people of different cultures.
N=2842

Q767 [RIdMon] *
CARD K5 AGAIN
(And how much do you agree or disagree that)
I identify with things like the monarchy, British traditions and ceremonies.
N=2842

Q768 [RBEmpl] *
CARD K5 AGAIN
(And how much do you agree or disagree that)
Being British matters to me because the British Empire was an important part of our history.
N=2842

Q769 [RDevol3] *
CARD K5 AGAIN
(And how much do you agree or disagree that)
I feel more British now that (Scotland has its own Parliament) (and) (Wales (has) its National Assembly).
N=2842

	[RAllUK]	[RPastAch]	[REthMin]
	%	%	%
Strongly agree	4.2	3.0	2.7
Agree	7.2	6.7	7.0
Neither agree nor disagree	1.4	2.3	1.9
Disagree	0.4	1.0	1.5
Strongly disagree	-	0.2	5.0
(Don't Know)	0.4	0.3	0.3
(Refusal/Not answered)	0.3	0.3	0.3

	[RimpHist]	[RDevol2]	[RNoDiff]
	%	%	%
Strongly agree	10.8	2.9	5.0
Agree	25.9	17.6	20.2
Neither agree nor disagree	4.9	15.3	4.6
Disagree	0.6	5.4	7.6
Strongly disagree	0.1	0.9	0.7
(Don't Know)	0.7	0.8	0.2
(Refusal/Not answered)	0.1	0.1	0.1

	[RIdMon]	[RBEmp]	[RDevol3]
	%	%	%
Strongly agree	2.4	2.0	0.4
Agree	5.9	5.1	2.1
Neither agree nor disagree	2.3	3.1	4.9
Disagree	1.9	2.0	4.4
Strongly disagree	0.7	1.0	1.2
(Don't Know)	0.3	0.3	0.5
(Refusal/Not answered)	0.3	0.3	0.3

VERSIONS A, B AND C: ASK ALL

Q770 [Ident1N] *   N=3228
CARD K6
People differ in how they think of or describe themselves. If you had to pick just one thing from this list to describe yourself - something that is important to you when you think of yourself - what would it be?

IF NOT 'None of these', 'Don't know' or 'Refusal' AT [Ident1N]
Q773 [Ident2N] *   N=3228
CARD K6
And what would the second most important thing be?

IF NOT 'None of these', 'Don't know' or 'Refusal' AT [Ident2N]
Q776 [Ident3N] *   N=3228
CARD K6
And what would the third most important thing be?

	[Ident1N]	[Ident2N]	[Ident3N]
	%	%	%
Working class	13.5	7.0	6.0
Elderly	3.3	2.8	2.4
A woman / A man	15.6	10.6	9.6
Not religious	1.5	2.3	4.0
A wife / A husband / A partner	8.4	18.7	12.8
A Catholic	0.9	1.1	1.5
A country person	2.6	3.3	5.8
A city person	1.4	1.8	3.0
A Protestant	0.4	0.8	1.2
A mother / A father	21.6	16.9	10.6
Middle class	2.8	3.9	4.0
Black	0.8	0.5	0.2
Retired	3.5	2.9	4.1
Religious	1.6	2.2	2.8
A working person	10.8	11.3	11.6
Young	3.5	4.2	3.2
White	1.5	3.0	5.6
Asian	1.4	1.2	0.5
Unemployed	0.3	0.6	0.9
Other (WRITE IN)	1.2	1.1	2.2
(None of these/No further answer)	1.9	1.8	5.5
(Don't Know)	0.5	0.5	0.2
(Refusal/Not answered)	0.0	0.0	0.5

IF NOT 'None of these', 'Don't know' or 'Refusal' AT [Ident1N]
Q779 [IdenWNat]   N=3228
CARD K7
Your (choice was / choices were):
(Respondent's answer to [Ident1N]) (if any))
(Respondent's answer to [Ident2N]) (if any))
(Respondent's answer to [Ident3N]) (if any))
If the list had also included the things on this card, would you have chosen one or more of these instead of the ones you did choose?

	%
Yes	34.0
No	64.0
(Don't know)	0.4
(Refusal)	0.7

Q780 VERSIONS A, B AND C: ASK WHERE 'Yes' AT [IdenWNat]
CARD K7 AGAIN   N=1162
Which ones?
DO NOT PROBE. CODE UP TO THREE
Multicoded (Maximum of 3 codes)

%
41.1 British   [NewIdBr]
38.7 English   [NewIdEn]
8.9   European   [NewIdEu]
1.6   Irish   [NewIdIr]
0.3   Northern Irish   [NewIdNI]
11.3 Scottish   [NewIdSc]
-     Ulster   [NewIdUl]
4.9   Welsh   [NewIdWe]
0.5   (Don't know)
3.0   (Refusal)

VERSIONS A, B AND C: ASK ALL BORN IN BRITAIN (I.E.
'England', 'Scotland' OR 'Wales' AT [WhrBrn]): IF NOT
'British not (English/Scottish/Welsh)', 'Don't know'
OR 'Refusal' AT [NatIdB]

Q802 [CultPol]   N=2842
CARD K8
Some people say that being (English/Scottish/Welsh) is
mainly about (England's countryside/Scotland's
landscape/Wales' countryside) and music,
(English/Scottish/Welsh) sporting teams,
(English/Scottish/Welsh) language and literature and
so on. Others say that being (English/Scottish/Welsh)
is mainly about, for example, the way
(England/Scotland/Wales) is governed, the (Westminster
Parliament/Scottish Parliament/National Assembly for
Wales) and how
(England/Scotland/Wales) runs its affairs.
Whereabouts would you put yourself on a scale between
these two positions?
(INTERVIEWER - IF RESPONDENT ASKS, IT IS THEIR
PERSONAL VIEW ON WHAT BEING ENGLISH/SCOTTISH/WELSH IS
ABOUT WE ARE INTERESTED IN)

%
7.0   Countryside, music, sport etc.
10.7 ...
19.3 ...
32.1 ...
12.4 ...
3.8   ...
2.6   How country is governed
1.5   (Don't know)
0.4   (Refusal)

Q803 [ImpCult] *
CARD K9
The last question asked you to decide whether cultural things, like countryside, music and sport, or political issues like how (England/ Scotland/Wales) runs its affairs, are more important to being (English/ Scottish/Welsh).
How important to you are, first, these cultural things?
(IF NECESSARY - this includes things like a country's countryside and music, sporting teams, language and literature).

N=2842

Q804 [ImpPol] *
CARD K9 AGAIN
And how important to you are these political issues?
(IF NECESSARY - this includes things like how the country is governed, its Assembly or Parliament and how it runs its affairs.

N=2842

	[ImpCult]	[ImpPol]
	%	%
Very important	31.5	20.5
Quite important	48.4	42.4
Not very important	8.4	21.4
Not at all important	0.5	4.5
(Don't Know)	0.9	0.9
(Refusal/Not answered)	0.2	0.2

VERSION A, B AND C: ASK ALL
N=3228

Q805 [AreaEDL]
CARD K10
Sometimes for their amusement, children give their address as Home Street, My area, This town, Localshire, My country, Britain, United Kingdom, Europe, The World. Thinking in this way about where you live now ...
Which one of the options on this card do you feel is most important to you generally in your everyday life?
CODE ONE ONLY.

%
9.6 The street in which you live
31.8 The local area or district
27.0 The city or town in which you live
9.1 The county or region, for instance, Yorkshire, Lothian or Glamorgan
8.5 The country in which you live, for instance, England, Northern Ireland, Scotland, Wales
4.5 Britain
5.2 The United Kingdom
1.2 Europe
0.9 (All equally important)
1.4 (None of these)
0.5 (Don't know)
0.2 (Refusal)

Q806 [AreaPrd]
IF NOT 'All equally important', 'None of these', 'Don't know' OR 'Refusal' at [AreaEDL]
How proud do you feel about living in (your street/your local area/your city or town/your county or region/your country/Britain/the United Kingdom/Europe)? Would you say ...
READ OUT

N=3240

%
33.0 Very proud
48.1 Somewhat proud
11.6 Not very proud,
2.7 Or, not at all proud?
1.2 (Don't know)
0.1 (Refusal)

Q807   **VERSION A, B AND C: ASK ALL**   N=3240
[AreaAbrd]
CARD K10 AGAIN
If you were abroad and someone who knew this country asked you 'where do you come from?', which one of the options on this card would you choose?
CODE ONE ONLY.
%
0.5 The street in which you live
6.9 The local area or district
29.4 The city or town in which you live
18.8 The county or region, for instance, Yorkshire, Lothian or Glamorgan
23.1 The country in which you live, for instance, England, Northern Ireland, Scotland, Wales
10.1 Britain
8.4 The United Kingdom
0.5 Europe
1.9 (None of these)
0.2 (Don't Know)
0.3 (Refusal)

Q808   **VERSION A, B AND C: ASK ALL IN ENGLAND**   N=2779
[BEngScW] *
CARD K11
I'd like you to think of a **white** person who you know was born in Scotland, but now lives permanently in England. This person says they are English.
Would you consider this person to be English?
Please take your answer from the **bottom** half of the card.

IF NOT 'Definitely would' AT [BEngScW]
Q809
[WEngAc] *
CARD K11 AGAIN
What if they had an **English accent**? Would you consider them to be English?

IF NOT 'Definitely would' AT [WEngAc]
Q810
[WEngPar] *
CARD K11 AGAIN
And what if this person with an English accent **also** had **English parents**? Would you consider this person to be English?
(INTERVIEWER - IF RESPONDENT ASKS, BY 'ENGLISH PARENTS' WE MEAN PARENTS WHO WERE **BORN IN ENGLAND**)

Q811   **VERSION A, B AND C: ASK ALL IN ENGLAND**   N=2779
[NWhEngSc]
CARD K12
I'd like you to think of a **non-white** person who you know was born in Scotland, but now lives permanently in England. This person says they are English.
Would you consider this person to be English?
Please take your answer from the **bottom** half of the card.

IF NOT 'Definitely would' AT [NWhEngSc]
Q812
[NWEngAc2] *
CARD K12 AGAIN
What if they had an **English accent**. Would you consider them to be English?

IF NOT 'Definitely would' AT [NWhEngAc2]
Q813
[NWhEngPa]
CARD K12 AGAIN
And what if this non-white person with an English accent **also** had **English parents**? Would you consider this person to be English?
(INTERVIEWER: IF RESPONDENT ASKS, BY 'ENGLISH PARENTS', WE MEAN PARENTS WHO WERE **BORN IN ENGLAND**)

	[BEngScW]	[WEngAc]	[WEngPar]
	%	%	%
Definitely would	15.1	5.0	16.9
Probably would	31.7	40.3	44.1
Probably would not	28.5	21.0	9.7
Definitely would not	21.8	16.2	7.0
(Don't Know)	2.4	2.0	1.9
(Refusal/Not answered)	0.4	0.4	0.4

	[NWhEngSc]	[NWEngAc2]	[NWhEngPa]
	%	%	%
Definitely would	15.0	3.9	11.0
Probably would	31.8	38.3	43.2
Probably would not	29.0	22.5	13.8
Definitely would not	20.6	17.4	9.9
(Don't Know)	3.1	2.4	2.6
(Refusal/Not answered)	0.5	0.5	0.5

Q814 **VERSION A, B AND C: ASK ALL IN SCOTLAND**
[BScEngW] * N=290
CARD K15
I'd like you to think of a **white** person who you know was born in England, but now lives permanently in Scotland. This person says they are Scottish. Would you consider this person to be Scottish? Please take your answer from the **bottom** half of the card.

IF NOT 'Definitely would' AT [BScEngW]
Q815 [WScoAc] * N=290
CARD K15 AGAIN
What if they had a **Scottish accent**? Would you consider them to be Scottish?

IF NOT 'Definitely would' AT [WScoAc]
Q816 [WScoPar] * N=290
CARD K15 AGAIN
And what if this person with a Scottish accent **also** had **Scottish parents**? Would you consider this person to be Scottish?
(INTERVIEWER: IF RESPONDENT ASKS, BY 'SCOTTISH PARENTS', WE MEAN PARENTS WHO WERE **BORN IN SCOTLAND**)

Q817 **VERSION A, B AND C: ASK ALL IN SCOTLAND**
[NWhScEng] * N=290
CARD K16
I'd like you to think of a **non-white** person who you know was born in England, but now lives permanently in Scotland. This person says they are Scottish. Would you consider this person to be Scottish? Please take your answer from the **bottom** half of the card.

IF NOT 'Definitely would' AT [NWhScEng]
Q818 [NWScoAc2] * N=290
CARD K16 AGAIN
What if they had a **Scottish accent**? Would you consider them to be Scottish?

Q819 **IF NOT 'Definitely would' AT [NWScoAc2]**
[NWhScoPa] * N=290
CARD K16 AGAIN
And what if this non-white person with a Scottish accent **also** had **Scottish parents**? Would you consider this person to be Scottish?
(INTERVIEWER: IF RESPONDENT ASKS, BY 'SCOTTISH PARENTS', WE MEAN PARENTS WHO WERE **BORN IN SCOTLAND**)

	[BScEngW]	[WScoAc]	[WScoPar]
	%	%	%
Definitely would	13.6	3.8	20.3
Probably would	30.5	43.9	42.1
Probably would not	29.7	21.9	10.5
Definitely would not	24.5	15.4	8.3
(Don't Know)	1.3	0.8	0.9
(Refusal/Not answered)	0.5	0.5	0.5

	[NWhScEng]	[NWScoAc2]	[NWhScoPa]
	%	%	%
Definitely would	11.7	3.8	16.7
Probably would	30.5	40.5	41.2
Probably would not	28.2	22.8	13.1
Definitely would not	27.3	19.4	11.4
(Don't Know)	1.8	1.4	1.5
(Refusal/Not answered)	0.5	0.5	0.5

Q820 **VERSION A, B AND C: ASK ALL IN WALES**
[BWelEnW] * N=159
CARD K19
I'd like you to think of a **white** person who you know was born in England, but now lives permanently in Wales. This person says they are Welsh. Would you consider this person to be Welsh? Please take your answer from the **bottom** half of the card.

Q821 **IF NOT 'Definitely would' AT [BWelEnW]**
[WWelAc] * N=159
CARD K19 AGAIN
What if they had a **Welsh accent**? Would you consider them to be Welsh?

Q822 IF NOT 'Definitely would' AT [WWelAc]
[WWelPar] *
CARD K19 AGAIN
And what if this person with a Welsh accent **also** had **Welsh parents**? Would you consider this person to be Welsh?
(INTERVIEWER: IF RESPONDENT ASKS, BY 'WELSH PARENTS', WE MEAN PARENTS WHO WERE **BORN IN WALES**).
N=159

Q823 VERSION A, B AND C: ASK ALL IN WALES
[NWhWelEn] *
CARD K20
I'd like you to think of a **non-white** person who you know was born in England, but now lives permanently in Wales. This person says they are Welsh.
Would you consider this person to be Welsh?
Please take your answer from the **bottom** half of the card.
N=159

Q824 IF NOT 'Definitely would' AT [NWhWelEn]
[NWhWelAc] *
CARD K20 AGAIN
What if they had a **Welsh accent**? Would you consider them to be Welsh?
N=159

Q825 IF NOT 'Definitely would' AT [NWhWelAc]
[NWhWelPa] *
CARD K20 AGAIN
And what if this non-white person with a Welsh accent **also** had **Welsh parents**? Would you consider this person to be Welsh?
(INTERVIEWER: IF RESPONDENT ASKS, BY 'WELSH PARENTS', WE MEAN PARENTS WHO WERE **BORN IN WALES**).
N=159

	[BWelEnW]	[WWelAc]	[WWelPar]
	%	%	%
Definitely would	9.7	5.2	29.7
Probably would	29.0	32.6	36.6
Probably would not	29.1	27.0	10.8
Definitely would not	30.9	24.2	6.8
(Don't Know)	1.3	1.3	1.0
(Refusal/Not answered)	-	-	-

	[NWhWelEn]	[NWhWelAc]	[NWhWelPa]
	%	%	%
Definitely would	11.9	6.2	18.7
Probably would	23.1	26.5	33.3
Probably would not	30.1	23.3	13.6
Definitely would not	33.6	30.8	15.3
(Don't Know)	1.3	1.3	1.0
(Refusal/Not answered)	-	-	-

Q826 VERSIONS A, B AND C: ASK ALL
[BrPP] *
CARD K13/K17/K21
How much do you agree or disagree with the following statement?
People from outside the United Kingdom who move permanently to (England/Scotland/Wales) to live and work here are entitled to describe themselves as **British** if they want to.
(INTERVIEWER: IF RESPONDENT ASKS, IT IS THEIR **PERSONAL VIEW, NOT THE LEGAL POSITION THAT WE ARE INTERESTED IN**)
N=3228

Q827 [NatPP] *
CARD K13/K17/K21 AGAIN
And would you agree or disagree that people from outside the UK who move permanently to (England/Scotland/Wales) to live and work here are entitled to describe themselves as (**English/Scottish/Welsh**) if they want to?
N=3228

	[BrPP]	[NatPP]
	%	%
Strongly agree	9.6	6.6
Agree	31.6	26.6
Neither agree nor disagree	15.7	16.2
Disagree	30.6	35.1
Strongly disagree	11.3	14.3
(Don't Know)	0.8	0.9
(Refusal/Not answered)	0.4	0.4

VERSIONS A, B AND C: ASK ALL

Q828 [SRSocCL1]   N=3228

Do you ever think of yourself as belonging to any particular class?

IF YES: Which class is that?

%
19.2 Yes, middle class
31.9 Yes, working class
1.2 Yes, other (WRITE IN)
46.9 No
0.4 (Don't know)
0.3 (Refusal)

IF 'Yes, other', 'No' or 'Don't know' AT [SRSocCL1]

Q831 [SRSocCL2]   N=3228

Most people say they belong either to the middle class or the working class. If you had to make a choice, would you call yourself ... READ OUT ...

%
17.1 ... middle class
27.4 or, working class?
3.7 (Don't know)
0.7 (Refusal)

Q832 [SRSocCL] (NOT ON SCREEN)   N=3228

Derived from SRSocCL1 and SRSocCL2

%
36.3 Middle class
59.3 Working class
4.4 No class given

VERSIONS A, B AND C: ASK ALL IN ENGLAND: IF 'middle class' OR 'working class' AT [SRSocCL1] OR [SRSocCL2]

Q833 [ENatClas]   N=2779

Would you say that you had more in common with (middle/working (same as resp)) class Scottish people or with (working/middle (opposite to resp)) class English people?

%
26.2 (middle/working (same as resp)) class Scottish
33.5 (working/middle (opposite to resp)) class English
24.7 (No preference)
5.7 (Depends on the individual)
5.6 (Don't know)
0.1 (Refusal)

VERSIONS A, B AND C: ASK ALL IN SCOTLAND: IF 'middle class' OR 'working class' AT [SRSocCL1] OR [SRSocCL2]   N=290

Q834 [SNatClas]

Would you say that you had more in common with (middle/working (same class)) class English people or with (working/middle (opposite to resp)) class Scottish people?

%
28.1 (middle/working (same as resp)) class English
16.8 (working/middle (opposite from resp)) class Scottish
3.6 (No preference)
2.7 (Depends on the individual)
- (Don't know)
- (Refusal)

VERSIONS A, B AND C: ASK ALL IN ENGLAND: IF 'middle class' OR 'working class' AT [SRSocCL1] OR [SRSocCL2]   N=159

Q835 [WNatClas]

Would you say that you had more in common with (middle/working (same class)) class English people or with (working/middle (opposite to resp)) class Welsh people?

%
34.0 (middle/working (same as resp)) class English
34.1 (working/middle (opposite to resp)) class Welsh
22.1 (No preference)
5.3 (Depends on the individual)
3.2 (Don't know)
- (Refusal)

Q836
VERSIONS A, B AND C: ASK ALL
[BrnUKPP]   N=3228
CARD K13/K17/K21 AGAIN
How much do you agree or disagree with the following statements?
Anyone who was **born** in the United Kingdom should be entitled to have a British passport, whether they live here or not.
(INTERVIEWER: IF RESPONDENT ASKS, IT IS THEIR **PERSONAL** VIEW, NOT THE LEGAL POSITION THAT WE ARE INTERESTED IN).
%
16.4 Strongly agree
50.8 Agree
9.2 Neither agree nor disagree
18.6 Disagree
3.0 Strongly disagree
1.6 (Don't know)
0.3 (Refusal)

Q837
[PBrnUKPP]   N=3228
CARD K13/K17/K21 AGAIN
(And how much do you agree or disagree that ...)
Anyone whose **parents** were born in the United Kingdom should be entitled to have a British passport, even if they weren't born here themselves.
(INTERVIEWER: AGAIN, IF RESPONDENT ASKS, IT IS THEIR **PERSONAL** VIEW, NOT THE LEGAL POSITION THAT WE ARE INTERESTED IN).
%
7.6 Strongly agree
40.4 Agree
17.2 Neither agree nor disagree
27.3 Disagree
4.6 Strongly disagree
2.6 (Don't know)
0.3 (Refusal)

Q838
VERSIONS A, B AND C: ASK ALL IN ENGLAND
[EngCult1]   N=2779
CARD K14
Here are some things which people sometimes say are important to English culture. Which one do you feel is the most important?
CODE ONE ONLY
%
7.0 English sporting achievements
12.4 The English flag (St George's Cross)
7.2 English music and arts
17.9 English sense of fair play
39.6 English language
10.9 English countryside
4.5 (Don't know/can't choose)
0.5 (Refusal)

Q839
IF NOT 'Don't know/can't choose' OR 'Refusal' AT [EngCult1]
[EngCult2]   N=2779
CARD K14 AGAIN
And the second most important?
%
10.1 English sporting achievements
12.4 The English flag (St George's Cross)
12.6 English music and arts
14.3 English sense of fair play
24.3 English language
19.7 English countryside
6.0 (Don't know/can't choose)
- (Refusal)

Q840
VERSIONS A, B AND C: ASK ALL IN SCOTLAND
[ScoCult1]   N=290
CARD K18
Here are some things which people sometimes say are important to Scottish culture. Which one do you feel is the most important?
CODE ONE ONLY
%
6.7 Scottish sporting achievements
11.5 The Scottish flag (St Andrew's Cross)
18.5 Scottish music and arts
23.4 Scottish sense of equality
11.7 Scottish language, that is, Gaelic or Scots
24.3 Scottish landscape
3.9 (Don't know/can't choose)
- (Refusal)

VERSIONS A, B AND C: ASK ALL

Q844   [BrCult1] *   N=3228
CARD K23
And what about **British** culture? Which one do you feel is the most important?

IF NOT 'Don't know/can't choose' OR 'Refusal' AT [BrCult1]

Q845   [BrCult2] *
CARD K23 AGAIN   N=3228
And the second most important?

	[BrCult1]	[BrCult2]
	%	%
British sporting achievements	7.0	11.2
The British flag (The Union Jack)	10.3	13.0
British Democracy	38.0	17.7
British Monarchy	22.3	16.9
British sense of fair play	12.4	24.6
British national anthem (God Save the Queen)	3.4	6.1
(Don't Know/can't choose)	6.1	4.0
(Refusal/Not answered)	0.4	6.5

VERSIONS A, B AND C: ASK ALL

Q846   [FathBorn]   N=3228
CARD K24
Please tell me where your father was born.

	%
England	66.2
Scotland	10.6
Wales	5.0
Northern Ireland	1.1
Republic of Ireland	2.1
Other	14.1
(Don't know)	0.5
(Refusal)	0.4

IF NOT 'Don't know/can't choose' OR 'Refusal' AT [ScoCult1]

Q841   [ScoCult2]   N=290
CARD K18 AGAIN
And the second most important?

	%
Scottish sporting achievements	9.7
The Scottish flag (St Andrew's Cross)	6.7
Scottish music and arts	18.1
Scottish sense of equality	18.5
Scottish language, that is, Gaelic or Scots	13.1
Scottish landscape	27.1
(Don't know/can't choose)	3.0
(Refusal)	-

VERSIONS A, B AND C: ASK ALL IN WALES

Q842   [WelCult1]   N=159
CARD K22
Here are some things which people sometimes say are important to Welsh culture. Which one do **you** feel is the most important?
CODE ONE ONLY

	%
Welsh sporting achievements	8.7
The Welsh flag (Welsh Dragon)	17.8
Welsh music and arts	8.3
Welsh sense of equality	12.0
Welsh language	37.0
Welsh landscape	10.7
(Don't know/can't choose)	5.4
(Refusal)	-

IF NOT 'Don't know/can't choose' OR 'Refusal' AT [WelCult1]

Q843   [WelCult2]   N=159
CARD K22 AGAIN
And the second most important?

	%
Welsh sporting achievements	21.0
The Welsh flag (Welsh Dragon)	14.0
Welsh music and arts	18.8
Welsh sense of equality	10.0
Welsh language	15.5
Welsh landscape	14.4
(Don't know/can't choose)	0.9
(Refusal)	-

Q847 [MothBorn]
CARD K24 AGAIN
And where was your mother born?   N=3228

%
66.8   England
9.7   Scotland
5.3   Wales
1.2   Northern Ireland
2.3   Republic of Ireland
14.1   Other
0.1   (Don't know)
0.4   (Refusal)

Classification

Prejudice (version A)

Q848   **VERSION A: ASK ALL**   N=1089
        [PMS] *
        CARD L1
        Now I would like to ask you some questions about
        sexual relationships. If a man and woman have sexual
        relations before marriage, what would your general
        opinion be?

Q849   [ExMS] *   N=1089
        CARD L1 AGAIN
        What about a **married person** having sexual relations
        with someone other than his or her partner?

Q850   [HomoSex] *   N=1089
        CARD L1 AGAIN
        What about sexual relations between two adults of the
        same sex?

	[PMS]	[ExMS]	[HomoSex]
	%	%	%
Always wrong	6.0	53.3	23.7
Mostly wrong	6.8	30.6	8.6
Sometimes wrong	11.7	10.4	10.5
Rarely wrong	10.3	0.6	10.5
Not wrong at all	59.8	1.5	38.1
(Depends/varies)	3.0	1.9	4.6
(Don't Know)	1.4	0.7	2.8
(Refusal/Not answered)	1.1	1.0	1.1

Q851 [CvPtRts] N=1089
CARD L2
How much do you agree or disagree with this statement:
Gay and lesbian couples should be able to have much
the same rights as married couples by entering into a
Civil Partnership
%
16.5 Agree strongly
41.4 Agree
13.3 Neither agree nor disagree
13.5 Disagree
13.3 Disagree strongly
1.2 (Don't know)
0.8 (Refusal)

Housing

ASK ALL
Q852 [Tenure1] N=4290
And now some questions about you and your household.
Does your household own or rent this accommodation?
PROBE IF NECESSARY
IF OWNS: Outright or on a mortgage?
IF RENTS: From whom?
%
31.5 Owns outright
39.4 Buying on mortgage
10.4 Rents: local authority
0.2 Rents: New Town Development Corporation
6.0 Rents: Housing Association
1.7 Rents: property company
0.4 Rents: employer
0.9 Rents: other organisation
0.4 Rents: relative
7.0 Rents: other individual
0.2 Rents: Housing Trust
0.5 Rent free, squatting
0.7 Other (WRITE IN)
0.2 (Don't know)
0.5 (Refusal)

Q856 [ResPres] N=4290
Can I just check, would you describe the place where
you live as ... READ OUT ...
%
9.4 ..a big city,
22.9 the suburbs or outskirts of a big city,
47.9 a small city or town,
16.1 a country village,
2.6 or, a farm or home in the country?
0.7 (Other answer (WRITE IN))
0.1 (Don't know)
0.3 (Refusal)

Religion and ethnicity

ASK ALL
Q866 [Religion] (NOT ON SCREEN) N=4290
Do you regard yourself as belonging to any particular
religion?
IF YES: Which?
CODE ONE ONLY - DO NOT PROMPT
%
45.8 No religion
9.6 Christian - no denomination
9.0 Roman Catholic
22.2 Church of England/Anglican
0.6 Baptist
1.8 Methodist
2.4 Presbyterian/Church of Scotland
0.3 Other Christian
1.4 Hindu
0.5 Jewish
3.3 Islam/Muslim
0.2 Sikh
0.2 Buddhist
0.4 Other non-Christian
0.1 Free Presbyterian
0.0 Brethren
0.1 United Reform Church (URC)/Congregational
1.4 Other Protestant
0.1 (Don't know)
0.3 (Refusal)

Q875   [Famrelig] **(NOT ON SCREEN)**   N=4290
In what religion, if any, were you brought up?
PROBE IF NECESSARY: What was your family's religion?
CODE ONE ONLY - DO NOT PROMPT

%
15.1   No religion
12.5   Christian - no denomination
14.4   Roman Catholic
38.9   Church of England/Anglican
1.1   Baptist
3.9   Methodist
4.7   Presbyterian/Church of Scotland
0.3   Other Christian
1.6   Hindu
0.6   Jewish
3.4   Islam/Muslim
0.3   Sikh
0.2   Buddhist
0.2   Other non-Christian
0.1   Free Presbyterian
0.0   Brethren
0.5   United Reform Church (URC)/Congregational
1.6   Other Protestant
0.0   (Don't know)
0.3   (Refusal)

IF RELIGION GIVEN AT [RelRFW] OR AT [RelFFW] AND NO
REFUSAL AT EITHER

Q877   [ChAttend]   N=4290
Apart from such special occasions as weddings,
funerals and baptisms, how often nowadays do you
attend services or meetings connected with your
religion?
PROBE AS NECESSARY.

%
12.1   Once a week or more
1.8   Less often but at least once in two weeks
4.8   Less often but at least once a month
8.1   Less often but at least twice a year
4.8   Less often but at least once a year
5.1   Less often than once a year
47.3   Never or practically never
1.4   Varies too much to say
0.1   (Don't know)
-   (Refusal)

ASK ALL
Q878   [Religiu2]
Would you say that nowadays you are ...READ OUT...   N=4290
%
7.9   ...very religious,
26.8   somewhat religious,
30.3   not very religious,
34.3   or, not at all religious?
0.3   (Don't know)
0.5   (Refusal)

Q879-   [NationU]   N=4290
Q887   CARD L1/L3
Please say which, if any, of the words on this card
describe the way **you** think of **yourself**. Please choose
as many or as few as apply.
PROBE: Any others?
%   Multicoded (Maximum of 9 codes)
66.3   British   [NatBrit]
59.2   English   [NaEng]
16.2   European   [NatEuro]
2.5   Irish   [NatIrish]
0.5   Northern Irish   [NatNI]
10.2   Scottish   [NatScot]
0.1   Ulster   [NatUlst]
5.1   Welsh   [NatWelsh]
3.7   Other answer (WRITE IN)   [NatOth]
1.0   (None of these)   [NatNone]
2.2   **EDIT ONLY:** OTHER - ASIAN MENTIONED   [NatAsia]
1.3   **EDIT ONLY:** OTHER - AFRICAN /CARIBBEAN
    MENTIONED   [NatAfric]
0.0   (Don't know)
0.5   (Not answered)

Q902

IF MORE THAN ONE ANSWER AT [NationU]   N=4290
[BNationU]
CARD L1/L3 AGAIN
And if you had to choose, which one **best** describes the way you think of yourself?

%
20.9   British
23.8   English
1.5   European
0.6   Irish
0.1   Northern Irish
4.0   Scottish
-      Ulster
1.8   Welsh
0.7   Other answer (WRITE IN)
0.2   (None of these)
0.5   OTHER - ASIAN MENTIONED
0.2   OTHER - AFRICAN /CARIBBEAN MENTIONED
0.1   (Don't know)
0.7   (Refusal)

Q906

ASK ALL   N=4290
[RaceOri2]
CARD L2/L4
To which of these groups do you consider you belong?

%
1.4   BLACK: of African origin
1.1   BLACK: of Caribbean origin
0.0   BLACK: of other origin (WRITE IN)
2.3   ASIAN: of Indian origin
1.3   ASIAN: of Pakistani origin
0.4   ASIAN: of Bangladeshi origin
0.5   ASIAN: of Chinese origin
0.9   ASIAN: of other origin (WRITE IN)
88.2   WHITE: of any European origin
1.0   WHITE: of other origin (WRITE IN)
1.2   MIXED ORIGIN (WRITE IN)
1.2   OTHER (WRITE IN)
0.0   (Don't know)
0.6   (Refusal)

Q917

VERSIONS B, C AND D: ASK ALL LIVING AS MARRIED (AT [MarStat5]
[MarrEvr]   N=348
Now a few questions about your household. Firstly, have you ever been married in the past?

%
30.5   Yes
68.3   No
-      (Don't know)
1.3   (Refusal)

Q918

VERSIONS B, C AND D: ASK ALL MARRIED (AT [MarStat5])
[MarrBfre]   N=1742
Now a few questions about you and your household. Firstly, have you ever been married before now?

%
17.0   Yes
82.4   No
0.1   (Don't know)
0.5   (Refusal)

Q919

VERSIONS B, C AND D: ASK ALL NOT LIVING AS MARRIED (AT [MarStat5])
[CohabEvr]   N=2857
(Now a few questions about you and your household/And have) you and a (woman/man) ever lived together as a couple without being married?

%
27.5   Yes
72.0   No
0.0   (Don't know)
0.5   (Refusal)

Q920

VERSIONS B, C AND D: ASK ALL LIVING AS MARRIED (AT [MarStat5]) OR 'Yes' AT [CohabEvr]
[CohbLong]   N=1144
IF HAS COHABITED: About how long did you live as a couple for with this (woman/man)? If you've lived as a couple like this more than once, just tell us about the longest period.
IF IS COHABITING: About how long have you and your partner been living together as a couple?
ALL: NOTE: ROUND UP/DOWN TO NEAREST YEAR
IF LESS THAN SIX MONTHS, ENTER O
Median: 3 years

%
0.1   (Don't know)
1.6   (Refusal)

Q921 [CohbOwn]   N=1144
IF HAS COHABITED: I now want to ask you a few questions about this time when you were living as a couple - again, think of the longest period if you've done this more than once. Firstly, did you or your partner ever own your accommodation while you were living together?
IF YES : Did you own it jointly or not?
IF IS COHABITING: Do you or your partner own your accommodation?
IF YES : Do you own it jointly or not?
ALL: IF BOTH OWNED JOINTLY AND NOT JOINTLY DURING PERIOD, CODE AS OWNED JOINTLY
%
32.8 Own - jointly
20.6 Own - not jointly
45.1 (Did/Do) not own
- (Don't know)
1.5 (Refusal)

Q922 IF 'Own - jointly' OR 'Own - not jointly' AT [CohbOwn]
[OwnAgree]   N=1144
(Did you have then/Do you have) any written agreement with your partner other than a will or mortgage about your share in the ownership of your home?
%
5.9 Yes
47.3 No
0.1 (Don't know)
1.5 (Refusal)

Q923 VERSIONS B, C AND D: ASK ALL LIVING AS MARRIED (AT [MarStat5]) OR 'Yes' AT [CohabEvr]
[ChngWill]   N=1144
(Did either you or your partner make or change/Have either you or your partner made or changed) a will because you were living together as a couple?
%
11.3 Yes
87.1 No
0.1 (Don't know)
1.5 (Refusal)

Q924 VERSIONS B, C AND D: ASK ALL LIVING AS MARRIED (AT [MarStat5])
[CoLegalA]   N=348
Have you or your partner ever sought legal advice about your legal position as a cohabiting couple? This could be advice from books, leaflets, or internet resources or advice from a Citizens Advice Bureau or solicitor
%
19.0 Yes
79.7 No
- (Don't know)
1.3 (Refusal)

Q925 VERSIONS B, C AND D: ASK ALL LIVING AS MARRIED (AT [MarStat5]) OR 'Yes' AT [CohabEvr]
[ChldCohb]   N=1144
IF HAS COHABITED: When you were living together as a couple with this (woman/man), did you and (she/he) have any children together? Again, please think of the partner you lived with for the longest period.
IF IS COHABITING: And, have you and your partner had any children together?
ALL: IF ADOPTED/STEP/FOSTER CHILDREN ONLY, CODE AS NO.
%
27.7 Yes
70.8 No
- (Don't know)
1.5 (Refusal)

Q926 ASK ALL WHO LIVED TOGETHER AS MARRIED IN THE PAST (I.E. 'Yes' AT [CohabEvr])
[GetMarr]   N=799
Did you and this partner ever get married?
%
55.5 Yes
42.5 No
- (Don't know)
2.0 (Refusal)

Education

ASK ALL

Q927 [RPrivEd] *   N=4290
Have you ever attended a fee-paying, **private** primary or secondary school in the United Kingdom?
`PRIVATE' PRIMARY OR SECONDARY SCHOOLS INCLUDE:
* INDEPENDENT SCHOOLS
* SCHOLARSHIPS AND ASSISTED PLACES AT FEE-PAYING SCHOOLS
THEY EXCLUDE:
* DIRECT GRANT SCHOOLS (UNLESS FEE-PAYING)
* VOLUNTARY-AIDED SCHOOLS
* GRANT-MAINTAINED (`OPTED OUT') SCHOOLS
* NURSERY SCHOOLS

IF NO CHILDREN IN THE HOUSEHOLD AGED 5 OR OVER IN THE HOUSEHOLD (AS GIVEN IN THE HOUSEHOLD GRID)
Q928 [OthChld3] *   N=4290
Have you ever been responsible for bringing up any children of school age, including stepchildren?

IF RESPONDENT HAS CHILDREN AGED 5 OR OVER IN THE HOUSEHOLD OR `yes' AT [OthChld3]
Q929 [ChPrivEd] *   N=4290
And (have any of your children / has your child) ever attended a fee-paying, **private** primary or secondary school in the United Kingdom?
`PRIVATE' PRIMARY OR SECONDARY SCHOOLS INCLUDE:
* INDEPENDENT SCHOOLS
* SCHOLARSHIPS AND ASSISTED PLACES AT FEE-PAYING SCHOOLS
THEY EXCLUDE:
* DIRECT GRANT SCHOOLS (UNLESS FEE-PAYING)
* VOLUNTARY-AIDED SCHOOLS
* GRANT-MAINTAINED (`OPTED OUT') SCHOOLS
* NURSERY SCHOOLS

	[RprivEd]	[OthChld3]	[ChPrivEd]
			N=4290
	%	%	%
Yes	11.4	35.9	8.7
No	88.1	34.8	56.0
(Don't Know)	-	0.0	-
(Refusal/Not answered)	0.4	0.4	0.5

ASK ALL
Q934 [Tea] **(NOT ON SCREEN)**
How old were you when you completed your continuous full-time education?
PROBE IF NECESSARY
`STILL AT SCHOOL' - CODE 95
`STILL AT COLLEGE OR UNIVERSITY' - CODE 96
`OTHER ANSWER' - CODE 97 AND WRITE IN

%	
26.3	15 or under
25.6	16
8.0	17
11.0	18
24.4	19 or over
0.4	Still at school
3.7	Still at college or university
0.1	Other answer (WRITE IN)
0.1	(Don't know)
0.5	(Refusal)

Q935 [SchQual]   N=4290
CARD L3/L5
Have you passed any of the examinations on this card?

%	
67.5	Yes
32.0	No
0.1	(Don't know)
0.4	(Refusal)

Q940 **ASK ALL**
[PschQual]
CARD L4/L6
And have you passed any of the exams or got any of the qualifications on **this** card?
%
56.0   Yes
43.5   No
0.1   (Don't know)
0.4   (Refusal)

Q936- **IF 'Yes' AT [SchQual]**
Q939   CARD L3/L5 AGAIN   N=4290
Please tell me which sections of the card they are in?
PROBE : Any other sections?
CODE ALL THAT APPLY
%   Multicoded (Maximum of 4 codes)

28.1   **Section 1:**   [EdQual1]
GCSE Grades D-G/Short course GCSE/Vocational GCSE
CSE Grades 2-5
O-level Grades D-E or 7-9
Scottish (SCE) Ordinary Bands D-E
Scottish Standard Grades 4-7
SCOTVEC/SQA National Certificate modules
Scottish School leaving certificate (no grade)
Scottish Access 1-3
Scottish Intermediate 1

47.3   **Section 2:**   [EdQual2]
GCSE Grades A*-C
CSE Grade 1
O-level Grades A-C or 1-6
School Certif/Matriculation
Scottish SCE Ord. Bands A-C or pass
Scottish Standard Grades 1-3 or Pass
Scottish School Leaving Certificate Lower Grade
Scottish Intermediat 2
SUPE Ordinary
N Ireland Junior Certificate

28.5   **Section 3:**   [EdQual3]
A-level, S-level, A2-level, AS-level
International Baccalaureate
Vocational A-level (AVCE)
Scottish Higher
Scottish SCE/SLC/SUPE at Higher Grade
Scot. Higher School Certif
Certif Sixth Year Studies/ Advanced Higher Grades
N Ireland Senior Certificate

3.5   **Section 4:**   [EdQual4]
Overseas school leaving exam or certificate
-   (Don't know)
0.5   (Refusal)

Q941-Q966   IF 'yes' AT [PSchQual]   N=4290
CARD L4/L6 AGAIN
Which ones? PROBE: Which others?
PROBE FOR CORRECT LEVEL
Multicoded (Maximum of 26 codes)

%		
17.3	Univ/CNAA first degree	[EdQual38]
2.4	Univ/CNAA diploma / Foundation Degree	[EdQual39]
5.9	Postgraduate degree	[EdQual36]
5.3	Teacher training qualification	[EdQual12]
2.8	Nursing qualification	[EdQual13]
0.8	Foundation/advanced (modern) apprenticeship	[EdQual26]
2.5	Other recognised trade apprenticeship	[EdQual27]
2.0	OCR/RSA - (Vocational) Certificate	[EdQual28]
1.3	OCR/RSA - (First) Diploma	[EdQual29]
0.8	OCR/RSA - Advanced Diploma	[EdQual30]
0.5	OCR/RSA - Higher Diploma	[EdQual31]
3.2	Other clerical, commercial qualification	[EdQual32]
5.3	City&Guilds - Level 1/ Part I	[EdQual22]
4.9	City&Guilds - Level 2/ Craft/ Intermediate/ Ordinary/ Part II	[EdQual23]
3.8	City&Guilds - Level 3/Advanced/ Final/ Part III	[EdQual24]
1.6	City&Guilds - Level 4/Full Technological/ Part IV	[EdQual25]
1.1	Edexcel/BTEC First Certificate	[EdQual33]
0.8	Edexcel/BTEC First/General Diploma	[EdQual34]
4.2	Edexcel/BBC/TEC (General/Ordinary) National Certif or Diploma (ONC/OND)	[EdQual10]
4.5	Edexcel/BTEC/BBC/TEC Higher National Certif (HNC)or Diploma (HND)	[EdQual11]
3.3	NVQ/SVQ Lev 1/GNVQ/GSVQ Foundation lev	[EdQual17]
5.4	NVQ/SVQ Lev 2/GNVQ/GSVQ Intermediate lev	[EdQual18]
3.8	NVQ/SVQ Lev 3/GNVQ/GSVQ Advanced lev	[EdQual19]
0.7	NVQ/SVQ Lev 4	[EdQual20]
0.3	NVQ/SVQ Lev 5	[EdQual21]
6.7	Other recogn academic or vocational qual (WRITE IN)	[EdQual37]
0.5	(Don't know)	
0.1	(Not answered)	

Q999   [HEdQual] **(NOT ON SCREEN)**   N=4290
Highest educational qual obtained

%	
18.5	Degree
11.3	Higher educ below degree
16.1	A level or equiv
18.7	O level or equiv
9.6	CSE or equiv
1.5	Foreign or other
23.5	No qualification
0.6	DK/Refusal/NA

ASK ALL
Q1000   [HEdQual2] **(NOT ON SCREEN)**   N=4290
Highest educational qual obtained (postgrad separate)

%	
5.9	Postgraduate degree
12.6	First degree
11.3	Higher educ below degree
16.1	A level or equiv
18.7	O level or equiv
9.6	CSE or equiv
1.5	Foreign or other
23.5	No qualification
0.6	DK/Refusal/NA

Partner's/spouse's job details

ASK ALL WITH SPOUSE/PARTNER WHO IS WORKING OR WAITING TO TAKE UP WORK

Q1003 [Title] **NOT ON DATAFILE**   N=1761
Now I want to ask you about your (husband's/wife's/partner's) (present/future) job.
What (is his/her job / will that job be)?
PROBE IF NECESSARY: What is the name or title of the job?
Open Question (Maximum of 80 characters)

Q1004 [Typewk] **NOT ON DATAFILE**   N=1761
What kind of work (do/will) (he/she) do most of the time?
IF RELEVANT: What materials/machinery (do/will) (he/she) use?
Open Question (Maximum of 80 characters)

Q1005 [Train] **NOT ON DATAFILE**   N=1759
What training or qualifications (are/were) needed for that job?
Open Question (Maximum of 80 characters)

ASK ALL WHO ARE MARRIED OR LIVING WITH A PARTNER (AT [MatSta2b1]

Q1006 [S2Employ]   N=1761
In (husband's/wife's/partner's) (main) job (is/will) (he/she) (be) ... READ OUT ...
%
83.2 ... an employee,
15.6 or self-employed?
0.1 (Don't know)
1.1 (Refusal)

Q1008 [S2Superv]   N=1761
In (his/her) job, (does/will) (he/she) have any formal responsibility for supervising the work of other (employees/people)?
DO NOT INCLUDE PEOPLE WHO ONLY SUPERVISE:
- CHILDREN, E.G. TEACHERS, NANNIES, CHILDMINDERS
- ANIMALS
- SECURITY OR BUILDINGS, E.G. CARETAKERS, SECURITY GUARDS
%
38.9 Yes
59.4 No
0.6 (Don't know)
1.1 (Refusal)

ASK ALL WITH SPOUSE/PARTNER WHO IS WORKING OR WAITING TO TAKE UP WORK AS EMPLOYEE ('employee' OR DON'T KNOW AT [S2Employ])

Q1011 [S2OcSec2]   N=1486
CARD H1
Which of the types of organisation on this card (does he/she work / will he/she be working) for?
%
61.1 PRIVATE SECTOR FIRM OR COMPANY Including, for example, limited companies and PLCs
2.1 NATIONALISED INDUSTRY OR PUBLIC CORPORATION Including, for example, the Post Office and the BBC
32.2 OTHER PUBLIC SECTOR EMPLOYER
Incl eg: - Central govt/ Civil Service/ Govt Agency
- Local authority/ Local Educ Auth (INCL 'OPTED OUT' SCHOOLS) - Universities
- Health Authority / NHS hospitals / NHS Trusts/ GP surgeries
- Police / Armed forces
2.4 CHARITY/ VOLUNTARY SECTOR Including, for example, charitable companies, churches, trade unions
0.4 Other answer (WRITE IN)
0.2 (Don't know)
1.6 (Refusal)

ASK ALL WITH SPOUSE/PARTNER WHO IS WORKING OR WAITING TO TAKE UP WORK

Q1019 [S2EmpWr2]   N=1761
IF EMPLOYEE: Including your (husband/wife/partner), how many people are employed at the place where (he/she) (works/will work) from?
IF SELF-EMPLOYED: (Does/Will) (he/she) have any employees?
IF YES: PROBE FOR CORRECT PRECODE.
(DO NOT USE IF EMPLOYEE/No employees)

```
%
 9.9
18.0   Under 10
11.8   10-24
10.7   25-49
 9.9   50-99
 9.7   100-199
 7.6   200-499
15.5   500+
 5.9   (Don't know)
 1.1   (Refusal)
```

Q1032 [S2PartF1]   N=1762
```
%
76.3   (Is/Was) the job ... READ OUT ...
       ... full-time - that is, 30 or more hours per week,
22.3   or, part-time?
 0.2   (Don't know)
 1.1   (Refusal)
```

Income and benefits

Q1063 [AnyBN3]   N=4290
CARD L5/L7
ASK ALL
Do you (or your husband/wife/partner) receive any of the **state** benefits or tax credits on this card at present?
```
%
57.9   Yes
41.3   No
 0.2   (Don't know)
 0.6   (Refusal)
```

IF 'yes' AT [AnyBN3]

Q1064-
Q1081 CARD L5/L7 AGAIN   N=4290
Which ones? PROBE: Which others?
Multicoded (Maximum of 18 codes)

%		
23.4	State retirement pension (National Insurance)	[BenefOAP]
0.8	War Pension (War Disablement Pension or War Widows Pension)	[BenefWar]
0.9	Bereavement Allowance/ Widow's Pension/ Widowed Parent's Allowance	[BenefWid]
1.6	Jobseeker's Allowance	[BenefUB]
4.5	Income Support (not for pensioners)	[BenefIS2]
3.8	Pension Credit / Minimum Income Guarantee / Income Support for pensioners	[BenefPC]
24.4	Child Benefit / Guardian's Allowance	[BenefCB]
43.1	Child Tax Credit	[BenefCTC]
6.0	Working Tax Credit	[BenefFC]
7.0	Housing Benefit (Rent Rebate/ Rent Allowance)	[BenefHB]
9.1	Council Tax Benefit (or Rebate)	[BenefCT]
4.3	Incapacity Benefit / Sickness Benefit / Invalidity Benefit	[BenefInc]
5.5	Disability Living Allowance (for people under 65)	[BenefDLA]
2.1	Attendance Allowance (for people aged 65+)	[BenefAtA]
0.5	Severe Disablement Allowance	[BenefSev]
1.5	Care Allowance (formerly Invalid Care Allowance)	[BenefICA]
0.5	Industrial Injuries Benefits	[BenefInd]
0.3	Other state benefit (WRITE IN)	[BenefOth]
0.1	(Don't know)	
0.8	(Not answered)	

ASK ALL

Q1103 [MainInc4]   N=4290
CARD L6/L8
Which of these is the **main** source of income for you
(and your husband/ wife/ partner) at present?

63.3	Earnings from employment (own or spouse / partner's)
8.5	Occupational pension(s) - from previous employer(s)
2.3	Private pension(s)
11.6	State retirement or widow's pension(s)
1.5	Jobseeker's Allowance/ Unemployment benefit
3.3	Income Support (not for pensioners)
0.6	Pension Credit/ Minimum Income Guarantee/ Income Support for pensioners
2.2	Invalidity, sickness or disabled pension or benefit(s)
0.7	Other state benefit or tax credit (WRITE IN)
0.8	Interest from savings or investments
1.5	Student grant, bursary or loans
1.9	Dependent on parents/other relatives
0.7	Other main source (WRITE IN)
0.2	(Don't know)
0.7	(Refusal)

Q1108 [HHincome] *
CARD L7/L9   N=4290
Which of the letters on this card represents the total income of your household from all sources before tax? Please just tell me the letter.

ASK ALL IN PAID WORK (AT [REconAct])
Q1109 [REarn] *   N=2443
CARD L7/L9 AGAIN
Which of the letters on this card represents your own gross or total earnings, before deduction of income tax and national insurance?

	[HHincome]	[REarn]
	%	%
Less than 4,000	1.7	2.5
4,000 to 5,999	4.2	4.5
6,000 to 7,999	4.2	4.3
8,000 to 9,999	4.3	4.2
10,000 to 11,999	4.6	5.4
12,000 to 14,999	5.8	8.8
15,000 to 17,999	4.6	8.6
18,000 to 19,999	3.0	5.1
20,000 to 22,999	4.0	7.6
23,000 to 25,999	5.0	7.1
26,000 to 28,999	5.1	5.8
29,000 to 31,999	5.0	4.8
32,000 to 37,999	6.7	6.8
38,000 to 43,999	5.3	2.9
44,000 to 49,999	4.5	3.0
50,000 to 55,999	4.3	2.1
56,000 and over	12.0	6.6
(Don't Know)	6.2	1.8
(Refusal/Not answered)	9.6	8.3

Administration

ASK ALL
Q1111 [SCXplain]   N=4290
The final set of questions are in this booklet. They will probably be easier to answer if you read them. All of them can be answered just by ticking a box.
(IF APPROPRIATE: You don't necessarily have to do them right now. I can call back for the booklet another day)
PLEASE MAKE SURE YOU GIVE THE RESPONDENT THE VERSION (A/B/C/D) (red/grey/yellow/purple) QUESTIONNAIRE
ENTER THE SERIAL NUMBER : (serial number)
...POINT NUMBER : (sample point)
...INTERVIEWER NUMBER : (interviewer number)
ON THE FRONT PAGE OF THE SELF COMPLETION.
THEN TELL US WHETHER IT IS TO BE ...

40.1	... filled in immediately after interview in your presence,
54.9	or, left behind to be filled in later,
4.5	or, if the respondent refused.
0.1	(Don't know)
0.4	(Not answered)

Q1113 [PhoneX]   N=4290
Do you have a telephone?

%	
96.5	Yes
3.0	No
0.0	(Don't know)
0.4	(Refusal)

Q1114 **IF 'Yes' AT [PhoneX]**
[PhoneBc2] N=4290
A few interviews on any survey are checked by my office to make sure that people are satisfied with the way the interview was carried out. In case my office needs to contact you, it would be helpful if we could have your telephone number.
ADD IF NECESSARY: Your 'phone number will **not** be passed to anyone outside the National Centre without your consent.
IF NUMBER GIVEN, WRITE ON THE ARF
IF MORE THAN ONE NUMBER, ASK WHICH WOULD BE MOST CONVENIENT FOR RECONTACT
%
89.6 Number given
6.6 Number refused
0.2 (Don't know)
0.5 (Refusal)

ASK ALL
Q1115 [PhoneX2] N=4290
(And, may we have your mobile phone number as well?
IF NO MOBILE:) Is there another phone number where you could (also) be reached?
IF NUMBER GIVEN, WRITE ON THE ARF
%
35.5 Number given
62.3 Number refused/not given (*/no mobile or second phone*)
1.4 (Don't know)
0.8 (Refusal)

Q1116 [ComeBac3] N=4290
From time to time we do follow-up studies and may wish to contact you again. Would this be all right?
%
80.3 Yes
19.1 No
0.0 (Don't know)
0.6 (Refusal)

Q1117 [ExeCmBk] N=4290
On part of this project we are working with academics from the University of Exeter. They may want to do follow up interviews with some people who have taken part in this study. If **they**, or a survey organisation on their behalf, wanted to contact you, would it be alright for us to pass on your details to them - by that, I mean your name, address, telephone number and some of the answers you have given me today?
%
60.1 Yes
20.2 No
0.1 (Don't know)
0.6 (Refusal)

BRITISH SOCIAL ATTITUDES 2006 SELF-COMPLETION QUESTIONNAIRE VERSION A

1. Please tick <u>one</u> box on each line to show how much you agree-or disagree with each of these statements

N=2813

PLEASE TICK *ONE BOX* ON EACH LINE		Agree strongly	Agree	Neither agree nor disagree	Disagree	Disagree strongly	Can't choose	Not Answered
[DisGov] a. The government is doing enough to help disabled people have equal opportunities in society?	%	1.8	26.6	28.8	32.3	4.7	4.1	1.8
[DisOpp] b. In general, disabled people have the same opportunities in life as non-disabled people?	%	1.4	11.9	13.7	52.2	15.7	2.2	3.0

2. And how much do you agree or disagree with each of these statements?

N=2813

PLEASE TICK ONE BOX ON EACH LINE		Agree strongly	Agree	Neither agree nor disagree	Disagree	Disagree strongly	Can't choose	Not answered
[FalsConf] a. A lot of false benefit claims are a result of confusion rather than dishonesty	%	3.5	20.5	19.8	40.8	10.6	2.9	1.9
[CheatPor] b. The reason that some people on benefit cheat the system is that they don't get enough to live on	%	4.8	25.1	16.5	36.5	12.0	2.8	2.3

[GovBen]

3. Which is it more important for the government to do?

*PLEASE TICK **ONE** BOX ONLY*

N=2813

	%
To get people to claim benefits to which they are entitled	31.5
OR	
To stop people claiming benefits to which they are not entitled	56.2
Can't choose	11.8
Not answered	0.5

[InformBn]

4. How much do you agree or disagree with this statement?

"People who know someone is cheating the benefit system should always report this."

*PLEASE TICK **ONE** BOX ONLY*

N=2813

	%
Strongly agree	29.0
Agree	41.0
Neither agree nor disagree	19.6
Disagree	5.2
Strongly disagree	0.6
Can't choose	4.0
Not answered	0.5

[Ben500]

5a. Consider this situation:

An unemployed person on benefit takes a casual job and is paid in cash. He does not report it to the benefit office and is £500 in pocket. Do you feel this is wrong or not wrong?

*PLEASE TICK **ONE** BOX ONLY*

N=2813

	%
Not wrong	2.5
A bit wrong	17.7
Wrong	49.2
Seriously wrong	26.0
Can't choose	3.1
Not answered	1.4

[Ben500Do]

b. And how likely do you think it is that **you** would do this, if you found yourself in this situation?

*PLEASE TICK **ONE** BOX ONLY*

N=2813

	%
Very likely	5.7
Fairly likely	15.9
Not very likely	31.9
Not at all likely	39.3
Can't choose	5.6
Not answered	1.6

[Pay500]

6a. Now consider this situation:

A person in paid work takes on an extra weekend job and is paid in cash. He does not declare it for tax and so is £500 in pocket. Do you feel this is wrong or not wrong?

*PLEASE TICK **ONE** BOX ONLY*

N=2813

	%
Not wrong	11.4
A bit wrong	31.8
Wrong	40.5
Seriously wrong	10.9
Can't choose	4.2
Not answered	1.2

[Pay500Do]

b. And how likely do you think it is that **you** would do this, if you found yourself in this situation?

*PLEASE TICK **ONE** BOX ONLY*

N=2813

	%
Very likely	8.4
Fairly likely	20.8
Not very likely	34.6
Not at all likely	29.1
Can't choose	5.6
Not answered	1.5

[Disab500]

7. And now consider this situation:
A person has been receiving extra benefit since a back injury stopped him working. Even though he is now well enough to do some types of full-time work he does not tell the benefit office and is £500 in pocket. Do you feel this is wrong or not wrong?

PLEASE TICK ONE BOX ONLY   N=2813

	%
Not wrong	1.4
A bit wrong	9.7
Wrong	55.1
Seriously wrong	30.0
Can't choose	2.6
Not answered	1.2

8. There are different ways of paying for road use. One way is to charge people a set amount of road tax regardless of how much they use the roads. Another way is to charge people according to how much they use them, which roads they use and when they use them. Please tick one box for each of these statements to show how much you agree or disagree.   N=2834

PLEASE TICK ONE BOX ON EACH LINE

	Agree strongly	Agree	Neither agree nor disagree	Disagree	Disagree strongly	Can't choose	Not answered
[BRPyMr] a. People who drive on busy roads should pay **more** to use the roads than people who drive on quiet roads	% 4.0	17.8	19.4	40.2	13.3	3.4	1.9
[BTPyMr] b. People who drive at the **busiest** times should pay more to use the roads than people who drive at other times	% 4.0	18.0	17.9	41.4	13.6	3.1	2.0
[BTNoAlt] c. People who drive at busy times, only do so because they have no other alternative	% 14.5	49.1	16.4	12.4	2.6	3.1	2.0
[CmplChrg] d. It is too complicated to charge drivers different amounts depending on when and where they drive	% 20.5	45.2	14.9	11.7	2.9	3.2	1.6

9. Please tick one box for each of these statements to show how much you agree or disagree.   N=1903

PLEASE TICK ONE BOX ON EACH LINE

	Agree strongly	Agree	Neither agree nor disagree	Disagree	Disagree strongly	I never/ rarely travel by car for less than 2 miles	Can't choose	Not answered
[CarWalk2] a. Many of the journeys of less than two miles that I now make by car I could just as easily walk	% 5.6	35.7	9.7	22.9	5.0	16.0	3.1	2.2
[CarBus2] b. Many of the journeys of less than two miles that I now make by car I could just as easily go by bus	% 4.5	25.1	9.7	31.9	12.9	9.8	3.2	2.9
[CarBike2] c. Many of the journeys of less than two miles that I now make by car I could just as easily cycle, if I had a bike	% 7.3	36.9	9.3	21.4	8.3	10.6	3.7	2.5

[ShrtJrn]

10. How many journeys of less than two miles do you make by car in a typical week?
PLEASE WRITE IN: N=2834

Median   3

%

	%
Or tick here if you <u>never</u> travel by car	12.2
not answered	7.6

11. Here are some things that could be done about traffic in residential streets that are not main roads. Please tick one box for each to show whether you would be in favour or not in favour.   N=971

PLEASE TICK ONE BOX ON EACH LINE

	Strongly in favour	In favour	Neither in favour nor against	Against	Strongly against	Can't choose	Not answered
[ResClose] a. Closing residential streets to through traffic	% 8.7	28.0	24.1	25.2	7.1	3.4	3.5
[Res20MPH] b. Having speed limits of 20 miles per hour in residential streets	% 22.8	53.1	8.2	9.3	2.1	1.8	2.7
[ResBumps] c. Having speed bumps to slow down traffic in residential streets	% 14.4	32.5	9.6	22.7	16.7	1.3	2.8

12. Please tick one box for each of these statements to show how much you agree or disagree.

N=971

PLEASE TICK ONE BOX ON EACH LINE		Agree strongly	Agree	Neither agree nor disagree	Disagree	Disagree strongly	Can't choose	Not answered
[DDNoDrv] a. If someone has drunk any alcohol they should not drive	%	58.0	24.4	6.2	8.4	1.0	0.2	1.8
[DD5YBan] b. Anyone caught drink-driving should be banned for at least five years	%	44.6	29.0	9.9	12.5	1.5	0.9	1.6
[DDNKLmt] c. Most people don't know how much alcohol they can drink before being over the legal drink-drive limit	%	25.1	41.5	6.2	18.8	5.3	1.1	1.9

13. From what you know or have heard, please tick a box for each of the items below to show whether you think the National Health Service in your area is, on the whole, satisfactory or in need of improvement.

N=1902

PLEASE TICK ONE BOX ON EACH LINE		In need of a lot of improvement	In need of some improvement	Satisfactory	Very good	Don't know	Not answered
[HSArea1] a. GPs' appointment systems	%	15.0	33.5	38.5	10.9	0.0	2.1
[HSArea2] b. Amount of time GP gives to each patient	%	10.4	24.4	51.2	11.8	0.0	2.3
[HSArea5] c. Hospital waiting lists for non-emergency operations	%	32.6	43.5	20.0	1.2	0.1	2.5
[HSArea6] d. Waiting time before getting appointments with hospital consultants	%	39.6	39.6	16.3	1.6	0.1	2.8
[HSArea7] e. General condition of hospital building	%	18.2	35.2	37.0	7.2	0.1	2.3
[HSArea13] f. Waiting areas in accident and emergency departments in hospitals	%	19.0	34.7	38.8	4.0	0.1	3.3
[HSArea14] g. Waiting areas for out-patients in hospitals	%	11.9	32.6	48.2	4.0	0.1	3.1
[HSArea15] h. Waiting areas at GPs' surgeries	%	5.1	15.9	62.2	14.0	0.0	2.7
[HSArea16] i. Time spent waiting in out-patient departments	%	19.7	48.2	27.5	1.3	0.2	3.1
[HSArea17] j. Time spent waiting in accident and emergency departments before being seen by a doctor	%	33.5	42.4	18.6	1.5	0.3	3.7
[HSArea18] k. Time spent waiting for an ambulance after a 999 call	%	7.6	28.5	45.1	11.0	0.1	7.6

14. Please tick one box for each statement to show how much you agree or disagree with it.

N=1902

PLEASE TICK ONE BOX ON EACH LINE		Agree strongly	Agree	Neither agree nor disagree	Disagree	Disagree strongly	Can't choose	Not answered
[MentHous] a. I would worry if housing were provided near my home for people with mental health problems leaving hospital	%	12.8	33.4	29.6	15.2	3.9	3.7	1.5
[MentFam] b. Serious mental health problems are just as likely to affect my family as anyone else's	%	16.2	59.2	14.4	5.1	0.9	2.7	1.5

15. In the last twelve months, have you or a close family member or close friend...

N=1902

PLEASE TICK ONE BOX ON EACH LINE		Yes, just me	Yes, not me but close family member or friend	Yes, both me and close family member or friend	No, neither	Not answered
[NHSDoc2] a. ...visited an NHS GP?	%	22.5	17.9	53.6	4.5	1.5
[NHSOutP2] b. ...been an out-patient in an NHS hospital?	%	21.0	29.8	18.0	28.8	2.3
[NHSinP2] c. ...been an in-patient in an NHS hospital?	%	11.0	25.5	5.8	54.1	3.7
[PrivPat2] d. ...had any medical treatment as a private patient?	%	5.7	10.6	2.7	78.4	2.7
[AETreat] e. ...had any medical treatment at an NHS accident and emergency department?	%	11.6	23.1	6.7	56.5	2.1

16. Sometimes public authorities intervene with parents in raising their children. Please show in each of the following cases how far you think public authorities should go in dealing with a <u>10 year old</u> child and his or her parents:

N=1843

PLEASE TICK ONE BOX ON EACH LINE

		Take no action	Give warnings or counselling	Take the child from its parents	Can't choose	Not answered
[ChldCre1] a. The child uses drugs and the parents don't do anything about it	%	0.4	68.9	26.0	2.6	2.2
[ChldCre2] b. The child frequently skips school and the parents don't do anything about it	%	0.4	89.9	5.9	1.7	2.0
[ChldCre3] c. The parents regularly let the child stay out late at night without knowing where the child is	%	2.7	73.2	17.9	4.0	2.2
[ChldCre4] d. The parents fail to provide the child with proper food and clothing	%	0.5	34.6	58.6	3.9	2.5
[ChldCre5] e. The parents regularly beat the child	%	0.4	11.8	83.2	2.1	2.5
[ChldCre6] f. The parents refuse essential medical treatment for the child because of their religious beliefs	%	3.5	40.1	41.0	13.3	2.2
[ChldCre7] g. The parents refuse to send their child to school because they wish to educate the child at home	%	34.5	45.9	4.4	12.9	2.2
[ChldCre8] h. The parents allow the child to watch violent or pornographic films	%	2.5	65.8	24.5	4.8	2.4

Public Authorities should

[TUPower]
17a. Do you think that trade unions in this country have too much power or too little power?
PLEASE TICK ONE BOX ONLY

N=2812

	%
Far too much power	3.8
Too much power	10.1
About the right amount of power	43.8
Too little power	17.6
Far too little power	2.6
Can't choose	20.5
Not answered	1.5

[BusPower]
b. How about business and industry? Do they have too much power or too little power?
PLEASE TICK ONE BOX ONLY

N=2812

	%
Far too much power	8.7
Too much power	29.8
About the right amount of power	36.4
Too little power	5.6
Far too little power	0.5
Can't choose	17.5
Not answered	1.6

[GovPower]
c. And what about the government, does it have too much power or too little power?
PLEASE TICK ONE BOX ONLY

N=2812

	%
Far too much power	15.9
Too much power	33.6
About the right amount of power	31.8
Too little power	7.4
Far too little power	0.7
Can't choose	9.0
Not answered	1.6

18. Please tick one box on each line to show how much you agree or disagree with each of these statements.

N=2812

PLEASE TICK ONE BOX ON EACH LINE	Strongly agree	Agree	Neither agree nor disagree	Disagree	Strongly disagree	Can't choose	Not answered
[DisNtEff] a. In general, people with disabilities cannot be as effective at work as people without disabilities	% 2.8	18.6	25.0	38.6	9.2	3.6	2.1
[DisPrej] b. The main problem faced by disabled people at work is other people's prejudice, not their own lack of ability	% 8.7	54.4	19.5	10.5	1.1	3.6	2.2
[DisNoAll] c. Employers should not make special allowances for people with disabilities	% 1.6	13.1	20.5	50.0	9.5	2.8	2.5
[OldPrej] d. The main problem faced by older people at work is other people's prejudice, not their own lack of ability	% 9.5	52.4	20.6	10.4	1.2	3.3	2.5
[OldAlw] e. Employers should not make special allowances for older people	% 2.2	29.4	28.0	30.7	4.5	3.0	2.2
[RaceProm] f. In general, Black and Asian employees are less likely to get promoted at work than other employees	% 3.4	22.4	30.5	30.6	5.4	5.5	2.1

19. Please tick one box for each line to show what you think about allowing people to smoke in each of the following places

N=971

PLEASE TICK ONE BOX ON EACH LINE	smoking should be…				
	…freely allowed	…restricted to certain areas	…banned altogether	Can't choose	Not answered
[SmkPlane] a. … on airline flights	% 0.6	9.8	87.7	1.3	0.6
[SmkTrain] b. … on trains	% 0.9	19.8	77.6	0.8	0.9
[SmkHospl] c. … in hospitals	% 1.0	9.3	88.4	0.5	0.8
[SmkWork] d. … at people's places of work	% 2.2	35.5	60.7	1.1	0.6
[SmkCinma] e. … in cinemas	% 0.9	10.5	87.0	0.9	0.7
[SmkRstnt] f. … in restaurants	% 1.8	21.9	75.0	0.7	0.7
[SmkPubs] g. … in pubs	% 9.0	38.4	50.2	1.3	1.1

20. Please tick one box for each statement to show how much you agree or disagree with it.

N=2813

PLEASE TICK **ONE** BOX ON EACH LINE

[WelfHelp]		Agree strongly	Agree	Neither agree nor disagree	Disagree	Disagree strongly	Not answered
a. The welfare state encourages people to stop helping each other	%	3.3	25.0	40.7	27.3	1.9	1.9
[MoreWelf] b. The government should spend more money on welfare benefits for the poor, even if it leads to higher taxes	%	4.3	30.8	34.0	26.6	2.6	1.8
[UnempJob] c. Around here, most unemployed people could find a job if they really wanted one	%	13.5	53.4	20.3	10.3	0.7	1.8
[SocHelp] d. Many people who get social security don't really deserve any help	%	4.3	24.5	37.0	29.5	2.6	2.1
[DoleFidl] e. Most people on the dole are fiddling in one way or another	%	6.2	25.8	36.7	26.6	2.6	2.0
[WelfFeel] f. If welfare benefits weren't so generous, people would learn to stand on their own two feet	%	8.8	37.8	26.1	22.8	2.2	2.1
[DamLives] g. Cutting welfare benefits would damage too many people's lives	%	6.5	40.2	34.0	16.2	1.3	1.8
[ProudWlf] h. The creation of the welfare state is one of Britain's proudest achievements	%	13.5	35.6	35.1	11.5	2.0	2.2

21. Please tick one box for each statement below to show how much you agree or disagree with it.

N=3744

PLEASE TICK **ONE** BOX ON EACH LINE

[Redistrib]		Agree strongly	Agree	Neither agree nor disagree	Disagree	Disagree strongly	Not answered
a. Government should redistribute income from the better-off to those who are less well off	%	7.4	26.2	26.9	31.0	7.0	1.4
[BigBusnN] b. Big business benefits owners at the expense of workers	%	9.5	41.1	31.6	14.4	1.7	1.7
[Wealth] c. Ordinary working people do not get their fair share of the nation's wealth	%	9.5	45.5	29.2	13.2	1.1	1.4
[RichLaw] d. There is one law for the rich and one for the poor	%	14.4	40.3	24.4	17.3	2.2	1.4
[Indust4] e. Management will always try to get the better of employees if it gets the chance	%	11.4	40.8	27.6	17.0	1.8	1.5

22. Please tick one box for each statement below to show how much you agree or disagree with it.

N=3744

PLEASE TICK **ONE** BOX ON EACH LINE

[TradVals]		Agree strongly	Agree	Neither agree nor disagree	Disagree	Disagree strongly	Not answered
a. Young people today don't have enough respect for traditional British values.	%	22.0	50.6	18.6	6.7	0.6	1.4
[StifSent] b. People who break the law should be given stiffer sentences.	%	31.0	47.3	15.1	4.9	0.3	1.4
[DeathApp] c. For some crimes, the death penalty is the most appropriate sentence.	%	28.3	28.5	13.8	16.4	11.4	1.5
[Obey] d. Schools should teach children to obey authority.	%	28.9	54.5	10.5	4.1	0.5	1.4
[WrongLaw] e. The law should always be obeyed, even if a particular law is wrong.	%	7.2	31.5	32.7	24.2	2.5	1.9
[Censor] f. Censorship of films and magazines is necessary to uphold moral standards.	%	16.8	48.7	18.3	11.7	2.6	1.9

[QTimeA]
23a. To help us plan better in future, please tell us about how long it took you to complete this questionnaire.

N=971

PLEASE TICK ONE BOX ONLY

	%
Less than 15 minutes	34.3
Between 15 and 20 minutes	39.0
Between 21 and 30 minutes	17.2
Between 31 and 45 minutes	4.7
Between 46 and 60 minutes	2.4
Over one hour	1.5
Not answered	0.9

[QDate]
b. And on what date did you fill in the questionnaire?

N=3744

PLEASE WRITE IN: DATE   MONTH   2006

24. And lastly just a few details about yourself.

[RSexChck]
a. Are you ....

N=3744

	%
Male	47.3
Female	51.6
Not answered	1.0

[RAgeChck]
b. What was your age last birthday?

N=3744

PLEASE WRITE IN: YEARS

Median	46 years
	%
Not answered	1.8

BRITISH SOCIAL ATTITUDES 2006 SELF-COMPLETION QUESTIONNAIRE VERSION B

[SCObeyLw]   N=932

1. In general, would you say that people should obey the law without exception, or are there exceptional occasions on which people should follow their consciences even if it means breaking the law?

PLEASE TICK ONE BOX ONLY

	%
Obey the law without exception	39.3
OR	
Follow conscience on occasions	54.0
Can't choose	5.8
Not Answered	1.0

N=932

2. There are many ways people or organisations can protest against a government action they strongly oppose. Please show which you think should be allowed and which should not be allowed by ticking a box on each line.

PLEASE TICK ONE BOX ON EACH LINE

	Should it be allowed?					
	Definitely	Probably	Probably not	Definitely not	Can't choose	Not Answered
[Protest1] a. Organising public meetings to protest against the government	% 52.4	33.1	6.4	3.8	2.8	1.5
[Protest3] b. Organising protest marches and demonstrations	% 36.9	39.6	11.5	7.1	2.4	2.5
[Protest6] c. Organising a nationwide strike of all workers against the government	% 11.7	21.7	29.9	29.9	3.8	3.0

N=932

3. There are some people whose views are considered extreme by the majority. Consider people who want to overthrow the government by revolution. Do you think such people should be allowed to ...

PLEASE TICK ONE BOX ON EACH LINE

	Definitely	Probably	Probably not	Definitely not	Can't choose	Not Answered
[RevMeet] a. ... hold public meetings to express their views?	% 17.4	28.2	22.3	28.0	3.4	0.8
[RevPub] b. ... publish books expressing their views?	% 16.0	34.3	25.2	16.7	4.4	3.4

[Justice]

4. All systems of justice make mistakes, but which do you think is worse ...

PLEASE TICK ONE BOX ONLY   N=932

	%
... to convict an innocent person,	51.3
OR to let a guilty person go free?	29.4
Can't choose	18.4
Not answered	0.9

5. Here are some things the government might do for the economy. Please show which actions you are in favour of and which you are against.

PLEASE TICK ONE BOX ON EACH LINE   N=932

	Strongly in favour of	In favour of	Neither in favour of nor against	Against	Strongly against	Can't choose	Not answered
[GovEcon3] a. - Cuts in government spending	% 10.0	24.8	28.5	22.4	7.0	4.2	3.0
[GovEcon4] b. - Government financing of projects to create new jobs	% 21.6	50.0	17.2	5.0	1.0	1.9	3.2
[GovEcon5] c. - Less government regulation of business	% 10.8	29.3	38.3	7.9	2.5	7.7	3.5
[GovEcon6] d. - Support for industry to develop new products and technology	% 25.7	55.3	11.7	1.3	0.3	1.8	3.9
[GovEcon7] e. - Support for declining industries to protect jobs	% 12.8	43.8	21.6	13.7	2.5	2.3	3.4
[GovEcon8] f. - Reducing the working week to create more jobs	% 6.8	21.2	32.5	24.9	7.5	3.6	3.4

6. Listed below are various areas of government spending. Please show whether you would like to see more or less government spending in each area. Remember that if you say "much more", it might require a tax increase to pay for it.

PLEASE TICK ONE BOX ON EACH LINE   N=932

	Spend much more	Spend more	Spend the same as now	Spend less	Spend much less	Can't choose	Not answered
[GvSpend1] a. The environment	% 12.3	40.5	37.8	2.5	0.5	2.2	4.1
[GvSpend2] b. Health	% 26.3	52.1	16.6	1.3	0.2	0.8	2.8
[GvSpend3] c. The police and law enforcement	% 15.1	42.9	34.4	2.2	0.6	1.5	3.3
[GvSpend4] d. Education	% 20.6	48.7	25.6	0.6	0.2	1.0	3.4
[GvSpend5] e. The military and defence	% 8.8	19.7	42.9	16.5	6.5	2.7	3.0
[GvSpend6] f. Old age pensions	% 23.1	46.4	25.3	1.5	0.1	1.2	2.5
[GvSpend7] g. Unemployment benefits	% 3.1	9.8	41.8	29.3	9.2	3.3	3.5
[GvSpend8] h. Culture and the arts	% 1.8	8.7	39.8	28.0	15.5	3.2	3.2

7. On the whole, do you think it should or should not be the government's responsibility to ...

PLEASE TICK ONE BOX ON EACH LINE   N=932

	Definitely should be	Probably should be	Probably should not be	Definitely should not be	Can't choose	Not answered
[GovResp1] a. ... provide a job for everyone who wants one	% 15.8	35.9	27.4	13.4	4.5	3.0
[GovResp2] b. ... keep prices under control	% 30.7	49.3	11.2	3.8	2.3	2.7
[GovResp3] c. ... provide health care for the sick	% 68.4	27.0	0.7	0.4	1.2	2.3
[GovResp4] d. ... provide a decent standard of living for the old	% 58.3	35.6	2.5	0.2	1.5	1.9
[GovResp5] e. ... provide industry with the help it needs to grow	% 27.3	54.3	9.9	2.2	3.8	2.4
[GovResp6] f. ... provide a decent standard of living for the unemployed	% 10.4	39.5	30.4	10.7	6.7	2.2
[GovResp7] g. ... reduce income differences between the rich and the poor	% 25.4	37.7	21.1	9.4	4.3	2.2
[GovResp8] h. ... give financial help to university students from low-income families	% 32.4	52.1	8.6	2.0	2.7	2.2
[GovResp9] i. ... provide decent housing for those who can't afford it	% 23.9	56.7	10.3	3.2	3.8	2.1
[GovResp0] j. ... impose strict laws to make industry do less damage to the environment	% 45.2	41.0	6.9	1.2	3.3	2.3

8. How successful do you think the government in Britain is nowadays in each of the following areas? N=932

PLEASE TICK **ONE** BOX ON EACH LINE

	Very successful	Quite successful	Neither successful nor unsuccessful	Quite un-successful	Very un-successful	Can't choose	Not answered
[GvOKHlth] a. Providing health care for the sick? %	3.8	46.0	23.7	18.6	4.8	0.8	2.2
[GvOKOld] b. Providing a decent standard of living for the old? %	1.8	26.3	35.3	24.4	8.0	2.1	2.0
[GvOKSec] c. Dealing with threats to Britain's security? %	4.8	35.7	28.0	17.7	8.6	3.0	2.3
[GvOKCrm] d. Controlling crime? %	1.6	18.4	29.8	32.2	14.4	1.1	2.5
[GvOKUnmp] e. Fighting unemployment? %	2.1	26.0	37.7	22.9	5.5	3.3	2.5
[GvOKEnv] f. Protecting the environment? %	2.0	16.1	39.4	26.1	9.5	4.6	2.3

9. Suppose the government suspected that a terrorist act was about to happen. Do you think the authorities should have the right to... N=932

PLEASE TICK **ONE** BOX ON EACH LINE

	Definitely should have right	Probably should have right	Probably should not have right	Definitely should not have right	Can't choose	Not answered
[TerGDetn] a. ...detain people for as long as they want without putting them on trial? %	34.2	29.6	18.3	12.5	3.5	1.8
[TerGTap] b. ...tap people's telephone conversations? %	32.6	40.6	13.6	6.8	4.3	2.1
[TerGSnS] c. ...stop and search people in the street at random? %	35.4	37.4	13.9	7.6	3.6	2.1

Now some questions about politics.

[Polintrst]
10. How interested would you say you personally are in politics? N=932

PLEASE TICK **ONE** BOX ONLY

	%
Very interested	9.9
Fairly interested	28.1
Somewhat interested	27.4
Not very interested	22.5
Not at all interested	9.8
Can't choose	0.7
Not answered	1.6

11. Please tick one box on each line to show how much you agree or disagree with each of the following statements. N=932

PLEASE TICK **ONE** BOX ON EACH LINE

	Agree strongly	Agree	Neither agree nor disagree	Disagree	Disagree strongly	Can't choose	Not answered
[GovNoSa2] a. People like me don't have any say about what the government does %	13.4	41.6	21.1	18.6	1.7	2.0	1.6
[InfluPol] b. The average citizen has considerable influence on politics %	1.9	13.0	22.2	47.1	11.3	1.8	2.6
[UstndPol] c. I feel that I have a pretty good understanding of the important political issues facing our country %	5.9	43.2	30.8	12.6	2.7	2.4	2.4
[InfPoli2] d. I think most people are better informed about politics and government than I am %	2.6	17.0	37.9	33.1	5.0	2.2	2.3
[MPPromis] e. People we elect as MPs try to keep the promises they have made during the election %	2.6	19.1	30.3	33.9	9.1	2.7	2.3
[CSTrust2] f. Most civil servants can be trusted to do what is best for the country %	1.4	20.3	37.1	24.9	9.8	4.5	2.0

[TaxHiSC]
12a. Generally, how would you describe taxes in Britain today?
First, for those with high incomes, are taxes ...

PLEASE TICK ONE BOX ONLY

N=932

	%
... much too high,	8.9
too high,	17.2
about right,	37.5
too low,	23.7
or, are they much too low?	3.6
Can't choose	6.9
Not answered	2.2

[TaxMidSC]
b. Next, for those with middle incomes, are taxes ...

PLEASE TICK ONE BOX ONLY

N=932

	%
... much too high,	9.0
too high,	33.6
about right,	45.8
too low,	3.0
or, are they much too low?	0.1
Can't choose	6.3
Not answered	2.1

[TaxLowSC]
c. Lastly, for those with low incomes, are taxes ...

PLEASE TICK ONE BOX ONLY

N=932

	%
... much too high,	21.9
too high,	40.3
about right,	27.9
too low,	1.7
or, are they much too low?	0.3
Can't choose	6.2
Not answered	1.8

[TrustFew]
13a. To what extent do you agree or disagree with the following statements.
"There are only a few people I can trust completely"

PLEASE TICK ONE BOX ONLY

N=932

	%
Agree strongly	24.2
Agree	48.9
Neither agree nor disagree	10.8
Disagree	11.2
Disagree strongly	2.5
Can't choose	1.7
Not answered	0.8

[TrustNon]
b. "If you are not careful, other people will take advantage of you"

PLEASE TICK ONE BOX ONLY

N=932

	%
Agree strongly	22.2
Agree	52.8
Neither agree nor disagree	15.0
Disagree	7.4
Disagree strongly	1.0
Can't choose	0.9
Not answered	0.8

[CrptAskR]
14a. Some people because of their job, position in the community or contacts, are asked by others to help influence important decisions in their favour. What about you? How often are you asked to help influence important decisions in other people's favour?

PLEASE TICK ONE BOX ONLY

N=932

	%
Never	39.1
Seldom	29.7
Occasionally	21.4
Often	4.0
Can't choose	5.2
Not answered	0.6

[CrptRAsk]
b.   And are there people you could ask to help influence important decisions in your favour?
PLEASE TICK ONE BOX ONLY

N=932

	%
No, nobody	41.4
Yes, a few people	36.6
Yes, some people	12.2
Yes, a lot of people	1.5
Can't choose	7.6
Not answered	0.7

[CrptFair]
15.   In your opinion, how often do public officials deal fairly with people like you?
PLEASE TICK ONE BOX ONLY

N=932

	%
Almost always	8.5
Often	27.2
Occasionally	29.8
Seldom	14.8
Almost never	7.7
Can't choose	11.3
Not answered	0.7

[CrptKnow]
16.   Do you think that the treatment people get from public officials in Britain depends on who they know?

PLEASE TICK ONE BOX ONLY

N=932

	%
Definitely does	16.1
Probably does	54.5
Probably does not	17.8
Definitely does not	2.3
Can't choose	8.8
Not answered	0.6

[CrptPol]
17.   In your opinion, about how many politicians in Britain are involved in corruption?
PLEASE TICK ONE BOX ONLY

N=932

	%
Almost none	4.6
A few	28.5
Some	29.7
Quite a lot	20.7
Almost all	5.4
Can't choose	10.5
Not answered	0.6

[CrptCiv]
18.   And in your opinion, about how many public officials in Britain are involved in corruption?
PLEASE TICK ONE BOX ONLY

N=932

	%
Almost none	3.8
A few	28.8
Some	33.9
Quite a lot	18.9
Almost all	2.5
Can't choose	11.3
Not answered	0.7

[CrptBrib]
19. In the last five years, how often have you or a member of your immediate family come across a public official who hinted they wanted, or asked for, a bribe or favour in return for a service?

PLEASE TICK ONE BOX ONLY

N=932

	%
Never	83.9
Seldom	5.8
Occasionally	2.5
Quite often	0.7
Very often	-
Can't choose	3.7
Not answered	3.3

20. Please tick one box for each statement below to show how much you agree or disagree with it.

PLEASE TICK ONE BOX ON EACH LINE

N=932

	Agree strongly	Agree	Neither agree nor disagree	Disagree	Disagree strongly	Can't choose	Not answered
[PolGift] a. Any individual who gives money to a political party should be allowed to keep their gift private if they wish. %	7.8	27.1	16.4	27.2	13.4	4.7	3.4
[PolLimit] b. There should be a limit on how much money a single individual can give to a political party. %	12.6	39.2	21.6	14.5	3.4	5.2	3.6
[PolFund] c. Political parties need to be funded by the government to do their job properly. %	6.8	29.0	30.8	16.1	6.9	6.9	3.5

21. Please tick one box for each statement below to show how much you agree or disagree with it.

PLEASE TICK ONE BOX ON EACH LINE

N=932

	Agree strongly	Agree	Neither agree nor disagree	Disagree	Disagree strongly	Not answered
[PCNoSolc] a. The police should be allowed to question suspects for up to a week without letting them see a solicitor %	6.3	13.5	13.9	44.8	17.8	3.7
[Refugees] b. Refugees who are in danger because of their political beliefs should always be welcome in Britain %	3.3	16.4	28.8	34.6	13.5	3.5
[PCCompln] c. Serious complaints against the police should be investigated by an independent body, not by the police themselves %	36.7	50.2	6.6	2.3	0.8	3.4
[IDCards] d. Every adult in Britain should have to carry an identity card %	19.1	32.2	22.2	13.3	9.8	3.6

[ContNo]
22. On average, about how many people do you have contact with in a typical week day, including people you live with. We are interested in contact on a one-to-one basis, including everyone with whom you chat, talk, or discuss matters. This can be face-to-face, by telephone, by mail, or on the internet. Please include only people you know.

Please select one from the following categories that best matches your estimate.

PLEASE TICK ONE BOX ONLY

	%
0-4 persons	12.8
5-9	19.8
10-19	25.6
20-49	22.7
50 or more	13.8
Can't choose	2.1
Not answered	3.3

Note: Questions 23 to 32 are the same as questions 1 to 10 on version A

33. Now some questions about air travel. Please tick one box for each statement to show how much you agree or disagree.

N=932

PLEASE TICK ONE BOX ON EACH LINE	Agree strongly	Agree	Neither agree nor disagree	Disagree	Disagree strongly	Can't choose	Not answered
[PlnAllow] a. People should be able to travel by plane as much as they like	% 14.4	54.9	17.0	7.6	1.5	3.5	1.1
[PlnTerm] b. People should be able to travel by plane as much as they like, even if new terminals or runways are needed to meet the demand	% 8.5	35.6	26.7	19.9	3.9	4.1	1.3
[PlnEnvt] c. People should be able to travel by plane as much as they like, even if this harms the environment	% 3.4	15.6	29.8	36.8	9.4	3.9	1.1
[PlnUpPri] d. The price of a plane ticket should reflect the environmental damage that flying causes, even if this makes air travel much more expensive	% 11.8	36.4	21.5	20.6	3.4	5.2	1.1

34. Please tick one box for each of these statements to show how much you agree or disagree.

N=932

PLEASE TICK ONE BOX ON EACH LINE	Agree strongly	Agree	Neither agree nor disagree	Disagree	Disagree strongly	Can't choose	Not answered
[CarTaxHi] a. For the sake of the environment, car users should pay higher taxes	% 2.8	18.7	19.5	44.2	10.6	3.0	1.3
[Motorway] b. The government should build more motorways to reduce traffic congestion	% 5.2	28.1	26.3	31.0	4.9	3.1	1.4
[BuildTra] c. Building more roads just encourages more traffic	% 4.9	40.8	22.9	24.7	2.8	2.6	1.4
[CarAllow] d. People should be allowed to use their cars as much as they like, even if it causes damage to the environment	% 3.5	19.1	32.8	31.9	6.8	4.2	1.8
[CarReduc] e. For the sake of the environment everyone should reduce how much they use their cars	% 13.1	52.8	19.9	8.5	1.6	2.9	1.2
[CarNoDif] f. Anyone who thinks that reducing their own car use will help the environment is wrong – one person doesn't make any difference	% 3.2	12.9	21.7	46.0	12.5	2.3	1.4
[CarEnvDc] g. People who drive cars that are better for the environment should pay less to use the roads than people whose cars are more harmful to the environment	% 15.7	50.5	17.5	9.4	2.1	3.6	1.3

35. Here are some things that some people have said about marriage. Please tick one box on each line to show how much you agree or disagree with each of these statements.

N=2774

PLEASE TICK ONE BOX ON EACH LINE	Agree strongly	Agree	Neither agree nor disagree	Disagree	Disagree strongly	Can't choose	Not answered
[MarVie14] a. Living with a partner shows just as much personal commitment as getting married to them	% 12.0	36.5	13.2	28.6	6.2	1.9	1.6
[MarVie15] b. These days a wedding is more about a celebration than about life-long commitment	% 9.9	42.8	16.3	22.9	5.1	1.5	1.5
[MarVie16] c. These days, there is little difference socially between being married and living together as a couple	% 10.5	55.1	12.4	15.1	3.8	1.5	1.6
[MarVie17] d. Many people stay in unhappy relationships because of money or children	% 12.4	62.6	13.9	6.8	0.8	2.1	1.5
[MarVie18] e. With so many marriages ending in divorce these days, couples who get married take a big risk	% 5.6	28.1	26.8	31.7	4.4	2.0	1.5

36. Do you agree or disagree ...?

N=2774

PLEASE TICK ONE BOX ON EACH LINE	Agree strongly	Agree	Neither agree nor disagree	Disagree	Disagree strongly	Can't choose	Not answered
[MarVie10] a. One parent can bring up a child as well as two parents together	% 8.0	34.0	14.2	33.1	7.9	1.3	1.6
[ChSingW] b. There's nothing wrong with a single woman who lives alone having a child if she wants one	% 6.9	37.0	18.7	25.0	9.2	1.4	1.8
[LATStRel] c. A couple do not need to live together to have a strong relationship	% 7.5	45.9	17.7	21.0	4.1	2.1	1.7
[LvAlone] d. People who choose to live alone just aren't good at relationships with others	% 1.2	8.4	25.7	46.3	13.9	2.9	1.7
[RelBtPar] e. Relatives will always be there for you in a way that partners might not be	% 7.2	33.3	24.9	27.3	3.4	2.0	1.8
[NoNeedP] f. You do not need to have a partner to be happy and fulfilled in life	% 11.9	57.0	16.4	10.1	1.4	1.5	1.7
[PChBICp] g. The relationship between a parent and their child is stronger than the relationship between any couple	% 12.1	29.8	31.7	18.3	1.6	4.6	1.9

37. Please tick one box on each line to show how much you agree or disagree with the following statements about divorce.

N=2774

PLEASE TICK ONE BOX ON EACH LINE	Agree strongly	Agree	Neither agree nor disagree	Disagree	Disagree strongly	Can't choose	Not answered
[Div16hrd] a. It should be harder than it is now for couples with children under 16 to get divorced	% 4.7	25.7	26.0	33.4	5.0	3.5	1.8
[DivChld] b. It is not divorce that harms children, but conflict between their parents	% 20.7	57.3	11.6	6.1	0.6	2.1	1.6
[DivPos] c. Divorce can be a positive first step towards a new life	% 7.5	55.3	25.6	6.0	1.1	2.9	1.6
[DivVint] d. If either partner is at all violent then divorce is the only option	% 25.8	38.0	17.9	13.3	0.8	2.5	1.6

38. Please tick one box on each line to show how much you agree or disagree with each of these statements.

N=2774

PLEASE TICK ONE BOX ON EACH LINE	Agree strongly	Agree	Neither agree nor disagree	Disagree	Disagree strongly	Can't choose	Not answered
[FrFam1] NEW a. Friends are for fun, not for discussing personal problems with	% 1.7	10.1	14.3	53.2	17.8	1.2	1.7
[FrFam2] b. When things really go wrong in life your family is more likely to be there for you than your friends	% 7.6	34.2	25.6	25.4	3.7	1.8	1.7
[FrFam3] c. People should make time for relatives like aunts, uncles and cousins even if they don't have anything in common	% 5.6	49.3	26.4	14.0	1.4	1.6	1.7
[FrFam4] d. People should make time for close family members even if they don't have much in common	% 9.2	58.6	20.1	8.0	0.9	1.3	1.9

39. Please tick one box on each line to show how much you agree or disagree with each of these statements.

PLEASE TICK ONE BOX ON EACH LINE

N=2774

	Agree strongly	Agree	Neither agree nor disagree	Disagree	Disagree strongly	Can't choose	Not answered
[LesCPar] a. A lesbian couple are just as capable of being good parents as a man and a woman	% 6.3	29.8	20.5	24.0	14.0	3.7	1.7
[GayCPar] b. A gay male couple are just as capable of being good parents as a man and a woman	% 5.7	25.7	20.3	25.7	16.8	4.0	1.8
[GLCommit] c. A same sex couple can be just as committed to each other as a man and a woman	% 12.9	49.9	19.3	6.6	5.5	4.0	1.8

[TeaGML2]
40. How suitable are gay men and lesbians for the job of primary school teacher?

PLEASE TICK ONE BOX ONLY

N=2774

	%
Very suitable	24.5
Fairly suitable	16.8
Neither suitable nor unsuitable	28.1
Fairly unsuitable	8.4
Very unsuitable	11.3
Can't choose	8.3
Not answered	2.5

41. Do you personally know anyone who is gay or lesbian?

PLEASE TICK AS MANY BOXES AS APPLY TO YOU

N=2774

	%	
No, I don't know anyone who is gay or lesbian	23.2	[KGMLNot]
Yes – a member of my family	9.4	[KGMLRel]
Yes – a friend I know fairly well	28.6	[KGMLPal]
Yes – someone I do not know fairly well	23.6	[KGMLAqqu]
Yes – someone at my work	17.9	[KGMLWork]
Yes – someone else	12.6	[KGMLElse]
Not sure	6.4	[KGMLNSur]
Not answered	2.1	

[CommLaw]
42. As far as you know, do unmarried couples who live together for some time have a 'common law marriage' which gives them the same legal rights as married couples?
PLEASE TICK ONE BOX ONLY

N=2774

	%
Definitely do	13.8
Probably do	36.9
Probably do not	22.4
Definitely do not	14.7
Can't choose	10.2
Not answered	2.0

43. And please tick one box to show how much you agree or disagree with each of these statements.

PLEASE TICK ONE BOX ON EACH LINE

N=2774

	Agree strongly	Agree	Neither agree nor disagree	Disagree	Disagree strongly	Can't choose	Not answered
[Marry1] a. Married couples make better parents than unmarried ones	% 9.3	18.6	28.0	32.4	7.7	2.0	2.0
[Marry3] b. Even though it might not work out for some people, marriage is still the best kind of relationship	% 13.3	41.0	20.7	17.5	3.8	1.5	2.2
[Marry5] c. Marriage gives couples more financial security than living together	% 13.4	47.8	19.1	13.1	2.2	2.1	2.2
[Marry6] d. There is no point getting married it's only a piece of paper	% 2.3	6.2	18.5	44.2	24.9	1.6	2.2

Note: **Question 44 is the same as questions 16 on version A**
Note: **Questions 45 to 47 are the same as questions 20 to 22 on version A**

[QTimeB]
48. To help us plan better in future, please tell us about how long it took you to complete this questionnaire.
PLEASE TICK ONE BOX ONLY

N=932

	%
Less than 15 minutes	10.3
Between 15 and 20 minutes	35.7
Between 21 and 30 minutes	26.7
Between 31 and 45 minutes	15.7
Between 46 and 60 minutes	5.1
Over one hour	5.2
Not answered	1.4

BRITISH SOCIAL ATTITUDES 2006 SELF-COMPLETION QUESTIONNAIRE VERSION C

Note: Questions 1 to 7 are the same as questions 1 to 7 on version A
Questions 8 to 17 are the same as questions 35 to 44 on version B
Questions 18 to 19 are the same as questions 17 to 18 on version A

20. We now have some questions about women.
Do you agree or disagree ... ?

N=1842

PLEASE TICK ONE BOX ON EACH LINE	Agree strongly	Agree	Neither agree nor disagree	Disagree	Disagree strongly	Can't choose	Not answered
[WWRelChd] a. A working mother can establish just as warm and secure a relationship with her children as a mother who does not work	% 11.6	52.3	11.8	17.4	2.1	2.1	2.5
[WWChdSuf] b. A pre-school child is likely to suffer if his or her mother works	% 3.6	31.6	20.2	36.0	4.2	1.8	2.6
[WWFamSuf] c. All in all, family life suffers when the woman has a full-time job	% 4.2	31.0	19.7	35.1	5.8	1.4	2.8
[WantHome] d. A job is all right, but what most women really want is a home and children	% 4.2	25.6	26.1	30.1	8.2	3.2	2.7
[HWifeFlt] e. Being a housewife is just as fulfilling as working for pay	% 7.9	35.9	27.1	19.1	4.0	3.5	2.6

21. And do you agree or disagree ... ?

N=1842

PLEASE TICK ONE BOX ON EACH LINE	Agree strongly	Agree	Neither agree nor disagree	Disagree	Disagree strongly	Can't choose	Not answered
[BothEar2] a. Both the man and the woman should contribute to the household income	% 17.7	49.0	20.7	8.7	1.0	1.7	1.2
[SexRole2] b. A man's job is to earn money; a woman's job is to look after the home and family	% 3.3	12.3	21.6	42.2	16.9	1.7	1.9

22. Do you think women should work outside the home full-time, part-time or not at all under these circumstances?

N=1842

PLEASE TICK ONE BOX ON EACH LINE	Work full-time	Work part-time	Stay at home	Can't choose	Not answered
[WWChd2] a. When there is a child under school age	% 3.6	36.9	39.5	18.6	1.3
[WWChd3] b. After the youngest child starts school	% 22.7	55.1	2.6	17.9	1.7

23. Do you agree or disagree ...?

N=1842

PLEASE TICK ONE BOX ON EACH LINE

	Agree strongly	Agree	Neither agree nor disagree	Disagree	Disagree strongly	Can't choose	Not answered
[ChdView2] a. Watching children grow up is life's greatest joy	% 31.5	46.2	14.3	2.6	0.5	3.9	1.1
[ChdView6] b. People who have never had children lead empty lives	% 3.0	8.5	22.2	45.8	15.6	3.6	1.2

[MardNow2]

24. Are you ...
PLEASE TICK ONE BOX ONLY

N=1842

%

... married or living as married 67.8 **ANSWER Q. 25**

or not? 30.6 **GO TO Q. 29**

Not answered 1.6

PLEASE ANSWER QUESTIONS 25 TO 28 IF YOU ARE MARRIED OR LIVING AS MARRIED

25. In your household who does the following things ...?

N=1278

PLEASE TICK ONE BOX ON EACH LINE

	Always me	Usually me	About equal or both together	Usually my spouse/partner	Always my spouse/partner	Is done by a third person	Can't choose	Not answered
[HhJob21] a. Does the laundry	% 25.3	16.5	16.9	21.9	15.3	1.0	0.2	2.8
[HhJob22] b. Makes small repairs around the house	% 20.1	25.6	14.3	23.3	11.2	1.9	0.4	3.1
[HhJob23] c. Looks after sick family members	% 11.3	15.6	43.9	13.8	5.0	1.0	5.7	3.7
[HhJob24] d. Shops for groceries	% 11.4	15.8	47.0	16.4	5.6	0.5	0.3	3.0
[HhJob25] e. Does the household cleaning	% 15.2	22.0	29.7	20.0	6.6	3.4	0.4	2.8
[HhJob26] f. Prepares the meals	% 17.0	21.0	27.2	22.7	8.7	0.7	0.2	2.6

[RHomeWrk]

26a. On average, how many hours a week do you personally spend on household work, not including childcare and leisure time activities?

N=1278

Median: 8 hours

not answered 7.0%

[SHomeWrk]

b. And what about your spouse/partner? On average, how many hours a week does he/she spend on household work, not including childcare and leisure time activities?

N=1278

Median: 8 hours

not answered 9.4%

[ChoreArg]

27. How often do you and your spouse/partner disagree about the sharing of household work?

N=1278

PLEASE TICK ONE BOX ONLY

%

Several times a week 6.2

Several times a month 8.9

Several times a year 10.1

Less often/rarely 35.5

Never 34.2

Can't choose 2.1

Not answered 3.0

[IncHigh]

28. Considering all sources of income, between you and your spouse/partner, who has the higher income?
PLEASE TICK ONE BOX ONLY

N=1278

%

My spouse/partner has no income 5.0

I have a much higher income 15.6

I have a higher income 19.4

We have about the same income 12.5

My spouse/partner has a higher income 26.9

My spouse/partner has a much higher income 9.5

I have no income 3.6

Don't know 2.7

Not answered 4.8

EVERYONE PLEASE ANSWER

29. Do you agree or disagree?

N=1842

PLEASE TICK ONE BOX ON EACH LINE	Strongly agree	Agree	Neither agree nor disagree	Disagree	Strongly disagree	Can't choose	Doesn't apply	Not answered
[TimeGen1] a. There are so many things to do at home, I often run out of time before I get them all done	% 12.6	39.2	16.0	22.5	2.5	4.1	1.1	2.1
[NoStres1] c. My life at home is rarely stressful	% 4.4	42.6	15.9	27.3	4.2	2.3	1.0	2.2
[NoStrs2C] c. My job is rarely stressful	% 2.0	18.4	12.1	26.4	9.8	26.6	1.2	3.6

30. How often has each of the following happened to you during the past three months?

N=1842

PLEASE TICK ONE BOX ON EACH LINE	Several times a week	Several times a month	Once or twice	Never	Doesn't apply/no job	Not answered
[HomeTrd] a. I have come home from work too tired to do the chores which need to be done	% 12.7	15.9	25.3	9.7	33.2	3.1
[HomeHard] b. It has been difficult for me to fulfil my family responsibilities because of the amount of time I spent on my job	% 4.7	8.3	19.8	27.1	36.2	3.9
[WorkTrd] c. I have arrived at work too tired to function well because of the household work I had done	% 0.8	2.5	13.2	45.2	34.6	3.8
[WorkDiff] d. I have found it difficult to concentrate at work because of my family responsibilities	% 1.0	3.1	20.0	36.4	35.8	3.7

[RUHappy2]

31. If you were to consider your life in general, how happy or unhappy would you say you are, on the whole?
PLEASE TICK *ONE* BOX ONLY

N=1842

	%
Completely happy	12.1
Very happy	39.0
Fairly happy	36.7
Neither happy nor unhappy	5.9
Fairly unhappy	3.1
Very unhappy	0.7
Completely unhappy	0.4
Can't choose	0.9
Not answered	1.2

[JobSat]

32. All things considered, how satisfied are you with your (main) job?
PLEASE TICK *ONE* BOX ONLY

N=1842

	%
Completely satisfied	6.6
Very satisfied	19.0
Fairly satisfied	26.7
Neither satisfied nor dissatisfied	5.7
Fairly dissatisfied	4.0
Very dissatisfied	1.8
Completely dissatisfied	1.0
Can't choose	32.5
Doesn't apply/no job	0.6
Not answered	2.2

[FamSat]
33. All things considered, how satisfied are you with your family life?
PLEASE TICK ONE BOX ONLY

N=1842

	%
Completely satisfied	19.6
Very satisfied	41.6
Fairly satisfied	28.3
Neither satisfied nor dissatisfied	4.0
Fairly dissatisfied	2.0
Very dissatisfied	0.6
Completely dissatisfied	0.2
Can't choose	2.1
Not answered	1.6

[MthrWrkd]
34. Did your mother ever work for pay for as long as one year, after you were born and before you were 14?
PLEASE TICK ONE BOX ONLY

N=1842

	%
Yes, she worked for pay	51.2
No	35.8
Don't know	11.6
Not answered	1.3

[ChldEver]
35. Have you ever had children?
PLEASE TICK ONE BOX ONLY

N=1842

	%	
Yes	68.6	ANSWER Q.36
No	29.6	GO TO Q.39
NA assume yes	0.4	
Not answered	1.4	

PLEASE ANSWER QUESTIONS 36 TO 38 IF YOU HAVE EVER HAD CHILDREN.

N=1270

36. Did you work outside the home full-time, part-time, or not at all...

PLEASE TICK ONE BOX ON EACH LINE	Worked full-time	Worked part-time	Stayed at home	Does not apply	Not answered
[RMarWrk2] a. When a child was under school age? %	46.4	20.0	25.0	6.4	2.3
[RMarWrk3] b. After the youngest child started school? %	44.2	26.3	7.8	13.9	7.7

37. What about your spouse/partner at that time – did he/she work outside the home full-time, part-time, or not at all?

N=1270

PLEASE TICK ONE BOX ON EACH LINE	Worked full-time	Worked part-time	Stayed at home	Does not apply	Not answered
[SMarWrk2] a. When a child was under school age? %	52.0	14.2	23.1	7.5	3.2
[SMarWrk3] b. After the youngest child started school? %	46.3	20.4	9.5	16.1	7.7

38. Please think now about the childcare you have used while your child/children were under school age. Apart from you and your spouse/partner at the time, which of these childcare arrangements have you used?
PLEASE TICK ALL BOXES THAT APPLY

N=837

	%
[CCParent] Child's parent not living with you	5.6
[CCrelpal] Other relatives or friends	50.5
[CCminder] Paid childminder	17.3
[CCNanny] Nanny/au pair	4.4
[CCNursry] Nursery	28.9
[CCPGroup] Playgroup	29.3
[CCOther] Other – PLEASE WRITE IN:	4.8
Not answered	16.8

EVERYONE PLEASE ANSWER

[PaidWrk]

39. Have you ever had a paid job?

N=1842

PLEASE TICK *ONE* BOX ONLY

		%	
	Yes	96.3	ANSWER Q.40
	No	2.4	GO TO Q.41
	Not answered	1.3	

PLEASE ONLY ANSWER QUESTION 40 IF YOU HAVE EVER HAD A PAID JOB

[FamWork]

40. How much, if at all, do you think your family responsibilities have got in the way of your progress at work or your job prospects?

N=1798

PLEASE TICK *ONE* BOX ONLY

	%
A great deal	3.3
Quite a lot	7.9
A bit	14.7
Not very much	20.9
Not at all	45.5
Can't say	5.5
Not answered	2.1

EVERYONE PLEASE ANSWER

41. How much do you agree or disagree with the following statements?

N=1842

PLEASE TICK *ONE* BOX ON EACH LINE

		Agree strongly	Agree	Neither agree nor disagree	Disagree	Disagree strongly	Not answered
[LadderWF] a. It is important to move up the ladder at work, even if this gets in the way of family life	%	1.8	10.9	24.6	52.9	7.9	2.0
[CopeWork] b. If a person cannot manage their family responsibilities they should stop trying to hold down a paid job	%	2.6	24.5	32.9	33.1	4.5	2.3

Note: Questions 42 to 44 are the same as questions 20 to 22 on version A

[QTimeC]

45. To help us plan better in future, please tell us about how long it took you to complete this questionnaire.

N=910

*PLEASE TICK *ONE* BOX ONLY*

	%
Less than 15 minutes	19.8
Between 15 and 20 minutes	37.2
Between 21 and 30 minutes	24.0
Between 31 and 45 minutes	11.3
Between 46 and 60 minutes	3.7
Over one hour	2.5
Not answered	1.5

BRITISH SOCIAL ATTITUDES 2006 SELF-COMPLETION QUESTIONNAIRE VERSION D

Note: Question 1 is the same as question 8 on version A

2. Please tick <u>one</u> box for <u>each</u> of these statements to show how much you agree or disagree.

N=931

PLEASE TICK ONE BOX ON EACH LINE		Agree strongly	Agree	Neither agree nor disagree	Disagree	Disagree strongly	I never travel by car	Can't choose	Not answered
[CarWalk] a. Many of the short journeys I now make by car I could just as easily walk	%	7.6	26.0	8.3	32.7	14.2	7.1	3.2	0.9
[CarBus] b. Many of the short journeys I now make by car I could just as easily go by bus	%	4.2	24.1	7.9	34.3	20.1	5.7	2.3	1.4
[CarBike] c. Many of the short journeys I now make by car I could just as easily cycle, if I had a bike	%	6.7	28.1	9.1	29.0	17.2	5.5	2.9	1.5

Note: Question 3 is the same as question 10 on version A

4. Please tick <u>one</u> box for <u>each</u> of these statements to show how much you agree or disagree.

N=931

PLEASE TICK ONE BOX ON EACH LINE		Agree strongly	Agree	Neither agree nor disagree	Disagree	Disagree strongly	Can't choose	Not answered
[SpeCamSL] a. Speed cameras save lives	%	14.4	40.1	15.3	19.2	7.1	1.7	2.2
[SpeCamMo] b. Speed cameras are mostly there to make money	%	17.9	32.8	19.5	22.2	3.1	1.9	2.6
[SpeCamTM] c. There are too many speed cameras	%	16.5	25.6	24.4	23.2	4.9	2.3	3.0
[SpeedLim] d. People should drive within the speed limit	%	47.2	45.1	3.3	1.7	0.1	0.4	2.2
[SpeCmInc] e. The number of speed cameras should be increased	%	7.2	13.8	27.2	30.3	16.5	2.8	2.3

5. Please tick one box for each of these statements
    to show how much you agree or disagree.

N=931

PLEASE TICK ONE BOX ON EACH LINE		Agree strongly	Agree	Neither agree nor disagree	Disagree	Disagree strongly	Can't choose	Not answered
[MobDSafe]								
a. It is perfectly safe to talk on a hand-held mobile phone while driving	%	3.1	1.7	2.4	28.9	61.4	0.4	2.0
[MobDDang]								
b. All use of mobile phones while driving, including hands-free kits is dangerous	%	23.7	34.9	11.6	20.3	6.7	0.7	2.2
[MobDBan]								
c. All use of mobile phones while driving, including hands-freekits should be banned	%	22.7	26.5	14.0	25.7	7.7	1.3	2.0
[MobDLaw]								
d. The law on using mobile phones whilst driving is not eproperly nforced	%	37.4	43.7	10.1	3.7	1.0	1.8	2.3

Note: **Questions 6 to 8 are the same as questions 13 to 15 on version A**
         Questions 9 to 17 are the same as questions 35 to 43 on version B
         Questions 18 to 19 are the same as questions 17 to 18 on version A
         Questions 20 to 41 are the same as questions 20 to 41 on version C
         Questions 42 to 43 are the same as questions 21 to 22 on version A

[QTimeD]
44. To help us plan better in future, please tell us about
     how long it took you to complete this questionnaire.

N=931

PLEASE TICK ONE BOX ONLY

	%
Less than 15 minutes	21.2
Between 15 and 20 minutes	35.5
Between 21 and 30 minutes	26.5
Between 31 and 45 minutes	10.0
Between 46 and 60 minutes	4.4
Over one hour	1.8
Not answered	0.5

Subject index